TRADITION AND ENLIGHTENMENT
IN THE TUSCAN ACADEMIES

1690 - 1800

TRADITION AND ENLIGHTENMENT IN THE TUSCAN ACADEMIES

1690 - 1800

by Eric W. Cochrane

The University of Chicago Press

Library of Congress Catalog Card Number: 60-14232

The University of Chicago Press, Chicago 37
The University of Toronto Press, Toronto 5, Canada
Edizioni di Storia e Letteratura, Rome, Italy

© 1961 by The University of Chicago
Published 1961. Composed and printed in Rome, Italy

To
DELIO CANTIMORI
Friend and Teacher

CONTENTS

PREFACE

The grand duchy of Tuscany, in 1700, covered almost the same area as the region of Tuscany today. It extended from the Apennine chain, separating it from the duchies of Parma and Modena and the Papal Legations in the north, through the wide, fertile valley of the Arno reaching from Pisa and Livorno in the west to Arezzo, Cortona, and Lake Trasimeno in the east, across the hill country of the Chianti, famous even then for its wine, to the barren mountains, green in the spring and red-brown in the summer and fall, that stretch from the south gate of Siena up to lofty Mt. Amiata and down to the wide, empty coastal plains of the Maremma as far as the borders of Latium in the States of the Church. Only a few autonomous areas in the far northwest, the tiny Republic of Lucca, and the Spanish forts along the Tyrrhenian coast remained outside the frontiers, to be absorbed one by one in the following century before the Grand Duchy itself was absorbed, in 1859, into the new Kingdom of Italy.

To be sure, the physical aspect of Tuscany has changed considerably in the last 250 years. In 1700, as today, stately villas and graceful cypresses dominated the countryside; but instead of the innumerable white houses recently constructed under the land-reform program, only a few isolated huts and an occasional flock of sheep broke the solemn solitude of the Maremma, while much of the lower Arno and Chiana valleys were abandoned to swamp and the bare mountains in back of Florence still showed the effects of deforestation. The same Medieval and Renaissance palaces lined streets of the several cities; but the façades had not yet been illuminated with neon, smokestacks had not yet risen above Prato and Pontesieve, and suburban apartments and villas had not yet begun to stretch up toward Fiesole and down from the hilltops of Siena. While agriculture seemed to provide almost the sole means of sustenance

*for the great majority of the population, the fields devoted largely
to the cultivation of grain had not yet given way to the great variety
of fruits, vegetables, vines, and olive trees growing on every inch of
arable (and not-so-arable) land for which Tuscany is well known
today.   Visitors at the turn of the eighteenth century would have
found rather a country of barely 850,000 people, living in and about
small, quiet towns and villages, and vast stretches of open land devoid
either of roads or inhabitants.*

*Yet Tuscany had not always been what it seemed to be in 1700 —
a forgotten corner of the continent far from the centers of political
and intellectual activity.   Other Europeans still remembered it as what
the* Encyclopédie *called the « mère des découvertes et des établisse-
ments utiles à l'humanité, » the home of Boccaccio, Brunelleschi,
Leonardo, Ficino, Michelangelo, and Machiavelli.   During the course
of the century, moreover, it once again attracted the attention of
foreigners, not only for its art treasures, as the same article in the*
Encyclopédie *went on to point out, but for the wise laws which in
a few years all but emptied the prisons and reduced the once-dreaded
Inquisition to silence.   Thus Tuscany in 1700 may have counted for
very little in terms of might, of wealth, or even, since the death of
Galileo, of wisdom; but Tuscany in the 1780's enjoyed a reputation
far greater than its modest size might indicate.   Not only was it
admired as the source of most of the "sciences, arts et métiers" that
since the fifteenth century had brought enlightenment to the whole
of Europe; it also was acclaimed as a "model country," in the words
of the French envoy, in which the most advanced tenets of the enlightened philosophers of the day had first been applied in practice
to laws and institutions.*

*Indeed, it is just this aspect of Settecento Tuscany[1] — the truly
remarkable transformation of the whole political and economic structure of the country, that is — which most impressed the first historians
of the period; for they, the immediate descendants of those who had*

---

[1] The Italian term *Settecento* is used here to avoid confusion with the usual connota-
tions of the English term *eighteenth century.*

made the history, looked to the past for precedents to the measures they were advocating in Tuscany of the early nineteenth century. It is not surprising, moreover, considering the nature of the events they described, that Gino Capponi and Antonio Zobi passed on their interests to somewhat more scholarly successors — to Abele Morena and Antonio Anzilotti in the last decades of the nineteenth and the first of the twentieth century, and to Niccolò Rodolico, Ernesto Codignola, Ettore Passerin d'Entrèves, and others, who have carried on their work in recent years. For seldom has a government adopted such sweeping changes in so little time under what seem to have been such adverse circumstances.

Politically and economically, Tuscany under the last two Medici (Cosimo III, 1670-1723, and Giangastone, 1723-1737) was little more than a petrification of what it had been in 1300. The Principato, established by the Medici upon the ruins of the last two urban republics a century and a half earlier, had simply transferred all final authority to the person of the prince and left untouched the innumerable magistracies and the intricate legal structure of the formerly independent city-states. The result was a hopeless confusion of conflicting jurisdictions — central and local, ecclesiastical and lay, civil and criminal, political and economic — a "chaos presque impossible à débrouiller," in the words of a Lorraine official in 1737, "a political, economic, and social structure in the process of exhaustion," in those of the historian Franco Valsecchi in 1953.

Yet by 1790 this chaos had given way, apparently, to order. During the course of the century the political attitudes and administrative policies that Cosimo I (1537-74) had bequeathed to his heirs was gradually abandoned — first by the government of Giangastone, at least in ecclesiastical affairs; then by that of the Regency, which ruled from 1737 to 1765 in place of the absentee Francesco Stefano (later Emperor Francis III, who had exchanged Lorraine for Tuscany upon the extinction of the Medici); and finally by that of Pietro Leopoldo, who arrived in Florence as a boy of eighteen and left, after twenty-five years, to succeed his brother Joseph II on the imperial throne in 1790. Within less than half a century the civil jurisdiction of the clergy, the internal and most of the external restrictions on commerce, the trade and manufacturing guilds, the inalienable land-holdings, and the entire structure of political and judicial administration had been abolished; and a regular hierarchy of local and appellate courts, a uniform system of municipal councils, a bureaucracy dependent directly upon the several royal ministries, and a body of economic legislation guaranteeing an almost complete freedom of production and exchange had been erected in their place. The prince and some of his assistants had even thought of complementing their work with a written constitution, the text of which was published early in the following century, and of extending it into purely ecclesiastical affairs through diocesan and national synods, the importance of which has since been illustrated by the many students of Italian Jansenism. Tuscany, in other words, had become a single state, rationally organized as much as any other in Europe at the time — for the explicit purpose of fulfilling the desires and serving the best interests of all its citizens.

The principal edicts and decrees by which this transformation was accomplished (at least on paper), as well as the objectives of several of the royal ministers charged with preparing them, have already been fairly thoroughly described. What still remains to be considered is the question of origins: where Tuscans, that is, who in 1700 seemed incapable of any kind of innovation, found the incentive and the inspiration to undertake, in the 1780's, what elsewhere would require centuries of slow development or a violent revolution. Historians have, it is true, suggested several possible answers. Some have attributed the reforms to external influence — to the efforts of a foreign dynasty to apply in Tuscany the principles of efficient administration practiced in Nancy and Vienna, or to the teachings of Montesquieu, Locke, the Physiocrats, and other Transalpine authors, whose works Italians cite with increasing frequency from the middle of the century on. Others have defended the indigenous character of the reforms, seeing them as the expression of the interests of a new middle class of entrepreneurs and functionaries, as the natural response of intelligent men to an economic situation rapidly approaching the point of disaster, or as one manifestation of what Gioacchino Volpe has called "a rise in the general tone of Italian life" evident from as early as the last decade of the seventeenth century.

But none of these hypotheses, valuable as it may be for the interpretation of a limited number of phenomena, is free of serious difficulties. The first, for example, does not account for the enthusiastic support given the Lorraine princes by their principal subjects; the second cannot explain why Italians of the Settecento should have been so much more receptive to foreign literature than their predecessors; the third overlooks the presence of members of the same noble families in important political positions throughout the century; the fourth is apparently contradicted by the failure of many of the reforms in practice; and the last has so far been unable to show any connection between the predominantly literary interests of the first part of the century and the political and economic interests of the last. The origins of the Tuscan reforms, in other words, and consequently, as Heinz Holldack has pointed out, the origins of the movement that was to culminate later in national unification and independance, still remain obscure.

The truth is that relatively little is yet known either about Tuscany or about Italy as a whole between the late sixteenth and the early nineteenth centuries. Most historians have so far preferred to study the more glorious moments of the Renaissance and the Risorgimento, and they have generally considered only those elements of the intervening period that seemed to correspond either to the well-known definitions of the Enlightenment in France and England or to the ideals of Italian patriots in the following century. Only very recently have scholars like Franco Venturi, Guido Calcaterra, Walter Binni, Mario Fubini, and Bruno Migliorini begun to examine thoroughly some of the more important aspects of Settecento culture — political economy, historiography, poetry, literary criticism, and linguistics. Only very recently have others, like Guido Quazza, Franco Valsecchi, Massimo Petrocchi, and Mario Berengo, begun to investigate the particular conditions, cultural as well as political and economic, of several of the Italian states.

Not until such inquiries have been extended to all the fields of contemporary thought and activity and not until they have been carried out in all the many regions in which Italy was still both psychologically and politically divided, will it be possible to understand either the general character of the age or the puzzling peculiarities of writers who thought of themselves primarily as Tuscans or Lombards, if not as Sienese, Pisans, and Pavesi. Not until then, moreover, will it be possible to approach the principal problem involved in the study of pre-Revolutionary Italy — whether the reforms, that is, in Naples, Parma, and Lombardy as well as Tuscany, are evidence of a continuing vitality or of the exhaustion of an indigenous cultural tradition. Meanwhile all attempts to push the Risorgimento back before Napoleon will remain as fruitless as searching for its beginnings in Vergil or the Etruscans, and all attempts to incorporate the Settecento into some sort of Europe française *must be limited to the observation of apparent similarities.*

This study does not pretend to give final answers to these questions even for Tuscany alone; such a task would require years of eyestraining labor. For students of the period have so far directed their attention almost wholly to the statute books, the official memoranda, the treatises of the economists, and the correspondence of the Jansenists; and they have only begun to penetrate the enormous mass of dissertations, pamphlets, notes, accounts, drawings, posters, poems, journals, clippings, and letters, which the Settecento letterati, *unwilling to throw away the least scrap of paper, carefully stored up in attics and archives, and which will eventually, as Gaetano Gasperoni suggested some years ago and as the admirable work of Mario Rosa has shown more recently, enable historians to reconstruct in some detail the social, economic, and cultural environment in which the reforms appeared.*

This study is based on only part of this material — upon the records of the academies, that is, some thirty-five of them in all, upon diaries, rolls, dissertations, and correspondence, most of which have lain forgotten ever since they were written on back shelves and in dusty closets in the several cities of Tuscany. Such a restriction in documentation has the obvious disadvantage, to be sure, of overlooking the importance of individual personalities and of omitting many of the more significant achievements of the age simply because they happened to take place outside the academies. Yet the very nature of these documents is such that they may well provide a kind of index to all the rest; for since the rolls of the academies include the names of almost everyone of any social or intellectual prominence, it is probable that the diaries reflect fairly accurately what most educated Tuscans were reading, writing, and thinking. By examining institutions rather than individuals, moreover, and by showing how a number of single persons for the first time in over a century spontaneously joined themselves together for the realization of common objectives, a study of the academies should provide further evidence for the "reawakening" noticed by some historians among the adherents of Arcadia and the professors at Pisa. By concentrating on the average rather than the exceptional, this study should show with some accuracy how far the ideas of a few brilliant minds (and the humdrum, unheroic Settecento produced very few of them indeed) filtered down to the ordinary literate citizens of what was rapidly becoming one of the more progressive states of Europe. By considering a kind of institution first established in the very different cultural and political circumstances of the late sixteenth century, it should give some further indication of the extent to which the eighteenth century built upon the heritage of the Renaissance. By following in detail the reactions of many Tuscans to the increasing influx of literature from beyond the Alps, it should clarify what contemporary writers meant by "Enlightenment" (Illuminismo) and should explain how a movement common, according to its chief representatives, to all Europe could be modified by contact with the peculiar historical traditions of one nation. By describing, finally, the way in which the would-be poets of the 1690's gradually became the political economists of the 1780's, this study should permit a more precise evaluation of the contribution of the Settecento to the Risorgimento of the nineteenth century.

The present volume describes the organization and the activities of all the academies as a whole, without accounting for each of them separately. The more interesting of the still unprinted diaries, rolls, dissertations, and charters, together with a brief history and complete bibliographical references for each of the academies will soon be published as a separate volume by the Edizioni di Storia e Letteratura.

This study has been many years in preparation. It began during an extended visit to Italy made possible by two successive Fulbright scholarships in 1951 and 1952. It grew, thanks in part to the encouragement of the late Professor Gaetano Salvemini, during the following years, as I was able, in spite of frequent interruptions, to continue my studies of the Settecento in various libraries in the United States, France, and Italy. Finally, in the spring of 1957 I was fortunate enough to revisit the Tuscan cities in which the academies once flourished and to complete my collection of documents. My thanks are due to the many librarians and archivists and to the officers of several of the academies whose kind cooperation made this work possible; it will be more appropriate to mention them individually in the following volume. Thanks are due also to the Department of History at Yale University, to which some of the material in the present work was presented as a dissertation for the Ph.D. degree in 1953, and to the Division of Social Sciences at the University of Chicago for the generous grant that enabled me to have the manuscript prepared in final form. Needless to say, the various fields of knowledge that this study touches upon are far too numerous, in these days when the Settecento ideal of enciclopedia *has become a mere dream, to fall within the competence of a single person, and I have had to depend in large measure on the advice and assistance of Professors Arnaldo Momigliano, Paul Oskar Kristeller, Franklin Baumer, Donald Lach, Ettore Passerin d'Entrèves, and Dr. Nicola Carranza, who have read some or all of the chapters, and who have most generously pointed out errors and suggested changes and corrections. Every word of this book has been subjected to the merciless scrutiny of Dr. Mario Rosa of Rome, whose intimate knowledge of Tuscan culture in the Settecento has made him intolerant of the least inaccuracy. Every paragraph has been read by and to my wife, whose sensitivity to tangled sentences, unclear expressions, and bad metaphors has rid the text of many of its original barbarisms. And most of the notes and quotations have been carefully checked by Dr. Nicla Capitini, whose resourceful imagination has enabled her to trace down even the most obscure references. To Monsignor Giuseppe De Luca my debt far exceeds the modest limits of historical erudition and cannot possibly be stated in this preface. Finally, I must express, however inadequately, my gratitude to Professor Delio Cantimori, from whose lectures, writings, and conversation I have constantly drawn inspiration and instruction. That my own work shows traces of his teaching is the greatest compliment I can hope for; and to him this book is respectfully and gratefully dedicated.*

Chicago, February 1960

A NOTE

ON CITATIONS AND ABBREVIATIONS

Records of the academies, of which a full description will be given
under each in the following volume, are referred to by the name of the
academy followed by the title of the document and the specific date, article,
or page number. References to and quotations from documents to be published
are marked with an asterisk (e. g., Crusca: *Diario, 3 December 1700 is
an entry for that date in the Diary of the Accademia della Crusca). Florentines clung to the Julian calendar (« stile fiorentino ») as adamantly as the
British in the first decades of the century, but I have used New Style throughout. I have where possible referred to the works of the political economists
in the collection of « Scrittori classici italiani di economia politica » (published
in Milan in the first years of the nineteenth century and here always abbreviated:
S.C.I.E.P.), in spite of occasional lacunae and inaccuracies, simply because
the works can be found in the major American libraries more readily in this
than in any other edition. I have quoted verse in the original, with the
translation in the footnotes, and prose in English, with the original in the
footnotes whenever it seemed necessary to convey the exact meaning or whenever the source was unavailable outside Tuscany — unless, of course, it will
be printed in the following volume. The reader will pardon the freedom
with which I have translated some passages when he notices the execrable
style of the original and when he realizes that almost nothing here quoted
has the slightest literary value. I have generally modernized punctuation,
and, except where relevant, I have shortened the titles of the many Settecento
books that try to cram a detailed table of contents and an elaborate dedication
onto the title page.

Manuscripts are indicated by the following abbreviations of the names
of the libraries or archives in which they are found:

Florence	Archivio di Stato	ASF
	Biblioteca Nazionale Centrale	BNF
	Biblioteca Marucelliana	Mar
	Biblioteca Riccardiana	Ricc
	Accademia della Crusca	Cr
	Accademia dei Georgofili	Geo
	Società Colombaria	Col
Siena	Archivio di Stato	ASS
	Biblioteca Comunale	BCS
	Accademia dei Fisiocritici	Fis

Cortona	Biblioteca dell'Accademia Etrusca	Etr
Arezzo	Biblioteca della Fraternità dei Laici	Laici
	Accademia Petrarca	Petr
Livorno	Archivio di Stato	ASL
Volterra	Biblioteca Comunale	BCV
Pisa	Archivio di Stato	ASP
Pistoia	Biblioteca Forteguerriana	Fort
Prato	Biblioteca Roncioniana	Ronc
Roma	Accademia dell'Arcadia — Biblioteca Angelica	Arc

The puslished transactions of the academies, of which the titles occasionally vary and of which none appeared with any regularity, are referred to without the date except when it is important and are abbreviated as follows:

Atti della R. Accademia de' Georgofili (Series I unless otherwise indicated)   *Atti Georgofili*

Memorie di varia erudizione della Società Colombaria   *Memorie Colombaria*

Atti dell'Accademia dei Fisiocritici   *Atti Fisiocritici*

Saggi di dissertazioni accademiche pubblicamente lette nella nobile Accademia Etrusca   *Saggi Etrusca*

The periodical *Giornale fiorentino di agricoltura, arti, commercio, e economia pubblica* is abbreviated *Giornale fiorentino di agricoltura;* Angelo Fabroni's *Giornale de' letterati* is always followed by the indication (Pisa) to distinguish it from the journals of the same name published in Venice at the beginning of the century and in Florence by Raimondo Adami from 1742 to 1762; and the *Magazzino toscano* (Livorno) is so designated to avoid confusion with the other *Magazzino toscano* published from 1770 in Florence. Edicts, decrees, and laws are usually cited in the collection entitled *Leggi e bandi di S.A.R.* (title varies slightly) published at irregular intervals (e.g., Vol. VIII,... *dal dì 11 luglio 1774 al dì 27 giugno 1776*) and referred to as *Leggi e bandi;* a few are cited in the incomplete collection *Leggi granducali* in the New York City Public Library.

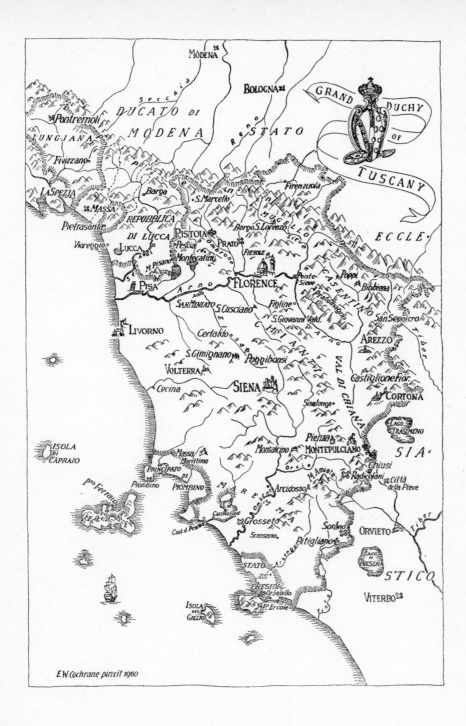

GRAND DUCHY OF TUSCANY

MÒDENA

BOLOGNA

Secchia

DUCATO DI MODENA

STATO

Reno

ECCLE·

Pontremoli

LUNGIANA

Fivizzano

LaSPEZIA

Barga

S.Marcello

Firenzuola

MASSA

Pietrasanta

REPUBBLICA

DI LUCCA

Borgo S.Lorenzo

Viareggio

LUCCA

PISTOIA

PRATO

MUGELLO

Pescia

Montecatini

FIESOLE

M.Pisano

CASENTINO

PISA

Arno

FLORENCE

Ponte Sieve

Poppi

Bibbiena

San Miniato

S.Casciano

Figline

Pratomagno

Livorno

Certaldo

S.Giovanni Vald.

San Sepolcro

Tiber

CHIANTI

VAL D'ARNO

AREZZO

S.Gimignano

Poggibonsi

VOLTERRA

Castiglione Fior.

Cecina

SIENA

CORTONA

Sinalunga

LAGO TRASIMENO

ISOLA DI CAPRAJO

VAL DI CHIANA

SIA=

Pienza

MONTEPULCIANO

Massa Marittima

Montalcino

Chiusi

PRINCIPATO DI PIOMBINO

M.Amiata

Radicofani

Città della Pieve

Pto Ferraio

Piombino

Orcia

Arcidosso

ELBA

MAREMMA

Castiglione

Grosseto

Sorano

ORVIETO

Tiber

Scansano

Pitigliano

Cast.d.Pescia

STATO DE'

PRESIDI

LAGO DI BOLSENA

S'TICO

Orbetello

VITERBO

ISOLA DEL GIGLIO

P.Ercole

E.W.Cochrane pinxit 1960

Chapter I

FROM THE CINQUECENTO TO THE SETTECENTO

The first page of the ponderous, six-volume fourth edition of the *Vocabolario degli Accademici della Crusca*[1] bears a small copper engraving: in a high-ceilinged room devoid of all decoration but a frieze of the members' academic seals along the rear wall, are seated some fifteen gentlemen, either in knee breeches, Louis-XIV wigs, and brocaded jackets, or in the simple black gown and white collars of an *abate*. In the rear center the *arciconsolo* presides from a raised platform, surrounded by four assistants, two *consiglieri* and two *censori,* and a secretary, who is writing at a desk. All listen, some more attentively than others, to one of their associates, who, at the far right, is delivering a *lezione,* or perhaps reading an original sonnet, from the *bugnola,* or rostrum.

This is the Accademia della Crusca in one of its regular weekly sessions. Ever since its foundation in 1582,[2] the Academy had included the leading men of letters of the city of Florence, from Lionardo Salviati, Benedetto Buommattei, Michelangelo Buonarroti the Younger, and Galileo Galilei, to Carlo Dati and Francesco Redi; and now, at the beginning of the eighteenth century, one might be able to recognize in a similar engraving the faces of Lorenzo Bellini, since 1668 professor of anatomy at Pisa, of Alamanno Salviati, soon to be called to Rome as cardinal by Clement XI, of Lorenzo Magalotti, diplomat, scientist, and author, of Vincenzo da Filicaia, senator,

---

[1] (Florence: D. M. Manni, 1729-33). Earlier editions hereafter cited by number and date.

[2] It is possible that the Academy existed, at least informally, somewhat earlier: such is the hypothesis proposed in the Settecento by Anton Maria Biscioni and discussed in the most thorough history of the early years of the Academy, Cartesio Marconcini, *L'Accademia della Crusca dalle origini alla prima edizione del Vocabolario* (Pisa: Valenti, 1910), pp. 43 f.

former governor of Pisa, and "the most famous composer of *canzoni* of our century," of Benedetto Averani, professor of humanities and "the greatest light ... of Latin or Tuscan eloquence in many centuries," and of Anton Maria Salvini, the leading Hellenist of his day and author of hundreds of published and still more unpublished verses, discourses, and translations,[3] not to mention Leone Strozzi, Pandolfo Pandolfini, Luigi Rucellai, Filippo Buonarroti, Cesare Ricasoli, Averardo Serristori, and many others, whose illustrious surnames had long been identified with the greatest moments of Florentine history. Professors, prelates, royal ministers, and landed proprietors, they all willingly took time from their normal occupations to participate in the work of the Academy — in the composition and criticism of verse, in the preparation of discourses, in the celebration of annual feasts, and, above all, in the compilation of the authoritative historical dictionary of the Tuscan language, which they already had published in three progressively augmented editions in the course of the preceding century and which had earned them recognition throughout Italy as arbiters in matters of linguistic usage. They felt themselves charged with a grave obligation, and they responsed with enthusiasm:

> You, most noble academicians, who busy yourselves all year 'round with literary exercises, you pay no heed to the discomforts of the season. Struck by the love of the Muses and seized by the furor of glory, you become ever more fervent in the virtuous contest; so that by your continual exertion you maintain this so noble, so famous Academy in the beauty, vigor, and freshness of ever-growing praises.... [4]

Neither the heat of summer, then, nor the stony chill of Florentine palaces in January had any importance beside the responsibilities to

---

[3] Angelo Fabroni, *Historia Academiae Pisanae* (3 vols.; Pisa: Mugnaini, 1791-95), III, pp. 538-63; Crusca: * Diario, 5 January and 30 July 1708; Carmelo Cordaro, *Anton Maria Salvini, Saggio critico-biografico* (Piacenza: Favari, 1906), and the many relevant biographies in the *Notizie istoriche degli arcadi morti* and *Le vite degli arcadi illustri,* ed. G. M. Crescimbeni (Rome: Rossi, 1721 and 1708-51).

[4] Anton Maria Salvini, « Per l'ultima accademia innanzi allo stravizzo », in his *Prose toscane* (2 vols.; Florence: Vol. I, Guiducci & Franchi, 1715; Vol. II, Manni, 1735); here quoted from Vol. I, pp. 358-59: « Voi, nobilissimi Accademici, tutto l'anno in letterarj esercizj indefessamente impiegandovi, non riguardate incomodi di stagione ... ; e percossi dall'amore delle Muse, e presi dal bel furore di gloria ... più, e più con virtuosa gara v'infervorate; acciocchè dalle continuate esercitazioni, bella, vigorosa, e fresca, e sempre in nuova, e nuova laude crescente si mantenga questa si nobile, e si riputata Accademia ... ».

language, literature, and the sciences that the Academy imposed upon them.

The same engraving might well have illustrated the four other societies which, in 1700, still survived from the two dozen or so founded in the several cities of Tuscany some hundred years before.[5] The oldest, "mother of all the Italian academies," was the Accademia degli Intronati of Siena, which was probably founded sometime in the early sixteenth century rather than in the fifteenth or fourteenth as its loyal Settecento eulogists, Girolamo Gigli and Uberto Benvoglienti, imagined. By 1700 its once extensive activities were largely limited to the production of plays and the preparation of the annual poetical and musical celebration of the Feast of the Assumption.[6] Its competitor (socially as well as intellectually, since its constitution excluded the nobility), the Accademia dei Rozzi, had been founded by a group of artisans and merchants about 1520, chiefly for the purpose of reciting poetry and comedies, and it still supervised the elaborate receptions customarily accorded by the city to visiting dignitaries and newly elected archbishops.[7] Of the three academies in Florence, one was older than the Crusca by some forty years — the Accademia Fiorentina, which had been founded under the protection of the first Medici grand duke in 1540 . It enjoyed not only the respectability of antiquity but also a semi-political position, first through its close connection with the Studio Fiorentino (the University of Florence), of which the *consolo* automatically became rector and the halls of which the members used for their sessions, and second through its functions as a tribunal for all civil cases arising in the book trade of the metropolis.[8] The other was of considerably more

[5] Cf. Michel Maylender, *Storia delle accademie d'Italia* (5 vols.; Bologna: Cappelli, 1926-30), and the indispensable *Repertorio alfabetico e bibliografico* of Giuseppe Gabrieli, published separately as an extract from the *Accademie e biblioteche d'Italia*, Vol. X.

[6] Girolamo Gigli to Antonio Magliabecchi on the origins of the Intronati, BCS Y.I.1; « Zucchini » degli Intronati BCS Y.I.3; and Benvoglienti's « Discorsi », BCS C.IV.4. Cf. Fabio Iacometti, *L'Accademia senese degli Intronati* (Siena, 1950).

[7] Giuseppe Fabiani, « Memoria sopra l'origine ed instituzione delle principali accademie della città di Siena . . . », in Calogerà, *Nuova raccolta d'opuscoli*, III, 3-104 (hereafter referred to as Fabiani, *Memoria*), and his *Memoria dell'Accademia dei Rozzi* (Siena: Pazzini, 1775).

[8] *Notizie letterarie ed istoriche intorno agli uomini illustri dell'Accademia Fiorentina*, with preface by Jacopo Rilli, the *consolo* (Florence: Matini, 1700). Salvino Salvini, *Fasti*

recent origin, although, like the Crusca itself, basically an outgrowth of the parent academy. The witty Lodovico Coltellini had founded the Accademia degli Apatisti in 1640 as a refuge of younger Florentines from what he considered stuffy pedantry in the other societies; and it specialized in an immensely popular brain-twisting game called the *Sibilla*, in which members were called upon to deliver an extemporaneous explanation, well padded with references to ancient and modern authors, of the meaningless response of a blindfolded child to a "question" posed by the president.[9] Besides the usual discourses and periodic meetings, then, each of these academies had succeeded in assuming special functions that prevented its absorption into the others and that saved it from the fate of the moribund Sepolti and Risvegliati, or of the by then extinct Emendati, Umorosi, Algerati, Accesi, *et al*.

In their structure and occupations, nonetheless, these societies resembled each other closely. All observed, first of all, some form of written constitution, more often resembling the preface, prologue, and thirty-one lengthy articles of the Intronati than the "brief, clear, few, substantial, useful, and necessary" laws of the Crusca.[10] These *statuti* or *capitoli*, as they were usually called, provided for the election of a president, known variously as a *consolo, principe, arcirozzo, arcintronato*, etc., and a large assortment of other officers, counsellors, custodians, secretaries, and censors, who held office for periods varying from six months to a year; they established the procedure for the selection of new and the commemoration of deceased members; they determined the frequency of meetings, the means for the financial support of academic activities, and the obligations of the individual members to the body as a whole; and they generally called for the preservation of the records of academic meetings and other important activities. Each academy, and many of the academicians as well,

---

consolari dell'A. F. (Florence: Tartini, 1717). Documents concerning litigations in the book trade: BNF Mag IX, 38.

[9] Memorie dell'A. degli A.: Mar A. 36. Many of the discourses are in A. M. Salvini, *Discorsi accademici ... sopra alcuni dubbj proposti nell'A. degli A.* (3 vols.; Florence: G. Manni, 1695, 1713, 1733). See further, E. Benvenuti, *A. Coltellini e l'Accademia degli Apatisti nel secolo XVII* (Pistoia, 1910).

[10] A. M. Salvini, *Prose toscane*, I, 213.

adopted an *impresa,* a decive like the grain filter and crank of the Crusca, together with a motto which supposedly symbolized the purpose and aspirations of the bearer and explained the appropriateness of such bizarre designations as "the Deafened" or "the Buried." [11] Most of them chose a princely "protector" as well as a celestial patron; and almost all invited "the nobility and the more learned of the people" to celebrate the patron saint's feast day, Carnival, or the harvest with a banquet, a ball, and effusions of *giocosi* sonnets and orations.

These merely formal or organizational matters, indeed, were of no mean importance. The selection of officers alone, for which the constitutions devised the most ingenious complications, often required a lengthy preparation: for the keeper of manuscripts in the Intronati, for instance, the counsellors and the censor each were to nominate one and the *arcintronato* two candidates, who were submitted one by one to a secret vote; the three receiving the greatest number of "white," or affirmative, ballots were then submitted at the next session to a final vote, unless one or more of them had received less than twelve "whites" at the first turn, in which case the process had to begin all over again: and all this left some ten other officers to be chosen each in a different manner.[12] Two or three formal proposals and a speech of thanks preceded the admission of new members, while special *accademie funerali,* with odes, eulogies, lighted tapers, and sometimes even a specially ordered portrait to adorn the academic halls, duly waved them on into the next world. A retiring president usually delivered an oration, to which the successor was expected to respond, or prepared a "defense" of his conduct in office against an "accusation" proposed from the floor. The selection of an *impresa* for each member required a careful consideration by the censors and then a series of speeches in open session which sought to demonstrate, for example,

[11] Mario Praz, *Studies in Seventeenth Century Imagery* (London: Warburg Institute, 1939), discusses thoroughly the entire literature on *imprese,* with many delightful illustrations in the text. See especially p. 50 for a definition; the epistolary debate between Camilli and Tasso over the appropriateness of that of the Intronati is described in note to p. 17. For those of the Crusca: « Catalogo . . . degli accademici che hanno imprese », in *Prose e rime inedite d'Orazio Rucellai, di Tommaso Buonaventuri e d'altri* (Florence: Magheri, 1822), pp. 329 f.

[12] Intronati: *Capitoli, Art. VI.

that since the shell-like form (the applicant) without the *cialda* (pure flour, or the Academy) within it remains empty; and since, on the other hand, when touched by the "fire" of academic discussion, it becomes light, risen, and warmed so as to offer nourishment to the intellect of others, therefore the name *Ripieno* (the Filled One) is appropriate — or is not.[13] A minor amendment to a charter necessitated, in the Crusca, the suspension of the usual academic activities and the nomination of two "regents" of a "general assembly," who were then compared in learned perorations to Solon, Lycurgus, or dictators ruling the Roman Republic.[14] And long rhapsodies on the delights of well-earned vacations and exhortations to "take up again (*ripigliare*) the usual academic business" closed or opened each academic season.

True, some of these activities had lost much of their original significance. It is evident, for example, that by the end of the Seicento the academic orators no longer attached to *imprese* the metaphysical and mystical powers attributed to them by the courtiers at Urbino, by Giovio, by Lucarini, by Bargagli, and by a host of others a century earlier. Even though the famous frontispiece to Vico's *Scienza nuova seconda* shows the continuing popularity of symbolic representations and their adaptability to other purposes several decades later, the traditional discussions of such subjects had already dwindled into mere routine.[15] But what counted was the routine itself — the program, the set orations, the formalities; for the academies, by surrounding their administrative procedures with pomp and ceremony,

---

[13] « Difesa » and « Risposta alle censure fatte dallo Smunto all'Impresa », *Lettere di Francesco Redi*, ed. Domenico Moreni (Florence: Magheri, 1825), pp. 207, 213 f.

[14] A. M. Salvini, *Prose toscane*, I, lezione 12 (pp. 213-17).

[15] Compare the well-known passage in Baldassare Castiglione's *Cortegiano* (e. g., edition of Giuseppe Prezzolini (Milan-Rome: Rizzoli, 1937), pp. 59 and 64), in which Unico Aretino proposes as a question of discussion the significance of the *S* on the forehead of Elisabetta Gonzaga. One of the most famous Cinquecento treatises on the subject is that of Paolo Giovio, *Ragionamento sopra i motti e disegni d'arme e d'amore che comunemente chiamano imprese*, published in Vol. V of the *Biblioteca rara* of G. Daelli (Milan: G. Daelli, 1863). For the Intronati: Alcibiade Lucarini, *Imprese dell'Officioso accademico intronato, raccolte dallo Sconosciuto, accademico unito* (Siena, 1629) on the *impresa* of Scipione Bargagli. Cf. Eugenio Garin, *L'umanesimo italiano* (Bari: Laterza, 1952), p. 163.

celebrated the vary fact of their existence as autonomous self-sufficient institutions, conscious

> che se noni vi si appon di die in die
> lo tempo va d'intorno colle force. [16]

All the academies, secondly, while protecting themselves against the threat of Dante's scissors, recognized an obligation to "the universal knowledge of the sciences and the liberal arts," and they had provided either by law or custom for the presentation of discourses, *lezioni* or *dicerie,* to be delivered periodically before the assembly.[17] Neither the names, to be sure, nor the constitutions of the surviving Seicento academies, called "della Crusca" or "degli Intronati" rather than "of Botany" or "of Agriculture" like those of the following century, made any specification concerning the discourses except that they be "virtuous." The *scienze* invoked by the founders of the Accademia Fiorentina still meant "the whole wide range of learning and of doctrine, . . . which the Greeks expressed by a specially coined word: Encyclopedia"; and the ideal academician was still a "universal man" — like Lorenzo Magalotti — whose "incommensurabile vastità" of knowledge would admit no separation of disciplines.[18] The speakers might in theory, therefore, speak about anything they pleased: some brought before the academies reports of their own extra-academic activities that often had very little in common with the vast majority of discourses, like Filippo Baldinucci in discussions of esthetics and the history of art and Francesco Redi, whose scientific treatises bore the seal of the Crusca.[19] Others — and this practice was far more

---

[16] A. M. Salvini, *Prose toscane,* I, 359 (lezione 31).

[17] Fiorentina: *Capitoli, proemio. The original is no more logical: « L'universal cognizione, e notizia delle scienze . . . », etc.

[18] « Tutto il bel giro dell'erudizione, e della dottrina . . . che i greci con un sol nome espressero fatto a posta, di Enciclopedia »: A. M. Salvini, « In morte di Benedetto Averani », *Prose toscane,* I, 375; Giuseppe Averani on Magalotti, Crusca: * Diario, 18 August 1712; Capitolo del Sollevato in lode dell'Imperfetto (cf. * Diario, 27 November 1698): Cr. A.24, fol. 129 f.

[19] Some of these discourses are published, e.g., Filippo Baldinucci, *Lezione . . . nell'A. della C.* (29 December 1691 and 5 January 1692) (Florence: Matini, 1692), with reference to his *Notizie de' professori del disegno da Cimabue in qua* (in many volumes with the seal of the Crusca; Florence: Franchi, 1688-1727) (hereafter referred to in the 2d edition of

frequent — simply reshuffled the usual quotations from Homer, Vergil, and Dante into a "burlesque discourse" with such titles as "the cold warmed up" and "the glories of ignorance" or into a response to one of the *dubbi* — "If the fire of love is awakened more by seeing the beloved laugh or cry" (answer: "laugh," because Beatrice smiles at Dante in Paradise) — in which they frankly disavowed the limitations of a specific subject.[20]   Any question, indeed, could serve the requisites of "learning" as long as it provided a cohesive framework for a number of "learned" quotations.

In practice, nevertheless, the great majority of academic discourses at the turn of the century fell under a very few specific headings. The *Favella toscana,* first of all, had been for well over a century the most avidly cultivated of the "sciences" in Florence and Siena; the Accademia Fiorentina, in fact, had from the very beginning adopted the study and codification of the vernacular as its principal responsibility.   Although by 1700 the attempt to "make Tuscan into a real language of learning" — and therefore one capable of replacing the Latin of the Quattrocento — had largely succeeded, the question of proper linguistic usage had once again become particularly urgent.[21] The third (1691) edition of the *Vocabolario* had clearly defined the long-standing position of the Florentine academicians: the only "Tuscan" suitable for literary expression was that formulated between 1300 and 1400,

Il buon secolo: in which in our country one spoke and wrote with complete purity, without that variety and barbarity brought on later by the inmixture of other dialects and by the study of Latin, which led thence to the neglect of the spoken tongue.

D. M. Manni; Florence: Stecchi & Pagani, 1767-74), and his *Vocabolario toscano dell'arte del disegno,* dedicated to the Crusca (Florence: Franchi, 1681).   For Redi, see Dino Prandi, *Bibliografia delle opere di F. R.* (Reggio Emilia, 1941).

[20] Ricc Cod. Moreniana 365, fol. 4-6; Discourses in the Apatisti and Crusca from 1663 to 1665.   A. M. Salvini, *Discorsi accademici,* II, lezione 83, and Crusca: *Diario, 2 January 1698.

[21] S. Salvini, *Fasti consolari dell'A. F.,* p. xx.   On the origins of the « Questione della lingua » and its development in the Cinquecento, see Thérèse Labande-Jeauroy, *La question de la langue en Italie* (Strasbourg: Istra, 1925); Robert A. Hall, *The Italian « Questione della lingua »: An Interpretative Essay* (Chapel Hill: University of North Carolina Press, 1942); Maurizio Vitale, *Le « Prose » di Pietro Bembo e le prime grammatiche del secolo XVI* (Milan:

To this perfect speech they were willing to admit the words of a number of later writers whom they judged to be faithful imitators of the *buon secolo* and to include as well the expressions still used both "by the people (*volgo*)" and "by the men of the court" in Tuscany. They specifically forbade the use of dialect or foreign words, which "rather than adding refinements, might introduce roughness into the language," and they condemned the travesties of "some affected youths,... who find nauseous anything that does not come from France."[22] For any attempt, they insisted, to modify the language of those who had given Italian its greatest masterpieces would limit the thought, impair the expressiveness, and dry up the imagination of all posterity. The compilers of the third *Vocabolario* had sought to silence the opposition to the first two editions by amplifying the citations, by quietly admitting Tasso as an "authority," and by conceding the qualification of a certain number of words as *voci antiche*. But alas! the compromise simply provoked another storm of protest. The critics objected first of all to the omission of many words used by the approved authors, of which Jacopo Facciolati of Padova listed "several hundred" from the "infinite number" he had found. They complained secondly of its refusal to admit the obsolescence of much Trecento language, which, though it might still be current in Florence as the Crusca claimed, simply gave less diligent non-Tuscan students an opportunity to disguise inadequate work with verbal flourishes.[23] And they denounced above all the exclusion of perfectly

La Gogliardica, 1954), esp. Part. III (beware of typographical errors in the bibliographies); and Bruno Migliorini, « La questione della lingua », in *Questioni e correnti di storia letteraria,* ed. A. Momigliano (Milan: Marzorati, 1949), pp. 1-75 (esp. pp. 38-41).

[22] *Vocabolario* (3d ed., 1691), Preface, p. 14: « Il buon secolo nel quale veramente nella nostra Patria e si parlò, e si scrisse con intiera schiettezza, e senza quella varietà, e barbarie, che indusse poi il rimescolamento cogli altri dialetti, e lo studio posto nella lingua Latina, che indusse per cotal guisa trascuranza della materna ». F. Redi to Carlo De' Dottori in Padova, 6 July 1681, in [Jacopo Facciolati], *Ortografia moderna e italiana* (2d ed.: Padova, G. Manfrè, 1723), Part II, p. 28. Cf. Renato Piattoli, « Storia editoriale di un gruppo di lettere di Francesco Redi attenenti a cose di lingua e al Vocabolario della Crusca », *La bibliografia,* LIV (1952), 116-19, which establishes the dates of some of the letters printed from 1724 by Manni.

[23] Facciolati, *op. cit.,* pp. i-ii. He might well have noticed, as has Guglielmo Volpi, that some of the words were simply invented by the editor: « Le falsificazioni di Francesco Redi nel Vocabolario della Crusca », *Atti della R. A. della C.* (1915-16), pp. 33-64.

good Lombard or Venetian expressions for which there was no Tuscan equivalent. A too rigorous limitation on the natural expansion of the language, they pointed out, would simply end in its petrification. The "Anti-Cruscans" still shared with the Crusca the general concept of language as a perfectly formed medium of communication to be imitated by aspiring authors; and it seems never to have occured to them, as it did to Minturno before them or Vico after, that words might simply emanate from the will of the creative human mind. Indeed, they denied neither the superiority of Tuscan over other dialects nor the authority of the Tuscan academicians as linguistic judges. Instead, they called upon the Crusca to fulfil its proper mission, deploring only those "puerile, inept *Cruscanti,* who claim to possess all alone the entire teaching authority for the literature of today," who scorned the perfectly expressive modern variants and dialect words of authentic Latin derivation which Benedetto Marcello would later imagine the Lombards, the Bergameschi, and *Il Seicentuccio* offering in homage to *Monna Cruschetta.*[24]

But the Cruscans refused to cede. In 1696 they intrusted the preparation of still another edition to a special committee which, except for an interruption between 1710 and 1714, was to meet bi-weekly until the completion of the fourth edition in 1729-38. They accepted the invitation of Pandolfo Pandolfini to respond to the latest attack, published in Venice under the name of the once formidable opponent Alessandro Tassoni, not by expressing their "resentment," but by considering carefully each of the criticisms and

---

[24] *Il toscanismo e la Crusca, o sia Il Cruscante impazzito* (Venice: Recurti, 1739), p. vi (reprinted the next year in Naples by the Stamperia Munziana. It is usually attributed to Marcello, although some catalogues and even such an authority as Carlo Calcaterra attribute it to Francesco Arizzi). Lodovico Vedriani, *Historia dell'antichissima città di Modona* (Modena: Soliani, 1666), II, 720. On the recognition of the authority of the Crusca, note the request of the historian and critic Lodovico Antonio Muratori for advice on proper usage: *Lettere inedite di L. A. M. scritte a toscani* (Florence: Le Monnier, 1854), pp. 126, 131, 161, etc., and especially his confession to Salvini (24 September 1700, *ibid.,* p. 128): « In somma, le Muse italiane scelsero il più maestoso ed ameno lor nido nella Toscana, molti secoli sono, e ve lo mantengono con grande felicità », as well as his delight over the *Annotazioni* (see next footnote), to Magliabechi, 24 December 1698, p. 72. On the philosophy of language in the sixteenth century, see further Riccardo Scrivano, « La posizione di Vincenzo Borghini nella critica cinquecentesca », *Rassegna della letteratura italiana,* VII (1958), 22-37.

reporting their conclusions in academic sessions.[25] And they set out, in innumerable discourses over the next two decades "in praise of the Tuscan language," to illustrate the subtlety of its nuances, the beauty of its accents, the logic of its syntax and grammar, and the richness of its vocabulary. Some undertook to clarify former definitions, answering in lengthy reports such questions as whether the word *grasce* pertained only to household goods; others dissected the Venetian *Annotazioni* or unearthed former critics as far back as Paolo Beni (1613) in order to "give him a good thrumping and pound down his insolence."[26] Polemics often became warm indeed, as "tenderness... turned into compassion, then laughter, and finally scorn of the scorners," [27] and as the Cruscans stooped to personal denigration, accusing Muratori, for instance, of trying to advance his own reputation by finding errors in Petrarch. But they considered

[25] *Annotazioni sopra il Vocabolario degli accademici della Crusca, Opera postuma di Alessandro Tassoni* (Venice: Rossetti, 1697) (cf. Crusca: * Diario, 11 December 1698): but note T. Casini, « A. T. e la Crusca », in *Rivista critica della letteratura italiana,* II (1885), pp. 93-94, and U. Renda, « A. T. e il Vocabolario della C. », *Miscellanea tassoniana di studi storici e letterari,* ed. T. Casini (Bologna-Modena: Formiggini, 1908), pp. 277-324. Even the wording of the preface *a chi legge* renders the authorship of the work suspect, by lamenting the loss of Tassoni's four-volume *Ragionamenti* « ne' quali... si scoprirebbero gli errori del cav. Lionardo Salviati, e di Diomede Borghesi, del Bembo, del Muzio, del Ruscelli [all the Cruscan 'saints,' in other words] e di tant'altri che hanno voluto prescriver leggi all'Italiana favella », and by claiming to base the publication on some documents discovered by Magliabechi, who would certainly have handed them over to the Crusca and to no one else.   The largely polemical intention of the book is confirmed by the anonymous editor's justification of printing the « annotations » eighty-four years after the appearance of the first edition to which they would have applied: the third edition, he remarks, has corrected less than one third of the errors found by Tassoni in the first. Names of the members of the committee appointed in 1698 are listed by Alamanni in *Atti dell' A. della C.,* I (1819), lxxxii, and a few records of their sessions remain in scattered, unmarked MS sheets in the present library of the Academy.   A detailed description of the preparation of the third edition is given in several letters of Alessandro Segni to Francesco Redi in 1680 in a copy from the originals once in the possession of Redi's nephew Gregorio: Cr IX Selva a/2.

[26] Salvini's original is far more expressive than the translation: « Dargliene una buona stropicciatura... e rintuzzar la sua sfacciataggine »: from « Progetto di risposta ... all'*Anti-crusca* di Mess. Paolo Beni », *Saggio di lettere di Orazio Rucellai,* ed. D. Moreni (Florence: Magheri, 1826), pp. 183-98. On Beni (1552-1627), his *Anticrusca, ovvero il paragone dell'italiana lingua: Nel quale si mostra chiaramente che l'antica sia inculta e rozza e la moderna regolata e gentile* ... (Padova: B. Martini, 1613, reprinted in 1619). Cf. letters of Rucellai of 1665-66 in *Saggio di lettere,* pp. 1, 2, 21, and 34.

[27] A. M. Salvini, *Censura d'una censura d'autore ignoto intorno alla nuova edizione del Vocabolario* (Nozze Tassinari-Rampi; Imola, 1850), p. 12.

their mission of vital importance, for such criticism threatened to
"ruin and render defective the most beautiful and perfect works" for
the "studious youth" and provide "foreigners" with just another opportunity "to offend our writers." [28] Thus Corsi, Forzoni Accolti, the
Salvini, and, above all, Benedetto Averani devoted thirty-five lectures
in the first decades to Petrarch alone, largely to the *canzoni* on
Laura's eyes; Marc' Antonio de' Mozzi dedicated some ten to the
exegesis of Canto I of the Purgatorio; Salvini and Buonaventuri
explained the quality of the later poets, from Ariosto and Tasso on,
by their conformity to Trecento models; and they all appealed to the
grammarians of the sixteenth and seventeenth centuries, to Pietro
Bembo, Giovanni Della Casa, and Benedetto Buommattei, in support
of the Academy's decisions. [29] Among the various cities of Tuscany
there may well have been a certain disagreement as to *whose* Trecento
was the better: the Intronati, for instance, found in the letters of
St. Catherine, which they were publishing for their colleague Gigli,
a model of linguistic purity unequaled by any Florentine author. [30]
But all agreed on the inadmissibility of any modification in the perfect
speech of the *secolo d'oro,* and none, needless to say, ever doubted

[28] Gio. Bartolommeo Casaregi, *Difesa delle tre canzoni degli occhi* ... *di Francesco
Petrarca,* published together with similar essays of Giovanni Tommaso Canevari and Antonio
Tommasi (Lucca: Frediani, 1709), p. 203. Note his rather discourteous comment on Muratori's criticism of the line « Di là non vanno dalle parti estreme »: « . . . a quei, che ben
intendono la forza del buon parlare toscano [i.e., Florentines], non riuscirà oscura la sud-
detta maniera di dire . . . »: p. 47.

[29] Crusca: *Diario, 20 July 1710, 5 July 1705, and 3 January 1709, *et seg.* (various
entries thereafter). Benedetto Averani, *Dieci lezioni composte sopra il quarto sonetto della
prima parte del "Canzoniere" del Petrarca* (Ravenna: Landi, 1707), beginning 21 August 1698
in the Crusca. A similar series of lectures by A. M. Salvini began on 5 January 1708
(Diario). Cf. Rozzi: Costituzione, published in appendix to Curzio Mazzi, *La Congreda
dei Rozzi di Siena nel secolo XVI* (2 vols.; Florence: Le Monnier, 1882). The one exception
to the universal Trecentismo among the Cinquecento academies was the provision of the
Rozzi, in their reformed charter of 1561, « che non si possi leggiere altro poeta che il nostro
M. Jacopo Sanazaro [*sic*] » (Art. XII) without special permission.

[30] *Le opere della serafica S. Caterina di Siena,* nuovamente pubblicate da Girolamo Gigli
4 vols.; Siena: Bonetti, and Lucca: Venturini, 1707-21). Gigli's request for financial
assistance in publication: an undated memorial (1702?) to the Intronati: BCS Y.I.19; his
« Orazione in lode della toscana favella » (1706), in his *Lezioni di lingua toscana* (Venice:
Giavarina, 1729), pp. 117 ff.; and the tribute of V. P. Carli in dedication to *Componimenti
teatrali del sig. G. G.* (Siena: Bonetti, 1759).

the value of devoting session after session to the consideration of such questions.[31]

Far from infringing on its traditional prestige, secondly, the glorification of Tuscan actually encouraged the study of ancient languages and literature, for which Florentines had once won the acclaim of all Europe. To be sure, the great days of Angelo Poliziano and Pier Vettori had long since past, and Tuscany had not escaped the general decline of these disciplines evident all over Italy from as early as the mid-Cinquecento. Nevertheless, Latin still remained the basis of elementary as well as advanced education (the Jesuits and the *Scolopi* had preserved at least this principle of humanist pedagogy), and Greek continued to be taught, not only in the schools, as, for example, in England, but also in the universities, which elsewhere in Italy had generally given it up during the course of the seventeenth century.[32] It is not surprising, therefore, that the academicians should have been so receptive to the discourses on Homer, Ulpian, Theocritus, and Plotinus that appear in the diaries.[33] For the professors of Greek at Pisa and Florence had always been among their most active members — Giovan Battista Doni, Alessandro Adimari, and Carlo Dati in the past, and now, in 1700, Benedetto Averani, whom Curione calls "the most celebrated Greek teacher of the Seicento," and Anton Maria Salvini, whose dedication to the "Greek muses" drew compliments even from the great Benedictine scholar Bernard de Montfaucon.[34]

---

[31] Crusca: * Diario, 7 January 1711 and 10 January 1704.

[32] See Alessandro Curione, *Sullo studio del greco in Italia nei secoli XVII e XVIII* (Rome: Tosi, 1941), chaps. i-iii, and M. L. Clarke, *Greek Studies in England, 1700-1830* (Cambridge: Cambridge University Press, 1945), chap. iii, and *Classical Education in Britain, 1500-1900* (Cambridge: Cambridge University Press, 1959), chaps, iii and v. While classical philology died out in Italy, in Germany the influence of Joseph Scaliger, Justus Lipsius, and Janus Gruterus remained alive all through the seventeenth century, in spite of a tendency to rather arid *Einzelforschungen*. See Conrad Bursian, *Geschichte der classischen Philologie in Deutschland* (Munich and Leipzig: Oldenbourg, 1883), p. 270, and the rest of Book III, chap. i.

[33] Crusca: * Diario, 7 January and 2 April 1707.

[34] Curione, *Sullo studio del greco*, p. 63 (with bibliography on Averani, p. 65); Bernard de Montfaucon, *Diarium italicum* (Paris: Anisson, 1702), p. 394: « Salvinus vero Florentiae ornamentum, litterariae rei peritia cum primis clarus, Graecas musas maximè colit . . . » (undoubtedly somewhat exaggerated for the benefit of Cosimo III).

To be sure, the curriculum of the schools had no place in the sessions of the academies, since the charters forbade the use of any language but Tuscan. But the academicians were nonetheless convinced of the utility of classical learning for their own purposes. It could contribute, for example, to "oratory and the poetical faculty"; it could clear up such equivocal passages in the Scriptures as John the Baptist's negative response to the question *propheta es tu?* (by making the reader conscious of the definite article in the original); and it was "necessary," as Angelo Maria Ricci, later Salvini's successor in the chair of Greek at the Studio, pointed out, for anyone aspiring to be "truly learned in any science whatever." [35]   There were also less serious reasons: a knowledge of the lives, customs, and beliefs of the ancients, of their concepts of the "Divine Essence," and of their burial rites, their banquets, and their use of iced beverages, could both instruct Cruscans on the proper conduct of their *stravizzi* and relieve their discomfort during hot summer sessions.[36]   But above all the academicians found that the study of ancient languages offered the most effective means of demonstrating the equality, if not the superiority, of their own to all other languages. Since Greek and Latin — and perhaps Hebrew, out of respect for the Sacred Sricptures — seemed to offer the only competition to Tuscan in richness of vocabulary and range of expression, they deemed it their obligation to "magnify... the greatness and dignity" of Tuscan by carrying out the injunction of the Fiorentina: to render "every good sentence from every other language into our own."[37]

[35] A. M. Salvini, « Apologia sopra la lingua greca », *Prose toscane,* I, lezione 48, and his defense of Domenico Lazzerini, professor of Greek at Padova (who later made rather harsh criticisms of Salvini's translations), Crusca: * Diario, 14 January 1712. Angelmaria Ricci, *Della necessità e facilità della lingua greca* (Florence: Albizzini, 1714), pp. 14, 24 (Apatisti: * Lezioni, 12 December 1714).

[36] Crusca: * Diario, 14 and 21 January 1706; 28 August 1710, *et al.* Giuseppe Averani, *Del vitto e delle cene degli antichi* (Milan: 1863) (first published as Vol. III of his *Lezioni toscane* [Florence: Albizzini, 1766], according to the Preface; but I have been unable to find this edition).

[37] Ricci, *op. cit.,* p. 9: « Ampliare . . . la grandezza e dignità »; Fiorentina: * Capitoli, « Constituzione dell'obbligo degli accademici . . . », 4 March 1546. The only translation done from modern languages during a period of some thirty years were: Filippo Corsini's translation of Antonio de Solis, *Istoria della conquista del Messico* (Florence: Cecchi, 1699), and *Cato, a Tragedy by Mr. Addison: Il Catone, tragedia del signor Addison, tradotta da*

Hence translation formed the principal occupation of the academic Hellenists and Latinists; and so eagerly did they pursue their task that they remained unrivaled, at least in quantity of production, until the outburst of translations (*ou de trahisons*) into Franch in the second half of the century.[38] They set themselves rigorous standards: a deep knowledge of both the original and Tuscan, a thorough understanding of the material treated, and a scrupulous exactness in finding just the word corresponding to each thought of the author.[39] That this *ad verbum* method usually produced cold, prosaic, inelegant translations — the kind Foscolo later gave the generic name of *Salvinian* — made little difference; indeed, many of them were well enough accepted to be reprinted several times during the eighteenth and even into the nineteenth century. Salvini and his colleagues were not primarily philologists. They took no part in the work of editing and emending texts that was just then beginning at Padova, and they paid little attention to the manuscript treasures in the Florentine libraries that were so to fascinate their immediate successors. Nor did they seek in the study of antiquity a stimulus to original reflections and speculations, either philosophical or political, as had their ancestors of the Quattrocento; indeed, they looked upon the *Antichi* not as real people living in historical time,

Anton Maria Salvini (Florence: Nestenus, 1725), parts of which were read to the Crusca: * Diario, 11 August 1701 and 5 December 1715. Note further * Diario, 17 July 1710, in which Salvini « turned then to praise English, and finally much more the Tuscan language »: *Prose toscane,* I, lezione 26.

[38] Compare the number of translations by Salvini alone, of which a list is given by his biographer Cordaro, in *A. M. S., saggio critico-biografico,* with the list in appendix to Clarke, *Greek Studies in England.* Maurice Badolle, *L'Abbé Jean-Jacques Barthélemy (1716-1795) et l'hellénisme en France dans la seconde moitié du XVIIIe siècle* (Paris: Presses Universitaires de France, 1926), pp. 173 f. (quoted. p. 173). That Salvini's translations were valued primarily as exercises in Tuscan is further indicated by the inclusion of his *Lucian* in the *Opuscoli inediti di celebri autori toscani, l'opere dei quali sono citate dal Vocabolario della Crusca* (3 vols.; Florence: Stamperia di Borgo Ognissanti, 1807), II, 5 ff.

[39] Carlo Dati, « Del traslatare i classici nel volgar nostro », in his *Prose scelte* (Venice: 1846), pp. 81 ff., and among many discourses « in lode del tradurre », Crusca: * Diario, 30 July 1705 (Salvini), 10 March 1708, 31 July 1710 (Tommaso Buonaventuri). Note further Introduction of Domenico Valentini to his *Il Giulio Cesare, Tragedia istorica di G. Shakespeare tradotta dall'inglese* (Siena: Bindi, 1756) (on which: Anna Maria Crinò, *Le traduzioni di Shakespeare in Italia del Settecento* [Rome: Edizioni di Storia e Letteratura, 1950]). Often the critical commentaries were as important as the text itself: note those by Regnier Desmarais to Salvini's *Teocrito volgarizzato,* ed. A. F. Gori (Arezzo: Belotti, 1754).

but only as abstract models from which to deduce "precepts" of virtue and eloquence. Nor, for that matter, did they weigh the relative merits of ancients and moderns, like the participants in the *Querelle* then raging beyond the Alps; they could admire Greek and Roman writers for their "simplicity" and "clarity" while applauding Tuscan writers for their language, and they concluded that all were equally worthy of respect.[40] For the academicians of 1700 studied ancient languages and literature largely for the sake of Tuscan. And they intended their work not as a means of popularizing texts that none of the members would admit not being able to read in the original, but of demonstrating that Theocritus, Anacreon, Aulus Persius, Xenophon, Isocrates, Sappho, Horace, Homer, Vergil, and all other ancient authors, good or bad, famous or obscure, could have expressed themselves in the language of the *Vocabolario* without any restriction or modification of their ideas.

With somewhat less pleasure, perhaps, but with more self-righteous satisfaction, the academicians applied their learning also to exegeses and commentaries on matters of faith. Pagan antiquity was, after all, pagan; and they realized fully the possibility of falling into "grave errors" through excessive affection for the "Gentile philosophers."[41] Many of the academicians were ecclesiastics; and all of them were more than willing to seize any occasion, the beginning of Lent, Holy Week, or the feast of the patron, to modify the usual eulogies of the "good authors" into recommendations for "the reading of spiritual books."[42] Some of the speakers commented on various elements of Catholic doctrine: the Conception of the Virgin, the Resurrection, and the Trinity. Others meditated on moments in the life of Christ, corroborating the accounts of the Passion in the Gospels with citations from Latin authors, underlining the ignominy associated with the Flagellation and the Crucifixion in Roman criminal procedure, or determining the exact measurements of the Crown of Thorns. Some deduced from the Scriptures rules of practical morality for the guidance of the "youth," showing, for example, that "dishonest loves

---

[40] A. M. Salvini, *Discorsi accademici,* II, 55; Crusca: * Diario, 4 December 1699.
[41] Giuseppe Averani, *Lezioni toscane* (2 vols.; Florence: Albizzini, 1766), I, 134 f.
[42] Crusca: * Diario, 27 March 1698.

lead to a very bad end," that through the "knowledge of one's self" one can best avoid "hypocrisy" and "simulation," and that it is better to merit than to possess a position of honor.   And still others simply composed *lodi* (praises) of the Christian religion indistinguishable, except for the anathemas hurled against "atheism" and "superstition," from the more usual *lodi* of poetry and of deceased members.[43]

The popularity of such questions in the academies apparently bore very little relation to the depth of religious sentiment or conviction among the members.   Orators and versifiers talked incessantly about sin and superstition, which contemporary records show to have flourished about them; but never did they give any more immediate an example than the pride of Alexander and the divination of the Romans.   They meditated at length on the instability of the City of Man as evident in the empires of Xerxes and Caesar; but never did it occur to them that the same instability might be found in the regime of Cosimo III de' Medici.   They intoned sonnets to St. Thomas and St. Augustine; but never did they suspect the existence of the doctrinal difficulties that were just then provoking such discussion beyond the Alps.   "Heresy" still meant Manichaeism, Donatism, and Arianism; the term "infidel" applied only to the followers of the "Impostor" Mohammed; and the gods of Olympus presented the only threat to Christianity worthy of the "protests" of submission to the Church printed in prefaces to verse collections and theater programs.   Theological inquiry among the academicians remained what it had been in about the sixth century A.D.   Not only did they pass in silence over such names as Copernicus, Galileo, Calvin, Jansenius, and Bayle, that had a certain polemical currency in their own times, they ignored as well all the great spiritual leaders of the Catholic Reformation from St. Ignatius on.   Reduced as it was to a repeated protestation of orthodoxy, to masses for deceased members, to poetical tributes to the patron saint, or, occasionally, to a pilgrimage to Loreto or the Madonna of Impruneta, religion in academic discussions often dwindled into idle casuistry — to solving such questions as "what, after God, most deserves our love?" and "what is more blameworthy,

[43] E.g., Crusca: * Diario, 2 April 1700, 2 September 1706, 13 September 1708, 2 March 1718; Apatisti: * Lezioni, 14 December 1698, 10 May 1699, 24 February 1718.

2

avarice or prodigality?" to haranguing against "idleness" or "ingratitude," and to praising "friendship" and "moderation." Seldom
did they offer anything more to practicing Christians of their day
than the vague assurance

> Che l'innata virtù non pur l'invita (the soul),
> ma spinge al Ciel;
> ne puote esser mai paga,
> di non perfetto Ben, voglia infinita.[44]

In order to demonstrate the "necessity of controlling human appetites"
or the relative ease of becoming "holy" or "wise," speakers would
bring forth the whole array of sacred and profane authors from Plato
and Pythagoras to St. Augustine, line up the opinions — preferably
in the original language — on both sides, and generally conclude that
the philosopher might derive more value from the study of the
orators, but that he really should read the poets as well.

Frequently such subjects strayed far from the strict exigencies
of practical morality: "It is more estimable to express a good thought
roughly or a mediocre thought with all the finesse of art?" But
all were in essence questions of conduct for which the answers were
already known, questions of social obligations that had not the re-
motest relevance to the stable, compact society of 1700, or questions
of the relation between man and God that offered little in either
emotional or intellectual content. In essence, religion in the academies
was as hopelessly confused with the other fields of "learning" as were
the respective functions of civil and ecclesiastical authorities in the
administration of the Grand Duchy; and moral philosophy only feebly
recalled the Neo-Platonic *questioni d'amore,* which at the time of
Pietro Bembo had contained elements of genuine, or at least sincere,
philosophic speculation, but which by the mid-Cinquecento had already degenerated into the sterile and interminable sentences of Benedetto Varchi.[45] While the academies, like the *confraternite* and the

---

[44] G. B. Casaregi, *Sonetti e canzoni toscane* (Florence: Albizzini, 1741), sonetto xxxiii
on « L'anima nostra va sempre in traccia di Dio »; « That innate virtue does not merely invite
it, but presses it toward Heaven; nor can infinite desire ever be content with an imperfect
Good » (p. xv).

[45] See Nesca A. Robb, *Neo-Platonism in the Italian Renaissance* (London: Allen and
Unwin, 1935), chap. vi, esp. p. 196.

guilds, recognized a moral and religious function in inspiring their members when alive and praying for them when dead, they could not deny that such subjects offered admirably respectable material for the recitations in *lingua toscana* imposed by their constitutions.[46]

The third principal activity of these literary academies consisted of applying the faith in the richness of the vernacular to original composition. The meetings of the Crusca and the Apatisti always ended with the recitation of a new sonnet, often an extemporaneous comment on the preceding discourse; and those of the Rozzi and the Intronati were, by 1700, dedicated almost exclusively to the consideration of songs and odes to be presented at public spectacles. Such exercises were subject to a rigorous discipline. From two to six censors in each academy met secretly every fortnight or so to examine the contributions deposited, usually anonymously, in a locked box known as the *tramoggia* or the *zucca*. The best were then selected for a formal line-by-line criticism (*critica*) and then an equally detailed defense (*difesa*), in which the speakers dwelt at length over such particulars as "that *sole sole* has a certain I-don't-know-what that ends by not quite pleasing my ear." [47] Finally, a vote of the assembly decided either to return them to the authors for appropriate correction or to transcribe them into one of the permanent books — the *stacciato* or the *fiore* in the Crusca — depending upon their relative merits. The writing of original verse, in other words, was intended not as mere entertainment. It was rather a means of stimulating creativity. The elaborate procedure prescribed by the academies was justified, therefore, by the assumption that constant practice in composition and careful adherence to the forms and words of Horace

---

[46] Like A. M. Salvini, whose *Prose sacre* (Florence: Tartini & Franchi, 1716), delivered on various occasions in the Cathedral, the Seminary, and San Lorenzo, are almost indistinguishable in tone and composition from his many other discourses. Similarly, Marc'Antonio de' Mozzi, *Discorsi sacri* (Florence: Manni, 1717). Note further the mixture of linguistic and religious interests in the Preface to the *Fioretti di San Francesco* (Florence: Tartini & Franchi, 1718).

[47] F. Redi to Vincenzo da Filicaia, 2 November 1686, in Filicaia, *Poesie toscane* (Florence: Maturi, 1707-8), cited here in 2d ed. (Venice, 1812), II, 280: « Quel sole sole à un certo non so che, che al mio orecchio non finisce di piacere »; and Tommaso Buonaventuri. « Sopra un sonetto della Tramoggia . . . », and « Difesa dell'istesso sonetto », in *Prose e rime d'Orazio Rucellai*, pp. 211 ff.

and Petrarch would eventually lead to something of comparable poetic value.

No one, in 1700, would ever have doubted the complete validity of this assumption. Indeed, the recent success of several academic poets seemed to have given it the full support of experience. The lively *Bacco in Toscana* of Francesco Redi, after all, had been conceived in the *Stravizzo* of 1666 and perfected during some twenty years of discussions in the Crusca. And the amorous sonnets of Lodovico Adimari, the lyrics of Benedetto Menzini, the spiritual meditations of Vincenzo da Filicaia, and the *Bucchereide* of Lorenzo Bellini had already been hailed as classics by their contemporaries and soon would be admitted as authoritative language texts by the editors of the fourth *Vocabolario*.[48] Thanks in part to the durability of the Cinquecento revival of the Florentine *volgare,* moreover, Tuscan writers had managed to maintain a considerable degree of cultural autonomy throughout the seventeenth century; and they consciously (and, according to modern critics, successfully) resisted the taste for extravagant metaphors and flamboyant euphuism spread all over Italy by the most applauded poet of the age, the Neapolitan G. B. Marino. Like the other Seicento *Antiseicentisti,* it is true, they failed to propose any but the traditional remedies to what they deplored as "the modern affectations of this depraved century."[49] Yet by carefully preserving the special characteristics of their own literary heritage, they provided a direct connection between the Petrarchians of the Cinquecento and those of the early Settecento and thus anticipated, at least in practice, the attack on "Marinism" and the demand for

---

[48] See Ferdinando Massai, *Lo « Stravizzo » della Crusca del 12 settembre 1666 e l'origine del « Bacco in Toscana » di Francesco Redi* (Rocca S. Casciano, 1916). Lodovico Adimari, *Poesie sacre e morali* (Florence: Cecchi, 1696), and *Sonetti amorosi* (n.d.) (on which note the rather harsh comments of Dino Provenzal in *La vita e le opere di L. A.* [Rocca S. Casciano, 1902]); Menzini, *Opere* (Florence: Tartini & Franchi, 1731-32), esp. I: *Poesie liriche.* On Filicaia, note Crusca: * Diario, 14 July 1707; Lorenzo Fabbri, *Orazione in morte del senator V. da F. . . . detta nell'Accademia degli Apatisti* (Florence: G. Manni, 1709); and Tommaso Buonaventuri, Orazione in lode . . .: Mar A. 277, 2-4. Redi's *Bacco in Toscana ed Arianna inferma* was first published by Matini in Florence in 1685 and several times thereafter; Lorenzo Bellini recited his *Bucchereide* (Florence: Stamperia Reale, 1729) in the Crusca from 12 December 1697 on (* Diario).

[49] Lorenzo Panciatichi (1674) quoted in the preface to Menzini, *Opere,* I, xv-xvi (« affettazione moderna di questo secolo depravato »).

strict conformity to the Trecento, Roman, and Greek classics which Arcadia soon elevated to the position of a poetic principle.[50]

Still, it would be hazardous to credit the academic exercises with the quality of the few pieces that still are read, enjoyed, quoted by banquet toastmasters, and included in anthologies today. That the *Bacco* preserved its spontaneous vivacity through all its many drafts, for instance, is probably due more to the genius of the author than to the assistance of his colleagues, which all too often consisted merely in requests to be mentioned in the text.[51] That the exercises produced verses, to be sure, is indeniable — thousands and thousands of them, which the vast quantity surviving among the papers of the academies represents but a part of those mentioned in the diaries. That they produced verses as Petrarchian as Petrarch or as Anacreontic as Anacreon is barely less questionable; for as Petrarch had written sonnets, so did the academicians — sonnets on love, birth, and death, sonnets on the soul of Christina of Sweden rising to God, sonnets on the coronation of Clement XI or the election of the doge of Genova, sonnets comparing the Spanish general Montemar to St. Jerome, sonnets celebrating the terror of the Infidels before the Venetian fleet, sonnets on the retirement of an *arciconsolo* or the beginning of academic vacation, all in impeccable Trecento speech and all adorned with elaborate footnotes explaining the oblique references to, say, the Fall of Troy or the hidden compliments to friends and relatives.[52] But whether or not quality corresponded to quantity is somewhat less certain. Most of what the academicians praised as poetry amounted

[50] See Walter Binni, « La formazione della poetica arcadica e la letteratura fiorentina di fine Seicento », *Rassegna della letteratura italiana*, LVIII (1954), 534-60; Umberto Limentani, « L'antiseicentismo nella letteratura della prima metà del Seicento », *La critica stilistica e il barocco letterario (Atti del II Congresso Internazionale di Studi Italiani)* (Florence: Le Monnier, 1957), pp. 253-60; and Riccardo Scrivano in « La posizione di Vincenzo Borghini nella critica cinquecentesca », *Rassegna della letteratura italiana*, LXII (1958), pp. 22-37, esp. p. 30.

[51] Note introductions to *Le più belle pagine di Francesco Redi*, ed. Piero Giacosa (Milan: Treves, 1925) and *Vita, opera iconografia, bibliografia, vocabolario inedito delle voci aretine e libro inedito dei « Ricordi » di F. R.*, ed. Ugo Viviani (Arezzo: U. Viviani, 1924-28).

[52] Much of the poetry of the Crusca is preserved in Cr A.26, A.27, A.28, and 14, and some other pieces in Laur 441: Raccolte di poesie. That of the Intronati for the annual feasts is in BCS Y.I.15-18, in four MS volumes; that of the Rozzi is described briefly by Fabiani in *Memoria dell'A. dei R.*

in fact to hundreds of perfectly balanced lines in which all the words had been carefully checked in the *Vocabolario,* in which imagery was limited to subjects of classical mythology, and in which metaphor was sacrificed to prosaic, abstract demonstration. The academies seem to have instilled in their members not so much a capacity for literary creativity as a habit of thinking automatically in rhyme and meter and an ability to dash off sonnets "in bits and pieces day by day" (*giornalmente alla spicciolata*). It is not surprising, therefore, that Anton Maria Salvini by 1723 had amassed an "infinite number" of his own compositions, of which the "few less bad ones" selected for publication added up to no less than 416.[53] But nor is it surprising that no edition of Salvini's poems has appeared since the early eighteenth century.

However frivolous some of these activities may appear two and a half centuries later, they were regarded at the time with the utmost seriousness, by visitors from abroad as well as by Florentines.[54] Unlike the other organizations that also bore the general name of *accademia* — the theatrical groups, the art and music societies (like the Accademia del Disegno), and the schools on one hand and the scientific societies of the following decades on the other — the Crusca, the Intronati, and the Apatisti made no pretense of instructing or edifying their fellow citizens. Instead, their members addressed only a select élite:

> Nel sentiero del volgo imprimer l'orme
> Non è saggio consiglio;
> E de' buoni è quaggiù piccola schiera:
> Che veder puoi a un sol rotar di ciglio
> Cangiarsi in mille forme
> La turba adulatrice, e lusinghiera...[55]

[53] A. M. Salvini, *Sonetti* (Florence: Tartini & Franchi, 1723), Preface.

[54] Compare the reflections of Milton and Lassels in « how far the Italians excel us in passing their time well... making of orations and verses instead of drinking of ale and smoking of tobacco »: quoted by Lacy Collison-Morely in *Italy after the Renaissance* (London: G. Routledge, 1930), p. 27, with the more common judgment (« corbellerie e buffonerie ») of Gaetano Imbert, *La vita fiorentina del '600* (Florence: Bemporad, 1906), chap. ix.

[55] B. Menzini, *Opere,* I, 4: « To fix one's feet in the paths of the vulgar, this is unwise advice. Here on earth the good are but a small band; and you may see in one sweep of the eye how the flattering mob changes itself into a thousand forms ».

This isolation from and disdain of the multitude was reflected above all in the current theory of the origin and nature of academic institutions. Salvini and Gigli still agreed substantially with Scipione Bargagli, who, in 1569, had found the original model for contemporary literary societies in the "virtuous conversations for the comfort, utility, and recreation of this our mortal life" held by the followers of Plato "among peaceful woods and pleasant fields" "a mile away from the city of Athens." The second academy arose, he had continued, when friends of "il gran M. Tullio" retired to his villa near Pozzuoli (?), "lovely and delightful and adorned magnificently with woods and terraces." Academies then reappeared when a few "gentle spirits, excellent in various kinds of doctrine" sought to "bury themselves," like the Sepolti of Volterra, from the confusion and uncertainty, from "all dull and idle thoughts," and from "all the other mundane cares" of their age. In conformity with this theory, the academies had all, ever since their foundation, limited their membership to those able to demonstrate exceptional talent, prohibited the attendance of non-members except upon very special occasions, and forbidden the publication of their proceedings.[56] For they assumed that an impenetrable barrier separated "learning" from the "world," and that once within the academy, the "gentle spirits" would leave behind such matters as taxation, planting, harvests, the cure of souls, and the price of bread — *cure mondane* which may well have troubled their "secular" lives, but which could neither contribute to nor be guided by the conversation of scholars. The older academies of Florence and Siena still remained in essence, over a century after Bargagli's definition,

an assembly of free and virtuous intellects, ready to look for knowledge with honest, and friendly emulation; who under prescribed laws and statutes exert

---

[56] A. M. Salvini, *Prose sacre,* p. 135; Gigli to Magliabecchi, BCS Y.I.1, fol. 1; Scipione Bargagli, *Delle lodi dell'accademie . . . recitata nell'Accademia degli Accesi in Siena* (Florence, 1569), p. 12. Intronati: *Capitoli, Dell'origine degl'Intronati; Rozzi: Costituzione, 1531 (in Mazzi, *op. cit.*) Arts. IX, XIII, and 1561, Art. XXI. Note the statement of Bartoli, that « il diletto o il piacere consiste maggiormente nella quiete, che nel moto » and the search for « tranquillity » in the Accademia Fiorentina, in Rudolf von Albertini, *Das florentinische Staatsbewusstsein im Uebergang von der Republik zum Prinzipat* (Bern: Francke, 1955), p. 290. Cf. A. Iacometti, *L'Accademia senese degli Intronati,* p. 4, and Domenico

themselves in different honorable studies, now learning, now teaching, in order to become each day more virtuous and more wise. [57]

In essence, therefore, the members of this "piccola schiera" meant their discourses, versification, banquets, and spectacles chiefly as "literary exercises," and they considered the academies above all as a means for their becoming individually "more virtuous and more wise." The applause of their peers gave them encouragement and inspiration; the lectures on Petrarch and Dante presented them with the models of perfection; the intimate conversations of closed sessions secured them the assistance of the best authorities of their times; and the minute *accuse* and *difese* of their original compositions guaranteed them freedom from the dangers of error and imperfection. The purpose of the "literary exercise" was threefold. First, it developed the participant's powers of expression and refined the "choice or property of [his] words" in order to render "even greater the acuteness and alertness of [his] genius." Second, it taught him "the necessity [of being] gracious and pleasing in conversation" and of avoiding "every act ... that might irritate any one of the senses, ... offend the appetite, ... or present to the imagination things that it would receive unwillingly." And above all it served to direct him along the *buona via* toward spiritual and moral perfection, "teaching, guiding, and assisting him, ... with the love of a father," by "the example of others ... [and] the counsel of his superiors," to rise in "this learned cloister" from the "low principles" common to most men "to an excellence such that he never could reach it alone." [58] Whatever trained the expressive faculties of the mind, according to this casuistry, also by definition gave pleasure; and whoever learned to appreciate

Maria Manni, *Memorie della fiorentina famosa Accademia degli Alterati* (Florence: Stecchi, 1748), on the members « non molti, tutti scelte, e dotte persone ».

[57] Bargagli, *Delle lodi dell'accademie*, p. 13.

[58] *Ibid.*, pp. 25, 28; Domenico Maria Manni, *Lezioni di lingua toscana* (2d ed.; Venice, 1758), I, 250 (note other remarks on Giovanni Della Casa's *Galateo* in the 1st ed. (Florence: Viviani, 1737), I, 18, 185, 233, 240, *et al.*); Cosimo Mei, « Lezione sopra la postiva gravità di ciascun corpo, recitata all'Accademia Fiorentina il 4 settembre 1738 », in Calogerà, *Raccolta d'opuscoli*, XX, 253-68 (quoted, p. 253); Filicaia, *Poesie*, II, canzone xiii. Cf. the exposition of exercices in oratory in the Preface to *Prose fiorentine* (below, note 61), Parte I, Vol. IV (Florence: Tartini & Franchi, 1731), pp. ix f.

precision of thought and to enjoy the delicacies of good food and clever jokes also made himself more worthy of God. Wisdom, pleasure, and virtue, in the restricted sense used by the academic orators, had become interchangeable.

Knowledge, therefore, had become identified with "discourse," of "the art of speech" (*l'arte del dire*), which Girolamo Gigli, like generations of rhetoricians before him, hailed as "the most noble and perfect" of all the activities of the intellect. And *orazione,* according to the most respected of the Cruscan linguists, Benedetto Buommattei, meant essentially "a fitting union of words, capable of expressing (*palesare*) the concepts of the spirit (*animo*)," and not the "ordered arrangement of rhetorical arguments for the purpose of persuading." Since they had no one to persuade, the academicians could well leave the latter to the "professors of rhetoric." [59] This exaltation of *orazione* explains first of all the preoccupation with the problem of language in so much of contemporary academic literature: language was the essence of knowledge and the generative force of all the sciences. Any relaxation, therefore, in the vigilance over the purity of the *lingua toscana* as formulated by the recognized masters of verbal expression would compromise irreparably their aspirations to either intellectual or moral perfection. It explains further the evident indifference of the academies toward the subject matter treated by their speakers. To be sure, many of them — Redi and Bellini above all — undoubtedly show a purely scientific interest in their own private studies, which they must cerainly have communicated to their listeners. But in general, no one believed that Averani's chronicle of the Passion or Casotti's condemnation of superstition would convert the doubtful or raise the level of popular devotional practices. No one expected to better his understanding of ancient civilization from Salvini's reflections on the Saturnalia. And, needless to say, no one cared how cold could be heated or whether a smile might more easily win a lady's affection than a frown. What mattered was not the

---

[59] Gigli, *Lezioni di lingua toscana,* p. 118; Crusca: * Diario, 12 January 1719; Benedetto Buommattei, *Della lingua toscana,* (5th ed. « degli Accademici della Crusca »; Florence, 1760), pp. 11-12, which suggests also the moral value of oratory.

subject of the discourse, but rather the mere fact of its composition and recitation:

> Raro ad udir, com'Ei dagli alti Rostri
> gran dubbj or solva, ed or come le ascose
> in maestrevol tuono
> origin delle voci apra, e dimostri;
> e udir qual nuovo alle Toscane Prose
> lustro Egli aggiunga, e dia più forti tempre; [60]

not the depth of feeling or the vivacity of imagery in a poem, but the balance of conceits and the choice of words; not what was said but how it was said. Finally, all the activities of the academies might fall equally under the category of "literary exercises." Joking and witticisms, for instance, could be as "learned and excellent" as formal dissertations:

Nor should anyone be surprised that things done so lightly and with so little trouble should turn out to be so learned, excellent, and gracious; for this is the sign of great men, of those who are sublime and who rise far above the level of the common herd: that even in their jokes and pleasantries all they do always shows what they themselves are; [61]

[60] G. B. Casaregi, *Sonetti e canzoni toscane,* canzone ix (p. 147), « In morte di Anton Maria Salvini per l'Accademia della Crusca »: « Rare it is to hear him, as from the high rostrums he now solves great *dubbj*; and now in masterful tones he opens and demonstrates the hidden origins of words; and rare to hear what new luster he may add to Tuscan prose, and how he may endow it with still greater strength ». The concept of translation principally as a « literary exercise » is suggested further by the repeated translations of the same texts: e. g., Menzini's *Lamentazioni del santo profeta Geremia,* printed together with Salvini's correction of the translation from Greek and his own from the Hebrew (Venice: Piacentini, 1736), and above all, Homer and Theocritus; and is shown in Gregorio Redi's rendering of the Psalms.: *I salmi di David esposti in versi toscani,* (2 vols.; Florence: Paperini, 1734) (many read before the Crusca) from Latin, printed opposite the translation, instead of from the original.

[61] Preface to Lorenzo Magalotti, *Lettere scientifiche ed erudite* (Florence: Tartini & Franchi, 1721, p .vii: « . . . Nè dee recar maraviglia, che cose fatte così di leggieri, e con sì poca cura, sieno poi così dotte, ed eccellenti, e vaghe riuscite, perciocchè questa è la condizione degli uomini grandissimi, che lungo tratto sopra la comunale schiera degli altri s'innalzano, e si sublimano, che negli scherzi ancora, e ne' divertimenti fanno sempre ritratto di quel che e' sono . . . ». Other editions: Florence: G. Manni, 1736, and Venice: Dom. Occhi all'Unione, 1740). Similar idea in S. Salvini, *Ragionamento sopra l'origine dell'Accademia della Crusca* (1711: Crusca: *Diario, 28 February; published by Moreni, Florence: Magheri, 1814), p. 19.

wine, song, and even leisure were as essential to the cultivation of
the spirit as sermons:

> Beato il vostro non oprar che appresta
> Opre più belle...
> Nobil quiete onde vostr'opra nasce,
> Altro non è che l'istess'opra in fasce; [62]

and the extemporaneous responses to the Apatisti's *Sibilla,* in which
the "subject" became nothing but a meaningless sound, provided
the most exacting test of precision and fluency:

> Non così nel Liceo versar torrenti
> Di scienza solean nei dì primieri
> Egregi Spirti, a far palesi intenti
> Sublimi filosofici misterj;
> Qual si sparge da voi nei dotti accenti
> Copia di arcani lumi e grandi e veri
> Che l'error fuga dalle umane menti,
> E su non dubbia via drizza i pensieri. [63]

Whether they discussed the conduct of retiring officers, deduced
"precepts" from Vergil and Petrarch, described the setting of the
Crucifixion, danced, drank, or relaxed, the academicians were certain
of conducting a "literary exercise." And any "exercise," whatever its
particular form or content, would ultimately contribute to their
mastery of verbal expression, and therefore to the perfection of their
minds and souls.

The obvious resemblance between the many discourses *in lode
dell'Accademia* at the beginning of the eighteenth century and that
of Scipione Bargagli in 1569 is no mere coincidence; for in substance,
the activities, interests, and attitudes of the academicians had changed

---

[62] Filicaia, *Poesie,* canzone xiii: « Alli Accademici della Crusca »: « Happy is your
not-working. which hastens still more beautiful works.   This noble repose from which your
work is born is nothing but the work itself in swaddling clothes ».

[63] *Poesie del cavaliere Anton Filippo Adami, raccolte e pubblicate per la prima volta
da un accademico fiorentino* (Florence: Stamp. Imp., 1755), p. 86: « Not thus did the excellent Spirits of the Lyceum, intent upon expressing sublime philosophical mysteries, pour out
streams of wisdom in the first days.   A quantity of light, great and true though hidden,
like that which shines forth among you in learned accents, will put error to flight from
human minds and direct our thoughts along the right path ».

very little in the interval. Save for a few minor amendments to admit practices into one already common to the others, the constitutions that governed the academies of 1700 were still those drawn up in the mid-sixteenth century. The complicated system of elections, the celebration of saints' days, the commemoration of the deceased, the adoption of *imprese,* the use of academic names, the feasts and *utili divertimenti* — such practices all date from the very foundation of the academies. The special dedication to the *volgare,* the exaltation of Petrarch, the formulation of "precepts" from the ancient and modern classics, the scriptural exegeses and moral discourses — such subjects indeed had steadily occupied the academies from the generation of Bembo to that of Anton Maria Salvini.[64] Above all, the theory of the "literary exercise" and the correlation of learning, pleasure, and morality reflect certain assumptions concerning the function of knowledge that had been current ever since the late Renaissance, and which have at least a parallel in the "spiritual exercises" of Bargagli's contemporary, St. Ignatius Loyola.

To be sure, the academies of the mid-sixteenth century were not wholly without precedent. Both the Rozzi and the Intronati, for

---

[64] Compare the records of the Alterati described by Bernard Weinberg in « Argomenti di discussione letteraria nell'Accademia degli Alterati (1570-1600) », *Giornale storico della letteratura italiana,* CXXXI (1954), pp. 175-94, and « L'Accademia degli Alterati: Literary Taste from 1570 to 1600 », *Italica,* XXXI (1954), pp. 207-14. Note the similarity between those of 1700 and the many academic orations and discourses published in *Prose fiorentine raccolte dallo Smarrito, accademico della Crusca* (Carlo Dati), by Santi Franchi, in 17 volumes from 1716 (the first volume alone was completely compiled by Dati and published in 1661; it was then reprinted as the first of the series), especially those of Lorenzo Giacomini Tebalducci, Pier Segni, Jacopo Soldani, and Lionardo Salviati in the Fiorentina, Crusca, and Alterati (Parte I, Vols. I-II), and the many *lezioni* in the first years of the Fiorentina in Parte II, Vols. I-II; others of the Seicento by Carlo Dati and Lorenzo Magalotti (1663) in the Crusca and seven of Benedetto Averani in the Apatisti in Parte II, Vol. III (1728); but note further their dissimilarity from those of Giovanni Della Casa in Parte I, Vol. I, orazione 1, and Vol. II appendix. See the observations of Luigi Baldacci in *Il petrarchismo italiano nel Cinquecento* (Milan-Naples: Ricciardi, 1957), esp. chap. i on Bembo, one of the most applauded Cinquecento heroes of the Cruscans of 1700. The Seicento academies are well described by G. M. Mazzuchelli in *Gli scrittori d'Italia* (Brescia: Bossini, 1753-63), Vol. I, Parte 2, p. 875 ff. Besides the work of Manni (note 53), records of the Cinque- and Seicento academies are in Etr Notti Coritane, IV, 12, 16, 34, and 112; BNF Capponi cxcii, pp. 118-55 (Origine dell'Accademia o adunanza nominata Arsura) and dxiv; for Siena: Edouard Cléder, *Notices sur l'Académie italienne des Intronati* (Bruxelles: Macquardt, 1864), with reservations of Iacometti, *op. cit.,* (above, note 6), and Lolita Petrarchi Costanzi, *L'Accademia degli Intronati di Siena e una sua commedia* (Siena, 1928).

instance, had been founded well before the final collapse of the Sienese Republic, and the earlier academic charter, that of the Rozzi of 1531, contains many provisions that suggest a conscious imitation of the republican constitution.[65] In Florence, various literary circles as early as an "Accademia di Santo Spirito" of 1421 described by Vespasiano da Bisticci and an "Achademia Fiorentina" in the home of Alamanno Rinuccini, or even perhaps that supposed to have taken place in 1389 in the *Paradiso degli Alberti* by Giovanni da Prato, undoubtedly provided a model for the organization of the later academies. The connection is more evident with the better documented Platonic Academy of Marsilio Ficino and with the Orti Oricellari, in which the leading writers and politicians of Florence, including Machiavelli, participated intermittently from 1502 to 1522; and these societies may well have been influenced in turn, as Kristeller has suggested, by such groups as the lay *confraternite* of quite different origin.[66] Even the literary forms adopted by the academies, like the *dubbio* and the discourse, as well as their interests in lexicography, textual exegesis, and the study of the Latin and Greek classics had been familiar all through the Quattrocento, if not earlier. The myriad of academies that followed the foundation of the Umidi in the late 1530's, then, arose largely from the coincidence of an intellectual and of a social phenomenon — that is, of a change in the interests and aspirations of the intellectual classes after the disastrous events from 1494 to 1530 and the consolidation of a form of organization that had gradually emerged during the preceding century. In Tuscany, at least, this channeling of intellectual activity into formal institutions accompanied, rather than followed, the triumph of political absolutism and the collapse of the urban republics.

[65] Especially Articles IV, V, VI, and IX, prescribing very precise limitations on the authority and the term of office of the Signor Rozo [Rozzo], setting up a complicated system of elections and committees, and excluding the nobility (in Mazzi. *op. cit.*). The constitutions of the republics may well have influenced to some extent the structure of all the academies, as will be pointed out in chap. ii, below.

[66] Paul Oskar Kristeller, « Lay Religious Traditions and Florentine Platonism », in his *Studies in Renaissance Thought and Letters* (Rome: Edizioni di Storia e Letteratura, 1956), pp. 99-122; Von Albertini, *Das Florentinische Staatsbewusstsein*, pp. 74 f., and in general, the still standard work of A. Della Torre, *Storia dell'Accademia Platonica di Firenze* (Florence: Carnesecchi, 1902).

But the similarities between the new academies of the mid-Cinquecento and the earlier circles of *letterati* extend no further than
matters of formal organization. Gradually over the course of forty
years citizen-humanists like Donato Acciaiuoli, who had played so
important a part in the culture of the Florentine Quattrocento, had
given way to scholar-functionaries like Benedetto Varchi and Scipione
Ammirati. By 1541 both the wide philosophical and theological
speculation of the Platonic Academy and the discussions of literature
and politics in the Orti Oricellari had largely disappeared. The
Florentine *letterati,* many of whom just a decade before had been
involved in the last desperate effort to restore the patriotism and
liberties of the Republic, were now addressing thanks to their "most
illustrious Prince" for his benevolence toward them; while just five
years after he had summoned Spanish troops to crush their century-
old freedom and independence, the Rozzi of Siena were praying
that "God grant a pacific and tranquil state" to their "invittissimo e
inlustrissimo principe." [67]   Cosimo I, still anxious in the first years
of his reign to avoid the recurrence of open opposition, was quick
to comprehend the immediate political advantages of the academies,
in which many of the former political leaders of the city were still
assembled as its cultural leaders. From 1542 to 1553, in order "to
reform and re-establish in better condition his most dear Academy."
he introduced changes in the statutes that in essence reduced the
officers to financial dependence upon his largesse. He provided for
the distribution of prizes and medals to the principal members, for
instance, and made the consul automatically a member of the Consiglio del Dugento (Senate) and Rector of the Studio, with all the
"authority, honor, privileges, rank, salary, and emoluments" belonging thereto. By securing the adoption, moreover, of such provisions
as that prohibiting speeches without the prior permission of the
consul and censors, he assured the undivided attention of the members

---

[67] Fiorentina. * Capitoli, proemio, which also defines the relationship of the new academy
with the Umidi. Rozzi: Constituzione 1561, proemio. Note M. Baccio Baldini, *Orazione
fatta nella Accademia Fiorentina in lode del serenissimo sig. Cosimo Medici Gran Duca di
Toscana, gloriosa memoria* (Florence: Sermartelli, 1574) and Bernardo Davanzati, « In morte
del Gran Duca di Toscana, Cosimo Primo, recitata nell'Accademia degli Alterati », *Prose
Fiorentine*, Parte I, Vol. I, No. 3.

to their politically harmless exercises and made them realize the im-
possibility of achieving "honor and recognition" except through his
grace.[68] Some of the original academicians, to be sure, found it possible for a time to disguise material of somewhat greater currency
under innocuous titles — like Pierfrancesco Giambullari, whose reflections on cosmography and reports of recent geographical discoveries
were submitted as a treatise on the site of Dante's Purgatory.[69] But
any exaggeration of such liberties quickly provoked sterner measures:
the Accademia degli Intronati, for instance, was closed soon after the
occupation of Siena, probably because the close contacts maintained
by its members with their exiled associate Fausto Sozzini ("Il Fra-
stigliato") had rendered it suspect of heresy.[70] But in general the first
grand duke avoided outright suppression. Instead he converted the
academies into instruments for extending his authority into the realm
of thought by elevating them into semi-official institutions. And all
this he accomplished without altering visibly the external forms of
autonomy or abbreviating the flourishes of flattery and affection that
padded each new decree.

While these measures may well have been partially responsible
for what Il Lasca (Antonfrancesco Grazzini, 1503-1584) complained of as

> Una turba infinita
> di poetacci...
> pedanti e correttori,
> che metton tutto il mondo sottosopra,...

---

[68] Fiorentina: *Capitoli, appendices for these years.

[69] His « Del sito del Purgatorio » is printed in his *Lezzioni . . . lette nell'Accademia
Fiorentina* (Florence: 1551, with the device of the Medici on the title page). That the chief
interest of the discourse is not in Dante is further indicated by the marginal comments of
the Cinquecento owner in the copy now in the University of Chicago Library, which all refer
to the non-philological arguments.

[70] Fabiani, *Memoria*, pp. 39-40, and BCS Y.II.27. See Delio Cantimori, *Eretici italiani del Cinquecento* (Florence: Sansoni, 1939), pp. 346-48, on the probability of heretical
opinions in the discussions of the Sienese academies. Letter of Fausto Sozzini to
G. Bargagli (« Il Materiale »), 20 April 1563, is published in Cesare Cantù, *Gli eretici d'Italia:
Discorsi storici* (3 vols:; Torino: Unione Tipografico-Editrice, 1856-58), II, pp. 491-96.
« Other letters » to Bargagli are mentioned in his letter to Bellisario Bolgarini of 30 October 1577, *ibid*. II 497.

dell'Accademia nostra Fiorentina,
che fa molte parole e pochi fatti, [71]

and while they certainly did not create an atmosphere particularly
conducive to intellectual vigor, they did succeed remarkably well in
achieving the political ends for which Cosimo I had principally intended them. Within a few years academies, most of them modeled
on the Accademia Fiorentina, had sprung up in all the cities of
Tuscany under the direct or indirect sponsorship of the government;
and they continued well into the following century to be the most
important institutions of cultural life. Never did they make any
pretense of investigating or questioning the established political and
ecclesiastical order; never did they permit themselves reflections upon
their studies of language and literature that might in any way have
touched matters now within the sole competence of the prince.

To be sure, the precise frontier between pure scholarship and the
affairs of state would vary considerably according to the relative broad-
mindedness of the Medici rulers. Under the protection especially
of Ferdinando II and Cardinal Leopoldo, the Crusca became a forum
for the exposition of the new hypotheses and experiments of such
illustrious linguists as Galileo and Torricelli. Even the Apatisti often
directed their usual *dubbi* to questions on the relative merits, say, of
Democritus and Pythagoras, in which they could discuss still controversial questions of astronomy and physics.[72] But in general, the
academies under the Principato bore all the marks of a still somewhat insecure monarchical regime — not only in express prohibitions

---

[71] « An infinite mob of poetasters, pedants, and correctors [of the Tuscan classics—reference to the expurgation of Boccaccio and others: see below, chap. iii, note 40], who turn
the whole world upside-down, . . . to the shame of our Accademia Fiorentina, which puts
out many words and few deeds » , from his madrigal « in morte di Lodovico Domenichi »,
quoted by Arturo Graf, *Attraverso il Cinquecento* (Torino: Loescher, 1888), pp. 66-67. Many
of his contemporaries attributed this decline of letters to the establishment of tyrannies, e.g.,
Campanella in a passage from *De libris propriis et de recta ratione studendi syntagma* (Florence: Bestetti e Tumminelli, 1927), pp. 80-82, quoted by Benedetto Croce, *Poeti e scrittori
del pieno e del tardo Rinascimento* (Bari: Laterza, 1952), I. pp. 62-63; but such a thesis
necessitates the dubious inclusion (as it does in Campanella) of even such writers as Poliziano
and Valla among the decadent.

[72] BNF Mag IX, 91 (2 June 1669).

"to speak, either with praise or criticism, of the things of state, [or] of anything belonging thereto," but also in provisions enjoining absolute obedience to the officers and establishing rules for precedence among the members. Such articles are in clear contradiction with the republican institutions upon which the earlier constitutions had been modeled.[73] Scipione Bargagli, in fact, prescribed as one of the four conditions for the flourishing of an academy "that the place [of its meeting] be possessed and governed by lords and princes"; for only "under the shadow ... of some great and good prince" — and only, he might have added, within the reach of his purse — could their members strive for wisdom, pleasure, and virtue safe from what the Intronati deplored as "weighty and troublesome worries of the world." [74] Thus when the pious hypochondriac Cosimo III, now for religious rather than for political reasons, decided that his responsibility for the safety of his subjects' souls could no longer permit free investigation in any of the sciences except medicine and botany, the intellectuals complied without a murmur; and they continued as before to address dedications and eulogies to their "most serene protector," who expected them simply to surround his throne with the decorum of "learning" traditional to his family and to leave philosophy to the theologians.

The five such academies that survived in 1700, therefore, had little in common, in interests, structure, or origin, with the scientific societies like the Lincei of Rome, the Royal Society of London, or even the short-lived Cimento of Florence.[75] They still responded to the intellectual and political conditions of over a century before, event though the principal of these conditions, the insecurity of the Medicean dominion, had long since passed away. In 1700, moreover, a new age was beginning, an age of which the reformation of poetry

[73] Intronati: * Capitoli, Art. XV; Fiorentina: * Capitoli, Art. XXIX; Crusca: * Leggi, Art. XVII.

[74] Bargagli, *Delle lodi dell'accademie,* p. 21; Intronati: * Capitoli, Art. XV.

[75] See Martha Ornstein, *The Rôle of the Scientific Societies in the Seventeenth Century* (Chicago: University of Chicago Press, 1928, 3d ed., 1938), on the Lincei and the Cimento. The dissimilarity in organization and purpose of the Cimento and either the literary academies or their successors in the Settecento was fully noted at the time and is discussed in the following chapter.

3

in Arcadia, the renewal of critical historical scholarship, the diffusion of foreign literature, and the legislative reform of the political and economic structure of the state represent but a few of the more prominent achievements. The survival of these institutions, then, would depend upon their ability to modify their structure, interests, and activities to meet the new requirements of an age far different from that in which they first had flourished.

Chapter II

TRADITION, ENLIGHTENMENT, AND CO-OPERATION

Indeed, the five ancient academies still flourished well into the eighteenth century. Although the official records have since been lost, the frequent references in contemporary literature confirm the continuation of regular meetings and the customary activities both in the Fiorentina and, except for the years just before 1748, in the Accademia degli Apatisti up until their dissolution by royal edict in 1783. Similarly the Crusca, by greatly expanding its membership from 1737 on, quickly recovered from the exhaustion that had afflicted the older members after the publication of the fourth edition of the *Vocabolario;* and there is little reason to suppose, in spite of the declaration to the contrary in the Edict of 1783, that a similar expansion in the 1770's would not have succeeded in arresting a second decline. Indeed, the new Accademia Fiorentina took over both the occupations and the objectives of the three older institutions that were incorporated into it, and, except for a brief silence during the Restoration of 1799, it held regular monthly sessions right up until the re-establishment of the Crusca in 1810.

The Cinquecento academies also lived on in Siena: not until the 1780's did the Intronati finally abandon their formerly diverse activities to concentrate wholly upon the management of their theater; and not until the monopolization of Sienese intellectual life by the reorganized Accademia dei Fisiocritici did the Rozzi apparently discard the occasional discourses and lectures that formerly had complemented their ceremonious receptions and balls. Both Sienese academies as well as the Crusca still exist today, although considerably modified in character and occupations; and their very existense still bears witness to the ability of these ancient institutions to survive the alterations of time and taste.

By the first decade of the new century, moreover, a number of other institutions had already sprung up in the cities of Tuscany that adopted the same title of "academy" used by the Crusca and the Intronati. The earliest had appeared in Arezzo as the Accademia dei Forzati (1683), which soon became the first of the many subsequent colonies of the Roman Arcadia. In 1690 the Sienese physician Pirro Maria Gabbrielli had gathered some twenty pupils and associates into the Accademia dei Fisiocritici, which soon after engendered a literary complement with the Arcadian name of Colonia Fisiocritica and which reopened after a twenty-year suspension under the presidency of the economist Sallustio Bandini in 1759. Two older academies were restored — the Affidati of San Miniato and the Risvegliati of Pistoia — while two new ones were founded — the Colonia Alfea in Pisa and the Infecondi in Prato, whose abundant records show a considerable activity until the latter years of the century. Thereafter the foundation of academies proceeded even more rapidly — the bibliophile Occulti (1726), the celebrated Accademia Etrusca (1727), the scholarly Notti Coritane, and the gay, if dubiously scientific Società Botanica in Cortona; the Accademia di Varia Letteratura (1744), the Enciclopedica (1749), and the Agricoltura (1788) in Pistoia; the Accademia Livornese, the Colombaria, and the Ierofili in Livorno, and, in Florence, the Società Botanica Fiorentina (1718), the Società Colombaria (1737), and the most famous of all, the Accademia dei Georgofili (1753), which still today is the principal association of Tuscan agriculturalists.

A still greater number of smaller, or at least more ephemeral academies appeared at various times in the capital, where the concentration of wealth, population, and intellect encouraged more frequent social intercourse; some, like the Rinascenti (1711) and the Teologi Dogmatici (1753), were founded within the Scuole Pie, and others, like Pompeo Neri's Accademia Legale and a Società di Medicina at Santa Maria Nuova, among the members and *dilettanti* of particular arts and professions. But even the more distant towns responded to the prevalent enthusiasm — from Volterra with its Accademia dei Sepolti, revived sometime before 1746 and still extant, to Montepulciano, and even, perhaps, to tiny, isolated Montalcino south of Siena.

Abundant records in print and manuscript still describe the various achievments of many of these organizations; a journalist's announcement or a single printed dissertation attests the existence of others; and undoubtedly silence now hides the names of some that may have flourished and disappeared without leaving any trace at all.[1] Nevertheless, enough documentation has survived to indicate the establishment in almost every Tuscan community of at least one institution for the co-ordination and promotion of the intellectual interests of its citizens during some part of the hundred years between the founding of Arcadia and the outbreak of the French Revolution, and to justify the attribute "academic" to the eighteenth as well as to the sixteenth century.[2]

To the multiplication of academies themselves, furthermore, corresponded a substantial growth in the number of academicians. By the middle of the century the some 150 Florentines who participated in intellectual organizations in 1700 had probably quadrupled: an official list of 1783 gives 840 resident members of the Fiorentina, Apatisti, and Crusca, without mentioning the many others associated only with the more recently-founded societies like the Botanica, Colombaria, and Georgofili; while by 1780 the eleven academicians of Cortona who had joined the Occulti in 1726 had sufficiently exceeded the statutory limit of 40 in the Etrusca to provoke a complaint from the secretary.[3] Similar increases undoubtedly occurred in the other cities, in Volterra after 1740, Pistoia after 1744, Siena after 1759, although the absence of lists showing the resident members at any given moment renders impossible any but general estimates. Mere arithmetical size, of course, gives no indication of the intensity of participation: from the 1720's on most of the academic rolls list a host of "members" — over 2,300 in the Intronati in 1770 —

---

[1] The documents concerning these and the other academies here referred to will be fully described in the companion volume mentioned in the Preface.

[2] This phenomenon was common to most of Italy at the time. « Not only every metropolis », noted Giambattista Chiaramonti in 1765, « but every important and almost every mediocre city of Italy as well has nourished its literary academy »: *Dissertazioni istoriche, scientifiche, erudite recitate . . . nell'adunanza letteraria del signor conte Giammaria Mazzucchelli* (2 vols.; Brescia: Rizzardi, 1765), I, 9.

[3] Etrusca: * Deliberazioni — note preceding 14 January 1780.

whose election obliged them to no more than a note of thanks. Nor did the resident members by any means attend all the meetings (no more than 40 ever attended the Crusca at the same time); and even they came more often to listen quietly to Ricci, Salvini, and Sarchiani, who monopolized session after session of the Crusca and the Fiorentina, or to observe the specimens of Micheli and Targioni Tozzetti, who did almost all the traveling and collecting for the Botanica.[4] And while a few academies met as often as weekly, some assembled no more than once a year, and others lapsed quickly into complete inactivity. But, subject to these reservations, the rolls still offer some indication of the extent of academic life at the time, especially when the corrected numbers are compared to population figures. Almost 1,000 persons enrolled in the five major and several smaller societies of Florence in 1760 represents a considerable percentage of a total population of some 75,000, as does 40-50 out of out of 14,000 in Cortona, 150-200 out of 16,000 in Siena, and similar proportions for the other cities. At least it is clear that in 1690 there were some 300-400 Tuscans formally associated with the literary and cultural institutions called academies and that by the middle of the century this figure had risen to somewhat over 1,500.[5]

These 1,500 academicians included, moreover, practically everyone of any importance, politically, socially, or intellectually, in each community. The bishops of Cortona were all members of the Etrusca, for instance, the Archbishop of Pisa was the "protector" of the Ierofili, the members of the Regency under Francesco Stefano were honorary members of the Crusca and the Fisiocritici, and almost all the royal ministers under Pietro Leopoldo were active in the Georgofili. The academies enrolled most of the university professors in Florence and all of those in Siena, most of the teachers in the Scuole Pie and episcopal seminaries, many of the leading ecclesiastics both regular and secular, a large number of physicians, lawyers, printers,

---

[4] Crusca: Diario, 17 August 1702 and July 1728.

[5] Population estimates based on the very detailed *Stati delle anime* by Giuseppe Parenti, *La popolazione della Toscana sotto la Reggenza lorenese* (Florence: Rinascita del Libro, 1937), and those based on the baptismal records in San Giovanni by Marco Lastri, *Ricerca sull'antica e moderna popolazione di Firenze* (Florence: Cambiagi, 1775).

and booksellers, and, finally, all those members of the landowning nobility who still accepted their traditional role as leaders and patrons of the cultural life of their cities. Numerically, then, the academicians may have been but a handful; actually they were the same few hundred Tuscans who guided the thoughts, actions, and livelihoods of the other 900,000.

The proliferation of academies and academicians during the first half of the Settecento certainly suggests a reawakening of intellectual activity in Tuscany, or at least a growing desire among Tuscans to engage in such activity. Such a "reawakening," indeed, has already been observed in the universities. Pisa above all, which during the first decades of the century trained almost all the political and intellectual leaders of the later decades, flourished intellectually as never before, thanks in part to several reforms in curriculum, to sizable gifts by private citizens and the grand dukes, to the appointment of several outstanding professors, and, after the death of Cosimo III, to the concession of a considerable measure of academic freedom.[6] But it is evident also in the formation of a number of informal *conversazioni*, which from the 1730's on assembled in private homes — like the Friday evening gatherings of the Rinuccini and Antonio Niccolini and, somewhat later, the *salotto* of the Countess of Albany, best known for its association with Alfieri.[7] It seems even to have affected bodies whose original purposes had nothing to do with literature

[6] See Niccolò Rodolico, *Stato e Chiesa in Toscana durante la Reggenza lorenese* (Florence: Le Monnier, 1910), chap. i (based on A. Fabroni, *Historia Academiae Pisanae* [above, chap. i, note 3], which is continued somewhat less happily by Everardo Micheli, *Storia dell'U. di P. dal 1737 al 1859* (Pisa: Nistri, 1877). Further: Antonio Anzilotti, « Le riforme in Toscana nella seconda metà del secolo XVIII (il nuovo ceto dirigente e la sua preparazione intellettuale », *Movimenti e contrasti per l'unità italiana,* ed. Luigi Russo (Bari: Laterza, 1930), pp. 60-129 (note, however, the unfavorable report of 29 October 1739 by Count Richecourt, head of the Regency, quoted by N. Rodolico in *Rassegna nazionale,* CLXXVIII [1911], 54-68, esp. p. 61). The forthcoming studies of Niccola Carranza should add considerably more evidence concerning the vitality of the University of Pisa in the early Settecento.

[7] Montesquieu, *Voyages* (2 vols.; Bordeaux: Gounouilhou, 1894-96), I, 187; Carlo Pellegrini, *La Contessa d'Albany e il salotto del Lungarno* (Naples: Edizioni Scientifiche Italiane, 1951), as well as the many anecdotes in Alessandro Ademollo, *Corilla Olimpica* (Florence: C. Ademollo, 1887). On « una lieta conversazione di persone culte e letterate » in the home of Pio Giannelli in Siena: *Novelle letterarie,* XXV (1764), 676-79.

and learning: religious orders, for instance, cathedral chapters, and even municipal councils. Many of the new academies, indeed, grew out of just such groups: from the dinner parties in Girolamo de' Pazzi's tower, for example, emerged the Società Colombaria; from Gabbrielli's classroom, the Fisiocritici; from the Order of the Bernabites in Livorno, the Ierofili. The deliberations of the City Council (*Consiglio Comunale*) of Volterra concerning the reorganization of the city's archives, similarly, may well have inspired the revival of the Accademia dei Sepolti; and the founders of the Etrusca may well have begun their literary and historical conversations in the Cortonese magistracies, whose incumbents all appear on the academic rolls.[8] So also the lay confraternities may have contributed to the formation of academies in the Settecento as they apparently had in the Cinquecento — at least in appearance and content such ceremonies as the *accademie autunnali* of the Confraternita di Santa Maria degli Alemanni in Cortona are indistinguishable from the annual feasts of the Etrusca, and many of the same persons participated in both.[9] For such organizations, which the waning of religious fervor and the transfer of all effective political responsibility to appointees of the prince had left with little to do, provided the only means, especially in the smaller towns, whereby citizens of like ambitions and interests might meet to exchange information and ideas. The growth of the academies, then, was but one manifestation of a quickening of Tuscan culture in the beginning of the Settecento. As intellectual life had declined in the Cinquecento partially from the hostility of the Principato toward any interference with its direct authority over each subject individually, so the revival in the Settecento led to an increased activity in whatever institutions had been permitted to survive.

[8] Lorenzo Aulo Cecina, *Notizie istoriche della città di Volterra* (Pisa: Giovannelli, 1758) (see below, chap. v, note 90), p. v.; members of the Council of Cortona are given in the agreements between the Academy and the Commune in Etr 471.1-2.

[9] Etr Notti Coritane, I, Appendix. Note Bianchini's orations for the priests of Prato and for the Infecondi: Mar A. 243, 11-12; the connection between the Barnabites and the Ierofili in petition of the Academy to the governor of Livorno: ASL Cose Livornesi, Busta I, Biblioteca pubblica, no. 1; and similar practices in the Sienese magistracies, e.g., *Discorso accademico concistoriale fatto dal cavalier Bernardino Perfetti, patrizio senese e poeta laureato, nel darsi il possesso alla nuova Eccelsa Signoria di Siena l'anno MDCCVI* (Venice: Lovisa, 1725).

Yet whenever the members of municipal councils or ecclesiastical corporations found it desirable to pursue more systematically their yet desultory discussions of arts and letters, they turned for help to the institutions that traditionally had been associated with learning rather than to those which first had brought them together. No other kind of organization, first of all, could so well provide the possibility of intercourse among many interested citizens. The private *salotto* in Tuscany never developed into anything like the *salon* in France — partially because women played a considerably less important role in Tuscan society and partially because informal groups could not fulfill the particular demands of Tuscan intellectuals as well as permanent organizations. Freemasonry, moreover, had very little of the influence in Tuscany that it enjoyed, say, in Naples; the little-known lodge established in Florence in the 1730's, probably on the initiative of some resident Englishmen, seems to have dissolved at the first sign of official disapproval.[10] At the same time, the very charters of the political, the religious, and, for that matter, the educational institutions prevented the admission of anyone not qualified in accordance with their particular purposes. The universities, indeed, seem to have afforded little chance for contact even among their members, for they consisted largely of a number of separate chairs or lectureships and never formed, as did some of those in England and Germany, a "body of scholars" of which the individual teachers might feel themselves a part. By maintaining the high quality of their faculties, it is true, the Tuscan universities never succumbed to the "intellectual fossilization" that elsewhere in Europe would drive anyone receptive to new ideas into different institutions;[11] but their functions remained limited almost wholly to teaching, and the academies grew up along side them without any evidence of rivalry or discord. While continuing, therefore, to carry on their professional obligations in the classroom, the professors at Pisa, Florence, and Siena — and at the

[10] Francesco Sbigoli, *Tommaso Crudeli e i primi Framassoni in Firenze* (Milan: Battezzati, 1884); its quick disappearance in also noted by the Cortonese Valerio Angiolieri Alticozzi in his *Relazione della Compagnia de' Liberi Muratori* (Naples, 1746), pp. ii-iii.

[11] Particularly the universities of Spain: note R. T. Shafer, *The Economic Societies in the Spanish world, 1763-1821* (Syracuse: Syracuse University Press, 1958), p. 20.

seminaries and public schools (*scuole pubbliche*) in other cities — also took part in the sessions of the Alfea, the Fiorentina, and the Fisiocritici. For only in the academies could teachers, as well as ecclesiastics, landowners, and magistrates, who were as much a part of the intellectual class as those with formal titles, enjoy the companionship of other "learned" citizens and express themselves on subjects other than those prescribed by their professions.[12]

No other kind of organization, secondly, was so well-known to Tuscans of the Settecento. From the beginning of the century on, a number of historical studies, like those of Jacopo Rilli and Salvino Salvini in Florence and of Uberto Benvoglienti, Girolamo Gigli, and Francesco Piccolomini in Siena, made them ever more conscious of the role the academies had played during the Cinquecento and ever more aware that no small part of the glory of the Tuscan cities derived from their having been "among the first in all Italy to institute literary assemblies." [13] These studies were carried on in the second quarter of the century by Andrea Alamanni, who filled session after session in the Crusca reading the diaries of former secretaries, by

---

[12] The inability of the university to fulfill the function of an academy is well stated by the *Provveditore* of the University of Pisa in a memorandum to the Regency of 20 March 1754 (ASF Reggenza 634): « The purpose of the University is above all that of instructing young students ». Rather than overburdening the professors with further academic duties, he recommends the creation of an « academy of sciences, like [that of] Bologna » (founded in 1711 for much the same reasons: see Carlo Calcaterra, *Alma mater studiorum* [Bologna: Zanichelli, 1948], p. 241). « In that case », he continues, « we could have annually a reasonable number of scholarly memorials and interesting dissertations to be published of the use of the public, this being the object of such academies », without interfering with the university curriculum. Note the further distinction between academies and other institutions by Chiaramonti in the beginning of his « Dissertazione istorica delle accademie letterarie bresciane », in *Dissertazioni istoriche, scientifiche, erudite recitate ... nell'adunanza letteraria del signor conte Giammaria Mazzuchelli*, I, 1-64, esp. pp. 9-10. Further: *Saggi scientifici e letterarj dell'Accademia di Padova*, I, (1786), iii-iv: « ... essendo per sua natura diverso l'oggetto di un'Accademia da quello di una università, e distinte e separate affatto le incombenze e gli uffizj di accademico e di professore ... ». The university is intended for « the instruction of the youth »; the academy, for « the enrichment and the propagation of its own learning ».

[13] Fabiani, *Memoria*, p. 3; and *Memorie Colombaria*, I, xi-xii (Gori). On academic histories, see above, chap. i, notes 6, 8, and 58 (Salvini's *Ragionamento*). Other histories: BCS Y.I.3: Turno Pipocci; V.II.3: Alcibiade Lucherini, Discorso; C.IV.24: Piccolomini, Lezione sull'origine ...; Y.I.19, 4: Baldasseroni, Dissertazione sull'origine ...; X.IV.11: Parere di Uberto Benvoglienti contro l'opinione del cav. Enea Piccolomini; C.IV.23: Notizie dell'Accademia ... cavate da Uberto Benvoglienti.

Anton Francesco Gori, who presented to the Apatisti the extensive notes he had gathered for an unexecuted history of the academy, and by Fabiani, who used the documents uncovered by his predecessors for a somewhat more judicious account of the Intronati and the Rozzi.[14] It is not surprising, therefore, that the new academies adopted constitutions strikingly similar to that of the Fiorentina, with the same elected officers, the same program of *lezioni,* verse recitations, eulogies, general assemblies, and even, in some cases, *imprese* and academic pseudonyms. In Florence and Siena, for one thing, the founders of new academies were often already active members of the older ones; in the other cities, where a former academy had since disappeared, they either revived its name or recovered its records for the guidance of their colleagues.[15] Moreover, the rolls of the Cinquecento and the Settecento academies often contain many of the same names; for in spite of having extended membership to many whose forefathers would never have pretended to be *letterati,* the Georgofili, the Colombaria, and the Fisiocritici still included representatives of the same families that had once furnished the leading members of the Alterati and the Accesi. So accustomed, indeed, did Tuscans soon become to this form of organization that they used it for almost every kind of collective endeavour — even (alas!) for such frivolous amusements as the *Veglie Piacevoli,* "pleasant vigils" of 1733-34, in which the discourses and poems were devoted quite frankly to nonsense. Thus the academies of Tuscany, unlike those of, say, Spain, were founded upon domestic, not upon foreign models.[16] For when,

---

[14] Crusca: *Diario, 3 August 1730, *et seq.;* Gori, *Memorie dell'Accademia degli Apatisti*: Mar A. 36, including one Discorso recitato nella celebre A. A., of 31 January 1744.

[15] D. M. Manni, *Memorie della . . . Accademia degli Alterati* (1748) (above, chap. i, note 53); Capitoli dell'A. degli Uniti: Col II.I.82; Etr Notti Coritane, IV, 12, 15, 34 f. (reception of the statutes of the Umorosi), and 57 (names of the Avidi). *Imprese* of the Crusca through the mid-eighteenth century in Cr 53 (small envelope).

[16] BNF Mag VI, 120 (Veglie Erudite). Cf. Shafer, *The Economic Societies in the Spanish World,* pp. 24-25. The only academy in which there is any evidence of imitating similar societies abroad is the Società di Medicina (1778); the petition for a charter (ASF Reggenza 1051, 41) includes a printed brochure entitled *Pièces concernant l'établissement fait par le Roi d'une Commission ou Société et Correspondence de médecine à Paris;* but the petition and even, indeed, the enclosed « Mémoire instructif » itself, refer more directly to the plan of an academy for experimental medicine proposed by Giorgio Baglivi (b. Ragusa, 1668; d. Rome, 1707) in *De praxi medica ad priscam observandi rationem revocanda* (Rome:

after some 150 years during which they had forgotten the art of spontaneous co-operation, Tuscans once again found it desirable to unite
their individual efforts in the pursuit of learning, they had only to
adapt an institution with which they had long been familiar to the
needs of a new generation.

Yet while taking over methods and procedures handed down
from the Cinquecento, the academicians were fully aware, as early
as 1690, that the institutions they were renovating or founding had
little other than their constitutions in common with the "useless and
perhaps even ridiculous societies that in bygone time [had] inundated
Italy." [17]   In order more carefully to distinguish themselves from
"those who, in complete accord with their merits, took pleasure in
calling themselves the Uncouth, the Deafened, the Obscured...,"
many of the new academies adopted titles somewhat more consonant
with their pursuits,[18] while the recognition that "with the change in
times some proportional change in the laws is necessary" led even
the older academies to modify their original charters.[19]   Meanwhile,
the academicians gradually discovered that similar institutions also
called "academies" had since been founded all over Europe: "a large
number of learned academies" in France, for instance, to which Lami
attributed much of the splendor of Louis XIV, the Royal Society of
England, to which several members of the Crusca and the Botanica
had been elected, and the Imperial Academy *Naturae Curiosorum*,

Cesaretti, 1696).   The proposed charter has further similarities with the German *Academia
Naturae Curiosorum,* of which the *Miscellanea curiosa medio-physica,* published in Leipzig
from 1670, had always been well known and received in Tuscany; several leading Tuscans
were members of the academy.

[17] Fisiocritici: Deliberazioni, 7 December 1694, on admission of Pietro Bruschieri of
Arezzo, and Pirro Maria Gabbrielli, « Notizie circa l'Accademia dei Fisiocritici », *Galleria
di Minerva* (Venice), II (1696), 181-85.

[18] Giovanni Cristofano Amaduzzi, *Discorso filosofico sul fine ed utilità dell'Accademie*
(Livorno: Enciclopedia, 1777), p. 11: « ... Voi non mi vedrete già perdermi dietro alle
proletarie accademie di coloro che, coerentemente ai loro meriti amarono di chiamarsi Rozzi,
Intronati, Offuscati, Erranti, od altri tali ... ».   Although by a non-Tuscan author, this
discourse was apparently widely read in Tuscany (a copy was presented to the Colombaria
on 1 March 1777 and appended to Annali 32; note also *Novelle letterarie,* N. S., VIII (1777),
167-70).   It contains much the same argument as that in the other treatises here cited.   Cf.
Filippo Venuti in *Magazzino toscano* (Livorno), II (1755), 473.

[19] Risvegliati: * Capitoli, proemio.

which, according to Fabiani, had inspired the founders of the Fisio-critici.[20] Hence, while academic orators continued to pay tribute to the institutions of their forefathers, they soon began introducing into their inaugural discourses long lists of "the famous academies of Europe," from Dublin to Petersburg, from Leipzig to Bordeaux, "who have restored and extended the arts and sciences."[21]

So ardently, indeed, did they seek to identify themselves with the enlightened institutions of an enlightened age that the arrival, in 1753, of a form letter from the Parisian printer Lottin — requesting information for a forthcoming dictionary of European academies — was sufficient to set all Siena astir. Unfortunately, the letter was addressed to the Intronati alone, an omission that flattered the recipients, to be sure, but one that brought forth the wrath of the insulted Rozzi, who were not above suggesting some misconduct on the part of their rivals. Failing in a formal demand that the letter be passed on to them, they conjured up one of their own, supposedly asking their secretary for corrections in the obviously biased and misleading communiqué already received from Siena; and they printed an elaborate reply under the false date of "Paris," all in order that the heirs of the artisan comedians of the sixteenth century might be included in the same list with the Académie Française.[22] Thus while Tuscans

[20] Lami in *Novelle letterarie*, VII (1746), 625; Fabiani, *Memoria*, p. 93; Crescenzio Vaselli, « Vita di Pirro Maria Gabbrielli, sanese », *Le vite degli arcadi illustri*, ed. Crescimbeni, II, 22-40.

[21] *Atti Fisiocritici*, I (1760), xvii; letter of Guido Savini, 22 January 1768: ASF Reggenza 669.28; oration to the Etrusca (anon.): BCS C.X.16, fol. 411; Ubaldo Montelatici (founder of the Georgofili), *Ragionamento sopra i mezzi più necessari per far rifiorire l'agricoltura* (Florence: Albizzini, 1752), p. 48 (on the Royal Society).

[22] Letters of Lottin to the Intronati, of the Rozzi to the Intronati (14 June 1754), and reply of the secretary of the Intronati, Pietro Pecci, to Lottin, all in BCS Y.I.19. The *Relazione storica dell'origine, e progresso della festosa Congreda de' Rozzi di Siena diretta al sig. Lottimj, stampatore in Parigi* dal maestro Lorenzo Ricci, mercante di libri vecchi (« Parigi » [but Siena: Moreni], 1757), is attributed to Pecci by the BNF catalogue and by Marino Parenti, *Dizionario dei luoghi di stampa falsi, inventati o supposti* (Florence: Sansoni, 1951), p. 161; but it is highly unlikely that Pecci would have spoken so harshly in a second letter of the accademy he had defended so eloquently in the first. A few grammatical errors (*le première*) and the misspelling of Lottin's name as *Lottimj* (with the Italian final *j*) in the supposed letter of Lottin to the Rozzi printed in the Preface, as well as the absence of an original, indicate rather clearly that the secretary of the Rozzi forged the letter as an excuse to issue a reply. Lottin (Augustin Martin, 1726-93) apparently never carried out the project;

followed purely local tradition in organizing their intellectual life, they sought to identify the academies that they founded on Cinquecento models with those across the Alps that they had since come to admire.

That the eighteenth century differed from all others because of its "enlightenment," *illuminismo,* no one doubted. "This is the century of philosophy," announced the academic orators, "the age of enlightened reason," in which "physics has been freed from the blindness and barbaric servitude of so many centuries," in which historians are exploring the recesses of the past, scientists exposing the mysteries of nature, and legislators abolishing the legal remnants of feudalism — "the philosophic century," in which Pisa, for example, "as if rising again to a new life, can be seen from one day to the next growing in population, being decorated with private and public buildings, being enlightened by knowledge, and becoming richer through the arts and through commerce." [23] The superiority of the eighteenth century, in other words, resulted both from the introduction of "philosophy" into all fields of intellectual endeavor and from the injection of "new life" into the society and the economy. Such an *illuminismo* was by this time, admitted the academicians, common to all Europe. But they claimed a special place for their own country: for it was precisely "on this fortunate soil," they insisted, that "the sciences have risen again; in fact, the happy revolution of the sciences itself, as everyone well knows, belongs to Tuscany." [24] Modern

there is no trace of such a catalogue among his works in the Bibliothèque Nationale, and it is not mentioned in Michaud. Other letters in Etr Notti Coritane, XI, 113 (17 December 1754), Cr A. 27, no. 1; BCS Y.II.7 (Libri delle deliberazioni . . . Accademia Intronata), p. 61, entry of Guido Savini (also secretary of the Fisiocritici), 12 April 1784.

[23] Attica: Discorso proemiale (1749) CASF Reggenza 842.15): « Quasi risorgendo a nuova vita, vedesi di giorno in giorno aumentar la popolazione, ornare di pubbliche e private fabbriche, illuminarsi colle scienze, arricchirsi coll'arte, e col commercio ». A. F. Gori, *Storia antiquaria etrusca* (Florence, 1749), p. xvi: « In questa nostra età (a cui sembra, che Iddio . . . abbia riservato tal dono, per maggior lustro, e vantaggio dell'ottime lettere . . . »; D. M. Manni, *Le veglie piacevoli* (Florence, 1767), I, x: « nostro secolo illuminato »; Angelo Fabroni in *Giornale de' letterati* (Pisa), I (1771), 21; the Georgofili's *Magazzino toscano* I¹ (1770), 148-49, and Anton Filippo Adami, *Della necessità di accrescere e migliorare l'agricoltura . . .* (Georgofili, 1767) (Florence: Bonducci, 1768), p. vii.

[24] *Giornale letterario di Siena,* Vol. I, No. 5 (15 January 1776), reviewing *Atti Fisiocritici,* Vol. V: « Le scienze hanno avuto in questo fortunato suolo il risorgimento; e la stessa loro felice rivoluzione . . . conforme è noto ad ognuno, alla Toscana appartiene ».

science had begun with the construction of the Florentine sun-dial in the mid-fifteenth century, modern philology with the establishment of the Crusca, modern historiography with the foundation of the Etrusca, "second to none in scholarship and doctrine," and the destruction of "the ignorance of so many centuries" with the rise of the Medici.[25] Similarly, so the argument runs, it was Tuscans who first established the institutions that by then had become chiefly responsible for the development and propagation of *illuminismo*: from the Crusca, "born in 1582, considerably before [the academies] of France and Spain,"[26] to the Lincei, founded largely through the initiative of Tuscans, and to the most important of all, the Cimento, from which all contemporary scientific societies ultimately derived.[27]

If the organization and activities, then, of the Accademia dei Georgofili frequently resembled those of the agricultural societies of Auch, Limoges, and Lyon, it was not because one had copied the others, but rather because all descended from the same archetype: the Accademia Fiorentina of the sixteenth century. Indeed, Tuscans insisted, whatever came from abroad was in essence but a further elaboration of truths and doctrines they themselves had first discovered. Such hypotheses, it is true, may well stray from strict historical reality. But their importance in Settecento Tuscany lies rather in their having facilitated the identification of traditional Tuscan institutions with the many contemporary *académies des sciences* and *des belles lettres* beyond the Alps and, above all, in having endowed the academicians with a consciousness of belonging to a new, and better, age.

It was, in fact, by making Tuscans members of an intellectual community extending far beyond the walls of their respective cities

---

[25] Leonardo Ximenes, *Del vecchio e nuovo gnomone fiorentino* (Florence: Stamp. Imp., 1757), p. iii.

[26] Lorenzo Del Riccio, tr., *Caratteri di Teofrasto, greco-toscani colle loro illustrazioni, varie lezioni, e note* (4 vols.; Florence: Moücke, 1761-63), I, 14; cf. Crusca: * Diario, 2 March 1748.

[27] *Atti Fisiocritici*, I, vi-vii; Neri Corsini (Lucumone) to F. Pancrazi, from Rome, 23 May 1750 (on the Etrusca), Etr 454, No. 9, and « obbligo personale » of 20 October 1760, Etr 449, No. 4; Antonio Cocchi in preface to his edition of Lorenzo Bellini, *Discorsi di anatomia recitati nell'Accademia della Crusca* (2 vols.; Florence: Moücke, 1741-47), II, 17-18. Lincei: Peruzzi in *Memorie Colombaria*, I, xxvii.

that the academies made one of their most valuable contributions to Tuscan, and to Italian, culture.[28] Tuscany had never been wholly isolated from the rest of the world, it is true: all during the Seicento the presence in the courts of Europe of Tuscan diplomats, many of them men of considerable learning, and the communications of Galileo and his disciples with colleagues abroad had lent at least some substance to the commonly held concept of a *Res Publica Litteraria,* sometimes embracing all Italy, sometimes transcending national, and even confessional, boundaries. But in general the absorption of most of the Tuscan *letterati* in the codification of the *volgare,* the composition of sonnets, and the pursuit of literary exercises closed their minds to the accomplishments of their foreign contemporaries — among whom, in turn, such activities could have had little appeal. The task, then, of reuniting Tuscany to Europe fell largely to those new institutions which, during the Settecento, would direct the attention of Tuscans to other occupations and which would make possible the extension of the limited contacts already enjoyed by a few to the literate classes of the whole country.

The academies began by opening their sessions to visitors from abroad, who arrived in ever increasing numbers from 1700 on — both to the resident foreigners like Sir Henry Newton, Horace Mann, and Louis Durfort and to travelers like Montesquieu, De Brosses, Mencke, Sherard, and Bedford.[29] They next created a special category for "honorary" membership, to be bestowed on whomever they considerd the more prominent men of letters of the age; and thus Caylus, Voltaire, Fréret, Barthélemy, Arthur Young, the Swedish metallurgist John James Ferber, the English anatomist William Thompson, and dozens of others (whose names the secretaries often misspelled and sometimes recorded simply as "Monsieur —?") all became at

---

[28] See Mario Fubini, « Illuminismo italiano e Illuminismo europeo », in *La cultura illuministica in Italia,* ed. Fubini (Torino: Radio Italiana, 1957), pp. 13-22, and E. W. Cochrane, « Le relazioni delle accademie toscane del Settecento con la cultura europea », *Archivio storico italiano,* CXI (1953), 78-108.

[29] Crusca: *Diario, 13 July 1710 (Newton), 8 July 1705 (commendation of a *Traité de la grammaire française* of François Regnier Desmarais (1632-1715) and letter to Pandolfini in BNF Capponi No. 521, cod. CLXXIII, 26-28.

least nominally associated with Tuscans of similar interests without ever setting foot in Tuscany. Some of the academies even established direct relations with academies abroad: the Crusca, for example, further strengthened the "bond of mutual affection with the Académie Française" it had established in 1662 through Regnier Desmarais, later *secrétaire perpétuel,* by exchanging a copy of the *Vocabolario* for one of the *Dictionnaire;* the Etrusca maintained connections with the Académie des Inscriptions of Paris and the Académie des Sciences of Bordeaux through Filippo Venuti during his long residence in France; and the Georgofili corresponded regularly with agricultural societies as far away as Stockholm and Madrid.[30] Most important of all, they contributed to the diffusion in Tuscany of literature of foreign origin — a task facilitated by an increasing familiarity with the French language and the "literary news" published in the gazettes, but still impeded by the high cost of transportation and the purely local organization of the book trade. Either they presented, as did the Georgofili from 1756 on, regular reports of new books and other "Transalpine news" in academic sessions, or they placed in their libraries such publications as Milton's *Paradise Lost,* the *Acta eruditorum,* and the *Journal des sçavans,* which they often received as gifts from honorary members. Needless to say, the contacts, both personal and literary, that the academies established with the rest of Europe were far from comprehensive: their records make no mention whatever of Berkeley, for instance, of Shaftesbury, of Helvétius, of Rousseau, of Jansenism, of speculative philosophy and social criticism in France, of moral theology in England; and their knowledge of English and German literature was usually limited to what had been

---

[30] Crusca: Alamanni to the Duc de Richelieu, 1 September 1748; Lorenzi to the Crusca, 5 February, J.-B. Du Bois (secretary of the Académie from 1722) to Lorenzi, 15 January 1748, *et al.,* all in Cr A. 29, nos. 172, 61-66. On Venuti: Hermann Weinert, *Filippo de' Venuti,* reprinted from *Annuario dell'A. Etrusca di C.* (1954). Among Etrusca elections: Barbet (president) and Loret of Bordeaux; Gros de Boze (1740) and Fréret (1744), secretaries of the Académie des Inscriptions. Georgofili: *Atti Georgofili,* Ser. V, Vol. III (1906), doc. iv (pp. 491-501) to article of Pietro Bargagli, 4 December 1755, 5 February 1756 (Madrid); *Atti,* IV (1801), 3-5: correspondence with John Sinclair (10 April 1797), president of the Bureau of Agriculture in England. On foreign members of the Crusca: Alfred von Reumont, *Dei soci esteri della A. C.* (Florence: Galileiana, 1855).

translated either into French or Latin.[31]   Such contacts were not
imposed from without; rather they were initiated by Tuscans themselves, among whom an unimpaired, if not somewhat complacent
pride in their own cultural and linguistic tradition prevented the acceptance of any novelty, except perhaps for fashions in dress, simply
because it came from abroad.   It is not surprising, therefore, that
what they learned from others tended to reflect what they themselves
already wanted to learn.[32]   Yet while perhaps not as open to foreign
influence as, for example, those of Milan, the Tuscan academies
shared with the many contemporary French provincial academies the
task of spreading to a wide audience the more advanced ideas of the
age.[33]   And they succeeded, during the course of the century, not only
in informing their members of the contributions of others to their
own fields of study, but above all in imbuing them with the willingness and the desire to look for suggestions and inspiration beyond the
borders of Tuscany.

The Settecento academies differed from those of the Cinquecento
also in the juridical relationship they established, at least tacitly, with

31 On English literature: E. W Cochrane, « Le accademie toscane nell'Illuminismo e
i loro rapporti culturali con l'Inghilterra », *Atti dell'Accademia Lucchese*, VIII (1952), 225-33.
In spite of statement in Arturo Graf, *L'anglomania e l'influsso inglese in Italia nel secolo XVIII*
(Torino: Loescher, 1911), chap. x, very few Tuscans knew English, especially in the first
part of the century—Salvini and Cocchi being the principal exceptions, though Gianfranco
Merli has noted close similarities between the *Magazzino toscano* (Livorno) and the *Spectator*
(at the BNF in French translation of 1754) in *Bollettino storico livornese*, N. S., I (1951), 67.
Note Paul Hazard and Henri Bédarida, *L'influence française en Italie au 18me siècle* (Paris:
Les Belles Lettres, 1934), and Alfred von Reumont, *Delle relazioni della letteratura italiana
con quella della Germania* (Florence: Galileiana, 1853).   On the *Encyclopédie* (published in
Livorno with dedication to Pietro Leopoldo: Ettore Levi-Malvano, « Les éditions toscanes
de l'Encyclopédie », *Revue de littérature comparée*, III [1923], 213-56), note remark in an
anonymous *ragionamento* delivered to the Crusca and published in *Magazzino toscano*, IV[1]
(1773), 65: « la più grandiosa collezione, che delle notizie alle scienze, e alle arti appartenenti sia mai stata fino ad ora pubblicata . . . ».   Further, Renato Mori, « J. J. Rosseau e
il pensiero politico toscano del Settecento », *Archivio storico italiano*, CII (1944), 82-105.   Note
provision for the « Mercurio » in the library of the Attica: ASF Reggenza 842.15, Art. XIV.
One of the very few references to the Society of Antiquaries is a tract by Filippo Venuti in
Colombaria: Annali 28, No. 5.

32 Note similar conclusion of Carlo Pellegrini in « Giovanni Lami, le *Novelle letterarie*
e la cultura francese », *Giornale storico della letteratura italiana*, CXVI (1940), 1-17.

33 On the Accademia dei Pugni of Verri, Beccaria, and Biffi, see Franco Venturi, « Un
amico di Beccaria e di Verri: Profilo di Giambattista Biffi », *Giornale storico della letteratura italiana*, CXXXIV (1957), 37 ff.   On the French academies: Georges Weulersse, *Le mouvement physiocratique en France* (Paris: Alcan, 1910), p. 19.

the state. To be sure, almost no one yet questioned the principle so rigorously applied by the first grand dukes: that any voluntary association among several persons for the pursuit of particular interests, be they as politically innocuous as the collection of ancient medals, was illegal, and consequently would be ineffective, and that all initiative within society ought to, and therefore did in fact proceed from the person of the prince alone. "Any plan of legislation," protested the Fisiocritici as late as 1767, "remains without value or authority unless it is given power by the venerable arm of the Sovereign." [34] Consequently, the new academies followed the customary procedure of making their constitutions and all subsequent amendments subject to royal confirmation, of submitting lists of members and programs of activity for prior approval, and of seeking, in petition after petition, to obtain both the privilege of assuming the title "royal" and the concession of financial assistance that previously had accompanied such titles.

Alas! all such efforts, the academies soon discovered, were inevitably thwarted by the "envy" of bureaucratic underlings; and if, after years of unexplained delay, the long-coveted approbation did at last arrive, it seldom entailed a *soldo* of subsidy.[35] For with the exception of Pietro Leopoldo, who paid for the prizes of the Georgofili, contributed toward the experiments of the Fisiocritici, and nominated the presidents of the Fiorentina, the grand dukes were no longer the Maecenases of the arts and sciences that the academic orators thought them still to be, nor, now that all opposition to the regime had become unthinkable, did they bother to maintain their once suspicious vigilance over the activities of their subjects. The academies also found, moreover, that the "benign hand" of the prince was ineffective in preserving their own institutions from the decline that at times afflicted the Crusca and the Fiorentina, in spite of the

[34] BCS L.III. 758-59: « qualunque piano di legislazione rimane senza valore, e senza autorità se non è avvalorato dal venerato braccio del Sovrano ». Similarly, the Petition of the Accademia di Varia letteratura, 19 February 1744 (ASF Reggenza 906.7); letter of the Avvalorati, 24 August 1790 (ASL 4332); and speech by the Arcirozzo of 1775 on « those blessings . . . conferred by our sovereigns » in preface of Acceso to Fabiani, *Memoria dell'A. de' Rozzi*, pp. 7-8.

[35] *Saggi Etrusca*, VII, vii-viii (though the Academy used the Palazzo Pretorio without paying any rent): Etr 449, « supplica » of 1 March 1727.

continuance of the traditional payments from the ecclesiastical tithes.[36] Hence, most of them were forced, however reluctantly, to go ahead with their plans alone — to meet their joint expenses by levying dues and to support their publications either by requiring honorary members to subscribe or, in one case, by selling off some of their extra furniture.[37] Gradually it became clear that the existence of an academy would depend upon nothing other than the will of its members; and gradually the academicians came to realize that their autonomy in respect to political authority was essential to the achievement of their goals. "These illustrious persons," concluded an anonymous speaker before the Etrusca, "deserve even greater praise," for they have undertaken works "profitable to the public, without the encouragement of the prince nor the direction of a magistrate."[38]

The admission of their autonomy and self-sufficiency in turn imposed upon the academies a new role within the body politic. The comparison of a literary gathering to a "popular republic," it is true, governed by an elected *consul* according to laws, "the fixed stars in the firmament of human polity," had been familiar to academic

[36] Payments to the Crusca: * Diario, 1760, intr., and Cr A. 27, 24, and 27.55; to the Apatisti and Fiorentina (for « cera e olio » and several public meetings, as well as for whitewashing and window repairs): ASF Reggenza 635.10 and 637.5; to the Intronati for rebuilding their burned theater: ASF Reggenza 662.9, petition requesting assignment to them of the subsidy granted by Ferdinando I to the by then extinct Filomati; to the Fisiocritici (contribution toward publication of the *Atti* and salary for a librarian): *Atti*, III, 760, and II, 67, and * Deliberazioni, 11 December 1759. Note Medicina: * Piano, Arts XXVII, XXX, XXXI.

[37] Note correspondence between the government and the Fisiocritici: ASF Reggenza 669.23. After 1759 the Academy received 40 scudi p.a. from the University to cover some of its experiments; the attached memorandum tells how « gli accademici entrarono spontaneamente nel fervore di fare una colletta fra loro » to build an adequate laboratory and requests further payments from the grand duke for custodian's salaries and publications. Etrusca: * Deliberazioni, 12 December 1780, 24 September 1784.

[38] *Saggi Etrusca*, IV, ix. In this again, in spite of many similarities, the Tuscan academies differed from the Spanish economic societies of the *Amigos del País*, which, though modeled after the earlier society in the Basque provinces (1764), spread all over Spain from 1775 on as the result of the encouragement and initiative of the government. See Shafer, *The Economic Societies in the Spanish World*, chap. iii; Richard Herr, *The Eighteenth-Century Revolution in Spain* (Princeton: Princeton University Press, 1954), pp. 154 ff.; and Jean Sarrailh, *L'Espagne éclairée de la seconde moitié du XVIIIe siècle* (Paris; Imprimerie Nationale, 1954), 2e partie, chaps. iv and v.

orators ever since the Cinquecento.[39] But not until the eighteenth century did anyone perceive that a "republic" of the learned might have some connection with that of the landlords, merchants, peasants, and beggars ruled by the heirs of Cosimo I with the help of a police force and taxation — the republic of the real world, that is, from which the citizens of the academies had sought to escape. The founders of Arcadia had stimulated such speculations by embodying the concept of a "civil society" in the *Leges Arcadum,* by speaking of a "single general will," in the words of Gravina, formed by a contract among several individuals, and by encouraging their successors throughout the century to think of themselves as members of a *corpo politico.*[40] Soon, then, such provisions in the charters of the older academies took on new meanings. Gigli had already pointed out that the substitution of a hierarchy of talent for one of birth was essential to the cause of the sciences and the arts; Cocchi now insisted further than in "subaltern bodies or colleges" a "more tempered power, not exercised by one alone," was essential also to the "public good."[41] Indeed, in Pompeo Neri's discourses on the "natural nobility" and in Francesco Gianni's observation that "equality is not a French invention [but] exists among us in many parts of our government," the structure of the academies seems to have suggested possible changes in that of society as a whole. Even the concept of a written constitution as prerequisite to the proper functioning of the commonwealth, after

[39] Intronati: Copia lettera (8 January 1703), BCS Y.I. 9, 432: « le leggi sono, è vero, le stelle fisse . . . nel firmamento dell'umana politica ». Bargagli, *Delle lodi dell'accademie,* p. 40.

[40] Angelandrea Zottoli, « Rousseau e l'Arcadia », *Atti della A. N. dei Lincei,* CCCL (1953), 3-20, quoting Gravina's speech of 20 May 1696: « in unum eundemque sensum coaluimus, ut, cum plures simus, una tandem mente universi ducamur ». Note also S. Salvini, *Fasti consolari dell'Accademia Fiorentina,* p. xxiii, comparing the academy, « una Repubblica di Lettere », to the Roman Republic, both of which were governed by consuls.

[41] Gigli to the Intronati, undated: ASF MS 740.41. A. Cocchi, report on Santa Maria Nuova (1747), cap. v, par. 2: ASF Reggenza 412: « Perché la felicità dell'universal governo della toscana porta, che dalla reale, e paterna provvidenza del suo Sovrano si possano sperare in qualunque parte del medesimo governo tutti i beni, che l'ottimo impero di un solo può produrre, è facile l'immaginarsi, che ne' corpi, o collegj, o università subalterne, una potestà più temperata, e non residente assolutamente in un solo fosse per essere più sicura, e più confacente al pubblico bene ».

all, was familiar among academicians long before its application in that proposed for all Tuscany by Gianni and Pietro Leopoldo.[42]

Thus the academies came to be defined as "societies within a society," similar to the municipal corporations envisaged in the Leopoldine reform of local government, charged with drawing forth the energies and talents of individual citizens for the good of the whole. First, by accustoming their members to speak in public and to participate actively in the "government" of their "republics," they established a kind of school of citizenship, somewhat like that sought by the reformers in introducing oral pleading into the law courts.[43] Second, by gathering together those most acquainted with the actual conditions of the country and those best equipped technically to deal with them, they provided a pool of intellect which the prince might draw upon for assistance. Indeed, from 1753 on, when the head of the Regency walked in on a meeting of the newly-founded Georgofili, the government used the academies for just such purposes. It regularly called upon them for advice on prospective legislation and for "all information that can contribute to increasing the natural riches of Tuscany"; while at the same time it permitted the academicians to criticize its measures free from "fear of offending the Sovereign Philosopher who promulgates [the law]."[44] Without ever questioning

[42] Gianni, * Ricordi (ASF Carte Gianni XIII, 302); Neri, « Sopra lo stato antico e moderno della nobiltà di Toscana » (1748), in J. B. Neri Badia (his father), *Decisiones et responsa juris*, II (Florence: Allegrini, 1776), 550-643. The draft constitution was prepared by Gianni and published in 1832 and 1847 with *Memoria sulla costituzione di governo immaginata dal gran duca Pietro Leopoldo da servire alla storia del suo regno in Toscana*, on which see N. Aglietti in *Rassegna nazionale*, CLXIV (1908), 273-95, 441-53. Note Montelatici on the « reggimento . . . democratico o popolare » in the Georgofili: *Atti Georgofili*, Ser. V. Vol. III (1906), 462, and Gio. Gualberto Uccelli before the Fiorentina (*Elogio di Alessandro Bicchierai* [Florence: Pagani, 1798], p. 10).

[43] On public speaking: compare A. M. Salvini, *Discorsi accademici*, II, lezione lviii, and Crusca: * Diario, 14 December 1714, with Gianni (« bisognava bene eccitare alla franchezza di arringare il pubblico quella gente, che per la costituzione doveva un giorno parlare nelle assemblee ») quoted by Aglietti, *op. cit.*, p. 287

[44] Rosemberg to the Georgofili, 20 March 1767: « tutti quei lumi, o notizie, che possono più contribuire ad accrescere le naturali ricchezze della Toscana »: ASF Arch. Tolomei 191, E. No. 2; query on taxation of 28 October 1771 quoted in the part by Mario Mirri in *Movimento operaio*, VII (1955), 187-88, and others in Geo II. ii. 1, 2, in ASF Arch. Tolomei 191. VI No. 6 (reply of the Academy to request of 24 April 1767); report of the Fisiocritici on conditions in the Hospital: *Atti Fisiocritici*, VI, 289. « Nemmeno ò timore di

the century-old belief in the prince as the source of all authority, then, the academies of the Settecento gradually assumed the very function from which those of the Cinquecento had expressly been barred: the function, that is, of intermediate bodies capable of transmitting to the prince the criticisms, the suggestions, and the desires of his subjects, and of communicating in turn to the subjects the will and the plans of the prince.

Yet the academies could never have accepted their reincorporation into the political order of their country had they not previously arrived at a new definition of the nature and purpose of knowledge. The change is apparent, in fact, from as early as the beginning of the century, as form gave way to content and as what a speaker said — about medicine among the Fisiocritici in the 1690's and about the works of Galileo among the Cruscans of 1718 — became more important than the mere fact of having spoken. Gradually the academies abandoned those elements of their programs extraneous to their more serious pursuits: masses for the dead, for instance, the *critiche* and the *difese* of sonnets, and the celebration of *stravizzi;* and they carefully avoided all controversies, like those of "the Epicureans, the Stoics, and the Academies," which, as Giulio Perini pointed out, could contribute no more to the "public good" of modern Tuscany than they had to that of ancient Greece.[45] Gradually the academicians came to realize that the success of their institutions would depend not so much on the qualities of the participants as upon a carefully defined plan of study.[46] The insistence upon the pursuit of knowledge as the principal, if not the only legitimate occupation of academic institutions, indeed, affected even the mythology of inaugural addresses. Thus while still repeating, in much the same words, Salvini's eulogies of Plato as the first of their number, the academic orators by 1730 would have nothing of the tranquil amenities of the Attic woods: the first academy, they now discovered, had been

offendere il Sovrano Filosofo » (by criticising recent laws on agrarian contracts): Gregorio Fierli (8 February 1792), in *Atti Georgofili*, III, 100. Similarly the Preface of the Arcirozzo to Fabiani, *Memoria dell'Accademia dei Rozzi*, pp. 7-8.

[45] Perini, Inaugural address.: ASF Reggenza 1052.58.

[46] Giovanni Targioni Tozzetti, *Ragionamenti sull'agricoltura toscana* (Lucca: Giusti, 1759), pp. 4-5; Gianni: * Ricordi (ASF Carte Gianni XIII.302).

not a haven for a retired élite but the center from which had radiated all ancient civilization, and its true heirs in more recent times were not the "assemblies of illiterates" that "dishonored learning" in the Seicento, but the Academy of Marsilio Ficino, the Lincei, and the Académie des Inscriptions — institutions, that is, animated by "the spirit of discovery" and dedicated to "the greatest utility of society." [47] Deprived of the possibility of influencing the real world of space and time, knowledge in the Cinquecento had become merely the basis for the literary exercises of a priviledged few; reinvested with such a possibility in the Settecento, it once again became "useful" as a means whereby all mankind might realize a fuller and a more comfortable life.

The academies now had an obligation not only to their own members, but to society as a whole — an obligation first of all to increase the content and widen the scope of knowledge. Accordingly, they took positive measures to prevent the enthusiasm of the founders from dwindling into routine and to assure a steady contribution to the arts and sciences from all those successively elected to membership. The Crusca and the Fiorentina had long been accustomed to Salvini's attempts to "reawaken spirits to ever new meditations and compositions," by recalling the examples of their forebears, by evoking their horror of "idleness," and by requesting their applause for the literary efforts of the "studious youth." [48] But the newer academies realized that oratorical exortations alone would be insufficient to realize the demands now made upon knowledge. Putting the members to work on a given project, they discovered, would stimulate their productivity much more effectively than advice to become "learned" in general; and they established a number of long-term projects — like the preparation of the *Vocabolario* in the Crusca and the anti-

---

[47] BCS C.X.2, 175-80 (Orazione accademica fatta nell'A. Etrusca sul vantaggio delle accademie, apparently written in 1730), and P. Guglielmo Della Valle, « Al chiarissimo sig. abate Giovacchino Pizzi, Custode Generale d'Arcadia, sopra l'utilità dell'accademia », in his *Lettere sanesi ... sopra le belle arti,* I (Venice: Pasquali, 1782), 27. Cf. Gigli to Magliabechi: BCS Y.I.1, and Etr Notti Coritane, IV (1747), 16.

[48] Crusca: * Diario, 17 December 1711 (Salvini, *Prose toscane,* I, 486, 492) and 20 February 1747 (Giovanni Bottari on « l'imitazione de' loro [ancestors'] gran fatti »). Further: Filippo Venuti in Etrusca: * Atti, 11 December 1751, and Salvini in the Apatisti: *Discorsi accademici,* II, 118, 331, etc.

quarian publications in the Etrusca — in order to harness the energy of those whose eagerness was not yet directed toward any particular goal. Some of them even resorted to force and adopted regulations providing for the expulsion or demotion of the inactive, for the submission of written compositions as a condition of admission, and for the compilation at the beginning of each year of a list, sometimes posted publicly to increase its effectiveness, bearing the names of those scheduled by lot to speak at the following meetings.[49] Money and honor might provide still another incentive, especially when the grand duke made an appropriate contribution; and after 1767 the Fisiocritici, the Georgofili, and the Etrusca adopted the practice, recommended by Nelli in 1756 and supported by the example of Transalpine academies, of offering prizes in competition.[50] The availability of equipment and information, moreover, might encourage those already engaged in a course of study; and first the Crusca, which in 1714 acquired new rooms in an adjoining building, then the Fisiocritici, which met in the chambers destined for their experimental equipment, and then the Botanica, the Colombaria, the Ierofili, and indeed most of the other academies founded libraries, laboratories, and museums for the use of their associates.[51] Finally, the academies sought to remedy such obstacles as the high cost of printing, the

[49] E.g., Risvegliati: Constitution of 1715, Art. V: Medicina: * Piano, Art. IX; Etrusca resolution 24 September 1784: Etr 449.110; Georgofili: Appunti (Geo II, ii, 1, 1, 5 February 1772 — drawing lots); Fisiocritici: Constitution of 1767, Arts. II, vii; IV, iv.

[50] Nelli in *Novelle letterarie*, XVII (1756), 481-85. List of prizes offered by the Georgofili printed in the first volume of the *Atti;* on that of the Etrusca, see below, pp. 175-76.

[51] Note of Alamanni in Crusca: Diario, 1714. Contents of the Library given in Cr A. 33 (very brief) and in an unmarked Indice de' libri of 1728; the collection passed to the Magliabechiana in 1783, hence does not form part of the present library of the Academy. Fisiocritici: see G. Gigli, *Diario senese . . . degli avvenimenti più ragguardevoli alla giornata . . .* (Siena: Quinza, 1722), I, 119 f., and Crescimbeni, *L'Arcadia* (Rome: De' Rossi, 1711), pp. 181-84. Colombaria: Annali 23, constitution, Cap. VI, and June 1757 (see Umberto Dorini, *Inventario dell'Archivio e degli altri manoscritti della S. C.* [Florence: Arte della Stampa, 1915]). Even the Intronati established a museum in their new theater: see Giovanni Antonio Pecci, *Discorso . . . sopra un'iscrzione nell'ideato museo . . .* (Siena: Quinza & Bindi, 1750), and in *Novelle letterarie*, XI (1750), 196-97 — not to be confused with the collection in the Opera of the Cathedral: BCS Y.I.12: Gl'inventari delle consegne delle robbe (1706-99). Gifts of cav. Giovanni Sansedoni of experimental equipment to the Fisiocritici and the foundation of a « piccolo museo » « di cose naturali » with gifts of other Sienese noblemen for the Academy are described in Dell'Accademia delle Scienze . . . : ASF Reggenza 669.28.

threat of censorship, and the difficulties of finding an adequate market, which would otherwise have discouraged their members from publishing the results of their researches and meditations. They subsidized a number of publications through dues and obligatory subscriptions.   They elected both the heads of printing houses — usually *letterati* themselves, who could be induced to accept manuscripts by being designated "printer to the academy" — and also the civil and ecclesiastical censors — most often such persons as Salvini, Marc'Antonio de'Mozzi, and Filippo Buonarroti, who could then be trusted to turn an imprimatur into a flattering recommendation. They offered little-known authors the possibility of advertising their works by placing the name of the academy on the title page. And they circulated among many potential readers the handbills by which publishers, before the emergence of a specialized retail trade, usually gave notice of the new books for sale in their shops.[52]

Some of these measures, to be sure, failed to achieve their intended results: publishing under the name of an academy, for instance, often involved such delays that only those authors hoping to sell a "language text" or to hide under a respectable anonymity could be induced to submit their works for approval.[53] All too often, moreover, the demand for productivity ended in the sacrifice of quality

[52] Note Guazzesi's complaints to A. M. Bandini of the difficulty of procuring books in Pisa in undated letter (1763): Mar B.2.27; similar complaints from Siena and Pecci's troubles with censorship in letters to Gori of 23 January 1747 and 6 December 1752: Mar B.7.25. Books from abroad paid a tariff of one-eighth the price (Pecci to Gori, 10 April 1747). Conditions of the book trade in 1704 can be gathered from the printed petition: *Per l'Università de' librai, stampatori e cartolai della città di Firenze*, signed by Gio. Vincenzo Cappi, in BNF Mag IX.38; conditions in 1767 from the several reports in ASF Reggenza 778.13.A. On censorship see further the Press Law of 28 March 1743 (*Leggi e bandi*, III) (a subject still largely unstudied). Printers and publication in Pisa and Livorno: Flora Vincentini, « Notizie sulle stamperie pisane dalle origini al 1860 », *Bollettino storico pisano*, XVIII (1939), 33-63, and Guido Chiappini, *L'arte della stampa in Livorno* (Livorno: Belforte, 1904), and in general (among many others): L. Piccioni, *Il giornalismo letterario in Italia* (Torino: Loescher, 1894). Note tribute of A. Cocchi to the printer Francesco Moücke in Preface to Bellini, *Discorsi di anatomia*, I, xx, and of Louis Durfort, French resident, to Cambiagi (« seul homme versé dans la connoissance de l'histoire . . . »): Archives des Affaires Etrangères, Paris, Toscane 143B, fol. 226. Examples of handbills in Colombaria: Annali, 1, Appendix.

[53] « È cosa notissima, che i Conservatori della Crusca fiorentina furono . . . un po' fastidiosi . . . . Però sono pochi a mio parere i libri sigillati dalla Crusca, e interessanti . . . »: Della Valle in Preface to his edition of Vasari's *Vite* (Siena: Carli, 1791-94), I, iv.

to mere quantity, especially when members heard themselves applauded for being able to "stretch out into a [whole] volume a world, so to speak, of rare erudition" from "one quite short inscription." [54] Yet the academies sought to increase the body of knowledge not so much by drawing forth the excellence of a few — a task they recognized beyond their competence — as by encouraging the greatest amount of activity among the greatest number of persons. While they may have erred in supposing that quantity would eventually produce something of quality, the flood of dissertations, poems, orations, and treatises that poured from their sessions during the century shows them to have been successful at least in overcoming what they considered to be the chief obstacle to the expansion of knowledge in their times: the lethargy, that is, that had afflicted all but a few Tuscans from the mid-Cinquecento on.

To the obligation for the increase of knowledge corresponded the further obligation for its diffusion; for, the academicians came to believe, the potential utility of knowledge depended upon its being placed at the disposal of all those capable of putting it into practice. They began, therefore, by attempting to arouse public interest in the subjects of their sessions — inserting notices of meetings in the literary gazettes and inviting the citizenry, through printed posters in the main squares of the city, to attend their "general assemblies." Some of them then sought to reach a still larger audience — first by publishing their transactions and then by issuing inexpensive editions or abridgements, with cheap paper, small print, and narrow margins, of works otherwise available only to the wealthy. [55] The Georgofili, indeed, appealed even to the uneducated, with publications like Marco

[54] D. M. Manni, in his « Lezione . . . nell'A. degli Apatisti » (1738), Calogerà, *Raccolta d'opuscoli*, VIII, 210.

[55] Examples of such posters in many parts of the Notti Coritane and in ASF Reggenza 669.23, doc. V (Fisiocritici). Proposal to publish *Atti* of the Georgofili, 1 July 1772; report of the committee, 4 August 1779: Geo II.ii. 1.1 (Appunti) — though the first volume did not appear until 1791, records of the sessions and many the dissertations were published periodically in the *Magazzino toscano* and the *Giornale di agricoltura* from 1770 on. *Vocabolario degli accademici della Crusca: Compendio formato sulla quarta edizione* (5 vols.; Florence: D. M. Manni, 1739), meant particularly for those who « o mancanti sono di ricchezze, o che per l'istituto della loro vita sono necessitati a cangiar spesso sede »: *Novelle letterarie*, I (1740), 149-50.

Lastri's "Calendars for the Peasants of Tuscany" containing little discourses against popular prejudices, extracts from academic proceedings, weather forecasts, "rustic proverbs," and advice on planting according to saints' days and phases of the moon.[56] By excluding their members from prizes offered in competition, the Georgofili drew support not only from the *letterati,* but also from farmers and *fattori* (estate managers) all over the country; and the Accademia di Agricoltura even invited "persons from the country" to their sessions in order to procure firsthand information for their discussions.[57] Many of the academies, moreover, protesting against the "restriction" of their studies "to a single class of persons" and recognizing "the just principle that it is the duty of every citizen to contribute to the good of his fellow citizens," opened their newly founded libraries and museums to the general public, while the Georgofili had, by 1775, adopted a policy of turning over all the publications it received "to the Magliabechiana, in order that they be read not only by the members, but also by those who frequent the [public] library."[58] A few, finally, undertook special programs of popular education — like the public lectures of the 1740's in Pistoia, and those of the 1780's and 90's in the Florentine Botanical Gardens, and, above all, the various projects of the Georgofili for "the education of the children of the country," through the publication of agricultural textbooks, through instruction by parish priests, and even through suggestions to "public

---

[56] *Lunario per i contadini della Toscana,* ed. Marco Lastri, published yearly (e. g., *per l'anno 1782 ovvero anno rustico nono*) by Bonaiuti. See announcement in the *Giornale di agricoltura,* III (1788), 249, of a *Corso di agricoltura pratica o sia ristampa dei lunarj per i contadini della Toscana* printed by Pagani.

[57] Agricoltura: * Atti, 9 January 1790.

[58] Serafini, Memoria of 11 August 1765: ASL Cose livornesi, Bibl. pubblica, No. 3, and Ierofili petition of 5 December 1756: ASF Reggenza 650.44.IV. Negotiations on the library of the Etrusca, opened « per il pubblico vantaggio . . . con il giusto principio, dovere ogni cittadino contribuire al bene dei suoi concittadini » (letter of 7 May 1774: Etr 451.2) by request of Orazio Maccari in donating his collection, augmented with the assistance of a grant of scudi 1,200 by the Ministero of Finance, Angelo Tavanti (sometime Lucumone), through the Commune, on the condition that the Academy raise an equivalent sum, and finally opened « to all civil and honest persons » three days a week from 8 until 2 o'clock: Etr 471.16-19 (Statutes: Etr 451). Compare Occulti: Supplica of 12 February 1727 in Etr 449.1 (for the nobility alone). Georgofili: Appunti (Geo II.ii.1.1), 17 May 1775. On open meetings: Georgofili: Regolamento (*Atti,* I [1790], 56-68), Cap. X, and constitution of 1767 (*Atti,* Ser. V, Vol. III [1906], 452), Art. 3.

masters of Latin" that they teach "the authors *de re rustica* along with the classics." [59]   The success of these projects, it is true, was considerably limited both by the naïve supposition that ordinary citizens would find pompous orations and heavily annotated treatises either useful or interesting and by the inability of the *letterati* in general to comprehend the mentality of anyone outside their immediate circle.[60] Lastri's *Lunario,* for instance, was so clumsily "written-down" that any of its intended readers who could understand it would (being Tuscans) certainly have been insulted; while the popular riots of 1790, and the bloody revolt at Arezzo in 1799 at least leave doubts about the effectiveness of the conscious effort of some five decades to bring "enlightenment" to the lowest classes of the population. Yet the very recognition by the academies of the necessity for popularization itself represents a notable achievement. For in appealing to all "those cultured and sensible persons" outside the cabinets of the specialists "who can distinguish truth from falsehood," [61] they convinced the scholars and scientists of their times that learning, no

[59] Enciclopedica: *Relazione.* Announcement of lectures in the Botanical Garden: *Giornale di agricoltura,* I (1786), 193 (by Andrea Zucchini); ASF Arch. Tolomei 191.VII.27 (703): Orto dell'Accademia; lectures of Ottavio Targioni Tozzetti published as *Instituzioni botaniche* (2 vols.; Florence: Carlieri, 1794-96). Progetto . . . d'un'accademia d'arti liberali . . . da erigersi in Siena sotto la direzione dell'Accademia Intronata: BCS Y.I.20. Ferdinando Paoletti, *Pensieri sull'agricoltura* (1767) (S.C.I.E.P.), pp. 12-14. Giulio Perini on proposal to erect a veterinary institute: *Giornale di agricoltura,* I (1786), 289. D. M. Manni, *Nuova proposizione per trarre dall'agricoltura un maggior frutto* (read to the Georgofili, 6 September 1775) (Florence: Vanni, 1775), on which: Marco Lastri, *Biblioteca georgica, ossia Catalogo ragionato degli scrittori di agricoltura* (Florence: Moücke, 187), p. 81 (see below, chap. iv, note 114). The work of the *medici condotti* (resident physicians maintained by the government in all the communes), many of them members of the Georgofili and the Fisiocritici, in spreading scientific information, is recognized in *Magazzino toscano,* II[3] (1771), 85 f. Note E. Garin, *Medioevo e rinascimento* (Bari: Laterza, 1954), 141-42, on proposals to popularize the sciences in the Cinquecento, especially that of Alessandro Piccolomini.

[60] As shown in their distaste for any literature meant principally for entertainment — c.g., Ottavio Del Rosso in *Magazzino toscano,* II[2] (1771), 115, on « certi libri che pieni di micidial corruttela . . . seducono appoco appoco il cuor degl'incauti . . . fomentano le passioni . . . ».

[61] Saverio Manetti, *Della inoculazione del vaiuolo* (Florence: Bonducci, 1761), p. vii: « quelle culte e sensate persone, che il vero dal falso facilmente discernono ». Note Introduction to *Memorie due lette nella Società degli Amatori della Storia Patria* (Florence, 1803), p. iii: « Dalle società letterarie, più che da qualunque particolare individuo, il pubblico ha diritto di esigere e lumi e instruzione ». Note Corrado Lazzeri, *Arezzo e la sua insurrezione del 6 maggio 1799* (Arezzo, 1934).

longer the monopoly of the few, was, or ought to be, the just possession of all.

Thus during the course of the Settecento the academies came to
assume functions and responsibilities that two centuries earlier would
have been considered incompatible with their nature and purposes.
The academicians were now interested not in perfecting the spiritual
and moral qualities of a select élite, but in stimulating intellectual
activity among their fellow citizens, in encouraging a greater unity
between state and subjects, in elaborating and communicating knowledge. They justified these new interests first, by insisting that they
were essential to the progress of society (thus assuming that such
progress was possible and desirable) and second, by claiming that they
could be pursued much more effectively and efficiently by collective than by individual activity. This thesis — that the co-operation of many minds in a permanent institution could accomplish
much more than even the most brilliant acting separately — was by
no means original among Settecento Tuscans. It had been familiar
even to Anton Maria Salvini at the very beginning of the century in
his frequent insistence that only such co-operation could make possible projects as vast as the *Vocabolario*.[62] But after 1720 it was gradually elaborated as new subjects were introduced into academic sessions — by Antonio Cocchi in the Società Botanica, by an anonymous
speaker of 1730 in the Etrusca, and by Domenico Maria Manni in
the Georgofili. Single persons, they granted, had at times made important theoretical discoveries and technological improvements. But
especially in such sciences as botany, agriculture, and history, which
require the amassing of large quantities of concrete data, "the combined abilities of many directed toward the same single goal" would
achieve infinitely greater results in far less time. Hence the weakness of the Cimento: it was an academy in name only, which never
succeeded in uniting its individual members into one body and which
fell apart as soon as the moderating hand of the princely protector

---

[62] *Prose toscane*, II, Lezioni 21, 29, 30. Similar argument in Risvegliati: * Capitoli,
proemio.

was withdrawn. An academy also made possible effective special-ization among its members by directing their particular studies toward the solution of common problems too complex to fall within the competence of each of them separately; and it prevented any "increase in knowledge" from being confined to "the minds of a few private persons" by providing the means for its communication to others.[63] Nothing, Guido Savini told the Fisiocritici in 1768, in so profitable for the advancement of learning as "the mutual assistance of exchanged knowledge"; and nothing, he added, is "so pernicious as the vain efforts of those isolated scholars who prefer darkness and reject com-pany." Without academies to "raise [them] from the ground," admit-ted the founder of the Toscolidi, "the spirit of segregation and solitu-de" would turn "great men" into what Amaduzzi called "misanthropic pedants." Without academies to co-ordinate and support the labor of individual scholars and scientists, learning would degenerate into irrelevant trivia and useless nonsense.[64] If the "science of govern-ment," said Gianni in 1796, still remained far behind botany, paint-ing, history, physics, and linguistics, the reason was obvious: no academy had yet undertaken the study of such matters.[65] Thus by

[63] Antonio Cocchi, « Discorso sopra la storia naturale » (inaugural address to the So-cietà Botanica of 3 September 1734), published first in *Dissertazioni e lettere scritte sopra varie materie da diversi illustri autori viventi,* I (Florence: Bonducci, 1749), 81-102, then in *Dei discorsi toscani del dott. Antonio Cocchi* (Florence: Bonducci, 1761-62), I, 133-70, and also in his *Discorsi e lettere* (Milan: Classici Italiani, 1824), I, 77-98. Orazione accademica fatta nell'Accademia Etrusca sul vantaggio delle accademie (1730): BCS C.X.2, 175-80 (above, note 47). D. M. Manni, Georgofili: * Discorso (Mar B.1.9.22). Note further the preface to Vol. III of *Saggi Etrusca* and Anton Filippo Adami, *Dissertazioni critiche* (Pisa: Pizzor-no, 1765) (below, chap. v, note 6), pp. xi-xii, in the necessity of co-operation in historiography.

[64] « Ragionamento sull'utilità de' corpi accademici », in his posthumous *Prose e poesie* (Siena: Rossi, 1800), pp. 51-63. *Saggio sulle accademie letterarie letto nella nuova Acca-demia dei Toscolidi* (Livorno: Giorgi, 1773), pp. 17 f.

[65] Gianni, Cicalata in memoria delle cose discorse nella conversazione a cena del di 20 9bre 1796 sulle società o accademie patriotiche: ASF Carte Gianni XIII.304. In spite of the coincidence of dates and names, Gianni is not speaking of the many contemporary « patriotic » societies inspired by the French Revolution (see Delio Cantimori, *Utopisti e rifor-matori italiani* [Florence: Sansoni, 1943], p. 54, on the Società degli Emuli di Bruto in Rome, and Pia Onnis, « Filippo Buonarroti e i patrioti italiani », *Rivista storica italiana,* Ser. V, Vol. II² [1937], 38-65); his references are all to the same « illustrious academies » mentioned by Amaduzzi and to the Georgofili, of which he was a member.

the end of the century the academicians could accept only the last of Bargagli's four conditions for the existence of academies, and that with severe modifications.[66] They considered collective activity superior to individual — not because it better developed the "virtue" of each participant, but because it more effectively contributed to the *pubblica felicità,* to the happiness and well-being of their fellow-citizens. An academy therefore was no longer a select band of *beaux-esprits* who "buried themselves" from the world to conduct "literary exercises"upon any subject from the wine of Montepulciano to the sonnets of Bembo; it was a "society within a society," a corporate body existing above and beyond its individual members for the elaboration of the arts and sciences useful to all men.

Thus the Cinquecento academies lived on into the Settecento and provided the model for the many other academies that, during the course of the century, sprang up in all the cities of Tuscany. Both were the principal cultural institutions of their respective ages; both followed much the same form of organization and procedure; both included as members almost all those Tuscans with the ability or the ambition to write and speak. But whereas the first had arisen largely because of the exhaustion or the suffocation of intellectual life in the late sixteenth century, the second arose because of a revival of intellectual life in the early eighteenth. The Settecento academies thus differed from their predecessors — first, in their inclusion of many persons whose pretensions to learning went little further than reading and listening to the words of others; second, in their consciousness of belonging to a cultural community comprehending all Europe; and third, in the definition of their role within society as autonomous corporations responsible for the expansion and diffusion of knowledge and for the mediation of desires and aspirations between the state and the citizens. Convinced, then, of the potential applicability of knowledge to the concrete social, political, and economic problems

---

[66] Bargagli, *Delle lodi dell'accademie,* pp. 21 f. The other conditions: a « pleasant » landscape and climate; a state ruled by « lords and princes », and the presence of « belle, amabili, et valorose » women.

of their age, sure of their ability to serve the interests of learning more effectively than individuals acting alone, and dedicated to the somewhat loosely defined ideal of "public happiness," the academies set forth to draw the minds of their members into fields of study and investigation that two centuries earlier would have been considered beyond their competence and contrary to their better interests.

CHAPTER III

POETRY, PIETY, AND PLAY

On the morning of 29 December 1794, the Accademia Fiorentina, into which the Crusca, the Apatisti, and the Sacra Fiorentina had been amalgamated in 1783, met in an "extraordinary session," with elaborate decorations and an orchestra.[1] The program attracted an almost unprecedented attendance; even many of those who did not generally consider their election as an obligation to attend the regular sessions of the academy turned up for this one. Their sudden interest had little to do with the crises of which almost all educated Tuscans — and many others as well — were fully aware: the riots in Pistoia and Prato of 1788, for instance, which had shattered the ecclesiastical reforms of Pietro Leopoldo's episcopal colleague, Scipione de' Ricci; the insurrections in Florence and Livorno just after the departure of the Grand Duke for Vienna in the spring of 1790, which had forced the frightened and unarmed Council of Regency to withdraw temporarily the careful legislative work of some twenty years; and now the increasing menace from beyond the Alps, which was to end, three years later, with the arrival of French armies and the eclipse of Tuscany as an independent state. What really mattered on this festive occasion was the visit to the capital of a young lady named Teresa Bandettini of Lucca, who possessed the extraordinary talent of being able immediately to transform any theme presented to her into rhyme and meter. And the *letterati* of all Florence gathered in their principal institution to pay tribute to this wonder of genius and to acclaim her one of the great poets of the age.[2]

[1] Fiorentina (1783): * Registro, 29 December 1794.

[2] Some of her verses were published, usually under her Arcadian psuedonym Amarilla Etrusca, e.g., *Saggio di versi estemporanei* (Pisa: Peverata, 1799); *Il giudizio universale, poemetto cantato all'improvviso sul tema datole da monsignor Sardi, arcivescovo di Lucca*

Extemporaneous versification was nothing new in the Italian literary tradition, to be sure. It may well go back as far as the *trobadori;* it certainly had been popular during the Renaissance, when Leonardo da Vinci, according to Vasari, performed before Lodovico il Moro; and it had flourished along with the Commedia dell'Arte for the two preceding centuries. But never had impromptu poets evoked greater enthusiasm than in the Settecento. This was the age of Bernardino Perfetti of Siena and of Maria Maddelena Morelli Fernandez of Pistoia, better known as Corilla Olimpica, the "Tenth Muse" of Arcadia, whose "ease and informality in improvising most elegantly on any subject whatever" — from sacred history and moral philosophy to physics and legislation — had won them Petrarch's laurels on the Campidoglio and the special blessings of the Pope.[3] This was the age of Pietro Metastasio, who began his spectacular rise to fame as imperial poet and the most celebrated librettist of all Europe when Gian Vincenzo Gravina, the jurist and playwright, found him declaiming on the streets of Rome, the ten-year old son of a humble shopkeeper. Still, the Accademia Fiorentina was not the market place, nor was it a private garden party. It was the official organization of Florentine scholars, whose constitution had pledged them to the serious pursuits of philology, historiography, and linguistics. And the year, moreover, was 1794, not 1708 — a century after Crescimbeni had denounced the emptiness of Seicento verse,

(Florence, 1796) (« The Last Judgment, a poem sung extemporaneously on the theme given her by Msgr. Sardi, archbishop of Lucca »); and *La teseide, Poema* (Parma: Mussi, 1805).

[3] *Atti della solenne coronazione fatta in Campidoglio della insigna poetessa D.na Maria Maddalena Morelli Fernandez, pistoiese* . . . (Parma: Stamperia Reale, 1779), p. 5 (from 1st ed.; Rome: Salomoni, 1775); cf. Gaetano Gasperoni, *La storia e le lettere nella seconda metà del secolo XVIII* (Jesi: Cooperativa, 1904), pp. 35 f., and A. Ademollo, *Corilla Olimpica* (above. chap. ii, note 7). The hundreds of verses that Perfetti (b. 1680, crowned by order of Benedict XIII in 1725, frequently a participant in the Sienese academies, d. 1747) composed orally during walks in the cloister of the convent of the Carmelitani Scalzi in Florence were considered « precious relics to be jealously preserved and exposed to the veneration of future centuries » by contemporaries: *Saggi di poesie, parte dette all'improvviso, e parte scritte dal cavaliere Bernardino Perfetti patrizio senese* . . . *raccolte e date alla luce dal dottor Domenico Gianfogni* . . . , *canonico dell'imperial Basilica Laurenziana ed accademico apatista* (2d ed.; Florence: Bonducci, 1774), p. vi. The Accademia Fiorentina held another session in honor of Corilla on 25 November 1800: *Onori dedicati alla memoria di Corilla Olimpica* (Florence: Stamperia del governo democratico [i.e., the same Cambiagi who had previously been « Stampatore Imperiale » and « Stampatore Granducale »], 1800).

fifty years after Goldoni had reformed the comic stage by forcing the actors to memorize their lines, and several decades after Parini and Alfieri had introduced more serious themes into Italian letters. The scholarly secretary of the Academy, Giulio Perini, vice-director of the Magliabechiana Library, who just eleven years before had condemned such occupations as the ruin of earlier academies,[4] must have been somewhat uneasy when Teresa mounted the rostrum of so distinguished an assembly. For he must have recognized, like Luigi Russo more recently,[5] that in the Settecento this sort of metrical gymnastics, entertaining though it might be, contributed nothing to real poetry and that its popularity had little to do with an intellectual curiosity about spontaneous creativity like that stirred up in our own times by Minou Drouet. Rather, it consummated the divorce, begun over a century before, between words and meaning, between form and content; and therefore, when cultivated by the self-styled leaders of the Republic of Letters, it represented the nadir of literary decadence.

Much as Giulio Perini might have hoped to "combine erudition with the philosophic spirit of the present century for the advantage of nations," the truth is that many of the same activities that had amused — or elevated the minds of — the academicians of the Seicento continued to maintain their appeal throughout the Settecento. Essentially, extemporaneous versification was but a slight modification of the usual practice of presenting and criticizing original compositions in academic sessions, which the academicians had always hoped would eventually engender a new Trecento in their own times. The foundation of Arcadia, indeed, merely strengthened these expectations. So sympathetic did the Florentine academicians find the Arcadian program to their own aspirations that, while adhering almost immediately to the new movement, they saw no need to supplement or supplant the existing academies with a separate "colony" like those established in other Tuscan cities.[6] For Arcadia, they thought, by calling upon

---

[4] Orazione proemiale (27 November 1783), ASF Reggenza 1052-58.

[5] Luigi Russo, Metastasio (3d ed.; Bari: Laterza, 1945), p. 2.

[6] Letters concerning the Campagna Fiorentina, the informal organization of Florentine Arcadians, are preserved in Arc Lettere a Crescimbeni.

all Italy to rescue Italian poetry from *Secentismo* and to return to the
models of the past was simply spreading to the four corners of the
peninsula the very principles that the Fiorentina and the Crusca had
been proclaiming for over a century.

While editing and republishing, then, those works of their immediate ancestors that seemed to substantiate the efficacy of academic
exercises,[7] the academicians of the Settecento continued to multiply
verses — verses presented for the annual feast of the Intronati, verses
composed to applaud the election of the Florentine Lorenzo Corsini
to the Papal throne, verses to rejoice in the marriage of the Archduke
Joseph to Isabella of Parma and to mourn the decease of such distinguished personages as Giangastone de' Medici and Benedetto
Averani.[8] Most of the new academies followed the example of the
older ones: not only the Arcadian colonies, which turned out volumes
of sonnets and odes to honor St. Ranieri, the protector of Pisa, or a
distinguished professor upon the completion of his lectures,[9] but even
the most gravely scientific societies. The Accademia Etrusca held
regular poetic contests on such themes as "The love of virtue in a hero
is insufficient unless coupled by a hate for vice"; the Società Botanica
of Cortona announced the opening of its gardens with printed son-

---

[7] Above, chap. i, notes 47 and 48; further: Redi, *Sonetti* (Florence: Brigonci, 1702);
Lettere, in his *Opere,* Vols. IV & V (6 vols.; Florence: Manni, 1724 & 1727) (the authoritative
text for the *Vocabolario* according to Vol. VII, Introduction, pp. 8-9; 2d ed., with device of
the Crusca, 2 vols.; Florence: Cambiagi, 1779). No separate edition of the *Bacco* seems to
have been published in Tuscany before that of Livorno, 1821; one did appear in Lucca in 1728.
The *Opere,* with a biography by Salvino Salvini, appeared in 3 vols. in Venice in 1712. See
Domenico Brogiani (a professor at Pisa), *Elogio di F. R.* (Pisa: Pizzoni, 1779).

[8] Cr 14: *Poesie originali trascritte nel farina,* nos. 5 & 7. Sigismondo Della Stufa, *Per
le felicissime nozze . . . Giuseppe d'Austria . . . Isabella di Parma: Lezione detta nella pubblica Accademia Fiorentina celebrata in Firenze . . . XIII maggio MDCCLXI* (Florence: Bonducci, 1761). Crusca: * Diario, 20 September 1724 and 11 April 1731. G. B. Casaregi,
Sonetti e canzoni toscane, canzone 9, p. 137.

[9] *Celebrandosi con divota magnificenza / la solenne triennale festa / in onore del
sempre glorioso / e gran protettore di Pisa / S. Ranieri / Poesie liriche dedicate all'eccelso
Senato, e valoroso popolo pisano* (Pisa: Stamp. archivescovile, 1759); *Applausi poetici al Signor Braccio da Filicaia, patrizio fiorentino e accademico della Crusca, e nell'Università
di Pisa lettore straordinario di legge canonica* (Pisa: Bindi & Nencioni, 1749), including
sonnets by Ranier Bernardo Fabbri, *vice-custode* of the Colonia Alfea. Note also Lorenzo
Ottavio Del Rosso, *Canzone recitata all'Accademia della Crusca nell'anniversario della morte
di Francesco I Imperatore* (Florence: Moücke, 1766).

nets;[10] and the Fisiocritici made specific provision in their first con-
stituition for the recitation of "poems of any kind, provided they concern the subject under consideration" — a condition that might be fulfilled by odes in honor of the patron saint or of a deceased president
as well as by eclogues "on the nature of the torpedo fish." [11] To be
sure, the academies were not alone in their addiction to verse recitations. Verse was one of the necessary accomplishments of an educated
man of the age, and it could properly be used to congratulate a
friend with due elegance, to warn one's wife of the natural weak-
nesses of her sex,[12] to complain, to joke, to laugh. Indeed, every event
of the least significance right up to the end of the century brought
forth a shower of *applausi poetici* — births, marriages, and funerals,
the monastic vows of a noble lady, the theatrical success of a popular
actress, the promulgation of the Leopoldine criminal code. As Gian
Carlo Passeroni complained,

> Oggi non si addottora alcun che prima
> la sua dottrina in versi non si canti;
> senza esser messo da più d'uno in rima
> oggi non si marita un par d'amanti;
> senza sonetti, senza questo clima,
> non fassi ufficio alle anime purganti. [13]

The academies simply ennobled a universally accepted means of
verbal expression by holding forth the promise that it might, with

---

[10] Etrusca: * Deliberazioni, 8 January 1744; Filippo Angelliere (*sic*) Alticozzi, *Effu-
sione di grato animo* ... *per le particolari grazie ottenute dalla somma clemenza di
S. A. R.* ... (Florence, 1766).

[11] Fisiocritici: * Capitoli, Art. VIII; Egloga sopra la natura del pesce torpedine, and
many others in BCS L.III.3, fol. 568 f., 743 f. Fabiani, *Memoria,* pp. 103-4. Cf. letter of
P. P. Pagliai to G. Gigli, 10 april 1717: BCS Y.I.19, 3-5: « Abbenchè non sia il principale
istituto della nostra Accademia dar giudizio sopra il purgato [idioma] toscano, ma solamente di cercare la verità per mezzo della vera moderna filosofia, non puote tutta volta
fare di meno scorrendo l'eruditissimo nuovo Vocabolario ... » (on which see below, p. 89).

[12] Gio. Battista Fagiuoli, *Rime piacevoli* (6 vols.; Florence: Nestenus & Moücke, 1729-
34), I, 262 f. Fagiuoli's popularity among the academicians is show by Andrea Pietro
Giulianelli, *Delle lodi di G. B. F.* (Florence: Albizzini, 1743), recited in the Apatisti 30 December 1743.

[13] *Cicerone,* no. iv, 13: « Today no one receives a doctorate without his learning
first being sung in verses; today no pair of lovers marries without being put into rhyme by
more than one; without sonnets, no office is said for the souls in Purgatory ».

sufficient practice and proper discipline, become poetry, and by showing its appropriateness in the exposition of scholarly as well as occasional themes.

A small number of these endless verses, to be sure, succeeded in
winning the approval of even the better contemporary critics. Teobaldo Ceva, for instance, an authority on what Arcadia considered
good poetry, found in such lines as these by Giovan Bartolommeo
Casaregi:

> O dolce vin, mio solo Amor, mia Dea,
> sommergitor d'ogni atra cura avversa:
> Viva Bacco, evoè, che il cuor mi bea:
> Eviì, spandi spandi, versa versa,

"particular elements of beauty, simplicity and fittingness of style,
obedient and prompt rhyme, and something indescribably extraordinary." [14] But on the whole the experience of the Settecento rapidly
dissipated the faith of the academicians, so high at the beginning of
the century, in the efficacy of their literary exercises. In vain did they
hope that the poetics of Arcadia, so similar to their own, would
nurture among them works of the quality of the few successful
Arcadian poets in other parts of Italy. Polyhymnia — alas! — had
fled the *Campagna fiorentina;* and all that remained was a vast assortment of mediocre variations on the same worn-out themes squeezed
into the same forms which better authors had sanctified in happier
centuries — the "academic poetry" lamented by Bettinelli, lashed by
Baretti, and ridiculed by Parini. Indeed, whatever of literary value

---

[14] Casaregi, *Sonetti e canzoni toscane* (1741), sonetto xxiii: « O sweet wine, my only
love, my goddess, submerger of every sharp, adverse thing. Long live Bacchus, *evoè!* who
makes my heart blessed; *eviì!* spread forth, pour, pour . . . »; and introduction to *Componimenti poetici toscani del canonico Salvino Salvini e del conte Gio. Bartolommeo Casaregi, accademici della Crusca* (Florence: Albizzini, 1750), p. xiii: « . . . Le sue particolari bellezze:
semplicità e proprietà di stile, che si accomoda al costume di chi parla: rime ubbidienti e
pronte, quantunque difficili: . . . in questo . . . io ci sento un non so che di straordinario . . . »,
quoted from Teobaldo Ceva, *Scelta di sonetti con varie critiche osservazioni ed un dissertazione intorno al sonetto in generale* (Torino, 1735), p. 218. Others of Ceva's remarks: on
A. M. Salvini: « soavissima immagine », « maestoso è il periodico giro del primo quader-
nario »; on Casaregi: « divini sono, e divinamente espressi i sentimenti di questo sonetto » (pp. 80 and 216). Note Mario Fubini, *Dal Muratori al Baretti* (2d ed.; Bari: Laterza, 1954), p. 54 (note) and pp. 102-3.

actually was written in Settecento Tuscany may well have owed its success to its liberation from academic principles. True, Ranieri de' Calzabigi was a member of the Etrusca, Pietro Bicchierai of the Fiorentina, and Cosimo Giotti of the Apatisti.[15] But they did not write for the *eruditi* of the Crusca, who would probably have been more pleased with Gian Vincenzo Gravina's painfully dull adaptations of Greek tragedy. Nor did they write for the partially theatrical academies like the Intronati and the Rozzi, who in the second half of the century turned over their theaters to professional companies from outside the city.[16] They wrote directly for the stage — which flourished in the Settecento as never before — and for the numerous audience whose taste was formed by Goldoni, Metastasio, and even Voltaire, rather than by the incomparable *Trecentisti*. "The tragedies of various great men of recent memory," noted Bicchierai in 1767, "bore even their own admirers. For a too close observance of laws sterilizes the fantasy, or closes it within narrow confines where it cannot extend its wings far enough to take flight." [17]

[15] Pietro Napoli Signorelli, for instance, in his review of Italian drama from Martelli to Alfieri, *Storia critica de' teatri antichi e moderni* (6 vols.; Naples: Orsino, 1787-90, from 1st ed. of 1777), VI, 115 ff., names only one Tuscan after Gigli, i.e., Pietro Bicchierai, whose *Virginia e Cleone* (published *con alcune considerazioni del medesimo sopra il teatro* by Stecchi & Pagani, 1767) was produced in Florence in 1767. Calzabigi, whose fame today rests largely on his libretto for Gluck's *Orfeo*, wrote an *Ode per le solenne feste callisteie celebrate dall'Accademia Etrusca di Cortona* (Florence: Paperini, 1740). On Cosimo Giotti (Adimeto Metoneo, P. A.), whose *Poesie toscane in morte di Maria Teresa* (Florence: Moücke, 1780) were probably recited in the Apatisti and who was a close friend of Corilla Olimpica and sometime protégé of Marco Lastri, as well as a member of the Apatisti, the Accademia Fiorentina, and the Intronati, see introduction to his *Gusmano d'Almeida, tragedia* (1786) (2d ed.; Venice: Rosa, 1804). A few pieces by Marco Coltellini of Livorno are published in Ottaviano Diodati's *Biblioteca teatrale italiana*, Vols. IV and V. The academicians might have cited the charming *favole* (some of which are available in the modern edition of Ugo Frittelli, *Favolisti toscani* [Florence: Vallecchi, 1930]) of Lorenzo Pignotti in support of their theory, for many of them were apparently recited in the Apatisti. But fables were not among the kinds of poetry sanctioned by the Crusca; and by Pignotti's time the theory had largely been abandoned. See Sir Henry McAnally, « A Contemporary of Alfieri, Lorenzo Pignotti », *Modern Language Quarterly*, VIII (1947), 408-18, for relevant bibliography.

[16] Intronati: Deliberazioni, 22 October 1777, 30 April 1778 (to the company of Giuseppe Mori for five years), 11 September 1778, May 1784 (proposals of Guido Savini), etc.: BCS Y.II.7.

[17] In « Alcune considerazioni », *Virginia e Cleone*, p. 2.

It would be unfair, certainly, to blame the academies alone for the dearth of literary creativity in Settecento Tuscany (indeed, the causes of such phenomena lie somewhat beyond the limits of historical inquiry). Even Vittorio Alfieri, after all, was brought up in Salvinian orthodoxy as much as any of his contemporaries.[18] Yet the Crusca and the Fiorentina can at least be charged with having inculcated a theory of poetry that offered would-be writers no other advice than that which their forefathers had enunciated almost two centuries before: that all good literature must conform to the standards of the Golden Age. Why, then, bother with anything written after 1400? — so wondered Giovanni Bottari, who had given years to the compilation of the *Vocabolario*. The invention of printing would be much more applauded today, he reflected in his preface to Franco Sacchetti, "if instead of putting out an infinite number of useless books, usually empty of doctrine and of eloquence, . . . and hence silly and harmful, there were printed the many valuable works passed down to us by wise antiquity . . . many of which are now rare." [19] No one can deny the superiority of fourteenth to eighteenth-century Italian literature, and undoubtedly Bottari and his friends might well have profited from an imitation of the creative spirit of their ancestors. But they were unimpressed by, or perhaps blind to, the more profound qualities of Trecento letters. What interested Biscioni, for instance, was whether or not Laura and Beatrice were real people — a question to which he dedicated almost his entire preface to the 1723 edition of the *Prose* of Dante and Boccaccio.[20] What interested Bottari was the *verisimiglianza* of the *Decamerone;* and he intended his innumerable commentaries before the Crusca as nothing more than so much proof that Boccaccio had recorded real events performed by historical personages without ever permitting his imagination to intrude.

[18] Principally through the textbook of Teobaldo Ceva cited above, note 14. See Carlo Calcaterra, « Teobaldo Ceva, il Muratori e un verso dell'Alfieri », *Studi petrarcheschi*, II (1949), 243-61.

[19] Franco Sacchetti, *Delle novelle* (2 vols.; Florence, 1724), Preface. The edition is anonymous and may be the work largely of A. M. Biscioni; but the Preface is attributed to Bottari in the reprint included in the *Novelle* published in Milan, 1815 (p. 1).

[20] *Prose di Dante Alighieri e di messer Gio. Boccaccio* (Florence: Tartini & Santi, 1723), Preface.

"Examples from the Sacred Scriptures and the Fathers of the Church," he found, could confirm "the probability and credibility" of the magical operations reported in some of the tales and thus "justify him completely from the accusations of some modern writers."[21] Moreover, insisted Manni, Boccaccio meant his true stories not as an attack upon the Church, as the "unbelieving" Protestants Thomas Pope Blount and Jerome Wolf had "calumniously" proposed, but as a means of promoting piety among his contemporaries, led astray, as Bellarmine himself had admitted, by the "religious in name only." Whereas formerly he had been admired as a "most delightful inventor of stories," "in the future he [would] be exalted to the skies as an ingenious teller of true stories for our [moral] profit."[22]

Poetry, then, had above all a moral function. The exclusion of poets from Plato's Republic, argued Felice Franchi of the Academia Fiorentina, could be justified only as a measure, like the Index, for the protection of the untrained "youth" who might confuse metaphor with reality. For Homer and Vergil, as any student of St. Augustine ought to know, possessd "a few rays of light concerning the existence of the true God" — enough, that is, to free them completely from the "vain and impious superstition" of their times. They wrote good poetry, therefore, because they taught, just like Bernardino Perfetti, St. Basil, and Alexander Pope, "the total destruction of our false idols, that is, of wantonness, of intemperance, of anger, of pride, of idleness, of obscenity."[23] Even satire was charged with "bringing out the character of perfect morality and pointing out the evil practices of the times," with the strict injunction that it abstain from "offending any

[21] Crusca: *Diario, 27 August 1755. This lecture is not printed in his Lezioni ... sopra il Decamerone (all given in the Crusca) (2 vols. in 1; Florence: Ricci, 1818).

[22] D. M. Manni, Istoria del Decamerone di G. B. (Florence: Ristori, 1742), pp. xviii-xx, xxiii. Cf. Alberto Chiari, « La fortuna di Boccaccio », Questioni e correnti di storia letteraria, ed. Attilio Momigliano, pp. 274-286, esp. pp. 281-83. Manni's reference is probably to Thomas Pope Blount, Censura celebriorum auctorum in qua virorum doctorum de clarissimis cuisque saeculi scriptoribus judicia traduntur (Geneva, 1694), pp. 437-39, of which a copy was available in the Magliabechiana.

[23] D. Felice Amadeo Franchi, monaco cassinese, lettore di Sacra Teologia nella Badia di Firenze, e accademico fiorentino, I pregi della poesia (approved by A. F. Adami, as consolo, 19 July 1758) (Florence: Bonducci, 1758), here quoted from pp. 336, 348-49, and xl.

particular person." [24]   Under no circumstances, finally, could anything be admitted as literature that sought merely to entertain.   The
academicians agreed wholly with Muratori when he warned that
even "not dishonest romances," like those of "the ingenious and wise
Mme de Scudéry" he read as a boy, might possibly put "the vain
maxims of the world" into "tender heads" — or at least distract them
from the pursuit of scholarship and good morals that ought to occupy
every moment of their waking hours. [25]   Thus Boccaccio and Sacchetti, the academicians concluded, were great writers because they
told the truth for the sake of virtue in impeccable Trecento Florentine.
Let modern writers do likewise.

Such was the academic theory of imitation in the Settecento, a
theory that Poliziano had long before compared to swimming with
a life-preserver. [26]   Imitation in the Quattrocento had produced the
Rusticus and the *Orfeo.*   Imitation even in the Seicento academies,
where letters could at times still amuse without edifying, had contributed to the gracious *novelle* of Carlo Dati and Lorenzo Magalotti. [27]
But imitation in the Settecento resulted in nothing above the level of
Bottari's own emasculated adaptations of stories from St. Jerome put
in Boccaccian forms, in which virtue and chastity triumph after ex-
cruciatingly shallow temptations and after pages and pages of interminable sentences. [28]   Incapable, then, of perceiving either the spirit
or the vivacity of the Trecento writers, and faithful to a concept of
literature as antiquated as Dante's *De vulgare eloquentia,* the academic
poets and novelists had little to say even to their own contemporaries,

[24] Bindo Peruzzi in Preface to *Memorie Colombaria,* I, xli.

[25] Muratori to Giovanni Artico, 10 November 1721, *Scritti autobiografici,* ed. T. Sor-
belli (Vignola: Fabbri, 1950), p. 30.

[26] *Angeli Politiani Opera omnia* (Basle, 1553), Epist. VIII, pp. 104-116, esp. pp. 112-116,
of which part is quoted by Giuseppe Saitta in *Il pensiero italiano nell'umanesimo e nel Rinascimento* (3 vols.; Bologna, 1949-51), I, 545.

[27] Cf. Giambattista Marchesi, *Per la storia della novella italiana nel secolo XVII*
(Rome, 1897), chap. vi.

[28] Bottari's program for a new *Decamerone* is given in his lecture of 6 March 1751
(Crusca: * Diario, *sub dat.*: « exhorted the academicians to compile a *Decamerone* of stories
and moral tales for the use of the youth »), and printed in his *Lezioni sopra il Decamerone,*
II, 230-47. The result is published in *Novelle di alcuni autori fiorentini,* ed. Gaetano Domenico Poggiali (London, 1795).

who were already convinced of the preferability of virtue to vice and
who could find nothing in these compositions that corresponded to
their own experiences in life. By the end of the century the academicians themselves admitted defeat. Simply "following the model of
those [ancient authors]," lamented Francesco Fontani before the Accademia Fiorentina in 1790, "in the form of sentences, and servilely
imitating the precise manner of their expressions" had made modern
writers "completely destitute of soul and sentiment." [29] And sentiment, they concluded in words similar to those of the Romantics,
must be incompatible with imitation.

The crisis of form and expression corresponded to a crisis of
content. What should the aspiring poets and novellists write about?
Arcadia had from the very beginning posed the question of subject
matter, and it had convinced the Tuscan academicians more than ever
of the iniquities of the "Marinists" in reducing poetry to mere sounds,
to "extravagant hyperboles, devoid of all learning or doctrine." [30]
Certainly, there were always important events to grace with song;
but somehow neither the election of Bandini to the presidency of the
Fisiocritici, the solemn *triduum* of 1769 for the recovery of Pietro
Leopoldo from a smallpox inoculation, nor for that matter anything
else that occurred during the Settecento was important enough to
ennoble the verse commentaries with any universal significance. The
academicians did what they could: Salvini, for instance, inveighed
against the exclusion of love themes by his more prudish contempo-

---

[29] *Elogio di Carlo Roberto Dati, recitato nella R. Accademia Fiorentina* (Fiorentina
[1783]: * Registro, 1-29 July 1790) (Florence: Cambiagi, 1794), p. 13: « . . . . Sebbene privi
di genio, crederono d'aver fatto tutto se modellandosi col giro di periodeggiare di quegli,
e con troppo servile impegno imitando le precise loro maniere, frasi e parole, . . . si resero
scrittori languidi, e destituiti affatto d'anima e di sentimento ». Note also the comment of
Del Furia on A. M. Bandini's *Epitalamion* [in Greek] *in nuptiis de Flawnes* [or *Hawnes*]
et Farmor (Florence: Paperini, 1744): « Quantunque un tale argomento per esser di sua
natura troppo trito e comune non offrisse che un campo sterile ed infecondo alla poetica
fantasia . . . »: BNF Palatino-Del Furia No. 43, fol. 5.

[30] « Istravagantissime iperboli . . . senza niuno apparato di erudizione, e di dottrina »:
*Le satire di Benedetto Menzini fiorentino, con le note di Anton Maria Salvini, Anton Maria
Biscioni, Giorgio van-der-Broodt e altri celebri autori* . . . (Bern, 1763), Satira IV: « Argo-
mento », p. 137.

raries — one less subject to inspire their pens.[31] They tried their hands at all the traditional genres — pastorals, odes, Anacreontics, satires — and they even, occasionally, attempted witty descriptions of contemporary manners, like those so successfully executed in the intermezzi of Gigli and the drawings of Francesco Guardi. Here indeed might be a good subject:

> Leggiadre Femmine
> pace del cuore,
> qual mai ritrovasi
> tema migliore
> che non annoi
> fuori di Voi? [32]

But what did the *abati* and the *professori* of the Crusca and the Apatisti know about love, women, and the ways of the world? Perhaps a good deal; but their compositions contain nothing but what they had learned from Petrarch and Bembo. There was only one means of escape: "learning and doctrine." But again the reconciliation of *utile* and *dulce* failed, for in the exposition of scientific theories and natural phenomena, the content became so important that it swallowed up everything of aesthetic value, and the "poems" on the rings of Saturn and the circulation of the blood belong more properly to the field of science than to that of literature.[33] Hence, just as it had obscured the real qualities of Trecento letters, so *Trecentismo* in the eighteenth century thwarted the search for a subject matter conducive to poetic expression.

---

31 A. M. Salvini, *Prose toscane,* I, lezioni 39-40; note his translation from Plotinus: « Ragionamento d'amore, tratto dall'Enneade Terza », published in the *Biblioteca rara* of G. Daelli, Vol. VI: *Mescolanze d'amore,* for some idea of what Salvini meant by « love ». Salvini's plea is the same as that of one of the foremost Arcadian critics, Tommaso Ceva, who warned, « the most lively and famous songs and sonnets are those that concern love »: introduction to his *Memorie d'alcune virtù del sig. conte Francesco Lemene,* dedicated to the Colonia Milanese (2d ed. [1st: 1708]; Milan, 1718) (pages not numbered).

32 Francesco Lambardi, *Saggio di poesie di vario genere . . . recitate nell'adunanze dell'Accademia degl'Ingegnosi di Firenze* (« Lausanne » [but probably Florence: Bonducci], 1777), p. 57: « Le mode delle donne, Anacreontica »: « Fair women, peace of the heart, what better theme can be found, which will not bore any but you? ».

33 See below, p. 117 ff.

While the one-sided adoration of the Golden Age ended by stifling whatever creative imagination the academicians might have had, it did perform one service to the cause of literature in inspiring the printing or re-editing of a great number of long-neglected texts. Many of these publications arose directly from the preparation of the fourth edition of the *Vocabolario,* which occupied the best scholars of Florence for over three decades. The establishment, once and for all, of definitive models for correct speech free from the cavillings of Tassoni required a careful examination of all those who from earliest times had most contributed to the formation of the language. Since the previously accepted editions of the classics occasionally contained errors and since many of the works of the Trecentisti still remained in manuscript, the editors set out to scour the archives of the city — the misspelling of one word in the 1581 edition of Matteo Villani, for instance, led after a long search to the uncovering of the original manuscript.[34]

The academicians began, as might be expected, with the *Tre Grandi,* the "Three Greats," Dante, Petrarch, and Boccaccio. The first, to be sure, received somewhat less consideration, in spite of the constant eulogies of him as the "Tuscan Homer"; for neither his subject matter nor his "rough" (*rozzo*) and often archaic language particularly appealed to the linguistic purists and literary classicists, still faithful to the teachings of Pietro Bembo and Lionardo Salviati, in the quiet, unheroic Settecento.[35] "Ohimé ohimé ohimé," sighed

[34] Andrea Alamanni, « Notizie storiche sulla quarta edizione del Vocabolario », *Atti dell'A. C.,* I (1819), doc. 14, pp. lxxx-cvi. Bottari, in letters to Apostolo Zeno of 23 and 30 Aprile 1746, *ibid.,* cvii-cxvi, discusses some of the new editions to be prepared in support of the *Vocabolario,* of which he was one of the principal editors.

[35] The nearest most of the academicians came to admitting Dante's language was Giuseppe Bianchini's attempt to prove that it really was not coarse after all (just the opposite of Lami's thesis, which insisted upon the poetic quality of his archaisms and borrowed words): *Difesa di Dante Alighieri* (Florence: Manni, 1718). In general, see Guido Zacchetti, *La fama di Dante in Italia nel secolo XVIII* (Rome, 1900) (and review by Michele Barbi in *Bullettino della Società Dantesca Italiana,* IX [1902], 1 f.); Francesco Maggini, « La critica dantesca dal '300 ai nostri giorni », *Questioni e correnti di storia letteraria,* pp. 123-66; and Umberto Cosmo, *Con Dante attraverso il Seicento* (Bari: Laterza, 1946). On the « unheroic » quality of Settecento literature, and the actual preference for gay, clear, agile verses in Arcadia in spite of the constant talk about the desirability of epic and tragic themes, note Walter Binni, « Sviluppo della poetica arcadica nel primo Settecento », *Rassegna della letteratura italiana,* LXII (1958), 323-44, esp. p. 327.

Anton Francesco Gori, "the youth of Florence cares not at all even to read [the *Commedia*]; and there are many who have not the slightest notion of what it contains." [36] Evidently the academicians themselves cared as little as the "youth," who unjustly took the blame for everything at the time. They took no part whatever, as institutions at least, in the vigorous polemics between Saverio Bettinelli and their own Giovanni Lami concerning the merits of Dante as a poet, and they made no effort to replace the standard edition of the *Commedia,* which by then was already over a century old.[37] Petrarch, on the other hand, whose works contained "no words, except for a few Provençal terms, that are not used and received today," whose verse reached everyone and not just [like Dante's] the learned," and whose "inimitable naturalness" and perfect clarity rendered commentary superfluous — Petrarch, the Tuscan Vergil, enjoyed even greater popularity in the Settecento, thanks in part to the influence of Arcadian Petrarchism.[38] Thus the interminable lectures on the *Canzo-*

[36] Anton Francesco Gori, Lezione sopra Dante nell'Accademia Fiorentina: Mar C.261 (fol. 5): « ... La Fiorentina gioventù . . . ne pur di leggerlo punto si cura; nè rari son coloro, che ne pure san notizia qual sia l'argomento delle cose, che in se racchiude ».

[37] See Paolo Giudici, « Dante e un giornalista del settecento », *Annuario del R. Liceo Scientifico 'L. Respighi' di Piacenza* (1930-32), pp. 59-91. The Crusca edition is of 1595. No others were published in Tuscany until 1821; several non-Tuscan editions of the Settecento still followed the Crusca original, e.g., *La divina commedia . . . già ridotta a miglior lezione dagli accademici della Crusca,* ed. Antonio Volpi (3 vols.; Padova: G. Comino, 1726-27). It may be that the academicians hesitated to republish the *Commedia* for reasons similar to those suggested in the prefatory remark of Pompeo Venturi, S.J., of Siena, in his Lucca edition of 1728, reprinted in Venice in 1793 (*La D. C. . . . tratta da quella che pubblicarono gli accademici della Crusca l'anno MDXCV,* p. 4): « We will not neglect to warn the reader of those sentiments of the poet that are occasionally not in strict conformity with good doctrine, and even less with the reverence due to the Roman pontiffs ».

[38] Salvino Salvini, *Che la lingua toscana è più obbligata al Petrarca che a Dante* (n. d.), p. 7 (Crusca: * Diario, 3 March 1708). The only copy in print I have been able to find of this discourse, which expresses the opinion to which the Crusca remained faithful for the next generations, is that included in Vol. XI of a *Raccolta di opuscoli scientifici e letterari* in the Biblioteca Nazionale of Rome. The MS is in BNF Mag IV.57. A. M. Salvini makes similar comments in Lodovico Antonio Muratori, *Della perfetta poesia italiana, con le annotazioni critiche di A. M. S.* (several editions; here referred to in that of Milan: Classici Italiani, 1829), IV, 42, 330. See above, chap. i, notes 28 and 29, and in general, Carlo Calcaterra, « Il Petrarca e il petrarchismo », *Questioni e correnti di storia letteraria,* pp. 167-273. See further Giovan Battista Baldelli, *Del Petrarca e delle sue opere* (Florence: Cambiagi, 1797-1804). One Tuscan edition of the *Canzoniere* was published, though not under academic auspices: *Rime di mess. Francesco Petrarca,* ed. Luigi Bandini (Florence, 1748); but the numerous errors in the text brought it little but adverse criticism.

niere begun by Benedetto Averani at the turn of the century were expanded during the following decades into the even lengthier and more minute analyses of single passages by Salvini, Casaregi, Francesco Forzoni Accolti, Lorenzo Del Riccio, and others. Similarly Boccaccio, the Tuscan Cicero, was exalted in almost as many lectures by Salvino Salvini and Giovanni Bottari as the master of narrative prose.[39] True, the academicians did not get around to republishing the *Canzoniere* or the *Decamerone* — the first, probably, because it was still readily available, and the second because they were too honest to commit such a sacrilege as reprinting the expurgated edition of 1582 and too timid to defy the still-binding prohibition *donec corregatur*. While defending their heroes against so many innocuous foreign and anonymous critics, moreover, they shunned their most important opponent, Giuseppe Baretti, whose attacks ("let's throw away Boccaccio and [Giovanni Della] Casa and every other author of the Good Centuries, and write whatever comes to us") threatened their entire literary tradition. Yet they served at least Boccaccio — or rather students and admirers of Boccaccio — perhaps even more effectively by editing and reprinting his minor *volgare* works, the often neglected and then little-known *Filocopo, Fiametta, Ameto,* and *Vita di Dante.*[40]

[39] Lectures of Bottari (Crusca: * Diario, 31 July 1727 *et seq.*) cited above, note 21. See Ettore Bonora, « Francesco Petrarca », and Giuseppe Petronio, « Giovanni Boccaccio », both in *I classici italiani nella storia della critica,* ed. Walter Binni (Florence, 1954), I, 95-166 and 167-228, especially the chapters on the Settecento. Petronio (pp. 191-92) show Bottari to have been largely isolated from the more advanced criticism of the age. See further Fubini, *Dal Muratori al Baretti,* chap. v, on Baretti.

[40] Giuseppe Baretti in *La frustra letteraria,* ed. Luigi Piccioni (Bari: Laterza, 1932), p. 87. Baretti's attack on the Cruscan hero Bembo is described by Luigi Russo in *Belfagor,* XIII (1958), 271 (« Pietro Bembo e la sua fortuna storica », pp. 257-72). Note A. M. Salvini's annotations to the records of the committee for the « correction » of Boccaccio: *Annotazioni e discorsi sopra alcuni luoghi del Decamerone . . . fatte da' deputati alla correzione del medesimo* (Borghini, Varchi, Bastaino, Antinori, *et al.,* of 1573) (4th ed. [there were none in the eighteenth century]; Florence: Le Monnier, 1857). It is strange that the Cruscans did not recall the verses of their much-praised forefather Il Lasca:

> Com'hai tu tant'ardir. brutta bestiaccia . . .
> Fiorenza mia, va, ficcati 'n un forno,
> S'al gran Boccaccio tuo con tanto scorno
> Lasci far tanti sfregi in sulla faccia.

> (« Contro Girolamo Rucellai »).

At the same time, the academicians went far beyond the classics. Not only Boccaccio and Petrarch, after all, as Ildefonso di S. Luigi pointed out, but "all authors, even the least elegant," of "that happy century of our speech" "bore gold in all they pronounced or wrote."[41] Therefore, insisted Manni, "while we are busy bringing forth the writings of the *miglior secolo,* we should not lose sight of all that which has remained in manuscript, especially those [works] whose subject matter has [moral] value," like the Trecento *volgare* translations of the lives of the Fathers.[42]   And Manni, who then owned a printing house, co-operated with the *Vocabolario* committee in publishing a long series of texts: pious stories and homilies like the *Vite di alcuni santi* and the *Volgarizzamento* of the sermons of St. Augustine, chronicles like that of Donato Velluti and Dino Compagni, moral reflections like those of Arrigo da Settimello.[43]   Many others accompanied these efforts — the *Specchio* of Jacopo Passavanti, for instance, revised by the Crusca in 1725 from its earlier edition of 1681, Bottari's edition of Sacchetti, and, above all, the voluminous *Delizie degli eruditi toscani,* edited by Ildefonso di S. Luigi under the sponsorship first of the Crusca, and then, after 1783, of the Accademia Fiorentina.   If the academicians were incapable of creating a new Trecento of their own, then, they succeeded admirably in bringing much of the old one to life again.

Still, the interest in the literature of the past and, in particular, the publication of "language texts" was not necessarily limited to the

---

Delle opere di messer G. B., cittadino fiorentino (6 vols.; Florence, 1723, with annotations of A. M. Salvini).   Documents concerning the prohibition and correction of the *Decamerone* are printed by Peter Brown in *Giornale storico della letteratura italiana,* CXXXIV (1957), 314 f. According to Mario Rosa, who has studied the MS diary in the Riccardiana, Lami himself thought of republishing the original *Decamerone* in 1747, but his request for approval was refused by Benedict XIV.   Editions were later published in Lucca in 1761 and by Masi in Livorno in 1789-90.   Salvini's appeal for a complete edition of Petrarch in Crusca: * Diario, 5 January, and 6 August, 1697.

41 Preface of Ildefonso di S. Luigi to Vol. I of his *Delizie degli eruditi toscani* (25 vols.; Florence: Cambiagi, 1770-89), pp. vii and cxi.

42 D. M. Manni in Introduction to *Vite di alcuni santi scritte nel buon secolo della lingua toscana* (Florence: Manni, 1732-35), I, vii.

43 The works published by Manni will be given in Crusca: * Approved Works.   The didactic poem of Arrigo da Settimello was issued in the Trecento *vulgarizzazione* called *L'Arrighetto,* of course, not in the original Latin.

authors of the fourteenth century, nor, for that matter, to Florentines. The Crusca had always maintained that the great merit of the *lingua toscana* consisted in its adaptability to all the possible concepts of the human mind, of which, obviously, the generation between Dante and Sacchetti had had time to consider only a small number. An adequate treatment of art, for instance, had to wait for Benvenuto Cellini and Filippo Baldinucci, and a full exposition of philosophy for Galileo. Accordingly, the fourth *Vocabolario* cited the later writers along side the terms they had introduced into the language.[44] The post-Trecento authors "approved" by the Settecento academicians fell roughly into three categories. The first comprised the poets of the Cinquecento — Bembo, whose Petrarchian sonnets carried into practice the rules he had drawn up for the *volgare;* Ariosto, whose epic was too widely read to be ignored; Tasso, who, according to Salvini, "is incomparable ... in everything he wrote";[45] Sannazzaro, from whose *Arcadia* the homonymous academy had taken its name and whose *De partu Virginis* offered Gori and Casaregi the opportunity to make pious reflections and learned references to Christian antiquities; Giovanni Della Casa, the "honor of the Tuscan tongue," whose unprinted letters and poems had been collected as early as 1656;[46] and, finally,

---

[44] Lists of cited texts are given in prefaces to each edition. Cf. Gaetano Domenico Poggiali, *Serie di testi di lingua stampati che si citano nel Vocabolario degli accademici della Crusca* (2 vols.; Livorno, 1813). Luigi Razzolini, *Bibliografia dei testi di lingua a stampa citati dagli accademici della Crusca* (Bologna, 1878), gives the full title of each work cited, though, unfortunately, not by the edition of the *Vocabolario.* The *Due trattati ... , uno dell'orificeria, e l'altro della scultura* of Benvenuto Cellini was published by Tartini & Franchi in 1731, though without mention of the Academy. Filippo Baldinucci (1624?-96) had been an active Cruscan: Vols. II and VI of the 1st edition of his vast *Notizie de' professori del disegno da Cimabue in qua,* published in 6 vols. between 1681 and 1727 (above, chap. i, note 19) (2d ed. by Manni, 21 vols. in 10; Florence: Stecchi & Pagani, 1776-74), bears the device of the Crusca; his *Vocabolario toscano dell'arte del disegno* (Florence: Franchi, 1681), is dedicated to the Academy as are his Lezioni of 29 December 1691 and 5 January 1692, first published by Matini in 1692 and included in the *Raccolta di alcuni opuscoli ... scritti in diverse occasioni da Filippo Baldinucci accademico della Crusca* (Florence: Bonducci, 1765). On Galileo, see below p. 112; his contributions to the language are discussed by Bruno Migliorini in the essay « Galileo e la lingua italiana », in his *Lingua e cultura* (Rome: Tumminelli, 1948), pp. 134-58 (a superbly written volume, by the way, which should show modern scholars how such subjects still can be made interesting).

[45] In note to Muratori, *Perfetta poesia,* IV, 332: « Il Tasso in tutte le cose, ma in particolare nelle canzoni, che sono il più alto genere di poesia, è incomparabile ».

[46] On Tasso, see the excellent chap. ii of Fiorenzo Forti, *L. A. Muratori fra antichi e moderni* (Bologna: Zuffi, 1953); Bottari published an edition of the *Opere* in 6 vols. (Flo-

Pier Vettori, Luigi Alamanni, and "our most gentle" Giovanni Rucellai, whose bucolic verses were to inspire the founders of the Georgofili.[47] The second group included the great number of verse and prose writers associated with the first Florentine academies: Benedetto Varchi, Antonfrancesco Grazzini ('Il Lasca'), and the many academic orators whose discourses were published in the voluminous *Prose fiorentine* from 1716 on — to which must be added the principal scientific writers from Galileo to Torricelli and Magalotti.[48] The third group comprehended the Tuscan poets of the late Seicento, in whose works, as has been pointed out, the literary aspirations of the Florentine academies had been most nearly fulfilled.

rence: Tartini & Franchi, 1724). On Ariosto, cf. Raffaello Ramat, *La critica ariostesca dal secolo XVI ad oggi* (Florence: La Nuova Italia, 1954). On Bembo: A. M. Salvini, *Discorsi accademici*, II, No. 33. Giovanni Della Casa, *Opere ... con una copiosa giunta di scritture non più stampate ...* (Florence: G. Manni, 1707), III, xi, of introduction by Giovanni Battista Casotti, *accademico fiorentino,* who tells of the plans of Carlo Dati und Egidio Menagio to accomplish the project, which just then was completed after a thorough search in Rome, Florence, and Montepulciano. Some letters were published just before by Antonio Bulifon in his *Lettere storiche politiche ed erudite,* I (Pozzuoli, 1685), which was known at least to Salvini, author of some of the notes to Casotti's edition. *De partu Virginis libri tres, etrusco carmine redditi a comite Io. Bartolomaeo Casaregio ... cum observationibus in quattuor veterum Christianorum monumenta ... cura et studio Antonii Francesci Gorii* (Florence, 1740), with seal and imprimatur of the Crusca.

[47] Montelatici in *Atti dell'Accademia dei Georgofili,* Ser. V, Vol. III (1906), pp. 414-15, and his *Ragionamento sopra i mezzi più necessari per far rifiorire l'agricoltura,* p. 39-41. Rucellai's *Dell'api* first appeared in Rome in 1524: it was reprinted together with Alamanni's *Della coltivazione* in Padova, 1718, and Verona, 1745, republished in *Raccolta di poemi georgici* (Lucca, 1785). Vettori's *Trattato della coltivazione degli ulivi* was published in Florence, 1718. Note also Giovanni Fabbroni, *Gli ozj della villeggiatura,* (« 2d ed. »; « Villa », 1800), pp. 3-4.

[48] The first volume is entitled *Prose Fiorentine raccolte dallo Smarrito accademico della Crusca: parte prima, contenente orazioni* (Florence: Santi Franchi, 1716). Carlo Dati (« lo Smarrito ») in fact gathered only the texts published in this first volume (see above, chap. i, note 64). The project continued through 17 volumes under the editorship of Giovanni Bottari and Ross'Antonio Martini, sometime secretary of the Crusca, until 1745, with slight modifications of the original title. On Galileo: Buonaventuri's « Prefazione universale » (cf. Crusca: * Diario, 14 July 1718) to the Crusca's edition of *Opere di Galileo Galilei nobile fiorentino ... nuova edizione* (3 vols.; Florence: Tartini & Franchi, 1718); on Evangelista Torricelli, whose *Lezioni accademiche* (Florence: Guiducci & Franchi, 1715) the Crusca approved for publication in 1715, note marginal comment of A. M. Salvini in the copy in the Marucelliana: « Il Torricelli, ne' suoi libri stampati, de' quali io lessi con grande avidità e soddisfazione quello delle sferali e mi ricordo che io leggeva dopo cena, e ammiravo la facilità, brevità, chiarezza, e universalità e fecondità sua » (on p. xlvi). Two editions of Magalotti's *Lettere familiari* (1741 and 1769) were published during the century in Florence.

These three groups were selected, in spite of the difference in their ages and places of origin, according to the same standards of excellence so rigorously applied in the academic exercises: conformity to the usage and vocabulary of the *Secolo d'oro*. Everything that did not wholly meet these standards was simply ignored — all the neo-Latin literature of the Renaissance, for example, most of the vernacular literature of the "decadent" Quattrocento, and all the authors of all ages who, like Castiglione and Tassoni, had embraced the heresy of Anti-Tuscanism. Thus everyone read the *Canzoniere,* but no one ever thought of reading the *Africa* or *De Ignorantia.* Manni published Capponi's *Commentari* on the Pisan War, but not Matteo Palmieri's *De captivitate.*[49] The Dantists commented frequently on the *Vita* by Boccaccio, but never on that by Bruni. And the Hellenist Salvini failed to recognize in Poliziano the same conscious blending of Attic and Tuscan grace that he was trying, somewhat less successfully, to promote in his own times.[50]

Even more surprising is the omission of all the Florentine prose writers of the early Cinquecento — Donato Giannotti, for instance, or even Guicciardini. Undoubtedly the submissive subjects of Giangastone and Pietro Leopoldo would have found little of interest in reflections on the crisis of the Republic; certainly they would have accepted only with severe reservations the identification of good language with that current at the time in Florence. Machiavelli, at least, suffered as well from the taint of "immorality," in spite of one attempt to prove that he had intended the *Prince* as a trap into which

[49] Muratori reproached the editors of the third edition for having omitted Palmieri: « E perchè non è questo sì bel libro mentovato nella Crusca? È egli forse perchè nè pure in Firenze non ve n'abbia veruna copia? [indeed there was one, but is was kept locked up in a safe until the nineteenth century] o perchè l'autore fu sospetto d'eresia? » [Probably the real reason]: to Magliabechi, 27 March 1697, in *Lettere inedite di L. A. M. scritte a toscani dal 1694 al 1749,* ed. F. Banaini, F. L. Polidori, Cesare Guasti, and Carlo Milanesi (Florence: Le Monnier, 1854) (hereafter referred to as *Lettere a toscani*), p. 29. Muratori had seen a copy of the *Città di vita* in the Ambrosiana (*Perfetta poesia,* I, 39), but did not know of the one in Florence.

[50] Note Salvini's praise of Chiabrera as the Italian Pindar, who, « quando volea lodare una cosa, . . . solea dire: Ella è poesia greca, facendo sinonimi poesia greca e cosa eccellente »: Muratori, *Perfetta Poesia,* I, 403 (note 36). Salvini contributed to the edition of Chiabrera's *Rime* published in the collection of *Rimatori italiani ultimamente stampati, le cui opere sono citate nel gran Vocabolario degli A. della C.* (3 vols.; Rome: Salvioni, 1718).

to lure tyrants by urging them on to absurd exaggerations. It was not until 1794, over a decade, that is, after Cambiagi had first published the complete works, that the Accademia Fiorentina discovered the political and historical — although not the literary — merits of Machiavelli.[51] It has not been until just recently, moreover, that linguists have finally dissipated the myth about the "decadence" of the *volgare* under the influence of the Quattrocento Latinists.[52] Some Settecento scholars, indeed, did render tributes to Poliziano and Lorenzo de' Medici,[53] and a few, notably Lorenzo Mehus, Angelo Maria Bandini, and Ferdinando Fossi, prepared editions of the previously unpublished letters of Quattrocento humanists with a critical insight and with a sensitivity toward the qualities of the texts that are still admired by students of the Renaissance today.[54] But none of this work took place

[51] Crusca: * Diario, 8 and 22 August 1750. *Opere di Niccolò Machiavelli* (6 vols.; Florence: Cambiagi, 1782; another edition by the same in 9 vols. [the ninth of which contains the letters published by Fossi], 1796-99. Gio. Battista Baldelli, *Elogio di Niccolò Machiavelli* (« London » [but Livorno], 1794) and Fiorentina: * Registro, 7 August 1794. The popularity of the Discorsi at the time of the French Revolution is noted by C. F. Goffis in W. Binni (ed.), *I classici italiani*, pp. 354-55. See below, chap. vi.

[52] Note P. O. Kristeller, « The Origin and Development of the Language of Italian Prose », *Studies in Renaissance Thought and Letters*, pp. 473-93; and remarks of Giovanni Nencioni, « Essenza del Toscano », *Rassegna della letteratura italiana*, LXII (1958), 3-12, esp. pp. 9-14, with bibliography. Note further introduction to Ghino Ghinassi, *Il volgare letterario nel Quattrocento e le 'Stanze' di Poliziano* (Florence: Le Monnier, 1957).

[53] Namely, by the indefatigable biographer Angelo Fabroni: *Magni Cosmi Medicei vita*, and *Laurentii Medicis Magnifici vita* (each in 2 vols.; Pisa: Landi, 1789 and 1784). On Poliziano: Filippo Venuti in Etrusca: * Atti, 14 April 1754. The Stanze were published several times elsewhere in Italy during the century, e. g., Venice, 1761, and Parma, 1792, but never in Tuscany.

[54] Lorenzo Mehus, (ed.), *Leonardo Bruni arretini (sic) epistolarum libri VIII ad fidem codd. Mss. suppleti, et castigati* (Florence: Rigacci, 1741), and *Epistolarum Ambrosii Traversarii* (Florence: ex Typographio Caesareo, 1759) (note particularly the Preface); Ferdinando Fossi, *Monumenta ad Alamanni Rinuccini vitam contexendam* (Florence, 1791) (of which there is now a modern edition of *Lettere e orazioni*, ed. V. R. Giustiani [Florence: Olschki, 1953]); and A. M. Bandini, *Cl. Italorum et Germanorum epistolae ad Petrum Victorum* (Vettori) (Florence, 1758). Bandini also published Giovanni Corsi's biography of Ficino as *Commentarius de platonicae philosophiae . . .* (Pisa: Pizzorno, 1771). One of the best of his scholarly works is the *Specimen literaturae fiorentinae saeculi XV in quo dum Christophori Landini gesta enarrantur virorum ea aetate doctissimorum in literariam remp. merita . . . Omnia ex codd. MSS . . .* (Florence: Rigacci, 1747). For opinions of modern scholars on these works: Hans Baron, *The Crisis of the Early Italian Renaissance* (Princeton: Princeton University Press, 1955), II, 514; P. O. Kristeller, *Studies in Renaissance Thought and Letters*, pp. 174,

within the academies. Their contributions to the preservation of the Italian literary heritage was indeed valuable; but it remained fixed within the bounds of Cruscan concepts of proper usage and uninspired by any purely historical interest in the works their members were reading and publishing.

Meanwhile, as the traditional dedication to *volgare* literature bore fruit, in the Settecento, in the extensive publication of "language texts," so also two other traditional practices of the older academies sufficiently met the demands of the new century to permit positive contributions to Italian letters. Translation, first of all, still remained one of the chief occupations of the academicians: indeed, they soon discovered that it could profitably be carried on far more extensively than their predecessors had suspected and, above all, that it could be used for quite different purposes. While most of them still recognized, with Scipione Maffei, the desirability of "enriching our language with new words, new expressions, [and] new phrases,"[55] they no longer needed any proof of the capacity of Tuscan to supply an abundance of "choice, expressive, meaningful, and appropriate" words for any idea that might appear in another tongue.[56] Maffei's new expressions, after all, already existed potentially in the *genio* of Tuscan, and the translator could easily "discover" them without having recourse to coinage.

Translators could now, therefore, give their attention principally to "vulgarizing" the contents of foreign literature in a manner "intelligible" to an Italian speaking audience.[57] Since what mattered was

192, and 323; Eugenio Garin, *L'umanesimo italiano,* p. 283, etc.; and in general, Alessandro Perosa, *Sulla pubblicazione degli epistolari degli umanisti,* published in *Le fonti del medioevo europeo* (Rome, Tipografia del Senato, 1954).

[55] Scipione Maffei, *Traduttori italiani, o sia Notizie de' volgarizzamenti d'antichi scrittori latini e greci che sono in luce* (Venice: Coletti, 1720), pp. 16-17. See also Filippo Argelati, *Biblioteca degli volgarizzatori* (5 vols.; Milan: Agnelli, 1757), esp. III, 68-69, on the translations of A. M. Salvini.

[56] Crusca: Diario, 20 January 1707, on speech of Tommaso Buonaventuri.

[57] Lorenzo Del Riccio, *Componimenti poetici del libero signore de Canitz volgarizzati da un accademico della Crusca* (Florence: Moücke, 1757), Preface, ix-x. (This, by the way, is one of the very few translations from German. On the reception of Friedrich von Canitz [the « Boileau della Germania »] in Italy, see Alfred Noyer-Weidner, *Die Aufklärung in Oberitalien* [Munich: Hueber, 1957], pp. 269 ff. — Del Riccio's translation is not mentioned).

not words but ideas and information, not the peculiar locutions of, say, Plutarch or St. Basil, but the "fundamentals of true wisdom" contained in their works,[58] there was no longer any reason to restrict translation to the three languages that the Accademia Fiorentina had long considered the only rivals of Tuscan.   Piety, for instance, could be found in Fénelon as well as in St. Gregory the Great; wisdom could be found in Pope as well as in Plotinus; and Addison and Racine could offer examples of literary excellence as valuable as those in Horace or Homer.[59]   Through their translations, then, the academies played an important part in the diffusion of contemporary French, and to some extent English and German literature that eventually had such a great effect on Settecento Italian culture.   They encouraged adaptations, like those of Gregorio Redi and Lorenzo Guazzesi, of French classical drama; some of them, especially the Etrusca and the Colombaria, published translations of contributions by their foreign correspondents; and the Georgofili, who became the most active translators after 1770, distributed popular versions of the principal medical, scientific, and agricultural treatises that reached them from beyond the Alps.[60]   For what had once been simply a literary exercise or a means of glorifying the *volgare* had now become

Such expressions can be found even in Salvini, e.g., on his translation of Plotinus (above, note 31), Crusca: * Diario, 2 April 1707, even though he generally did not practice what he preached.

[58] Angelo Maria Ricci, *Tre fondamenti di vera sapienza . . . ritrovati in tre nobilissimi ragionamenti di Plutarco, S. Basileo e S. Gregorio Nazianzeno* (Florence: Moücke, 1731). See especially pp. 21 and 22 on the purpose of the translation, and p. 174 on the « commune utilità de giovani ».

[59] *Lo spirito del sacerdozio di Gesù Cristo . . . modello di perfezione proposto a tutti quegli ecclesiastici, che sono chiamati alla vita apostolica, tradotto dal francese* [of Fénelon] *nell'italiano da un accademico della Crusca* [Giovanni Giraldi] dedicated to Msgr. Francesco Maria Ginori, Bishop of Fiesole, and approved by the Academy on 5 August 1742, published in 2 vols. in 1744. The *Essay on Man* was translated by Anton Filippo Adami as *I principj della morale, o sia Saggio sopra l'uomo,* published in Venice in 1765 and 1784, and republished in the polyglot edition *Essai sur l'homme, Poëme philosophique . . . en cinq langues* (Strasbourg: König, 1772).   A. M. Salvini's translation of Addison is cited above, chap. i, note 37.   Among the many translation of Racine in Tuscany may be mentioned Gregorio Redi's *Andromaca* (1766), Lorenzo Guazzesi's *Ifigenia,* and Filippo Venuti's *La religione* (read in the Etrusca: * Atti, 16 August 1748).

[60] Above, pp. 48-50.   Examples: *Magazzino toscano,* I¹ (1770), 53 (on smallpox) and 63 f. (Tissot); II⁴ (1771), 65 f. (Linnaeus).

a way of transmitting to a wider audience information and ideas previously available only in a language not its own.

Similarly, the age-old battles over the *questione della lingua* raged on as before. The new century opened, as has been seen, with the Florentine academicians engaged in a two-front war. On one front, that of internal sedition sponsored by the Intronati of Siena, they succeeded in winning an undisputed victory within two decades. Incapable of resisting the temptation of satire that had made him famous as a dramatist, Girolamo Gigli soon followed up his already polemical edition of St. Catherine's letters with his *Vocabolario cateriniano,* filled with acrimonious attacks on Florentines in general and on the Crusca in particular. Unfortunately the belligerent lexicographer weakened his own position by permitting *campanilismo* (local patriotism) to infringe upon the exigencies of pure scholarship: many of the "words" (*vocolezza* and *gecchimento,* for instance) [61] had no other foundation than his own extravagant imagination; and his determination to gain the adherence of all Italy for his crusade led him to forge letters of approval and to invent a number of purely fictitious "academies" whose support he vaunted in an appendix. [62] The counterattack of the Crusca was swift and decisive: on 2 September 1717, in the presence of forty members,

having seen the recently-published book by a certain Girolamo Gigli, unfortunately elected many years ago to membership; having recognized the same book

[61] Examples from the *Vocabolario cateriniano,* first published up through the letter *R* partly in Rome, partly in Lucca, in 1717 analyzed by Migliorini, *Lingua e cultura,* p. 181, in an excellent essay entitled « Il 'Vocabolario cateriniano' del Gigli », pp. 167-190. Cf. Maria Carmi, *Pier Jacopo Martello: Studi* (Florence, 1906). On the Cruscan position in general during the eighteenth century, see now the excellent survey of Maurizio Vitale, *La questione della lingua* (Palermo: Palumbo, 1960), pp. 112 ff.

[62] The second edition contains the subtitle « con l'aggiunta della Retrattazione [*sic*] del medesimo . . . e delle lettere di quasi tutte le accademie d'Italia in approvazione della locuzione della Santa: A Manilla nell'Isole delle Filippine » [but Lucca, n. d.], a copy of which is now in the Biblioteca Vaticana, but nowhere in Florence to my knowledge. The « academies » include one in Cortona that certainly never existed and one in Montalcino that very probably did not. These letters are printed in Francesco Corsetti, *Vita di G. G.* (Florence: All'Insegna di Apollo, 1746); and Gigli's whole turbulent career is recounted in Temistocle Favilli, *G. G. senese* (Rocca S. Casciano, 1907). On 3 April 1717 the Fisiocritici (Deliberazioni) nominated Bernardino Perfetti and Cesare Scotti to draft a letter to Gigli approving the « nuova opera sopra l'idiotismo senese ». The Deliberazioni contain transcriptions under the entry of Gigli's letter of 13 March and Pagliai's response of 10 April 1717.

as most injurious, and full of false slander against our Academy; and having presented, through the *arciconsolo,* the most just complaints of all the Academy to His Royal Highness; [the Academy has decreed] by the unanimous vote of all members that the said former member be dismissed, erased, and removed from our Academy, on account of the deep injury and horrible crime by which he has lacerated most wrongly the bosom of his most loving Mother, who is guilty of no other error than of having once admitted him among the number of her own. [63]

On 9 September Gigli's *Vocabolario* was "publicly burned by the hand of the executioner in Piazza di S. Apollinare"; [64] and the Academy persuaded the grand duke to inform the victim, who by then had made himself *persona non grata* also in Rome, that his presence within the dominions of H.R.H. would no longer be desired. The furious patriot had to spend almost four years cooling off in the quiet of Viterbo, until "a printed retraction, in which he excuses himself of all the imprecations and calumnies [he had] spread about against any kind of person or order" abated the wrath of the offended Florentines. [65] Meanwhile the protests and excuses of Gigli's supposed supporters poured in: from Pier Jacopo Martello, "with proof of never having written a letter to Gigli," from Apostolo Zeno, who branded "completely false and apocryphal a letter circulated under his name," from the Innominati of Bra, from the Risvegliati of Pistoia, and from others. [66] The insurrection of Gigli was the last, flamboyant flourish

[63] Decree of 2 September 1717 in Crusca: Diario, Memorie per servire di continuazione al Diario dell'Accademia . . . : « veduto un libro . . . pubblicato modernamente . . . da un tal Girolamo Gigli eletto per disgrazia molti anni sono nostro accademico, il qual libro è stato riconosciuto per molto ingiurioso, e ripieno di false calunnie contro la nostra Accademia: e dal . . . nostro arciconsolo portate all'A. R. . . . le giustissime doglianze di tutta l'Accademia . . . il detto già nostro Accademico . . . a viva voce di tutti è stato cassato, raso è rimosso dalla nostra Accademia, pel capo d'una profonda malizia [the last word is crossed out in the MS] ignoranza, d'una stolta temerità, d'una perfida malignità, e d'una orribile fellonia, lacerando a gran torto il seno della sua amorevolissima Madre, rea non d'altra colpa che d'averlo una volta ammesso nel numero de' suoi ».

[64] Diario, 9 September 1717: « pubblicamente abbruciato per mano di Boja sulla Piazza di S. Apollinare ».

[65] *Ibid.,* 21 August 1721: « Una ritrattazione stampata . . . nella quale si disdice di tutta le maldicenze, e calunnie . . . contro qualsivoglia persona, ed ordine disseminate ».

[66] *Ibid.,* 18 March 1718 (« in giustificazione di non aver mai scritta una lettera al Gigli ») and 20 January 1718 (« del tutto falsa ed apocrifa una lettera divulgata sotto il suo nome »). Zeno was elected to the Crusca on 17 March 1722. Letter of the Innominati was received 30 December 1717 (Diario, *sub dat.*) and others of 5 and 22 February 1718 accompanying

— almost in parody — of the once promising Sienese school of Claudio Tolomei, Scipione Bargagli, and Celso Cittadini, whose merits as linguists even the third edition had admitted. After the defeat, no one ever again bothered to insist upon the preferability of *tenche* to *tinche;* and Sienese retreated forever to the unpretentious position of a charming and respectable, but purely local, variant of Tuscan.[67]

But on the other front, that of Anti-Tuscanism or "Italianism," the opposition was more formidable. To some extent the fourth edition of 1729-38 answered the critics of the third — not only by its greatly augmented volume, but also by its careful correction of previous errors, its vastly broadened list of authorities, its inclusion of many more modern, nay, even contemporary authors (like Salvini), and the admission of many more words as "antiquated," which the Committee had warned as early as 1712 should be used only "with parsimony and reserve."[68] The exhaustive efforts of the principal Florentine *letterati* during almost a quarter century did at least succeed in maintaining some of their "innocent despotism" over "the speech of Italy."[69] Manuscripts still arrived for their criticism even from such distinguished scholars as Mazzuchelli; literary duelists still submitted to their mediation; non-Tuscans still sent in questions about proper definitions and usage; and some writers still attempted, like Paolo Gagliardi in 1741, "to overcome the disadvantage of birth" (in Brescia) by "placing

a gift: Cr A.39, 17-18. The original letter of the Risvegliati in enthusiastic support of Gigli is in BCS Y.I.19; that to the Crusca of 29 December 1717 has disappeared, but is mentioned in Pandolfo Pandolfini's acknowledgment of 29 February 1728.

[67] In general, see Carlo Battisti, *La parlata senese e S. Caterina* (reprinted from *Studi cateriniani*, XI [1935]), and Migliorini, « Voci senesi », *Lingua e cultura*, pp. 219-22. Sienese, still has its defenders today, to be sure. Note the hope expressed in *Bullettino senese,* Ser. III, Vol. I (1942), (a speech to the Accademia degli Intronati) that St. Catherine's letters in a new edition « sottraggono alla voracità del tempo le pure e pittoresche espressioni che ancora fluiscono dal labbro dei nostri popolani, e dall'altro pongano o ripongano in luce i testi degli autori senesi », as well as the disapproval of the « invasione di tanti neologismi inutili e peggio, di tanti barbarismi . . . », pp. 150-51.

[68] MS (without numerical indication) Cr: Diario delle sessioni che si anderanno facendo per la nuova edizione del Vocabolario, at the sole entry for 16 March 1712. Cf. Preface to Vol. I of the fourth edition. On the whole question of language, see now the long Introduction of Mario Puppo to his *Discussioni linguistiche del Settecento* (Torino, U T.E.T., 1957).

[69] Giulio Rucellai, *Discorso . . . recitato . . . per le augustissime . . . nozze . . . Giuseppe Arciduca d'Austria . . .* (Florence: Stamperia Imperiale, 1761), p. 4.

in front [of their works] the honored name of the most noble and famous Accademia della Crusca, the flower of all Italy." [70]

But these tokens of submission were not enough; for possession of a "perfect" speech proved incapable of preventing the passage of intellectual leadership in Italy to other, more vigorous centers. The dissent of Muratori and Benedetto Marcello (1739) had swelled by the middle of the century into the vigorous attack upon "Cruscanism" by all the best critics of the Peninsula — by Giuseppe Baretti, Francesco Algarotti, and Saverio Bettinelli. Heaping ridicule upon "the sovereign tribunal, which at its own pleasure inserts or expels letters from words and moves the afflicted vowels forward or backward," and inventing absurd speeches to be delivered by ignorant pedants upon admission to the academy, they ended by proclaiming, with Alessandro Verri, the "solemn rejection of the purity of the Tuscan language." [71] They might admire the magnitude of the fourth edition; but they quickly recognized that the concessions in detail had left the basic Trecento principles of Bembo, Salviati, and Salvini untouched. "The Italians have for a long time borne the yoke imposed upon them by the Florentines," [72] complained the herald of "ration-

70 Cf. Crusca: *Approved publications. Correspondence of the Crusca with Mazzuchelli in Cr A.29, 68-72, et al. P. Gagliardi to G. Bottari, 29 June 1741 and 10 May 1742 in Lettere del canonico P. G., accademico della Crusca (2 vols., Brescia: Pianta, 1763), II, 243-44, 245, submitting his translation of the Confessions of St. Augustine approved by the Crusca in 1742. Crusca: Diario, 23 January 1738, records the receipt of a request from Tommaso Perrone of Lecce for the Academy's approval of his translation of Marco Girolamo Vida's Cristiade (Naples, 1733), to which « gli fu ordinato, che rispondesse lettera di ringraziamento, scusando l'Accademia dall'interporre in quest'opera di già stampata il suo giudizio . . . ». Also, ibid., 19 July 1742, on a letter from « un certo Borga di Bergamo [Anton Maria, 1724-68] per muoverla a giudicare un piato, ch'egli diceva essergli stato suscitato da un suo avversario . . . faceva istanza d'avere il giudizio dell'Accademia »: Minute e lettere riguardanti un parere il alcuni Accademici . . . sopra l'intelligenza della voce Infognito, richiesto da Venezia, e colà mandato. March 1757: Cr A.36.

71 See above, chap. i, note 24. Pier Jacopo Martello quoted by Walter Binni in « P. J. M. e le sue commedie 'per letterati' », Rassegna della letteratura italiana, LXI (1957), 52-61, p. 54, Note Baretti's « Diceria di Aristarco Scannabue da recitarsi nell'Accademia della Crusca il dì che sarà ricevuto accademico », La frustra letteraria, No. XXV (pp. 252-62), now reprinted in Puppo, Discussioni linguistiche del Settecento, pp. 213-19. Verri cited by Migliorini in Questioni e correnti di storia letteraria (above, chap. i, note 21), pp. 45-46 (with a good summary of the whole question). Cf. Vincenzo Vivaldi, Storia delle controversie linguistiche in Italia, I (Catanzaro: Mauro, 1925), chap. vi.

72 In preface to Carlo Innocenzo Frugoni, Opere poetiche (Parma: Stamperia Reale, 1779), I, xlvi: « Gl'Italiani si sono lasciati porre il giogo da' Fiorentini assai per tempo.

alist" poetry, Carlo Gastone Della Torre di Rezzonico in 1779, and the perfection of the language demands that, like Greek, it freely admit contributions from all its dialects. "Every word that can be understood by all the inhabitants of Italy," proclaimed Pietro Verri in the *Caffè,* "is an Italian word: the authority and the consent of all Italians, in matters of their speech, is greater than [that] of all the grammarians." [73] The Trecento, in other words, was to be relegated to an honorable place in history, and "Tuscan" was to give way to "Italian."

The Florentines did what they could in self-defense. They insisted again and again on "the advantages of the Tuscan language and on the importance of expanding it ... for the good of society, ... philosophy, and all the liberal arts"; they proclaimed linguistics to be on "the level of the sciences"; and they even, at times, dedicated themselves to excruciating analyses of minute linguistic questions with a scientific seriousness that would have surprised Anton Maria Salvini, and with an aridity that would certainly bore the enthusiasts of the *Défense de la langue* columns in modern French newspapers.[74] Some of them — most especially Domenico Maria Manni in a series of lectures delivered to the Florentine Seminary in 1736 and published with the imprimatur of the Crusca the following year — set out to codify the extensive observations of Buommattei a century earlier into "methodical" Tuscan grammars, which added considerations of syntax to the previous dissertations on letters and cases, and which succeeded in introducing the study of Tuscan as well as Latin grammar into the secondary schools.[75] Ross'Antonio

e lo scuoterlo sarebbe impresa temeraria ». The policy of the Filopatridi and the Patria Società Letteraria in Piedmont in adopting Tuscan as their official language (instead of French or dialect, but carefully differentiated from the peculiar usages of contemporary Tuscany) is described by Carlo Calcaterra, *Le adunanze della « Patria Società Letteraria »* (Torino: Internazionale, 1943), pp. xxiv f.

[73] Cited by Nino Valeri, *Pietro Verri* (Milan: Mondadori, 1937), p. 162.

[74] Crusca: *Diario, 2 September 1762 (Antonio Ricasoli); Giulio Perini, Lezione inaugurale: ASF Reggenza 1052.58. Cf. Ildefonso di S. Luigi, *Dissertazione sopra il vero significato della voce Antenati* (Florence: Cambiagi, 1784) (with approval of the Accademia Fiorentina).

[75] *Lezioni di lingua toscana di Domenico Maria Manni, accademico fiorentino, dette da esso nel Seminario arcivescovile di Firenze* (Florence: Viviani, 1737; 2d ed. under author's supervision, Lucca: Rocchi, 1773). *Della lingua toscana libri due* of Benedetto Buommat-

Martini, secretary of the Crusca, proposed as early as 1741 the initiation of further researches in preparation for a fifth edition of the *Vocabolario;* while one of his colleagues called, in 1743, for the publication of a supplementary *Vocabolario delle arti* covering the specialized vocabulary of the fine arts, agriculture, and printing.[76]

Unfortunately these proposals produced little in the way of positive results. Linguistics might indeed have expanded into the study of the historical development of the language, for which the editors of the fourth edition had collected ample documentation. Instead, it never advanced beyond the already tiresome issue of just what language was to be spoken and written. Grammar might have included a philosophical or logical investigation of parts of speech in the manner of, say, Du Marsais or Vico. Instead, it remained at the level of mere description — long discussions of whether to say *abici* or *abece* (ABC) and endless tautologies on the use of each letter, on declensions, on pronouns, reminiscent of Molière's Monsieur Jourdain. Hence, the much-heralded fifth edition bogged down in unenthusiastic statements of good intentions: the presentation of a concrete proposal by the Accademia Fiorentina in 1784; the appointment of a committee in 1785; the delivery of

tei, first published in 1643, was re-edited and published in 1760 (« Impressione quinta rivista e corretta dagli accademici della Crusca »; Florence: Stamperia Imperiale), with the biography by Gio. Battista Casotti of Prato, first published by Guiducci & Franchi in 1714, and the approval of the Crusca dated 1757. Note also the first « lezione » of Gigli in his *Lezioni di lingua toscana*; and in general Ciro Trabalza, *Storia della grammatica italiana* (Milan: Hoepli, 1908), chaps xiii-xiv. The best-known is P. Salvadore Corticelli (1690-1758), *Della toscana eloquenza discorsi cento,* published in Bologna in 1752 with the blessings of the Crusca, supplemented by his *Regole ed osservazioni della lingua toscana ridotte a metodo* (Bologna: Volpe, 1745), and many editions throughout the century, which earned him election to membership on 20 February 1747. A few grammatical treatises of Benedetto Varchi were published in the *Opuscoli inediti di celebri autori toscani, l'opere dei quali sono citate dal Vocabolario della Crusca* (1807: above, chap. i, note 39), I, 102 f. (« Frammento di grammatica ») and III, 138 f. (« Tempi dei verbi » — recited in the Accademia Fiorentina in 1551).

[76] Crusca: *Diario, 9 March 1741, published as *Ragionamento presentato all'A. della C. . . . per norma di una nuova edizione del Vocabolario toscano* (Florence: Piatti, 1813); a *Vocabolario delle arti* had been proposed by Salvini as early as 1698 and by Bottari in 1704 (21 February); the proposal here referred to is that of Ferdinando Carlo Capponi: *Diario, 27 July 1743; it is spoken of as « già di gran tempo da lei [the Academy] meditato » by Martini in a letter to Samuel Johnson, 15 September 1755: Cr A.27.125. See Gio. Battista Zannoni's discourse of 9 May 1815, published in *Atti dell'Accademia della Crusca*, I, (1819), 202-38.

a few "lezioni sulla lingua toscana" after the turn of the century; and even a precise resolution of the enigmatic Accademia Italiana di Scienze Lettere ed Arti in 1808 to undertake "the compilation of a dictionary of the language." [77] But in 1794, when the exhaustion of the fourth edition on the market made such a project financially attractive, the Fiorentina dismissed the challenge and simply granted permission for its reprinting.[78] For the truth is that no one was really much interested in such questions any longer. The drop in the attendance of the Crusca meetings after 1730 suggested already that one generation would have to pass away before Martini's proposal could be fulfilled.[79]

> Donna del più puro Italo accento,
> che sugli altri Idiomi, e splendi, e regni,
> qui sol [in Tuscany] par che non curi i tuoi gran pregi...

complained Casaregi in 1749.[80] Most of the new academies had found the Etruscan alphabet more interesting than the Tuscan and Micheli's new botanical specimens more challenging than Salvini's ardent appeals to put commas over handwritten *e*'s. The Crusca itself disappeared in 1783; and the new Accademia Fiorentina soon became so engrossed in the other parts of its ambitious program that it forgot about its original promise to carry on the work of its predecessor. Thus, a final attack on "Cruscanism" launched in 1785 by Melchiorre Cesarotti encountered almost no effective resistance; [81] and when Domenico Moreni began, after the Restoration,

[77] Much of the concrete documentation has disappeared. The proposal of 1784 is mentioned by G. B Zannoni, *Storia dell'Accademia della Crusca* (Florence: Tipografia del Giglio, 1848), p. 16; the committee of 1786 by D. Moreni in his preface to S. Salvini, *Ragionamento sopra l'origine dell'A. della C.*; Fiorentina (1783): * Atti, 20 May, 1 & 8 July 1802, et seq.; and *Atti dell'Accademia Italiana di Scienze, Lettere ed Arti*, II, (1810), viii.

[78] Zannoni in *Atti dell'Accademia della Crusca*, I (1819), xix. Other unofficial printings of the fourth edition appeared in Naples in 1746-48 and in Venice in 1763 and 1797.

[79] Note by Alamanni in Crusca (Diario, 30 August 1742): «... o siasi che le condizioni de' presenti tempi ispirassero negli animi della gioventù sentimenti diversi da i passati ...», etc.

[80] « Lady of the purest Italian accent, — who rulest in splendor over the other idioms; — it seems that only here your great merits are neglected »: G. B. Casaregi, Sopra l'A. dellla C., Sonetto (9 August 1749): Cr A.35, 6.

[81] Melchiorre Cesarotti, *Saggi sulla filosofia delle lingue e del gusto* (1785), reprinted in Vol. I of his *Opere* (Pisa: Capurro, 1814), p. 16. See further Part III, sec. 9 (p. 94) for

to publish the letters and discourses of his famous predecessors, the question had largely retreated from the domain of polemics to that of pure scholarship.

In one issue, however, the Tuscan academicians won the support even of some of their more determined adversaries. No one, to be sure, objected to the influx of books from France that increased rapidly from the middle of the century on. Indeed, several volumes, including the *Encyclopédie* itself, issued from Tuscan presses in the original language during this time; a bookstore dedicated exclusively to the sale of Transalpine publications flourished in Florence; and one academy even addressed its petitions to the Regency in the same delightful variety of incorrect French that the Emperor-Grand Duke used in his messages from Vienna.[82]. Everyone of any education at least read the language that was fast displacing Latin as the means of international communication, although Filippo Venuti's care to include an Italian translation with his prize essay for publication in the Etrusca's *Saggi* suggests that a knowledge of it was often somewhat superficial.[83]

What the academicians objected to was not French itself, but Gallicisms. Substantially they employed the same arguments originally applied by the humanists of the Quattrocento against the "vulgarization" of Latin and by those of the Cinquecento against the Latinization of the *volgare*: two perfectly valid and expressive linguistic media would deteriorate if commingled. Gradually the usual *lodi della lingua toscana* altered the object of their criticisms to such words as *visaggio, portreto,* and *regrettare,* which soon became sufficiently current in some circles to be satirized in the *Raguet* of Scipione

the criticism of Salviati; and Part IV for the attack on the Crusca and the *Vocabolario*; and in general, Mario Puppo, « Storicità della lingua e libertà dello scrittore nel 'Saggio sulla filosofia delle lingue' del Cesarotti », *Giornale storico della letteratura italiana,* CDIV (1956), 510-43.

[82] *Stances pour la fete (sic) de Saint Louis roi de France ... Eglise de S. Antoine de Florence,* printed by Moücke in 1758 and 1759, preserved in Colombaria: Annali 26 and 27. Adami on the French bookshop, together with Pecci's report on the book trade, in ASF Reggenza 778.13. Lettre des Accademiciens [*sic*] de Pistoie au S. A R., 19 February 1744: ASF Reggenza 906.7.

[83] Filippo Venuti in *Saggi Etrusca,* IV (1743), x.

Maffei.[84] In 1761, Filippo Venuti, himself a sometime resident of Bordeaux and author of several works in French, gravely warned his compatriots against "the abuse of admitting into [another] living language like Tuscan "words and expressions borrowed from the French." Such practices, he insisted, threatened to split Italy into two separate linguistic nations by introducing terms among the learned "incomprehensible to the greater part of the population"; and, moreover, this "affectation" was "unnecessary" among a people with a fully developed language and literary tradition of its own.[65] The pursuit of *eloquenza toscana* thus became a patriotic obligation.[86] Certainly the Tuscans pressed the point too far. Cesarotti, for instance, picked out a number of "perfectly good Tuscan terms, all authorized by the examples of Boccaccio, Villani, and other writers of the Golden Age," which in fact had been Gallicisms at the moment of their introduction; and, indeed, the Cruscans evidently forgot the observations of their own Bembo on the role of Provençal in the formation of Tuscan in its infancy.[87] But although the complete isolation of Italian from other tongues proved to be as hopeless as freezing it to antiquated models, the reaffirmation of the value of an autonomous national language prevented its permanent contamination by many of the more bizarre adaptations of the Settecento Francophiles.

As the principal occupation of the academies turned from literary exercises to the diffusion of knowledge, finally, the very nature of the *questione della lingua* underwent a notable modification, especially among the newer societies dedicated to particular branches of learning. All of them agreed, first of all, with the basic premises of the Accademia Fiorentina concerning the preferability of Tuscan to Latin in conducting academic business: the "Tuscan language," as the founders of the Accademia Etrusca insisted, was fully capable of

---

[84] Cf. Ferdinand Brunot, *Histoire de la langue française des origines à 1900* (Paris: Colin, 1934), VIII[1], 132-37, for a full disscussion of these terms, and more briefly Giacomo Devoto, *Profilo di storia linguistica italiana* (Florence: La Nuova Italia, 1953), p. 105.

[85] Crusca: * Diario, 17 September 1761. On Venuti, see H. Weinert, « Filippo de' Venuti », *Archivio storico italiano*, CXIII (1954), 348-76.

[86] Crusca: * Diario, 13 March 1756.

[87] Cesarotti, *Saggi sulla filosofia della lingua* (*Opere*, I), p. 100. Pietro Bembo, *Prose della volgar lingua*, ed. Mario Marti (Padova: Liviana, 1955), p. 20, and elsewhere.

treating "any science whatsoever." [88]   But their reasons differed from those of their Cinquecento ancestors.   Latin, they admitted, might well assist a few scholars and scientists in communicating specialized information to learned colleagues in other countries among whom a knowledge of Italian could not be expected.   It might even, as Luigi Lanzi still maintained at the end of the century, be more fitting than the vernacular for commemorative inscriptions or monuments.[89] But when Lami, Bellini, and Micheli, for instance, sought to transmit their learning to their associates in the academies, they preferred the language most readily understood by their listeners.   The choice of language, therefore, depended wholly upon the audience to be addressed.   Most of the academies accordingly discouraged the presentation of papers in Latin — not because of any quarrel with the Quattrocento, but simply because of the desire of the members to benefit from what was being read to them.

The same insistence upon easy comprehension determined further a change in the style of the *volgare* itself.   No longer would aspiring philologists or botanists suffer the page-long sentences interrupted by incessant subordinate clauses and doubled adjectives that had delighted the Cruscans and the Apatisti of earlier generations; and no longer were they sufficiently charmed by imitations of Latin syntax to wait patiently through the whole complicated structure before the orator arrived at the verb.   Such sentences as this: "I do not deny, that the Latin orators, and poets, as much as they could, the Greeks imitated ... » [90] might make interesting exercises, but they were little

---

[88] *Saggi Etrusca,* VII (1958), xviii; « essendo capace la nostra lingua di trattare qualunque scienza nel suo idioma ».   Note further A. M. Salvini's justification of the study of Latin for its contribution to the appreciation of Tuscan: « Sopra la lingua toscana », in *Discorsi accademici,* Vol. I, No. 62, pp. 239-44, Vol. II, No. 77, pp. 423-27, and Vol. III, No. 21, pp. 62 f.: « Se sia meglio nel comporre usare il latino o il volgare ».

[89] Note Lami: « Latine scribere elegi, quia non solis Italis, sed & aliis nationibus res nostrae innotescerent, sine invidia & liberaliter volui ... », in *Sanctae Ecclesiae Florentinae monumenta* (Florence: Ex Typ. Deiparae ab angelo Salutatae, 1758), I, i. On Lanzi, see Giulio Natali, « Il Settecento, secolo di latinisti », *La cultura,* VII (1927-28), 391-400. The passion for Latin verse elsewhere in Italy described by Natali seems to have been much less strong in Tuscany.

[90] « Io non nego, che gli Oratori, e Poeti Latini, il più che poterono, i Greci imitarono ... »: A. M. Ricci, *Della necessità e facilità della lingua greca* (in the Apatisti, 13 December 1714), p. 240.

suited to teaching peasants how to plant vines or citizens how to read medieval chronicles. Words came to be valued less for themselves alone and more for their capacity to explain a given matter to "every kind of person"; and Gabbrielli and his fellow physicists sought accordingly to "write minutely and with the familiarity of the spoken style, without any [superflous] erudition." [91]

Such demands did not necessarily conflict with the program of the Trecentisti: who, after all, could write with more "familiarity" than Sacchetti or Passavanti? A good writer might still adhere to the language of the *Secolo d'oro,* which the editors of the *Vocabolario* had always held to be perfectly comprehensible to ordinary Sienese and Florentines. But above all, he must search for brevity and precision; and he must avoid "immoderate use of metaphor" and the "cold, insipid poetic nonsense" that so burdened the meaningless literature of the Seicento.[92] "I have chosen the popular language," stated the sometime president of the Società Botanica, Giovanni Targioni Tozzetti, "and a simple, narrative style, intelligible to all; for I write ... for my countrymen of every state and condition, ... and not only for men of letters." [93] Thus the academies of the Settecento adopted officially the consciously concise and simple style that Galileo had used so effectively in his scientific works but that his immediate disciples had not always imitated in theirs; and, more important still, they proclaimed this style to be appropriate not only for explanations of natural phenomena, but for all prose writing in general.[94]. Language was no longer simply a perfectly formed

---

[91] Gabbrielli, *L'eliometro fisiocritico* (Siena, 1705), p. 3; *Atti Fisiocritici,* V (1774), iv.

[92] Antonio Cocchi on Micheli's « stile alieno affatto del soverchio uso delle metafore », in his *Discorsi toscani,* I, xxxvi; Perini in ASF Reggenza 1052.58; *Saggi Etrusca,* III (1741), ix. In general: G. A. Pecci, *Sopra le più giuste regole per parlare e scrivere toscano* (Siena, 1767), Preface, pp. iii-vi; and Amaduzzi's comments on the relation of language to the sciences in *Discorso filosofico,* 26-27.

[93] *Relazioni d'alcuni viaggi fatti in diverse parti della Toscana per osservare le produzioni naturali e gli antichi monumenti di essa* (1st ed., 1751-54; here cited in 2d ed. in 10 vols.; Florence: Cambiagi, 1768-77), I, xiv.

[94] See Enrico Falqui, « La prosa scientifica del Seicento italiano », and Raffaello Spongano, « Galileo scrittore », both in *Il Sei-Settecento* (Florence: Libera cattedra di storia della civiltà fiorentina, 1956), pp. 23-88 and 107-122; and Raffaele Colapietra, « Stile e scienza nei discepoli di Galileo », *Convivium,* XXII (1955), 533-56.

structure to be preserved as a catalyst for the poetic imagination; it was now primarily a means of communication.

Meanwhile, the other favorite subjects of the older academies gradually faded away. Greek and Latin studies, first of all, did not long survive the death of Salvini, now that their justification in terms of the *volgare* no longer inspired the translators. To be sure, translation continued: Lorenzo Del Riccio, for instance, filled session after session in the Crusca with readings from his Demosthenes and his *Characters* of Theophrast, and he was frequently joined by others, like Marc'Antonio de' Mozzi with his Prudentius and Bindo Simone Peruzzi with his *Astronomica* of Marcus Manilius.[95] The Sacred Scriptures still furnished ample material for academic exercises, especially the Psalms, the Lamentations, and the Book of Ezekiel, which could serve also as texts for religious devotions.[96] Homer above all maintained his traditional prestige: Salvini's *Iliad* of 1723 was followed, from 1744 on, by that of Angelo Maria Ricci, which the translator supplemented with a three-volume commentary, in part read to the Crusca, for the use of his students.[97] Yet it never occurred

[95] Crusca: *Diario, 6 September 1731 (Demosthenes), *et seq.*, and 7 March 1748 to 24 March 1759 (published as *Caratteri di Teofrasto, greco-toscani* [above, chap. ii, note 26]; imprimatur of the Crusca: 22 December 1759), 9 July 1721, and 10 February 1742. Further: *Diario, 9 July 1746: Ricci on the study of Greek.

[96] Gio. Maria Luchini, accademico fiorentino, *Le lezioni di Giobbe ed il Cantico di Ezecchia* (Lucca: Marescandoli, 1731); [Anton Filippo Adami — according to Lami in *Novelle letterarie*, IX (1748), 235-36], *I cantici biblici, ed altri salmi esposti in versi toscani da un accademico apatista* (Florence: Giovannelli, 1748); G. B. Casaregi, *I Proverbi del Re Salomone tradotti in versi toscani* (Florence: Stamperia Imperiale, 1751) (Crusca: *Diario from 19 July 1742); Gregorio Redi, *I salmi di David esposti in versi toscani nel senso letterale*, approved by the Crusca and published by Paperini in 2 vols. in 1734.

[97] Salvini's *Iliade d'Omero tradotta dall'original greco in versi sciolti* (Florence: Tartini & Franchi, 1723) (but planned long before: Crusca: *Diario, 29 July 1700); *Odissea* (Florence: Tartini & Franchi, 1723). Ricci began reading his translation, which never seems to have been published, on 18 July 1744. Some eighteenth-century translations were published together by Masi in Livorno in 1805 (*Le opere tradotte in versi da varii*, 5 vols.). Ricci's *Dissertationes homericae habitae in Florentino Lyceo* (3 vols.; Florence: Albizzini, 1740-41) were probably read in translation to the Crusca from 7 March 1744. Some of his Italian « Ragionamenti omerici » read in the Academy are preserved in Laur 655. He also published school texts on Latin grammar, like *Regole Fondamentali della grammatica latina* (Florence: 1736), and manuals from which students might learn to imitate the grace of Latin in writing Tuscan: *Calligrafia plautina e terenziana*, contenente le più pure e nitide locuzioni di latinità ... corrispondenti ad altrettante volgari disposte per alfabeto ed espresse cogl'idiotismi

to the academicians that the methods they so arduously applied to the *Vocabolario* might be of service to the Latin as well as the Tuscan language, and, with other Italians, they went on using old-fashioned dictionaries like that of Ambrogio da Calepio (fifteenth century) until Egidio Forcellini's great *Lexicon* finally replaced them in 1771.[98]

Nor, moreover, do they appear ever to have been affected by the popular, if unscholarly, wave of enthusiasm for all things Hellenic (or pseudo-Hellenic) that swept across France after 1770.[99] Arcadia, after all, was too firmly rooted in the Italian literary tradition to produce an effect like that of the French translation of Gessner in 1760; Rousseau was too little known in Tuscany to have awakened an appreciation for the "simple, natural" Greeks or a passion for Plutarch; and no self-respecting Tuscan would ever have conceded, as will be seen, any glory to Greece that might have been reserved for Etruria. To some extent Greek scholarship suffered, in Tuscany as in France and England, from the inability to understand, or at least to sympathize with centuries less polite than the eighteenth. The Achilles of Salvini and Ricci, for instance, would have felt as much at ease in the sessions of the Crusca as would the Hector of Pope and Parnell in a London club or the Agammemnon of Mme. Dacer and Rochefort in a Paris salon. And no one suspected, even decades after Giambattista Vico's *Discoverta del vero Omero* (of which the Tuscan academicians apparently knew nothing), that Homer had been anything but what the eminent antiquarian Marcello Venuti in 1750 called "the delight of princes, the support of priests, and the admiration of men of letters."[100] Tuscany was not without accomplished Latinists and Hellenists in the eighteenth century — Alessandro Politi,

---

della lingua fiorentina . . . , opera utilissima per gli studiosi della lingua latina e toscana . . . per uso specialmente delle scuole delle comunità . . . (Florence: Tartini & Franchi, 1735).

[98] See John Edwin Sandys, *A History of Classical Scholarship* (Cambridge: Cambridge University Press, 1908), II, 373 f.

[99] See Badolle, *L'Abbé Jean-Jacques Barthélemy*, pp. 165 f.

[100] Marcello Venuti in an « Esordio d'un panegirico sopra la natività d'Omero », a rough draft in Etr 456, no. 14, probably of the speech recorded in Etrusca: * Atti, 5 July 1749. In general, note Gianni Gervasoni, *Linee di storia della filologia classica in Italia* (Florence: Vallecchi, 1929), pp. 27 f. On Homer in France: E. Egger, *L'hellénisme en France* (Paris: Didier, 1896), II, 131 f., and Badolle, *op. cit.*, p. 170; in England, Clarke, *Greek Studies in England*, pp. 124-28.

for instance, Anton Francesco Gori, Giovanni Lami, and, above all, Odoardo Corsini; but the academies took notice of their work only insofar as it bore upon what was becoming one of their chief interests: history, that is, and archeology. Thus in general the academies in Tuscany took little part in the revival of Greek and Latin philology that would soon culminate in Germany in the *Prolegomena* of Friedrich August Wolf and elsewhere in Italy in the volumes of Bartolommeo Borghesi, Angelo Mai, and Ennio Quirino Visconti.

The discussion of religious and moral questions, secondly, failed to advance beyond the point at which Anton Maria Salvini had left them. A few pamphlets on the Jesuits in France and Paraguay, it is true, were copied or pasted into the *Annali* of the Colombaria, although there is no evidence that the members ever pondered the issues involved. A "sharp, biting invective" delivered in 1730 "against the brutality of the members of the Curia toward their clients" brought a sharp rebuke from the Crusca for what it considered "blind, disordered passion" and a slighting of "so many celebrated and honored persons." In 1771 a speaker in Prato instructed the Infecondi on the errors of Jansenism.[101] And some of the controversy over ecclesiastical and doctrinal matters published in the first volumes of the *Novelle letterarie* may well have proceded from conversations in the Apatisti, of which Lami was a leading member — although the documents regarding this period have disappeared.[102] Otherwise the academicians just repeated the usual *lodi* of saints, doctrines, and abstract virtues — tributes to St. John the Baptist, "the great champion of justice, zealous upholder of the truth"; comparisons of the life of man to "a kind of war... in which we have to do not only with

---

[101] Colombaria: Annali 26 (18 February 1759); 27 (8 August 1759): pamphlet entitled *Raccolta di alcune notizie giustificative della condotta de' MM. RR. PP. Gesuiti nel Paraguay e nel Portogallo* (Trent, 1759); 29 appendix (Brief of Clement XIII of 9 June 1762 copied in Italian translation and marked simply « veduto », 5 September 1762); and 33 appendix (decrees or 25 and 28 August 1781 on reform of the monasteries in Tuscany). Crusca: * Diario, 18 July 1750. Infecondi: * Atti, 27 September 1771.

[102] See Mario Rosa, *Atteggiamenti culturali e religiosi di Giovanni Lami nelle « Novelle letterarie »*, (reprinted from the *Annali della Scuola Normale Superiore di Pisa*, Ser. II, Vol. XXV (1956), fasc. iii-iv), p. 14.

invisible enemies and with malignant spiritual powers, but even with impious men"; [103] meditations on the misery of human existence

> Ove ch'io vada, ove ch'io volga il ciglio,
> fuor che nemici intorno a me non veggio;
> chi servitù minaccia, e che periglio,
> e il mal fuggendo, mi spaventa il peggio

ending up with the comforting thought

> O strana pugna ov'è il morir salute! [104]

Evidently the attempts to vivify religion by talking incessantly about it suffered from the same difficulties that had prevented the emergence of poetry from mere versification — that is, from an inability to perceive the connection between the universal and the particular and from a limitation of concrete experience to what was written in certain books. The academicians might indeed have found some stimulation in the literature of the hallowed Trecento. Unfortunately their preoccupation with language blinded them either to the often profound spirituality of, say, Passavanti, or to the ideal of *docta pietas* in the Latin works of Petrarch. Hence, in their own times, neither the fiery sermons of that Seicento Savonarola P. Segneri nor the violent fervor of the reforming bishop Scipione de' Ricci at the end of the Settecento left any trace among them. Piety and ethics in the Republic of Letters remained throughout the eighteenth just what it had been during much of the seventeenth century: a mere branch of oratory.

Still, the constant intrusion of these themes into academic discourses may well have been responsible for the absence, among

---

[103] A. M. Salvini, *Prose sacre*, orazione v: « Giovanni, gran campione del Giusto, e zelatore, e mantenitore della verità . . . »; « È la nostra vita . . . una specie di guerra sopra la terra; nella quale non solamente con i nemicî invisibili, e colle spirituali maligne potestà . . . abbiamo che fare; ma non con gli uomini ancora empj . . . » (p. 51).

[104] Casaregi, *Sonetti e canzoni toscane* (1741 ed.), son. xxxix: « Wherever I go, wherever I turn my gaze, I see nothing but enemies about me; I am threatened by servitude and by danger; and, fleeing the bad, I fear the worse . . . O strange blow, where death is salvation! ». Typical of all this literature is Salvini's « Sonetti XIV sopra il Pater Noster fatti . . . il giorno dell'Ascensione l'anno 1721 nel tempo della sua gotta, per divozione del giorno, e per alleggerimento di quella », in *Opuscoli inediti di celebri autori toscani*, I, 157 f.

Tuscans, of any of the open hostility between science and orthodoxy that raged beyond the Alps. By "discovering the necessary attractions of matter and the forces of every body," insisted Antonio Cocchi, for instance, scientific researches contributed "more than all other studies to human happiness"; experimental physics, according to the Fisio-critici, "led to the knowledge of God"; and smallpox inoculations were "favorable to charity and consequently to religion." [105] Every branch of learning was, to some extent, a part of theology. The botanists, the naturalists, and the astronomers so consistently justified their respective disciplines in terms of their Christian faith that they could search the heavens and classify plants and fossils without ever questioning the accepted accounts of the Creation, the Nativity, or the miracles of the saints. And should any problem remain "hidden" in "this world here below," they need only wait for God to unveil the Truth about all things — from the meaning of a Roman inscription to the economic function of middlemen — in the World to Come. [106] This rather naïve faith in a sort of pre-established harmony between Christian doctrine and whatever new ideas they might entertain contained, to be sure, a good dose of bigotry. It required them to close their minds, that is, to many of the new ideas that reached them from abroad, or at least to dismiss anything apparently "offensive to the Catholic religion" as worthless *ipso facto*. [107] Yet at the same time this faith served well the cause of learning among them, for it enabled them to turn their whole attention to the "vast kingdom of the sciences" without ever worrying about the perfect orthodoxy of their conclusions.

The humor, the amusements, and the festivities, finally, that had occupied so large a part of the programs during the Seicento still

[105] Antonio Cocchi to the Botanica, in « Discorso sopra l'istoria naturale » (*Discorsi e lettere*, p. 79); Discorso del can. Gio. Batt. Fraticelli in difesa dell'A. de' Fisiocritici nel quale dimostra che le ricerche fisiche sperimentali conducono alla cognizione di Dio: BCS L.III.1; MS treatise entitled « Se l'innesto del vaiuolo repugni o non repugni alla religione », in Colombaria: Annali 31: « Più favorevole alla carità, ed in conseguenza alla Religione ».

[106] « Sonetto recitato . . . A. della Crusca . . . dal sig. abate Francesco Donato Marini », *Magazzino toscano*, II³ (1771), 164: « Al vasto Regno della scienza volse Giovanni il passo . . . . Ciò ch'è nascosto al frale uman desio / nel basso Mondo, oggi nel Cielo accolto / tutto rimira disvelato in Dio ».

[107] Note Orazio Maccari in Etrusca: *Atti, 31 May 1755.

appear in some academic documents through the first half of the
following century. The game of the *Sibilla,* for instance, retained
its popularity among the Apatisti well after 1748, when Goldoni
listened to an "abbé d'environ quarante ans, gros et gras," who spent
almost an hour showing how the blindfolded child's utterance "paille"
explained the riddle "pourquoi les femmes pleurent plus souvent et
plus facilement que les hommes." [108] Arcadia, indeed, had encouraged
the search for pleasure by associating "the use of the mind" with
"the pleasantness of the climate" and an "inclination to tranquility";
and even the Fisiocritici, in the early years of their existence, flavored
their usual medical and physical dissertations with the consideration
of such questions as "the origin and cause of laughter" and "happiness
(*allegrezza*) as the cause of some deaths." [109]

Certainly the Accademia Etrusca of Cortona surpassed all the
others in gaiety. From 1728 on it held annual celebrations on such
themes as "the ancient Anacletarian feasts intended by the Romans
for applauding the glories of their sovereigns," in which the officially
historical interests of the members might blend with the observance
of, say, the elevation of Francesco Stefano to the imperial throne.
An "istrepitosa sinfonia" generally opened the ceremonies, attended
by all the Cortonese nobility and their guests from out-of-town; the
distribution of printed sonnets and songs then gave way to the recitation of poetry and a formal discourse, sufficiently "learned" to please
"the scholars" and sufficiently witty to avoid "boring the many ladies
present"; and after a musical finale the company stayed on to the
small hours of the morning at a grand ball offered by the governor
"with copious and generous refreshments." [110] Occasionally, indeed,

[108] *Mémoires pour servir à l'histoire de sa vie* (1st ed.; Paris: Duchesne, 1787; here
cited in that of Venice: Vigentini, 1883), p. 417.

[109] Michele Morei, *Memorie istoriche dell'adunanza degli Arcadi* (Rome: Rossi, 1761),
p. 3. Fisiocritici: * Deliberazioni, 15 March 1699 and 18 July 1701.

[110] Etrusca: * Atti, 21 October 1745. Note descriptions in * Atti, 8 January and 17 February 1744; complete accounts for each feast are in Etr 457-59: Feste letterarie degli accademici etruschi. That entitled *Relazione della festa eseguitasi in Cortona nel martedì 14 ot-
tobre 1777 nel celebrarsi in essa le feste erée* was printed by Bellotti in Arezzo, 1777; and
the *Ercole in Cielo* of Stanislao Canovai, « componimento drammatico per le feste erée del-
l'A. E. », by Albizzini in Florence, 1777. Others (19 October 1732, 18 October 1741) in
print are preserved in Etr Notti Coritane, I, 86 f. and Appendix, p. 8. The dissertation
of Gio. Battista Bonsi in the « Tricennali » of May 1757 « sopra le feste e il vantaggio che

such innocent diversions infringed upon the public peace: the Carnival ball of the Rozzi in 1752, for instance, ended with the intervention of the civil authorities because of hurt feelings and drawn swords over a confusion of identity among the masked participants.[111]

In general, however, these activities rapidly disappeared after the turn of the century. In 1710 the Crusca celebrated its last *stravizzo* and thereafter held only a solemn "public assembly" each September; and except for the Colombaria, which recognized the need for "honest relaxation," [112] most of the newer academies omitted the once universal constitutional provisions for entertaining as well as instructing their members. They found nothing "amusing" about botany, agriculture, or, for that matter, any of the other branches of the arts, sciences, letters, and commerce; and even the Arcadian Forzati of Arezzo after 1748 forgot all about the amenable stage settings which Morei still was defending in Rome and in which their fellow *pastori* in Pisa still held their poetical festivities. Only in Cortona and, perhaps, in Pisa, did the academies still attempt after the middle of the century to provide a center for the social life of the community.[113] The members of the Georgofili, the Fisiocritici, and the Agricoltura of Pistoia took themselves and their studies with the utmost seriousness, and they surrounded their activities with the same air of almost pompous solemnity that Gianni and the other Leopoldine ministers were then applying to the affairs of state. Undoubtedly the cause of learning benefited in the long run from the exclusion of conscious frivolity from academic curricula. But the price was high; for it deprived the *eruditi* of the precious art that had so humanized Tuscan letters in the generations between Galileo and Redi — the art, that is, of smiling at themselves.

The intellectual interests of Tuscans had changed, and continued discussion of the old subjects had largely ended in sterility. Anton

apportano le accademie alla repubblica letteraria » « incontrò . . . il gradimento degli eruditi, senza arrecare alcuna noia alle molte dame »: In Colombaria: Annali, 26, with a description of the feast.

[111] Police record addressed to « Sacra Maestà Cesare » (!) in ASS Governatore, filza « Intronati e Rozzi », gives a full report on the incident.

[112] Constitution, Art. XI in Colombaria: Annali 1.

[113] The one notable exception is in Attica: * Statuti, cap. XV.

Filippo Adami in an official report on the press in 1767 warned gravely that "culture can no longer be spread or increased" by the "crowd of inept poetic rhapsodies, empty sermons, pedantic miscellanies, and other miscarriages of the intellect"; printers would either put forth works of "good sense and solid science" or face a well-deserved bankruptcy.[114]   Indeed, the academicians could moan "sweet flower torn from the world" just so many times as the daughter of a noble family entered a fashionable convent; they could sigh "Oh muse what shalt thou do, now that your greatest light is spent" just so many times as the members assembled to commemorate a deceased associate; they could send out half of Olympus to greet new popes, new princes, new bishops; they could sing of nymphs and green bowers just so often — and then such themes began to lose their freshness.   They could continue to multiply treatises on the difference between good and bad, but they soon found it impossible to come to any more meaningful conclusion than that reached long before by their forefathers: that virtue was to be admired and that vice was to be "defeated, despised, rejected, and unbendingly resisted." [115] And most of them came to realize in the course of the Settecento that they would have to find something else to talk about.

[114] Supplica e memoria sulla Stamperia Granducale (1767): ASF Reggenza 778.13: « la folla delle inette rapsodie poetiche, dei verbosi e vacui sermoni, delle farragini pedantesche, e di simili aborti intellettuali, et a dilatare congiuntamente il buon senso, e la scienza solida . . . ».

[115] « La detestazione, e il dispregio, il rigettamento, e la resistenza inflessibile al vizio »: Ildefonso di S. Luigi in *Delizie degli eruditi toscani*, VII, xxii-xxiii.

CHAPTER IV

NATURE, SCIENCE, AND THE COSMOS

In spite of the relatively narrow intellectual interests of the Cinquecento academies, their constitutions, as has been seen, never imposed upon the members any limitation of subject matter other than a certain discretion in matters of religion and politics. At first the new academies of the Settecento attempted specifically to remedy what they held to be vagueness in the curriculum of their predecessors by identifying themselves with a single field of learning. But instead of promoting specialization, the emphasis upon content that became prevalent in the intellectual world after 1700 simply encouraged the application of Salvini's ideal of *enciclopedia* to all the other fields admitted to the body of "learning" during the century. As late as 1748, for instance, Lami could still applaud Cipriano Targioni as an "encyclopedic physician," whose "principal occupation" with medicine, experimental physics, and natural history did not prevent his being able to "speak with good sense" about "all the other fields of learning." Eleven years later the Società Botanica could praise Antonio Cocchi as "an incomparable man," not satisfied merely with perfection in one profession and a superficial acquaintance with all the others, but one "in whom all parts of human knowledge were united"; and in 1756 Guido Savini, sometime president of the Fisiocritici, found nothing contradictory about mixing speculations on "original and absolute Beauty" with problems in logarithms.[1]

The academies in turn had no choice but to follow the "encyclopedic" ambitions of their members, even at the price of revising the instructions of their founders. Eighteen years after Micheli had dedicated the new Società Botanica to the study of the specimens

---

[1] *Novelle letterarie*, IX (1748), 404 (on Targioni); « Elogio di Antonio Cocchi » (in the Botanica, 1759), in Preface to Cocchi, *Discorsi e lettere*, p. vii, Fisiocritici: * Deliberazioni, 16 May 1765 (Savini).

planted in the Florentine Gardens his successors had found that the "love of truth" and the "variety of talents" among them had so extended their vision "to all the parts of natural history and physics" that they could "no longer be satisfied with botany alone" nor with the modest appellation of "botanica"; and both the Forzati of Arezzo and the Ierofili of Livorno eventually enlarged their original programs of Arcadian verse and "the sacred sciences" to include "agrarian arts, physics, moral philosophy, education..., history, art," and "everything comprehended... under the name of philosophy."[2] Especially in the smaller towns, where the literate class was too small in numbers to permit the establishment of several specialized societies, the new charters frankly envisaged the pursuit of all the "sciences, fine arts, and commerce" and admitted that "there is no field of learning which this academy does not cultivate."[3] The three largest academies in the second half of the century tried to meet the needs of intensified research by dividing the members into "classes"; but even this experiment soon floundered, first when the multiplication of classes surpassed the limits originally adopted by the academy as a whole, and second, when the members themselves refused to be bound by their assigned subjects. Accordingly, the Georgofili published sonnets and antiquarian notices in the *Magazzino toscano,* while the Accademia Fiorentina welcomed discourses on agriculture and economics in fulfilment of its constitutional articles on the intimate interdependence of "the study of the classics" and "modern scientific knowledge."[4] Indeed, the vast expansion of what was considered to be "learning" during the century demanded that the academies maintain the "en-

[2] A. Cocchi in *Dissertazioni e lettere scritte sopra varie materie,* (above, chap. ii, note 63), II, 99 (on the Botanica); *Novelle letterarie,* XIII (1752), 19, and XXI (1760), 275; letter of the Ierofili to the Reggenza, 5 December 1764: ASF Reggenza 650.4. Decreti dell'Accademia Aretina, Petr 4: « esercitar la ragione su vari oggetti dell'arte agraria, della fisica, della moral filosofia e dell'educazione relativa ai soggetti e circostanze della Patria, della storia, dell'arte, e di tutto ciò che viene abbracciato oggi giorno sotto il nome di filosofia ».

[3] ASF Reggenza 842.15: Petition of the Attica; Accademia di Varia Letteratura: Petition to the Grand Duke, without date, confirmed 10 September 1755: ASF Reggenza 906.7. Cf. Gori in *Memorie Colombaria,* I, xxi.

[4] E.g., *Magazzino toscano,* I¹ (1770), 131, 155. *Constituzioni della R. Accademia Fiorentina* (Florence: Cambiagi, 1783), Art. VIII (p. 5): « collo studio de' classici, e con i lumi delle moderne cognizioni scientifiche ».

cyclopedism" which few of the individual members could any longer hoped to attain.[5] For only by preserving the "liberty to discuss any subject in any manner whatsoever" could they, in the words of Domenico Maria Manni, "open the way" to the "great things beyond measure" upon which the happiness of society depended.[6]

Unrestricted, then, either by custom or by their charters, those academicians of the Settecento who had grown weary of the usual linguistic and moral questions set out in search of new subjects for their verses and discourses. They quickly noticed that many fields of learning had long enjoyed considerable favor in the Tuscan intellectual tradition, even though they had seldom occupied the attention of academic institutions. The systematic study of botany, for instance, dated from the reign of Cosimo I, who had founded the botanical garden (1557) in Florence that Cosimo III turned over to the Società Botanica in 1718; another had long been kept by the hospital of S. Maria della Scala in Siena, which Gabbrielli, as director, greatly expanded by incorporating with it the private collection of Pier Andrea Mattioli, later his associate in the Fisiocritici; and, indeed, it was the famous Cinquecento naturalist Andrea Cesalpino of Arezzo whose works first inspired the father of the Settecento botanists, Pier Antonio Micheli.[7] Modern astonomy, Leonardo Ximenes pointed out, went back to the fifteenth century when the Florentine sundial was constructed; scientific geography dated from the "first discoverer [of America] and the first inventor of a method... to

[5] Cf. Franco Venturi, *Le origini dell'Enciclopedia* (Rome-Florence-Milan: Edizioni « U », 1946), pp. 30-31.

[6] *Istorica notizia dell'origine e del significato delle Befane* (Lucca: Giusti, 1766), pp. 4-5: « Quella libertà che nell'Accademia degli Apatisti si gode, di ragionarvi di qualunque materia, e in qualunque modo... ha aperto la via, e dato i primi aiuti a cose grandi oltre misura ».

[7] Summary of the history of Tuscan botany in Lami's review of P. A. Micheli, *Catalogus plantarum* (below, note 72), *Novelle letterarie*, XIII (1752), 1-5, 17-22; Crescenzio Vaselli, « Vita di Pirro Maria Gabbrielli », in *Le vite degli arcadi illustri*, II, 35; and Giovanni Targioni Tozzetti, *Notizie della vita e delle opere di Pier'Antonio Micheli, botanico fiorentino*, ed. Adolfo Targioni Tozzetti (Florence: Le Monnier, 1858), p. 51. On Cesalpino, note further Ottaviano Targioni Tozzetti, *Istituzioni botaniche* (Florence: Carlieri 1794), p. 4; a « Vita » in *Magazzino toscano* (Livorno), II (1758), 220-29 and 273-81; and the tribute of the French botanist, J. F. Séguier, whom Maffei brought back to Verona, in his *Plantae Veronenses* (Verona: Typis Seminarii, 1745), p. xiv.

determine longitude," Amerigo Vespucci of Florence; experimental agriculture in modern times, initiated by Giovanni Soderini and the georgic poets of the Cinquecento, had been encouraged by the Medici princes ever since they had transferred their wealth from banking to land; and even most of the instruments, finally, upon which research in these disciplines depended — eyeglasses, the telescope, the clock, the thermometer, the barometer — had been invented, or at least perfected, by Florentines.[8] Such subjects, concluded the Cruscans and the Apatisti, were admirably "Tuscan"; why, then, should they not be introduced into the curriculum of the Tuscan academies?

As a matter of fact, they already had been. Most of the "natural philosophers" of the preceding century had joined at least one of the literary academies, to which some had even communicated their scientific discoveries. Evangelista Torricelli, for instance, had expounded his theories of motion and gravity to the Crusca, and the reflections of Galileo on the three comets of 1618 had been read to the Accademia Fiorentina.[9] To be sure, the speakers generally brought "science" down to the level of their audience, which evidently looked to them more for entertainment than for instruction. As Torricelli compared the strength of materials under pressure to Horatio at the bridge and illustrated the nature of weight by conjur-

---

[8] L. Ximenes, *Del vecchio e nuovo gnomone fiorentino* (cf. *Novelle letterarie*, XIX [1758], 49); *Saggi Etrusca*, IX, xv (on Vespucci), and Soderini, *Tratto della coltivazione delle viti, e del frutto*, republished by D. M. Manni in 1734 from the first edition by F. Giunti in 1600. In general, see Girolamo dei Bardi, *Prospetto sugli avanzamenti delle scienze fisiche in Toscana* (Florence: Tofani, 1808), and note Montelatici in *Atti Georgofili*, Ser. V, Vol. III (1906), 414-15 (cf. above, pp. 83-84). On inventions: D. M. Manni *De florentinis inventis commentarium* (Ferrara, 1731), and *Degli occhiali da naso inventati da Salvino Armati gentiluomo fiorentino* (Florence: Albizzini, 1738). The question of eyeglasses had been long debated. Note Francesco Redi's *Lettera intorno all'invenzione degli occhiali* (Florence: Onofri, 1678) (seal of the Crusca), and the treatise of Carlo Dati, « Inventione degli occhiali, se sia antica o no . . . », published by Giovanni Targioni Tozzetti in his *Notizie degli aggrandimenti delle scienze fisiche accaduti in Toscana nel corso di anni LX del secolo XVII* (also a very valuable source for the history of science) (3 vols.; Florence: Bouchard, 1780), II[1], 49.

[9] Paolo Frisi, *Elogio del Galileo* (Livorno: Enciclopedia, 1775), p. 51. On Torricelli: above, chap. iii, note 48. Other academic lectures by Galileo were published by Ottavio Gigli in his *Studi sulla Divina Commedia di Galileo Galilei, Vincenzo Borghini, ed altri* (Florence: Le Monnier, 1855).

ing up an academy of mermaids on the bottom of the sea, so Bellini
deliberately avoided "exact descriptions" of anatomy for fear of being
"boring and difficult" and "brought to the imagination examples of
a navy..., an orchestra, *scherzi d'acqua,*" and the like" in order to
provoke marvel and delight rather than [a taste for] science in the
minds of his listeners." [10]   But as much as Antonio Cocchi may later
have disapproved of the degradation of science into literary exercises,
these members of the Crusca and the Fiorentina who had been also
natural philosophers at least set a precedent, to which the academicians
of the Settecento would constantly refer.

Indeed, from the turn of the century on, the invocations of the
memory of the Seicento scientists increased continually.   To be sure,
the pride of Tuscans in the accomplishments of their famous compatriots, some of whom were still living in 1700, had never really
waned; but the cloud of ecclesiastical disapproval still hung over
the work of the greatest of them all, Galileo, and by extension over
the work of his disciples as well.   Still, already in 1691 Gabbrielli had
discussed the possibilities of reprinting Galileo's principal treatises;
in 1715 the anonymous editor of Torricelli's *Lezioni* filled the Preface
with praises of "quel pellegrino ingegno," although with reference
exclusively to his discoveries in dynamics and mathematics; and in
the meantime Anton Maria Salvini repeatedly praised him as a master
of style: "not everyone can be a Galileo," he decided, "such sublime
spirits are not born every day." [11]   The name of Galileo had been
conspicuously missing in Rilli's biographical history of the Accademia
Fiorentina of 1700; it was conspicuously present in *Fasti consolari* of
1717, in which Salvino Salvini published the biography — somewhat more eulogistic than accurate — composed in 1654 by Galileo's
pupil, Vincenzo Viviani. [12]

10 Torricelli, *Lezioni accademiche,* pp. 11 and 30; Cocchi, « Prefazione alla prima parte
dei Discorsi di anatomia di L. B. », in Bellini, *Discorsi di anatomia* (cf. Crusca: * Diario
25 January 1697), reprinted in Cocchi, *Discorsi e lettere,* pp. 147 f., here quoted from pp. 172,
170, and 166.   On Bellini, note A. Fabroni in *Historia Accademiae Pisanae,* III, 538-63.

11 Francesco Redi to Gabbrielli, 6 October 1691: Mar Redi 8.140; Torricelli, *Lezioni
accademiche,* Preface, viii (the author in fact was the same Tommaso Buonaventuri who
wrote the Preface for the Crusca edition of the works of Galileo: below, note 13); A. M. Salvini, *Prose toscane,* I, 490.

12 Note Antonio Favaro, « Sulla veridicità del 'Racconto istorico della vita di Galileo'

Finally, in 1718, appeared the long-awaited *Opere,* under the sponsorship of the Crusca and through the efforts chiefly of Benedetto Bresciani and Guido Grandi, who had kept alive an interest in Galilean philosophy at the University of Pisa all during the years following its banishment from the classrooms.[13] True, the editors prudently omitted the still controversial *Dialogue of the Two Systems,* even though it had been published anonymously, and without the obligatory civil and ecclesiastical approbation, just eight years earlier.[14] But Tommaso Buonaventuri's *Prefazione universale,* read by the author to the academy before its publication, stated the purpose clearly: this was more than just a "language text"; it was a manifesto of Galilean science, a call for the study of nature by means of "geometry," its "sole faithful interpreter," and a condemnation of the "opinione del volgo" that so long had obscured the truth.[15] By 1737 the admiration of Galileo had grown into a cult, when the Società Colombaria held a special celebration for the transfer of his bones to Santa Croce, and when one of their members, Giuseppe Bianchini, was moved to compose a "Sonnet... upon seeing the finger of the great Galileo."[16] Thenceforth no academic *prolusione* could possibly win approval without a lengthy tribute to "that immortal man," the "in-

dettato da Vincenzo Viviani », *Archivio storico italiano,* LXXIII[1] (1915), 323-80. Rilli and Salvini cited above, chap. i, note 8.

[13] Galilei, *Opere,* cited above, chap. iii, note 48. On Grandi, note his *Risposta apologetica ... alle opposizioni di A[lessandro] M[archetti] ... si difendono con tale occasione il Galilei ed il Viviani e s'illustrano molte dottrine circa la resistenza de' corpi duri e circa la forza dell'infinito* (Lucca: Frediani, 1712) (Viviani's unfinished commentary on Galileo's theory of resistance was completed by Grandi before its inclusion in the 1718 edition [III, 195 f.]), and Gabriel Maugain, *Étude sur l'évolution intellectuelle de l'Italie de 1657 à 1750 environ* (Paris: Hachette, 1909), p. 171. Cf. Antonio Pacinotti, *Sulla perenità della memoria del Galileo in Pisa* (Pisa, 1893).

[14] *Dialogo di Galileo Galilei linceo ... dove nei congressi di quattro giornate si discorre sopra i due massimi sistemi del mondo, tolomaico e copernicano* (2d ed.; Florence: 1710), with no other name than that of Cellenio Zacclori in the dedication. Possibly, as suggested in the *Biblioteca galileiana* of A. Carli and A. Favaro (Rome: Bencini, 1896), p. 100, it was really printed at Naples, although the only evidence in the text for this hypothesis is the dedication to Carlo Caraffa-Paceco [i.e., Pacheco], duca di Maddaloni. It includes the condemnation and abjuration.

[15] *Opere,* Preface, viii. Cf. Crusca: * Diario, 14 July 1718.

[16] Dorini, *La Società Colombaria* (Florence, 1935), p. 18. Mar A.15, 43; Sonetto al dott. A. F. Gori composto dopo aver veduto il dito del gran Galileo.

exhaustible source of wise and useful speculations";[17] nor could any academic orator afford to neglect the names of his disciples, from Viviani to Torricelli and Borelli, in the roll of his intellectual fore-bears. Accordingly, all the academies, whatever their particular interests among the "sciences," carefully added the Cimento to the usual genealogy of academies descending from Plato's to their own. For all the Tuscans now joined in rendering tribute to their great ancestors, whose names alone showed "how much had been done in this country for the development of physics." [18]

Gradually, then, the members of both the new and the old literary societies began introducing scientific subjects into their usual *lezioni*. They found, for instance, that a long disquisition on the deification of the sun among the ancients might well include notes on the latest calculations of its distance from the earth. After having fully per-suaded his fellow Cruscans of the appropriateness of the sun as a symbol of the Divinity, Giuseppe Averani went on to show how his own experiments with a magnifying glass corroborated the anti-Aristotelian hypotheses of Cicero, Seneca, Manilius, St. Basil, St. John Chysostom, St. Ambrose, St. Justin the Martyr, Copernicus, Tycho Brahe, etc., etc., concerning the nature of the heavens and the source of heat and light.[19] An exposition of the *Divine Comedy,* similarly, could lead to the conclusion that Dante had made some interesting and remarkably accurate astronomical observations, and a careful examination of Theophrast could provide comparisons of certain fossils recently discovered in Switzerland with those mentioned in the ancient text.[20] Thus in 1739 even the Rozzi of Siena modified

[17] P. Stanislao Canovai in *Atti Fisiocritici,* VII, 19: « sorgente inesausta di dotte ed utili speculazioni ».

[18] Note of G. Targioni Tozzetti to a brief index of Cimento writings he prepared in 1760, included with the letter of Giuseppe Scaramucci, 3 April 1789: ASF Reggenza 1054, Fasc. B, No. 5, reporting on the government's (unsucessful) attempt to recover the sixteen MS volumes of notes of the Cimento, mentioned by Targioni Tozzetti in the inclosed note, but subsequently lost. Targioni Tozzetti had already published much of the material in his *Atti e memorie inedite dell'Accademia del Cimento* (3 vols.; Florence: Tofani, 1780).

[19] Giuseppe Averani, *Lezioni toscane,* I, 30 f., and II, lezioni i-iii. See Crusca: *Dia-rio, 30 August 1725.

[20] Carlo Dati in Crusca: *Diario, 4 September 1721 and 17 July 1722; Del Riccio in *Diario, 6 August 1757. Note the tribute of Marco Lastri to Theophrast as an agricultur-alist in the preface to his *Biblioteca georgica,* pp. vi-vii (below, note 114). Theophrast

the usual tone of their festivities by staging an "allegorical conflict between shepherds and farmers" in which "the Academy attempted to illustrate... the application of the Sienese citizenry to the speculative and mechanical sciences." [21]   The intrusion of such new disciplines, to be sure, occasionally required a formal justification — that only a "knowledge of natural truth," for example, could engender "the quiet and the perfection of the heart and the mind." [22]   But in general the blending of science with the more traditional occupations of the academies and the use of the latest astronomical or medical discoveries to illuminate passages from classical, ecclesiastical, and Trecento authors quickly obtained the *placet* of all the academies; and indeed, discourses of this nature were still applauded in the Accademia Fiorentina as late as 1806. [23]

If science provided timely assistance to the academic orators, it rescued the poets from imminent exhaustion.   Again Arcadia stimulated an indigenous process by suggesting the integration of the literary and scientific activities that the authors of *Bacco in Toscana* and *La Bucchereide* had hitherto kept distinctly separate.   Magalotti, Redi, Bellini, and Malpighi had been among the first to follow Crescimbeni into the haunts of the shepherds; and Crescimbeni in turn knew enough of their works to appreciate fully the "marvelous effects in the kingdoms of nature — the mineral, the sensitive, and the vegetable" — that his colleagues were revealing in Siena.   Indeed, the "effects" produced by Boyle's vacuum pump might serve admirably to rid Italian letters once and for all of the kind of "effects" concocted by Marino, especially when arranged graciously into a "fisherman's eclogue." [24]   All other Tuscans agreed; and some fifty

---

as a botanist was a popular theme in the Società Botanica: note Gio. Domenico Civinini, *della storia degli agrumi*... *Lezione accademica* (Florence: Moücke, 1734), identifying certain plants mentioned in Theophrast by their modern names.

[21] Fabiani, *Memoria dell'Accademia dei Rozzi*, p. 67.

[22] A. Cocchi in *Dissertazioni e lettere scritte sopra varie materie*, II, 95. Cf. Fisiocritici: * Deliberazioni, 16 September 1694.

[23] Fiorentina: * Registro, 2 August 1804, *et seq.*, and 27 June 1805, *et seq.* Cf. remarks of Torricelli on St. Augustine and St. Jerome as mathematicians, in *Lezioni accademiche*, p. 64.

[24] Crescimbeni, *L'Arcadia*, p. 204, and his praise of Gabbrielli in a letter of 6 October 1699: BCS L.III.3. Note admission of Alessandro Marchetti on the basis of his scientific

years later they still insisted that "true literature [could] not be dis-
connected from rational philosophy" and that "it is not possible to
arrive at any grade of excellence in poetry without... a thorough
knowledge of the sciences." [25]

The academic versifiers seized upon such subjects with delight.
They adapted the stanzas of Martial and of Anacreon to explanations
of the chemistry of fireflies and sense of smell:

> Quindi il nervo olfattorio dal pericranio scende,
> e alla pituaria i rami suoi distende; [26]

they composed quatrains on the appearance of Jupiter and on its
position among

> Gli ordini, le distanze, e i giri immensi
> de' globi sparsi per l'eterea mole....[27]

They showed how acids and alkalis combined in a solution "as
revealed by the experiments of the most wise and acute Boyle"; they

work: letter to Crescimbeni, 30 September 1695: Arc Lettere a Crescimbeni, II. « Un eloga
pescatoria dove si spiegavano l'esperienza che in fine dell'Accademia si fecero con la macchina pneumatica boiliana, con applauso universale »: Fisiocritici: Deliberazioni, 7 December 1699.

[25] Crusca: * Diario, 16 May 1749; Forzati: Atti e decreti, 9 February 1760.

[26] Dell'odorato e degli odori, capitolo in versi martelliani, by Timagene Balirio, P. A.
della Colonia Alfea [Giovanni Francesco Lami of Siena], recitato nella adunanza...
17 July 1755, verse 19: « Therefore the olfactory nerve descends from the peracranium and
stretches out its roots to the pituitary »: MS appended to Colombaria: Annali 26, together
with his « Sopra i fosfori lampiride ». Note the verses on the circulation of the blood by
Bernardino Perfetti in his Saggi di poesie (1774 ed.), pp. 195-96. One of the most complete
and charming examples in the Esercizio accademico sopra la sfera armillare da farsi pubblicamente nel Collegio de' Padri delle Scuole Pie di Volterra (in which many of the Sepolti
were teachers), 28 August 1755, dedicated to the Governor Francesco Della Rena (Florence:
Giovannelli, 1755), in Colombaria: Annali 1, including a canzone in which « sarà mo-
strato quale sia la cagione del moto nei corpi celesti, esponendo brevemente le quattro ipotesi
più famose del Keplero, del Cartesio, del Leibnizio e del Neuton », an « anaceontica » on
« l'opinione del Gassendo », etc. On scientific poetry in general, see Emilio Bertana, L'Arcadia della scienza, (Parma: Battei, 1890).

[27] « The orders, the distances, the immense orbits of the globes spread through the
aetherial mass... »: Il sistema planetario, poema filosofico, probably by Giuseppe Targi
(Fisiocritici: * Deliberazioni, 12 September 1759), Fis MS Memorie Fisiocritici (1759), no. 9.
Cf. Mattia Damiani, « De' satelliti di Giove, componimento filosofico... detto nell'Accade-
bia de' Sepolti », in his Delle poesie (Florence: Bonducci, 1756-57), I, 24-20.

demonstrated the revolution of the sun about its axis and attributed its heat to the still little-known substance "electricity":

> Al tuo cenno Reale il Sole aggira
> sovra d'un'Asse immobile invisibile
> sua vastissima sfera, e in sen bollendo
> d'un'elettrica fiamma inestinguibile
> di sua lucida vampa irraggia il Cielo...[28]

They expounded Cartesian philosophy in imitations of *De rerum natura,* from which the Fisiocritici had taken the motto for their *impresa;*[29] and they celebrated Newton in pastoral song:

> ...nelle Britanne selve
> vivemmo entrambi, fra la Gente Artoa
> fra cui sovra d'ogn'altra avventurosa
> produr colui fu dato
> che dalla Notte oscura
> in cui giaceva immersa
> l'Alma Natura, e le sue Sante Leggi,
> alto voler de Numi, al dì tradusse...[30]

Such poems may indeed fall somewhat short of what would be considered true poetry in other ages. But the truth is that the academic "poets" valued them less for their aesthetic than for their didactic qualities, in spite of Damiani's solicitude in obtaining Metastasio's acceptance of his *Muse fisiche.* They looked upon rhyme and meter chiefly as a means of transmitting philosophic ideas or specialized information to a wide lay audience in the most pleasant manner possible. Should any of their readers fail to grasp the specific

[28] « At your royal beckoning the sun moves its most vast sphere about an immobile, invisible axis: and boiling within by an inextinguishible electric flame, it sends forth its bright rays throughout the heaven »: Carlo Stendardi, *Inno della natura ad imitazione degl'Inni d'Orfeo* (presented to the Colombaria, 25 May 1763) (Florence: Paperini, 1762) p. v.

[29] Fisiocritici: * Deliberazioni, 13 June 1760; Savini, *Prose e poesie,* pp. 44 f., holding up as an example his fellow Fisiocritico Benedetto Stay and probably referring to his *Philosophiae recentioris versibus traditae libri X* (Rome: Palearini, 1755).

[30] « In the woods of Britain we dwelt, among the Artoan folk, to whom it was given, above all other favors, to produce the One who from night obscure in which she was hidden drew forth to day Alma Natura and her Holy Laws, the high will of the gods »: Damiani, *Delle poesie,* I, 86-88, with other pastoral poems like « Della vicendevole gravità de' corpi, o sia Delle forze attrattrici: Componimento filosofico » (p. 53), « Del suono » (pp. 120-48), « Dell'azione de' corpi celesti » (pp. 20 f.), etc.

"truth" behind any metaphor or image, he need simply glance down at an ample footnote beneath the slender text for a full exposition. Although it may have damaged poetry, then, the presentation of botany, physics, and astronomy in the garb of verse served admirably to popularize among the academicians subjects which, as Bellini had feared, might have bored them in an unadorned prose dissertation.

The literary academies thus made an important contribution, through their publications, their orations, and their verses, to stimulating the interest of the Tuscan public in the natural sciences. But although the blending of literary and scientific themes had facilitated the revival of the Galilean tradition, the scientists of the Settecento eventually arrived at definitions of the nature of natural philosophy that demanded a recognition of its autonomy. Those Cruscans and Intronati, therefore, who were attracted to the new disciplines joined in the foundation of the Accademia dei Fisiocritici and the Società Botanica in the belief that their studies would be better served by institutions independent of those in which they continued to pursue their literary activities. As early as 1695, for instance, a certain Dr. Pietro Bruschieri of Arezzo described to the Fisiocritici how, having been admitted to the Accademia degli Oscuri, but still "adhering to the experimental philosophies, he desired ardently to be included in [their] assembly." [31] Thus the "youth of Tuscany," as Cocchi boasted, was led from the "Regno dell'Eloquenza" secured by their illustrious forefathers "in search of a more sublime and more beautiful knowledge: that of things"; and by 1741 he was willing to excuse Bellini's occasional debasement of anatomy before the Crusca only by conceding an intellectual immaturity among the audiences of 1700 that would be inadmissible twenty years later in the Botanica.[32]

What, then, did the academicians mean by "science" or "natural philosophy"? The definitions they proposed, first of all, almost alway impied a definite concept of the general structure and nature

[31] Fisiocritici: Deliberazioni, 25 June 1695.

[32] « In cerca del saper più sublime e più bello, quale è quel delle cose »: Cocchi, « Discorsi sopra l'uso esterno dell'acqua fredda », Dei discorsi toscani, pp. 76-132, p. 131, and in his preface to the discourses of Bellini, in his Discorsi e lettere, pp. 171 f.

of the universe. At the beginning of the century, to be sure, the
problem of cosmology still remained somewhat uncertain, at least
among the Fisiocritici, who were busy inquiring into the possibility
of knowing external objects, the nature of motion, and the relation
of celestial to terrestrial bodies. They did agree at least on what to
exclude from the sciences — for they repeatedly denounced the attribution of natural effects to such qualities as "attraction," "sympathy,"
or "fear of vacuum." They insisted that "experimental" philosophy
alone could permit an understanding of the physical world; they
ridiculed the "nonsense" in Plutarch and Pliny that unfortunately
had been accepted "for entire centuries by learned men"; and they
found Aristotelian metaphysics to be misleading even for the solution
of such questions as the exact geographical location of the Garden of
Eden.[33]

But just which of the current philosophical systems to adopt was
still an open question. They discussed the atomic theory, first of all,
which Alfonso Marsili had introduced into learned circles as early as
1663 and which may have enjoyed some currency in Tuscany as late
as 1727, when Niccolò Averani brought out an edition, still frequently
cited by historians of philosophy, of the works of Gassendi;[34] they
occasionally spoke of Leibniz, although in terms that suggest only
a secondhand knowledge of his works; and at the same time they

33 Fisiocritici: *Lezioni, 5 July 1691; 13 April 1693; 9 July 1693; 6 September 1694;
19 January 1696; 7 December 1699, et al., some of which are cited in Francesco Spirito,
R. A. dei F: Per la solenne inaugurazione del 250° anno accademico (Siena, 1940). Cf. Set-
timo Corti, « Il pensiero filosofico dei Fisiocritici », Giornale critico della filosofia italiana,
X (1934), 216-22.

34 Alfonso Marsili, Discorso filosofico circa alli atomi, in appendix to Fisiocritici:
*Lezioni, Vol. I. Petri Gassendi ... Opera omnia in sex tomos divisa, curante Nicolao
Averanio advocato florentino (Florence: Tartini & Franchi, 1727); note especially Averani's
Preface and biographical introduction, as well as the « Typographus philosophiae studiosis ».
Antoine Adam cites this edition as evidence of an interest in Gassendi in Florence, but
I have found no other signs of such an interest in Tuscan literature at the time. Ave-
rani's purposes may have been already more historical than scientific. It may be possible that the chief attraction of Gassendi in Tuscany was the frequency of his compliments to Galileo. See Centre Internationale de Synthèse, Pierre Gassendi: Sa vie et
son oeuvre, 1592-1658 (Paris: Michel, 1955), pp. 158, 172-73. There is not a word about
the influence of Gassendi in Italy in the Actes du Congrès du tricentenaire de P. G. (Paris:
Presses Universitaires de France, 1955), except the observation of Adam (pp. 7-8), based
on some remarks by Giannone, that it was probably much stronger in Naples than elsewhere.

looked favorably upon Descartes, whom Pagliai credited in 1698 with the best account of projectiles and whose dichotomy of matter and mind the founder of the Accademia Enciclopedica, Gian Domenico Stellanti, was to defend so vociferously as late as 1743.[35] But they carefully avoided those traditional villains, Epicurus and Democritus, whose names Gabbrielli scratched out of a dissertation in 1694; they shunned any specific commitment to the still suspect heliocentric explanation of planetary motion; and they limited their excursions into cosmological polemics to an abjuration of "systems" in general and to a somewhat vague exaltation of "experimental philosophy." [36]

Gabbrielli's colleagues, indeed, had done well to reserve judgment on such questions; for by the third decade of the century — after the pamphlet wars of Guido Grandi and the scientific publications of the Crusca — they had been so satisfactorily settled in the minds of most Tuscans that some now found the once applauded books written "to combat the philosophy of the Peripatetics and the fallacious method of the ancient schools" rather "boring" (*noiosi*). Even those few of timid conscience who still deferred to less enlightened provincial bishops or superiors did not hesitate to print full, enthusiastic expositions of Copernicus under a cautious qualification of "mere hypothesis." [37]

The academicians believed, then, that the universe consisted of purely quantitative matter arranged at one moment by "the Divine Maker" (*Artefice*) in exact mathematical relationships:

> Bella, perfetta, armonica struttura,
> opra di Magistero alto, e superno

---

[35] [Stellanti], *Le sensazioni e la immaginazione vindicate all'anima umana* (Lucca: Marescandoli, 1743), esp. pp. 19-20. Note A. M. Salvini, *Prose toscane,* I, 372 f., on Benedetto Averani's plans for a new translation of Ptolemy.

[36] Fisiocritici: * Lezioni, 13 April 1694, and Crescimbeni, « Della maniera di filosofare d'Eusifio », *L'Arcadia,* V, 200-201, on Democritus and Epicurus « per quanto comporta la nostra Religione ».

[37] Se l'innesto del vaiuolo . . . , in Colombaria: Annali 31 (above, chap. iii, note 105). Even as late as 1767 Damiani noted (*Delle poesie,* note 3 to p. 87) « Tutto quello, che in questo componimento è stato esposto secondo il sistema copernicano, intendasi detto per ipotesi, e non per tesi ». Similarly the fathers of the Scuole Pie in Volterra (above, note 26) proposed « l'ingegnoso sistema copernicano come semplice ipotesi », but they made no reservations whatever about the satellites of Jupiter or the spots of the sun.

and operating according to a few simple, "eternal, and invariable laws," which so corresponded to the rules of human logic that man, providing his mind was not obscured by artificial impediments, could eventually comprehend them.[38] This universe, moreover, was beneficent — or rather was not hostile to man and could be rendered beneficent simply by being known. The perception of its purely mechanical principles, the academicians thought, had been frustrated throughout the centuries by the "romanzieri della natura" and the metaphysicians in search of "qualities"; and not until just recently had the prophecies of such great forerunners as Bacon and Cesalpino finally been fulfilled by the two geniuses of modern times — first by Galileo, the "divino ingegno" to whom

> Giove disse: A voi tutto rivelo
> tosco Signore: voi meraviglie nove
> farete in Terra, e scoprirete in Cielo;[39]

and then (always in that order) by Newton, whom the academicians, as convinced as ever of the priority of Tuscans in the realm of the sciences, quickly applauded as his worthy successor. Finally their disciples — Malpighi, Redi, Benedetto Averani, and Tournefort — had completed the revelation by demonstrating that the "eternal force, without which nothing was ever done, and which exercises its constant rule over all the arts and the functions of nature," operated in botany and in medicine as well as in physics and in astronomy.[40] The real universe of "quantity and size" had suddenly replaced a false universe of qualities and final causes; and the "systems" devised by the philosophers, concluded Guido Savini before the Fisiocritici, had given way to another which he insisted was no system at all,

---

[38] « Beautiful, perfect, harmonious structure, the work of a high and mighty Author »: A. F. Adami, sonnet iii of « Le prove dimostrative della religione cristiana », in his translation of Pope, *I principi della morale,* 161; and Domenico Bartaloni in *Atti Fisiocritici,* V, 383 (« La Natura è un libro sempre aperto . . . »). Note Carlo Taglini, *Lettera filosofica* (Florence: Manni, 1729), p. 39, on how the « incomparable Galileo » had made further definitions of motion unnecessary.

[39] Savini, *Prose e poesie,* pp. 44-45. Sonnet of P. Pastorini, S.J., of 1737 in L. Cantini, *Iscrizioni che si trovano negli Atti dell'Accademia Colombaria di Firenze* (2 vols.; Florence: Albizzini, 1800-1801), II, 312: « And Jove said. To you I will reveal everything, Tuscan gentleman: you will make new marvels on earth and great discoveries in heaven ».

[40] Note of Cocchi in Bellini, *Discorsi di anatomia,* I, xiv; Manni in Preface to Redi, *Opere,* VI, 14; A. M. Salvini, *Prose toscane,* I, 303 (« In morte di Benedetto Averani »).

and which he supposed to have been perfectly verified by the "method
of experiment" and "the language of reason."[41]

Science, then, meant also a method of investigation. The process
of learning began with doubt, or "Socratic ignorance" as one Cruscan
called it,[42] concerning all previous explanations of natural phenomena
— and the academicians sometimes even exaggerated the importance
of initial doubt by hastily relegating the reports of new discoveries,
like the "fossil carbon of England," along with Lucian's cork-footed
men walking on water to the usual list of "absurd and extravagant
assertions." [43] Careful observation of the particular part of nature
under question, the part of the process known as *esperienze,* or experiment, formed the second step: a great number of apparently
similar phenomena (for instance, the symptoms which Cocchi found
in several anemic patients) were gathered together for examination
and for classification according to common characteristics.[44] In the
third step, then, the individual data thus collected were submitted to
"reason," which abstracted from them hypotheses concerning their
nature and the physical causes of their appearance: thus Cocchi could
conclude that his patients all suffered from the same *vermi cucurbitini* also described by Malpighi, Redi, and Antonio Vallisnieri. Reason moreover, meant not "simple speculations" but "geometry" and
"mathematics"; and when these hypotheses had been checked by a
repetition of the experiment or by further observation of similar
phenomena, it could be concluded that they conformed to a natural
law of universal applicability. The experimental scientist could then
proceed to a final step: that of determining in what way the newly
recognized truth might be made "useful" — how Cocchi's patients

[41] Savini, *Prose e poesie,* p. 57.

[42] Crusca: *Diario, 11 January 1720. The best of the many expositions of the
purposes and methods of science is in the Preface to Vol. V (1774) of the *Atti Fisiocritici.*

[43] Crusca: Diario, 19 August 1758. *Carbone fossile* (coal) was no longer a modern
myth some decades later when Pietro Leopoldo sent Attilio Zuccagni to look for deposits
in the Maremma: note G. Bardi, *Elogio del professore Attilio Zuccagni* (Florence, 1808:
read in the Georgofili, 31 August 1808). The search was rather successful: see Giorgio
Mori, « L'estrazione di minerali nel Granducato di Toscana durante il periodo delle Riforme », *Archivio storico italiano,* CXVI (1958), 207-46 and 322-45.

[44] Address to the Società Botanica of 1734 entitled « Sopra i vermi cucurbitini del-
l'uomo » in *Discorsi e lettere,* p. 139-46.

and all others similarly afflicted thereafter, that is, could be cured of the worms. For the sciences were intended "not to exhibit ingenuity with useless pomp, but to be of service to navigation and manufacturing [arti]." [45]

This method, to be sure, rested upon the assumption that the senses provided the only possible contact with the physical world; that this contact, if carefully guided by mathematical principles, could furnish the mind with a perfect representation of individual natural phenomena; and, finally, that human reason, by examining these data correctly, could arrive at the immutable laws that did in fact govern their existence, motion, and change. The academicians seldom worried about the soundness of this epistemology. It had been implied, after all, in the works of the "divine" Galileo; it had been expressly proclaimed by the Fisiocritici as early as 1691; it had been successfully demonstrated by a host of scientists ever since; and, finally, it had been confirmed theoretically by John Locke, whose works became known, indirectly at least, during the first half of the century. [46] Hence, the "natural philosophers" could comfortably leave the intellectual details to a few metaphysicians like Giovan Gualberto De Soria and accept "this new manner of examining the laws and the phenomena of nature" as the infallible method revealed to men by the Creator in order that they might at last apprehend the order in which He manifested His perfection. [47] "The theories of pure philos-

---

[45] G. Rucellai, *Discorso . . . per le augustissime nozze*, p. 15.

[46] On Locke: Fisiocritici: * Deliberazioni, 28 February 1768. Only one of Locke's works was translated in Tuscany, the *Ragionamento sopra la moneta, l'interesse del denaro, le finanze e il commercio*, by Francesco Pagnini and Angelo Tavanti (Minister of Finance under Pietro Leopoldo) (2 vols.; Florence: Bonducci, 1751); but the rest were well known through French translations, which abound in all the libraries. On the diffusion of Lockean philosophy and epistemology in Tuscany, see Giulio Natali, *Il Settecento* (2 vols.; Milan: Vallardi, 1944), I, 186-87, and Giovanni Gentile, *Studi sul Rinascimento*, 2d ed.; Florence: Sansoni, 1936), pp. 287-89, which emphasizes the important role played by Giovan Gualberto De Soria (especially in his *Opere filosofiche italiane* [Lucca: Benedini, 1750]).

[47] *Atti Fisiocritici*, V (1774), xiii, and Fisiocritici: * Lezioni, 12 February 1692: « Il mondo . . . fu dall'Artefice sovrano esposto all'esame dell'humani [sic] intelletti ». One of the few discourses on cosmography later in the century is the Latin exercise of Daniele Melandri, « Meditationes nonnullae de machina hujus mundi, ejusque conservatione per vires in initio concessus », *Atti Fisiocritici*, V (1774), 1-26.

ophy, which do such honor to our Galilean school, [had] by now become axiomatic."[48]

The unconditional faith that the academicians placed in the Galilean and Newtonian cosmos and in the method by which it had been discovered explains in part some of the peculiarities of the scientific work undertaken by their institutions. It explains first of all their intolerance of any attempt to deduce explanations of particular natural phenomena from intellectually-perceived first principles. Tuscans may have looked to their own Galileo and Torricelli for their arguments rather than to Condillac and Voltaire; but the Age of Reason was as much a "Revolt against Rationalism" in Tuscany as elsewhere in Europe.[49] Not only did they ridicule unceasingly the "chimera" of "innate ideas" and the "Aristotelian phantasms" of Antiquity; they also rejected more recent systems like the "whirlpools dreamed up" by Descartes, although with due appreciation for his contributions to optics and mathematics;[50] and they viewed with the greatest suspicion, in 1767, the latest product of the "furor to reduce everything to simplicity" — the "rather bizarre system," that is, of a certain "modern writer," who, "on the heels of an illustrious French naturalist," was "of the opinion that most animal species [had] descended from ... a very few in very remote times."[51]

This faith explains further the crusading spirit with which the academic scientists attacked all ideas and practices based solely upon

[43] G. Targioni Tozzetti, from his *Alimurgia, o sia Modo di render meno gravi le carestie, proposto per sollievo de' poveri* (Florence: Moücke, 1767), chap. v, reprinted as *Vera natura, causa e tristi effetti della ruggine* by Gabriele Goidànich (Rome: Reale Accademia d'Italia, 1943), here quoted from p. 64.

[49] See Peter Gay, *Voltaire's Politics: The Poet as Realist* (Princeton: Princeton University Press, 1959), pp. 26-27.

[50] In Bellini, *Discorsi di anatomia*, I, xviii. « Sistema delle idee innate essendo una macchina puramente chimerica »: Stendardi, *Inno della natura*, p. 5. On Aristotle: G. Averani in Crusca: * Diario, 30 July 1698; and Gaetano Giorni of Prato in an inaugural address in Ronc 115.Q.III.36. The theses of Louis Berthé de Besaucèle, *Le cartésiens d'Italie: Recherches sur l'influence de la philosophie de Descartes dans l'évolution de la pensée italienne aux XIIe et XIIIe siècles* (Paris: Picard, 1920), must be accepted only with considerable reservations: see review by Calcaterra in *Giornale storico della letteratura italiana*. LXXXII (1923), 380-81. See also G. B. Gerini, « I seguaci di Cartesio in Italia sul finire del secolo XVII e il principio del XVIII », *Nuovo risorgimento*, IX (1899), 426-43.

[51] Savini, *Prose e poesie*, p. 47.

"authority" — whether upon the "fabulous opinions of the ancients" or upon popular tradition; for "botanical observations" had "proved incorrect" not only Vergil's advice to soak seeds in a lime solution but also the belief that garlic planted next to a rose bush would improve the scent of the flowers.[52] It explains similarly the sense of mission among the Fisiocritici, who bade the whole world "come and see" (*venite e vedete!*) the newly discovered wonders.[53] Indeed, the enthusiasm at times burst forth into somewhat extravagant proposals to apply the same method to literature, ethics, law, and even "the knowledge of divine things" — exaggerations that brought the sharp reminders of Pompeo Neri and Giulio de' Mozzi that such disciplines did not necessarily proceed, as did the natural sciences, from the "eternal order of nature."[54] It explains finally the preoccupation of the botanists, physicians, and physicists with the individual and particular, their fascination with minute descriptions of single phenomena or events, the passion with which they amassed and assembled collections of almost everything, from plants to sea shells, and their almost unimaginative reluctance to advance any generalization or to entertain any speculation beyond the immediate data of observation. Thus the Georgofili, for instance, who had declared their "principal purpose" to be "the conservation, correction, and increase of *Tuscan* agriculture" — and not agriculture in general — always hesitated to accept the conclusion and theories of the authors of "the various agricultural treatises published abroad" and therefore "not [necessarily] applicable in this country" until they had been tested on its soil.[55] For the general structure and composition of the

---

[52] Ottaviano Targioni Tozzetti, *Lezioni di agricoltura, specialmente toscana* (4 vols.; Florence: Piatti, 1802-3), I, 96-97. Giovanni Lapi in *Giornale fiorentino di agricoltura,* I (1786), 257 (11 August: Georgofili).

[53] *Atti Fisiocritici,* V (1774), xv.

[54] « Orazione » of Carlo Antonio Andreini, *Magazzino toscano* (Livorno), III (1756), 147 ff. *et seq.* Note criticism of Pompeo Neri in Neri Badia, *Decisiones et responsa juris,* p. 516, and similarly in « Lettera sopra la misura ed il calcolo dei dolori e dei piaceri », *Dissertazioni e lettere scritte sopra varie materie,* I, 114 f., and G. De' Mozzi in Crusca: * Diario, 2 August 1755, all insisting that the methods of mathematics were not necessarily applicable to some other fields, notably, ethics and law. Such opinions agree with that of D'Alembert in the « Discours préliminaire » to the *Encyclopédie* (in the Livorno edition: I, vi).

[55] Georgofili: * Inaugural address (Mar B.I.9.22); Ottaviano Targioni Tozzetti, *Lezioni*

universe and the basic laws according to which it operated were
already known beyond all possibility of doubt; and nothing was left
for the scientists of the Settecento but to complete the description,
begun by Newton and Galileo, of the physical world in all its mani-
fold parts and to search for those truths about nature, as the Fisiocritici constitution of 1767 enjoined, which still remained to be
discovered.[56]

Potentially, then, all nature lay open to their gaze; and quite
naturally, in the generation of Magalotti and the Averanis, they
began where the Cimento had left off: with physics, that is, with
mathematics, and with astronomy. The Fisiocritici constructed a
vacuum pump on the designs of Robert Boyle and a "Torricellian
tube," or mercury barometer, upon which they based their discussions
of weight, gravity, and the density of the atmosphere; and Gabbrielli
had a meridian line drawn across the floor of the hall of the Fisiocritici in the University with which to calculate the motion and the
position of the earth.[57] Several of his colleagues made experiments
in optics, breaking down light rays through a prism and concluding
that they consisted of particles of matter; while Giuseppe Averani
succeeded in condensing sunlight with a parabolic lens (about 4,000
times, he estimated) in such a way that he could observe the crystal-
line structure of diamonds and melt many other precious stones.[58]

di agricoltura, I, iii: « I diversi trattati di agricoltura pubblicati fuori di quì non bene
si conformano al nostro Paese ».

[56] Note *Saggio del Real Gabinetto di Fisica e di Storia Naturale di Firenze* (Rome:
Zampel, 1775), p. 2: « scoprire delle verità finora ignote al Filosofo Newton) », and remarks
of Lorenzo Pignotti, *Elogio storico di Angelo Tavanti* (Florence: Vanni, 1782, here cited
in 2d ed.; Florence: Cecchi, 1846), p. 8.

[57] Fisiocritici: * Lezioni, 27 April 1692, 27 March 1705, etc. Cf. Gabbrielli, *L'eliometro fisiocritico* (above, chap. iii, note 91). Such experimental apparatus was eventually
installed in most Tuscan schools. Note *Gazzetta toscana*, XXVII (1784) under « Castiglion
Fiorentino », 6 July, describing the installation of a « pneumatica » made by Gaetano Cari
of Pistoia in the Collegio at Castiglion Fiorentino. Another *linea meridiana* was drawn
across the floor of the Cathedral at Pescia: Innocenzo Ansaldi, *Descrizione delle sculture,
pitture ed architetture della città e diogesi* [*sic*] *di Pescia* (Bologna, 1772), p. 21 (2d ed.,
Pescia, 1816, *emendata e accresciuta*). The voluminous and somewhat prolix *Storia del
metodo sperimentale in Italia*, by Raffaello Caverni (6 vols.; Florence: Civelli, 1891), gives
sample background information under each of the specific sciences, although unfortunately
few of the chapters extend much beyond 1700.

[58] Fisiocritici: * Lezioni, 9 February 1708, and 1711. G. Averani, *Lezioni toscane*,
II, lezioni ii-iv, and pp. 119 ff.: « Esperienze fatte con lo specchio ustorio ».

In 1706 a letter from William Derham of the Royal Society to Lorenzo Magalotti provoked a number of tests — with the cannons in the Fortezza da Basso in Florence and special pendulum clocks invented for the purpose and placed at various distances on quiet summer nights — which resulted in more accurate determinations of the speed of sound and the rejection of an hypothesis about its variability between northern and southern climes.[59]

Some of these questions, indeed, grew eventually into permanent occupations of the academies: from Gabbrielli's observations on atmospheric pressure in the 1690's, for instance, may have come the interest in meteorology that induced the Fisiocritici, after 1760, to appoint a permanent officer to record the annual rainfall in Siena; and the orations on the mathematical basis of all truth probably inspired the many dissertations on technical points of calculus and solid geometry presented to several of the academies later in the century.[60] But on the whole the principal contributions of Tuscans to these fields after 1700 took place outside the academies, which did little but provide a forum for the consideration or admiration of what had been done elsewhere. For one thing, they lacked the necessary apparatus. Certainly the limitation of astronomy in their sessions to occasional reports sent in by colleagues in the University can, in part, be attributed to their unwillingness or inability, unlike the Istituto delle Scienze of Bologna, to construct anything beyond the modest meridian line of the Fisiocritici; and almost all astronomical research accordingly centered around the observatory that Francesco Stefano was induced to finance at Pisa.[61] Even meteorology

[59] Averani, *Lezioni toscane*, II, xvii and pp. 191 f.: « Esperienze intorno alla natura, e velocità del suono ».

[60] Fisiocritici: * Deliberazioni, 28 March and 29 September 1760; 27 February 1761. *Atti Fisiocritici*, II, 225 f., III, 1 f. & 273 f., *et al.* Meteorological data were published periodically from 1786 to 1788 in Luigi Targioni's *Giornale fiorentino di agricoltura*. Note [L. Ximenes?], *Notizie de' tempi ad uso degli eruditi italiani e de' viaggiatori per l'anno 1752* (Florence: Paperini, 1751) (eclipses, phases of the moon, positions of the planets, etc., all reduced to a « useful » manual). Note also the several mathematical problems published in *Atti Fisiocritici*, VII, and the problems in physics and astronomy of Gregorio Fontana, *Ibid.*, V, 55 ff.

[61] Giuseppe Gaetano Bolletti, *Dell'origine e de' progressi dell'Istituto delle Scienze di Bologna* (Bologna: Volpe, 1767), pp. 98 f., and table 2 of the appendix. Note observations of lunar and solar eclipses presented by Ximenes to the Fisiocritici, * Deliberazioni, 25 June

received its chief impetus from Leonardo Ximenes, who, with the help of the government, established the weather station in Florence that still bears his name, while the most prominent mathematicians, from "le plus savant mathématicien de l'Italie," Guido Grandi, to Ottaviano Cametti and Stanislao Canovai, seldom contributed anything to the academies of which they were members beyond their reflections on purely literary or historical subjects.[62] Physics, on the other hand, undoubtedly suffered from the unqualified acceptance of the formulas of Galileo and the Cimento; and chemistry, long associated with alchemy and hindered by a minsunderstanding of the nature of the elements, did not "rise to the level of an exact science" in Tuscany until the "Revolution" of Lavoisier and until the Fisiocritici began applying it to their experiments in mineralogy.[63] Thus the Cruscans listened attentively to the reports of Averani's experiments and the Fisiocritici watched with fascination the evacuation of cylinders — in order not so much to correct or to further the work of their

1761, and *Atti,* III, 186 and 90. A good, brief history of astronomy in Settecento Tuscany is given in *Giornale de' letterati* (Pisa), I (1771), 204 f., with remarks on the *Observationes siderum habitae Pisis in Specula Academica ab anno LXV vertentis saeculi XVIII ad annum labentem LXIX iussu et auspiciis R. C. Petri Leopoldi M. E. D. in lucem editae* (Pisa: Pizzorni, 1769). Probably the best-known astronomer in Tuscany at the time was Paolo Frisi of Monza, sometime collaborator of the Verri on the *Caffé,* for eight years professor at Pisa, and author, while in Tuscany, of the eulogy of Galileo several times cited in this study.

[62] Note list of experiments, all of which had often been performed before, described by Carlo Alfonso Guadagni in a program for his associates entitled *Indice di esperienze che saranno mostrate ... nel corrente anno MDCCXXXV* — all evidently intended for demonstration alone, not for original research. On Grandi: Charles de Brosses, *Lettres familières écrites d'Italie à quelques amis en 1739 et 1740,* ed. H. Babou (2 vols.; Paris: P. Poulet-Malassis et de Briose, 1858), I, 291. His textbooks, e.g., *Aritmetica pratica* (17400), were widely used in the schools. Of Canovai, note his *Elementi di fisica matematica* (Florence, 1788), his translation of Gardiner (1782) and of J. F. Marie (1802). Of Ottaviano Cametti, *Synopsis trigonometriae planae,* and review by A. Fabroni in *Giornale de' letterati* (Pisa), II (1771), 227-33.

[63] Giuseppe Gazzeri, « Della necessità ed utilità dello studio della chimica » (report to the Georgofili, 5 May 1802), in Ildebrando Imberciadori, *Campagna toscana nel '700* (Florence: Accademia dei Georgofili, 1953), appendix XV, pp. 379 f.; Fisiocritici: * Lezioni, 7 December 1699; *Indice d'esperienze chimiche che saranno mostrate da Niccolò Bianchi ... nel laboratorio della Spezieria del Cignale in Mercato Nuovo per uso di alcuni associati* (Florence: 1752), on which *Novelle letterarie,* XIII (1752), 241. Among the chemical-mineralogical studies of the Fisiocritici: Giuseppe Baldassarri, « Osservazione sopra l'acido vetriuolico trovato naturalmente », *Atti Fisiocritici,* V, 140 f., and Domenico Battini, « Sopra i mezzi di determinare l'esistenza e quantità dell'aria epatica nelle acque minerali », *Ibid.* VII, 69 f.

predecessors as to rejoice in still one more demonstration of a natural law that they already accepted without question. Convinced, therefore, of the fruitlessness of further investigation into the general principles of terrestrial and celestial motion, they turned their attention to those parts of nature apparently more conducive to original research.

No branch of science, certainly, offered more people the opportunity to isolate and identify new "truths" about nature, however small, than did botany. A supposedly infallible system of classification — that of Tournefort — had just replaced, at the turn of the century, the rather disordered miscellanies still carried on in the tradition of Cesalpino and Rivinus; and Tuscan herbologists could now set forth, like Adam and Eve in the Garden, to name each of the plants in their own country according to its position among Tournefort's 10,146 species and 696 genera. No branch, moreover, was more suitable to academic organization, for it dependent upon the co-ordination of great quantities of precise information from many places, and it required capital expenditures beyond the means of a private investigator. No branch, finally, better satisfied the century-old passion of the Florentine nobility for collections of rarities; and several of its most distinguished members — Pandolfo Pandolfini, Carlo Strozzi, Filippo Buonarrotti — were the first, in 1716, to respond to the appeal of a bright young botanist of humble birth, Pier Antonio Micheli, for the formation of the Società Botanica.[64] Indeed, "this and the other natural sciences... enjoyed a universal esteem at the time," as Targioni Tozzetti observed some years later.[65]

Tuscan botany in the Settecento began with Micheli; and it passed into the next century with Ottaviano Targioni Tozzetti, after winning the devotion of such productive students as Giovanni Targioni Tozzetti, the father of Ottaviano, Saverio Manetti, and Michelangiolo Tilli, to mention but the more prominent names. Not all their work, to be sure, can be attributed solely to the initiative of the academies: the garden at Pisa, for instance, of which Tilli was for many years the director, always remained under the immediate

64 Botanica: * Roll.
65 *Notizie della vita e delle opere di Pier Antonio Micheli*, p. 32.

supervision of the University rather than of any autonomous institution.[66] But much of it would have been impossible without the
encouragement and the assistance of their colleagues. Botany required
first of all a tract of land in which a large variety of specimens could
be cultivated and observed — not perhaps the "immense estates"
demanded by Ottaviano,[67] but certainly an extensive and well-tended
garden; and the Società Botanica began by restoring and greatly
expanding the long-neglected Orto Sperimentale in Florence turned
over to it by Cosimo III in 1718. Botany required secondly the union
of practical experience and scientific principles, which the Società
achieved by bringing together the scholars, landlords, and scientists
of the city. Botany finally required experiment; and the Società
assumed the responsibility of collecting and distributing the funds
necessary to supplement the inadequate donations of the Grand Duke
and the University toward the innumerable voyages, which before
1716 had cost Micheli so much fatigue and personal sacrifice.[68].

The effort was rewarding. Some of the members had their
names immortalized in the vegetable world as salvinia, bonarota,
targionia, and tillea.[69]. All of them acquired an intimate knowledge

[66] A. Fabroni, *Historia Academiae Pisanae*, III, 236-39. Note also the brief notices
on Michelangiolo Tilli (1655-1739) by A. F. Gori in Mar A.15.296, and U. Nomi Pesciolini,
« Per la biografia d'uno scienziato . . . , M. T. », *Miscellanea storica della Valdelsa*, XIX
(1911), 1-21.

[67] « Memoria del sig.re dott.re Ottaviano Targioni Tozzetti sulla miglior direzione
e amministrazione dell'Orto Sperimentale . . . » (28 February 1801), from Geo Letture Accad.
fol. III, printed by Imberciadori in *Campagna toscana nel '700*, pp. 377-78.

[68] Besides that of Targioni Tozzetti already cited, see also the *Vita* by A. Cocchi
in his *Discorsi e lettere*, I, 99-137 and in his *Discorsi toscani*, II, 171-238, that by Angelo
Fabroni in *Vitae italorum doctrina excellentium qui saeculis XVII et XVIII floruerunt*
(20 vols.; Pisa: G. Ginesius, 1778-1805), IV, 111-72, and the recent « P.A.M., botanico » of
Giovanni Negri in *Atti della Società Colombaria* (1937-38), pp. 47-67. After the Orto was
ceded to the Georgofili in 1784, regular reports were made by its director to the Academy —
e.g., by Zucchini in 1786 and 1787, *Giornale fiorentino di agricoltura*, I (1786), 125 and 353,
II (1787), 321, etc.

[69] The price for such a favor seems to have been a subscription to Micheli's *Nova
plantarum genera*. Note the letter of Scipione Maffei to A. F. Gori, 4 December 1723:
Mar B.7.18 (now printed in the *Epistolario* of Maffei edited by Celestino Garibotto [2 vols.;
Milan: Giuffrè, 1955], I, 464-65), complaining that he had given money for one of the
plates but that he had yet heard nothing of the publication of the volume. As a matter
of fact, the enormous cost of publication, which Cosmo III had just refused to cover, forced
Micheli to wait another six years until he had received enough private contributions. He

of the varied flora of their country, either through the collections of their associates, like the beautifully illustrated descriptions of the Cortenese presented to the Etrusca by P. Mattia Moneti from 1735 to 1751, or through the public lectures sponsored by the Georgofili in the Orto in the 1780's and 90's.[70] At the same time they became familiar with the works of leading botanists all over Europe, whom their own authors and speakers quoted at length and some of whose works (most notably those of Linnaeus, whose system of classification eventually replaced that of Tournefort) they had published in new editions.[71] Meanwhile, the Tuscan botanists succeeded in introducing many previously unknown foreign plants, in identifying a great number of those native to Tuscany (even too many, perhaps, Albrecht von Haller suspected), and in establishing a new class (graminum) to account for some that had not been observed by Tournefort; and all of this data they carefully recorded in the several immense catalogues compiled from the time of Micheli on.[72]

also hoped that Micheli would change the plate he had paid for in order that a new plant might bear his name; but when Micheli's *Nova plantarum genera juxta Tournefortii methodum disposita* (Florence: Paperini, 1729) finally appeared, Maffei's name was given simply as the donor of the plate of « Glaucoides » and « Anagallidastrum » (Plate XVIII). Other names here cited: Plates LVIII, XV, III, XX.

   70 Etr 400-402. Cf. D. Biagio Bartalini, *Catalogo delle piante che nascono spontaneamente intorno alla città di Siena* (Siena: Rossi, 1776). The lectures of Ottaviano Targioni Tozzetti in the Florentine gardens are published in his *Istituzioni botaniche*. Other information in ASF Archivio Tolomei 191.VII.27 (703): Orto dell'Accademia. The botanical interests of the Colombaria are shown by the regular reports on the Giardino de' Semplici of Pisa, e.g., Annali 26, 21 January 1759 and 27 January 1760.

   71 *Caroli Linnaei Regnum vegetabile iuxta Systema naturae in classes, ordines et genera ab eodem constitutum*, curante Xaverio Manetti (Florence: Viviani, 1756). Manetti was successor of G. Targioni Tozzetti as director of the Orto for the Società Botanica and of Montelatici as secretary of the Georgofili.

   72 Albrecht von Haller (1708-77), *Biblioteca botanica, qua scripta ad rem herbariam facientia a rerum initiis recensentur* (Zurich: Orell, Gessner, Füssli, et Socios, 1771-72), II, 186-87. He calls the *Nova plantarum genera* « nobile & memorabile opus » and Micheli « hortulanus illiteratus [i.e., Salvini had to help him with his Latin] & pauper, sed plantarum spontanearum studiosissimus ». Séguier on the other hand praises Micheli for having enumerated some 1,900 new species (*Plantae Veronenses*, pp. xxviii-xxix, where he speaks of other Tuscan botanists as well). The more important of the catalogues are: P. A. Micheli, *Catalogus plantarum Horti Caesarei Florentini*, ed. G. Targioni Tozzetti (Florence: Paperini, 1748), with a long Preface on Micheli and the Società Botanica; Michelangiolo Tilli, *Catalogus plantarum Horti Pisani* (Florence: Tartini & Franchi, 1723) (of which the Preface pays tribute to the Società Botanica); Attilio Zuccagni, *Synopsis plantarum quae virescunt in Horto Botanico Musei R. Florentini* (Florence, 1806), and Ottaviano Targioni

Much of this work, admittedly, failed to rise above the level of a mere search for curiosities and a taste for the exotic, like that which had inspired the founders of the Orto in the days of Cosimo I and which still attracted enthusiasts for rare American trees at the end of the eighteenth century. Much of it, furthermore, was devoted wholly to replacing colloquial terms with the Latin equivalents, which were then set forth in lists that must have tried even the most patient audiences. But certainly in "certifying and fixing the names of plants," the Tuscan botanists achieved the essential first step in transforming "herbology" into an exact science, from which they correctly insisted "it is impossible to separate nomenclature." [73] On at least two occasions, moreover, they arrived at important discoveries, which won them the applause of their contemporaries and the recognition of posterity. Fungi, first of all, had always been considered a genus apart from other vegetables because of the apparent absence of seeds; Micheli, after years of careful observation, succeeded in overthrowing the traditional classification by accurately demonstrating the process of reproduction by spores. Most plant diseases, secondly, and especially the disastrous grain rust that wrought such havoc on Tuscan harvests, had usually been attributed to the condensation of humidity or the drying of sap on the leaves, even by such outstanding botanists of the age as Haller, Tscharner, and Tillet. Targioni Tozzetti, after untiring investigations in the Orto, proved them to be caused rather by various species of microscopic parasites, whose spores spread through the air. The discoveries of Micheli brought him the salutation of Boerhaave as "without any dispute the prince of the botanists of our age"; those of Targioni Tozzetti, supported by a

Tozzetti, *Catalogo delle piante coltivate nell'Orto Botanico-Agrario detto dei Semplici di Firenze* (Florence, 1841). For the collection of the Società Botanica in Cortona: « Catalogus brevissimus plantarum quae in horto sicco continentur », printed by Giuseppina Dragoni Testi, « Un ignorato centro di studi scientifici del secolo XVIII: La Società Botanica Cortonese e l'opera di Mattia Moneti », *Annuario dell'Accademia Etrusca* (1936-39), pp. 24-26. This article gives a complete history of the little-known society, as well as considerable information on the history of botany in Tuscany. On new plants: Antonio Targioni Tozzetti, *Cenni storici sulla introduzione di varie piante nell'agricoltura ed orticoltura toscana* (Florence: Galileiana, 1853) (unfortunately arranged by plant rather than by year of introduction).

[73] O. Targioni Tozzetti in the *Memoria* cited above, note 67.

precision of observation truly remarkable considering the equipment at his disposal, were finally confirmed by Tulasne and De Bary in the following century, although only recently has he received due credit as the "true precursor of modern phytopathology."[74]

Yet in spite of these noteworthy achievements, no one would have presumed to justify the study of botany apart from its practical utility "for agriculture, for the arts, and principally for medicine."[75] Indeed, it always had been closely associated with, if not dependent upon, the art of "rendering easier the manner of preventing, alleviating, and removing the illnesses of the human body," which several Settecento academies recognized as one of their main concerns.[76] Most of the botanical gardens, after all, still belonged to the public hospitals; and most of the botanists were at the same time practicing physicians. Like botany, medicine could claim many illustrious ancestors, whose works were frequently invoked and passionately defended — from Benivieni, Leonardo da Vinci, and Vesalius to Redi, Marcello Malpighi, and Pietro Andrea Matteoti — even too many, perhaps, in the Seicento, when Benedetto Buommattei complained that there were more practitioners than patients.[77] Like the physical sciences, medicine entered the Settecento with a newly perfected method: the "medicina meccanica" of Lorenzo Bellini, and

[74] Note the tribute to Micheli in James Edward Smith, *A Sketch of a Tour on the Continent in the Years 1786 and 1787* (3 vols.; London: J. Davis, 1793), I, 298, and more recently by Arthur Buller « Micheli and the Discovery of Reproduction in Fungi », a presidential address before the Royal Society of Canada, in *Transactions*, Ser. III, Vol. IX, sect. 4 (Ottawa, 1915), pp. 1-25. On Targioni Tozzetti, see above, note 48, and Introduction of Goidànich to *Vera natura, causa, e tristi effetti della ruggine*. Boerhaave's compliment is transmitted by Scipione Maffei in *Osservazioni letterarie*, III, (1738), 102 f., in a lengthy review of *Nova plantarum genera*. Note also Lastri's experiment in fertilizing fruit trees: *Magazzino toscano*, IV² (1773), 27-36.

[75] O. Targioni Tozzetti, *Istituzioni botaniche*, p. 1.

[76] Medicina: * Piano, Art. I.

[77] Among the reference to the precursors, note *Vita di Pietro Andrea Matteotti* [of Siena — recounting his researches in syphilis], *raccolta delle sue opere da un accademico rozzo* [probably Giuseppe Fabiani] (Siena, 1759), reprinted in the *Elogi degli uomini illustri toscani* (4 vols.; Lucca, 1771-74), III, lx-lxviii. On Bartolomeo Corte (1666-1738), see his *Notizie intorno a' principali ritrovamenti fatti in medicina dagl'Italiani* (Milan, 1718). Redi's medical letters, it will be remembered, were published as Cruscan « language texts » in the 1720's. From Buommattei, « Sopra l'imprese », in *Prose fiorentine*, Parte II, Vol. II (1728), pp. 199.

the program of Giorgio Baglivi (1668-1707) for the pursuit of "experimental medicine," upon which the Accademia di Medicina based its proposed constitution as late as 1778.[78]

Medicine, moreover, blended admirably with the other interests of the academicians, for it permitted them to compare poisons in ancient Massilia to one recently observed in Arezzo, and to point out how the owners of the "magnificent villas that pleasantly adorn the vales and hills of Tuscany" could contribute to the "public health" by imitating the "illustrious Romans [in] introducing these new kinds of fruits and vegetables... so that the people might enjoy the results of their scholarly opulence." But the middle of the century, indeed, no academic eulogy could properly be delivered without a report on the post-mortem of the honored deceased.[79] It its not surprising, therefore, that medicine flourished in Tuscany as it did all over Europe; for Tuscans were conscious of living in the same century with Boerhaave in the Netherlands, with Hoffmann and Kellner in Germany, with Haller in Switzerland, and with Antonio Vallisnieri of Padova, Bartolomeo Corte of Milan, and "His Anatomic Majesty," Gio. Battista Morgagni.[80] Hence, Gabbrielli's appeal in 1690

---

[78] Cocchi, *Discorsi e lettere,* pp. 147, and 175-76 (a purely physical explanation of Micheli's hypochondria), and speech of P. P. Pagliai in Fisiocritici: *Lezioni, 5 July 1691. Many editions of Baglivi's *Opera omnia medico-practica et anatomica* (Lion: Rigaud, 1704) were published during the century, although none in Tuscany. Note Medicina: *Piano, Art. XXIX (on which above, chap. ii, note 16). It is somewhat surprising that Haller scorns Bellini as much as he admires Redi (p. 147), calling him inept, conceited, full of pompous language, « acris in alios, sui laudator »: *Biblioteca medicinae practicae* (Basle, 1766) (which unfortunately goes only up to 1707, hence omits most of this period), p. 124. Settecento Tuscans did not share this harsh opinion. See further, below, note 82.

[79] On Massilia: P. F. V. ([Proposto Filippo Venuti?] the MS is not among his papers at Cortona), in *Magazzino toscano* (Livorno), III (1756), 504-14. Among the many « eulogies », note Fiorentina: *Registro, 22 September 1808.

[80] Note the interesting Introduction of Luigi Belloni to Morgagni, *Gli inventori anatomici del XVI secolo nel carteggio col medico milanese Bartolomeo Corte,* published by the Società Italiana di Anatomia (Milan, 1953), and Davide Giordano, *Giambattista Morgagni* (Torino: Unione Tipografico-editrice, 1941); Bruno Brunelli, *Figure e costumi nella corrispondenza di un medico del Settecento (Antonio Vallisnieri)* (Milano: Mondadori, 1938); Joseph Franchini, « Antonio Vallisnieri on the second centenary of his death », *Annals of Medical History,* N. S. III, Vol. I, pp. 58 f. — among the many studies on Vallisnieri. On medicine elsewhere in Italy, see Henri Bédarida, « La Gazzetta Medica di Parma: Contributo alla storia della medicina nel secolo XVIII », *Archivio storico per le provincie parmensi,* N. S. XXV (1925), 179-222; in Tuscany: Andrea Corsini, *Antonio Cocchi: un erudito del '700* (Milan: Agnelli, 1928).

brought forth an immediate response from the professors and students of the University and of S. Maria della Scala in Siena, who formed most of the academic body of the Fisiocritici in the early years; and observations of "an enormous tumor on the right arm of a girl in the convent of the hospital," of "white blood," and of fevers cured by quinine (*china china*) became a normal part of academic routines.[81]

Experimental medicine began with description; and description in turn began with the human body under normal conditions: the digestive system, the nerves, the heart, and the circulation of the blood. Indeed, perhaps it was the very descriptive character of anatomy, as well as the honorable position of surgery in the university faculties, that account for the frequency with which it appears in the the records of the academies, from the lectures of Bellini in the Crusca to those of Ferdinando Manotti and Pietro Tabarrani in the Fisiocritici.[82] Description then passed to the various irregularities introduced into the body by disease — from swelling and head wounds on patients at S. Maria della Scala to the symptoms of the fever epidemics of 1764 and 1767 [83] — the *istorie mediche,* that is, in which the literature of the age abounds, each devoted to an exact, thorough account of all the visible manifestations over a period of time of one specific affliction in one single person. Frequently, to be sure, these descriptions went somewhat beyond the requirements

[81] Fisiocritici: * Lezioni, 18 January 1694, 13 April and 30 June 1695, and 12 March 1696, *et al.*, and *Discorso letto nell'Accademia Botanica di Cortona* (n.d.), proving among other things that women were indeed the first to concoct poisons among the Romans.

[82] E.g., *Atti Fisiocritici,* II (1763), 175, IV (1771), 233 f., and the large appendix on « le cose anatomiche » of Tabarrini in III (1767). Bellini's most important anatomical work is published in his *Opera omnia,* cum praefatione Joannis Bohnii medicinae doctoris (Venice: Hertz, 1708). Note *idillo* on the operation of the heart, Fisiocritici: * Deliberazioni, 11 December 1759, and the remarks of J. E. Smith on the Sienese anatomists in *A Sketch of a Tour,* I, 327.

[83] Fisiocritici: * Lezioni, 18 January 1694, 13 December 1696, and * Deliberazioni, 31 January 1767 and 9 September 1764 (Pietro Cornachini, already the author of *Lettere fisico-mediche* [Siena: Quinza, 1751], and *Osservazioni alla lettera sopra a certi effetti morbosi attribuiti all'immediata traspirazione* [Quinza, 1749], touching on this subject), and Giovanni Targioni Tozzetti, *Prima raccolta di osservazioni mediche* (Florence: Stamperia Imperiale, 1752). On plagues, attributed to « una mancanza di spirito dell'aria, imbrattata da' corpicciuoli nemici all'umana natura »: Lorenzo Fabbri, *Lezione intorno alla cagione e alla natura della peste* (Florence: Nestenus, 1722), p. 86 (Crusca: * Diario, 20 March 1722).

of pure science. Like Francesco Redi's delightful *consulti* on a "hysteric-hypocondriac affection of a corpulent lady," the several discourses of the Fisiocritici on the effects of drunkenness and on a boy whose hair became curly after a shock seem to have been intended more for entertainment than for instruction, while the lurid reports of "a foetus born with most of its members doubled" presented to the Accademia Etrusca and of "a monstrous foetus recently born near Cesena" published in the *Magazzino toscano* evidently catered more to a delight in horrors than to any desire for illumination.[84]

A few more responsible authors attempted to justify these exaggerations — either by tracing "the origin and progress of the sciences" to "a certain natural pleasure in searching out the difficult and the marvelous," or by attributing to "our great Galileo" the observation "that human intellects usually turn toward marvels and excesses" and then applauding as his most faithful followers those who "fix their attention on ... the most strange and defective objects that nature can show." [85] But others frankly admitted that "physics and natural history" could also furnish innumerable "objects of pleasure," and they sought to "enrich the history of monsters" with illustrated nightmares chiefly "to satisfy those who are curious about nature." [86] It may be, indeed, that the perfect order of the Galilean-Newtonian universe at times became a bit tedious, or at least that it engendered

[84] Redi, *Opere*, VI, 90; Fisiocritici: * Lezioni, 30 June and 7 July 1695; Luigi Stampini, *Descrizione d'un feto umano nato colla maggior parte delle membra raddoppiate* (Rome: Stampini, 1749), presented to the Accademia Etrusca (* Atti, 7 May 1749) and appended to the volume of the Notti Coritane for that year; « Osservazioni sopra un feto mostruoso ultimamente stato partorito nelle vicinanze della città di Cesena », *Magazzino toscano*, I¹ (1770), 152 ff.

[85] *Giornale de' letterati* (Pisa), XXIX (1778), 98: « L'origine ed i progressi delle scienze umane son dovuti ... alla curiosità ... e ad un certo natural piacere di andare in traccia del difficile e del maraviglioso »; Giovanni Gentili, *Relazione di un individuo della specie umana fino all'età di anni 13 creduto femmina e poi riconosciuto legalmente per maschio* (Florence: Della Rovere, 1782), Introduction: « Si rivolgono gli intelletti umani, ove si scuopre la maraviglia, e l'eccesso ... e si fissano molto sopra gli oggetti i più difettosi ... che la natura ci mette in mostra » (pp. 3-4).

[86] In « Istoria di un mostro raniforme, scritta in forma di lettera dall'abate Carlo Girolami [of the Rozzi] al sig. cav. Antonio Vallisnieri », 23 March 1726, in Calogerà, *Raccolta d'opuscoli*, II, 471-90. Cf. comments of W. Binni, *Preromanticismo italiano* (Naples: Edizioni Scientifiche Italiane, 1947), pp. 172 f., on horror in the theater and in literature.

a particular passion for any sign that "Nature had been playing tricks" (*scherzato*). For while the academicians contemplated the harmony of the cosmos with awe and contentment, they seized with delight upon the exceptions, the inexplicable spectacles, the uncommon sights, the horrors, and the "terrible, violent forces and contrasts of the elements among themselves" that apparently contradicted its basic principles.[87] Thus medical histories, especially when adorned with elaborate, costly plates, took the place, in the Settecento, of the romantic travel literature of the sixteenth and seventeenth centuries and of the mystery stories and science fiction of the nineteenth and twentieth. Nevertheless, they performed an invaluable service to the growth of medicine, particularly in its years of infancy; for only by accumulating a vast quantity of specific data on the external effects of various diseases would physicians be able to diagnose correctly the new cases brought before them.

From diagnosis, then, experimental medicine proceeded to the cure, first by isolating the supposed causes of a disease and then by attempting to remove them. Admittedly, many of the prescriptions are somewhat disturbing to modern sensitivities, for Settecento physicians applied the experimental method somewhat freely. To an "illustrious lady" suffering from a "bilious matter held in the intestines" (probably a uterine tumor), for instance, Targioni Tozzeti prescribed first pulverized mother of pearl mixed with nut-water, then a broth of pigeons, then dried orange flowers, then a few spoonfuls of distilled water from the ashes of small Neapolitan lemons. When still he obtained no palliative consequences, he tried a broth of carbonized poppies, and behold! the patient at least stopped coughing. Here, he concluded, was at last the proper cure for this part of the ailment, as proved by "experiment," and he carefully marked it down in the "medical history" for the guidance of his fellow practitioners. Little wonder, then, that after several weeks of bleedings, purges, *passate d'acqua,* leeches, and compresses of

---

[87] Remark of Francesco Caluri in « Relazione sopra un preteso ermafrodito ». *Atti Fisiocritici,* V, 167-202, p. 169, and *Dei vulcani o monti ignivomi più noti . . . Osservazioni fisiche e notizie istoriche di uomini insigni di vari tempi* (Livorno: Calderoni & Faina, 1779), II, v: « Questi troppo terribili, e violenti sforzi, e contrasti degli elementi fra loro . . . ».

oatmush, patients usually found the only really efficacious medicine to be the Last Sacraments; but they could at least comfort themselves with the thought that the post-mortem on their bodies would be read all over Italy.[88] Nevertheless, even these recipes represent a considerable advance over the speculations on the balancing of humors and the "contraction and withdrawal of the animating spirit" in sleep, in which a few academicians still indulged as late as 1752.[89] The Settecento pathologists, moreover, cannot be held responsible for a knowledge of bacteria and psychology a century before Pasteur and Freud; nor can they be blamed for failing to wipe out malaria a century and a half before DDT finally rid the Maremma of its last mosquito. And even the most extravagant formula, after all, was at least drawn from "experience" and not from a metaphysical principle; while the encouragement of vegetable diets, cold baths, and the nursing of children by their mothers must have had a salutary effect, considering the customs of the time, even if the reasons were taken from Pythagoras rather than from science.[90]

The accomplishment of the physicians in the academies was first of all negative — that is, like Alessandro Bicchierai, one of the sponsors of the Accademia di Medicina, they consciously "banished

[88] Most of these examples are taken from the works of Cocchi and Targioni Tozzetti, especially the description by the letter of « un tumore follicolato vastissimo, trovato nell'ovario sinistro d'una donna » in *Prima raccolta di osservazioni mediche*.

[89] Fisiocritici: *Lezioni, 28 September 1692, 27 April and 28 September 1792; Lorenzo Fabbri in the Crusca: *Diario, 25 September 1751 and 14 March 1752; and further in the question of *il sonno*, Fisiocritici: *Deliberazioni, 12 September 1759. Note also: « Dissertazione recitata nella Sacra Accademia Fiorentina dal D. G. P. nella quale si esamina se le forze della immaginazione possano alcuna volta nelle malattie nostre la perduta sanità restituirci », *Dissertazioni e lettere scritte sopra varie materie*, II (1750), 131 f. It should be noted further that these prescriptions are no more extravagant than those written by the best physicians in England at the time, many of which are described in chap. x of Lester S. King, *The Medical World of the Eighteenth Century* (Chicago: University of Chicago Press, 1958).

[90] « Dissertazione sulle funeste conseguenze della nutrice mercenaria » translated by an « Accademico fiorentino » in *Magazzino toscano*, II[4] (1772), 65-88. Cocchi, *Del vitto pittagorico per uso della medicina* (Florence: Moücke, 1743) (Crusca: *Diario, 30 August 1743, and Etrusca: *Atti, 12 April 1744), and « Sopra l'uso esterno appresso gli antichi dell'acqua fredda sul corpo umano », *Saggi Etrusca*, II (2d ed., 1742), No. X; and Giovanni Bianchi of Rimini, sometime professor at Siena, *Se il vitto pittagorico di soli vegetabili sia giovevole di conservare la sanità e per la cura d'alcune malattie* (Venice: Pasquali, 1752). Passage from Cocchi, *Discorsi toscani*, II, 84.

from the clinic so many useless and harmful remedies." [91]   They gravely pointed out the dangerous effects of opium, especially when administered to children; they proved the absurdity of tracing epidemics to bad sausages, overeating, or freshly cut flax; and they finally succeeded, by the end of the century, in removing bleeding from normal medical prescriptions, even though its administration by such outstanding physicians as Cocchi and Targoni Tozzetti apparently gave patients some relief.[92]

But the accomplishment was also positive: they clearly recognized, for instance, the importance of preventive medicine, and they established rules of cleanliness and hygiene in the public hospials most of which would still be acceptable today. They successfully introduced the use of mercury, especially in the treatment of syphilis, after considerable hesitation over its possible poisonous results. They confirmed some of the beneficial effects long attributed to the mineral waters for which several Tuscan springs are famous even today. Finally, after the researches of Targioni Tozzetti, they fully realized that the ever recurring fever epidemics in the Pisano and the Valdinievole would cease only when reforestation and drainage canals had dried up the swamps, even if they failed to understand just how the "noxious exhalations" could lead to death.[93]

[91] G. G. Uccelli, *Elogio di Alessandro Bicchierai* (Fiorentina [1783]: * Registro, 27 April 1797), p. 42: « aver banditi dalla sua clinica tanti inutili, e dannosi rimedi . . . ».

[92] Lorenzo Fabbri, *De somno, de medicamentis somniferis, et de natura hominis in somno,* with the Italian version (Lucca: Benedini, 1753), p. 31 (Crusca: * Diario, 25 September 1751, *et seq.*).   G. Targioni Tozzetti, *Ragionamento . . . sopra le cause e sopra i remedi dell'insalubrità d'aria nella Valdinievole* (Florence: Stamperia Imperiale, 1761), Part V, pp. 361 f. Fisiocritici: * Lezioni, 12 September 1679 and 19 January 1702 (on bleeding).

[93] Note instructions of Cocchi in « Della tabe polmonare » in *Discorsi e lettere,* pp. 255 f., and Relazione dello spedale di S. Maria Nuova . . . 23 December 1742, in ASF Reggenza 412; Marco Covoni, *Regolamento dei RR. Spedali di S. Maria Nuova e di Bonifazio* (Florence, 1789); and finally, *Rapporto sopra lo stato degli spedali del Granducato di Toscana* (Florence, 1818). On mercury, L. Fabbri, *De somno,* pp. 1 f., and *Dell'uso del mercurio sempre temerario in medicina* (Colonia [Florence], 1749); Giuseppe Maria Saverio Bertini, *Dell'uso esterno e interno del mercurio* (in the Botanica, September 1744) (Florence: Giovannelli, 1744); and Roberto Gherardi, *Riflessioni sopra l'uso del mercurio nella medicina* (Lucca: Benedini, 1751). On mineral springs: Alessandro Bicchierai, *Dei bagni di Montecatini* (where Pietro Leopoldo built an *établissement* for the sick) (Florence: Cambiagi, 1788); Giuseppe Baldassarri, *Delle acque minerali di Chianciano* (Siena: Bindi, 1756), and *Osservazioni ed esperienze intorno al Bagno di Montalceto* (Bindi, 1756); A. Cocchi, *Dei bagni*

Over one of the more deadly scourges of mankind, moreover, they were almost triumphant. Tuscan physicians were among the first in all Europe to respond to the appeal of Condamine in 1754; by the time of his missionary voyage to Rome a year and a half later, the professors in the Florentine and Sienese hospitals, assisted by *medici condotti* (state-employed physicians) from all over the country, had already begun the inoculations against smallpox that were to be fully described in the first volume of the *Atti* of the Fisiocritici. The still "experimental" nature of the inoculations, to be sure, was sufficient to spread terror among the population: those conducted by the rector of the hospital, for instance, were proclaimed a great success because of the sixteen persons who submitted to the usual dreadful "purga" and an inoculation by incision on 19 August 1756 and then suffered seventeen days of face boils and fever, only one actually died. But let the timid be warned: two out of seven natural cases reported at the same time ended fatally, and the other five experienced intense suffering. The propaganda was so strong and the consent of the medical profession, backed up by all the academies, was so universal that any opposition melted away.[94] All conditions of men, from the Crown Prince to peasants, submitted quietly to the operation

---

di Pisa (Florence: Stamperia Imperiale, 1750); *Atti Fisiocritici*, II, 79 f. and 100 f.; VI, 253 f., and 330 f.; VIII, 109 f. and 192 f., *et al*. On swamps and fevers: Targioni Tozzetti in *Ragionamento* (above, note 92), pp. 107-110; *Atti Fisiocritici*, IV, 357; and Felice Fontana, *Ricerche fisiche sopra l'aria fissa* (Florence: Cambiagi, 1775).

[94] In general Arnold H. Rowbothan, « The Philosophes and the Propaganda for Inoculation of Smallpox in Eighteenth-Century France », *University of California Publications in Modern Philology*, XVIII (1935), 265-90; Umberto Benassi, « Per la storia del progresso italiano nel Settecento: l'inoculazione del vaiuolo principalmente nei ducati parmensi », *Bollettino storico piacentino*, XVII (1922), 3-19; and Andrea Corsini, *I primi innesti pubblici del vaiolo in Firenze* (Florence, 1912). The earliest academic discussion of small pox is in Fisiocritici: * Lezioni, 18 January 1692; Condamine's *Memoria sull'inoculazione del vaiuolo* of 24 April 1754 was translated and published in *Magazzino toscano* (Livorno), II (1755), 74-81, 145-62, and 193-204. The Florentine experiments are described in G. Targioni Tozzetti, *Relazioni d'innesti di vajuolo fatto in Firenze nell'autunno dell'anno 1757* (Florence: Bonducci, 1757); those in Siena in the entire *Atti Fisiocritici*, I (1760). Pompeo Neri, in reporting to the Grand Duke on the publication of this volume, noted that « in Siena, which is a small city, many more experiments in inoculation have been made in proportion to the population than in any other place in Italy »: ASF Reggenza 669.23. Pietro Verri also praised the work of the Fisiocritici in his « Sull'innesto del vaiuolo », *Opere varie*, ed. N. Valeri (Florence: Le Monnier, 1947), pp. 214 f.

that apparently proved once and for all the efficacy of Galilean methods when applied to the care of the human body.

If medicine, then, justified the study of botany by putting its methods and discoveries to practical use, both fields joined, in the Settecento, in engendering a completely new branch of science. For it was none other than the director of the Società Botanica, Micheli, who, while searching for plants at Radicofani, first noticed the striking resemblance of the rocky terrain of Mt. Amiata to that around Vesuvius and discovered thereby the phenomenon of extinct volcanoes. His own collection of shells and rocks inspired his successor and heir, Targioni Tozzetti, to broaden the scope of the specific commissions for the botanical gardens; and the voluminous *Voyages in Various Parts of Tuscany* finally transformed the traditional Italian taste for "picturesque" and artistic details of distant lands into a dedication to "natural history." [95] By 1754 the new science had received a complete program of research, when Targioni Tozzetti, following the example of Antonio Vallisnieri of Modena, called for the careful and systematic description from firsthand investigations — and not merely random, if perceptive observations in the manner of Aeneas Sylvius Piccolomini or Pietro Bembo — of the flora, fauna, soil, mineral deposits, water courses, climate, and mountain chains of every corner of the country. The "scientific travelers" set forth, guided by newly published textbooks on "what to look for on voyages in relation to geography, natural history, and commerce" and inspired by the works of the principal English and French naturalists of the

[95] G. Targino Tozzetti, *Relazioni d'alcuni viaggi* (above, chap. iii, note 93; see also his speech on presenting Vol. III (lst. ed.) to the Crusca: * Diario, 20 May 1752). On Micheli's discoveries at Mt. Amiati: G. Targioni Tozzetti, « Dei monti ignovomi della Toscana », in *Dei vulcani, o monti ignovomi*, Vol. I, no. 1. In general, see the interesting selections from original texts published by Francesco Rodolico, *La Toscana descritta dai naturalisti del Settecento* (Florence: Le Monnier, 1945), with an excellent introduction; chap. viii (on Spallanzini) of Pietro Vaccari, *Storia dell'Università di Pavia* (Pavia: Il Portale, 1948); and the texts and introduction in *Letterati, memorialisti e viaggiatori del Settecento*, ed. Ettore Bonora (Milan: Ricciardi, 1951). Elsewhere in Italy, to be sure, natural history was somewhat older as a discipline, thanks to Marcello Malpighi, Luigi Marsigli, Antonio Vallisnieri, and others, much of which is described by Carlo Calcaterra in chaps. vi-vii of *Alma mater studiorum*.

time, to discover the nature of the country in which they lived, preferably that part of it in the immediate environs.[96]

Many of their findings were indeed revolutionary. By 1747 the large number of fossil shells observed in the surroundings of Florence had aroused the curiosity even of the Accademia della Crusca. Where did they come from? There was only one way to find out, as Targioni Tozzetti explained in 1749: to reason backward in time from "the present situation of the same [shells] and from an examination of the quality and nature of the terrain." Perhaps, thought Giuseppe Dini, subterranean waters brought them in from the sea, whence the heat of the earth forced them to the surface. Or more probably, he continued, since the sea had actually receded in historical time from the Port of Pisa, all Tuscany had once been under water.[97] Then in 1751, Targioni Tozzetti reported to have seen in the upper Valdarno not only shells, but petrified wood, reindeer horns, and elephant tusks: Tuscany, evidently, had not always enjoyed a temperate climate but had once been both arctic and tropical.[98] Within a few years the Sienese naturalist Giuseppe Baldassarri had found further evidence for both the volcanic and maritime past of Tuscany in a chemistry laboratory: by placing ground fossil shells in a solution of "acido marino" (HCl) he precipitated a "sal neutro deliquescente," different from that produced with "acido del nitroso"

[96] G. Targioni Tozzetti, *Prodromo della corografia e della topografia fisica della Toscana* (Florence, 1754), of which parts are published in F. Rodolico, *op. cit.*, 320-24; *Riflessioni sopra l'utilità dei viaggi*, tr. from French by Giuseppe Antonio Luigi Noger (?) (Pisa: Pieraccini, 1785); « Saggio d'istruzioni per viaggiare utilmente, dove si vede ciò che si dee esaminare nei viaggi, per rapporto alla geografia, all'istoria naturale, al commercio », *Magazzino toscano* (Livorno), I (1754), 394-99, 433-42, and 463-617. Note review of Buffon's *Oeuvres complètes* in *Giornale letterario di Siena*, I (1776), xxxiii.

[97] Crusca: * Diario, 28 August 1747, 23 August 1749, and the descriptions by Gaspero Cerati of his trips through Lombardy and the Veneto, 9 September 1762, *et seq.* A special section of the Notti Coritane was devoted to « storia naturale ». The speculation on subterranean waters formed part of a long discussion « ne' nostri tempi con tanto calore per l'Italia agitata » of the origin of springs and fountains — see Carlo Girolami, accademico rozzo, « Istoria di una sorgente... » (26 August 1726), in Calogerà, *Raccolta d'opuscoli*, V, 89-112 (here quoted from p. 91).

[98] Crusca: * Diario, 11 September 1751.

(HNO$_3$), although identical to that found in the tufa outside the city.[99]

But beyond this the Tuscan naturalists proceeded with caution. Either they retreated into pure conchology, explaining how one fossil shell had got inside another but not why the pair had been found in the mountains of Elba, or else they accepted Targioni Tozzetti's simple exclamation: "Where has all the water gone? wise is he who can explain it!" Always they heeded Baldassarri's warning that scientific truth would emerge only from sufficient evidence and that neither the fossilized jawbones of the Senese nor the vertebrae of tropical animals of Siberia, although suggestive of considerable climatic changes on the earth's surface, would in any way justify "totally imaginary and hypothetical systems." The academicians simply recorded the "fact" of a geological evolution over a time span far greater than six millenia, without ever becoming particularly excited or upset over the idea, and without ever reflecting upon its possible incompatibility with biblical chronology.[100] Their faith in the harmony of religious orthodoxy and science remained unshaken; and while they closed their minds to the somewhat more daring deductions then being made from similar evidence beyond the Alps, they quietly dismissed with a smile the occasional attacks by a few bigots at home who insisted that all "the New Philosophy" would inevitably lead them to heresy.[101]

[99] « Considerazioni sopra i principj costitutivi della pietra amianto », *Atti Fisiocritici*, IV, 217 f. See further Giuseppe Baldassarri in *Ibid.*, II, 3 f., and his *Osservazioni ed esperienze intorno al Bagno di Montalceto* (Siena, 1779) (on which: *Giornale de' letterati* [Pisa], XXXVII [1780], 278 f.), and Paolo Mascagni, *Dei lagoni del Senese e del Volterrano, Commentario . . . al sig. Francesco Caluri* (Siena, 1779).

[100] Francesco Caluri in *Atti Fisiocritici*, III, 262 f.; Baldassarri, « Descrizione della mascella fossile straordinaria trovata nel territorio senese », *ibid.*, 243 f., and Targioni Tozzetti, *Relazioni d'alcuni viaggi* (2d ed.), III, 45, cited by F. Rodolico, *op. cit.*, p. 27. Compare the very different reaction to these and similar discoveries in France at the time described by Daniel Mornet, *Les sciences de la nature en France au XVIIIe siècle* (Paris: Colin, 1911), esp. Part. I. One way out of the evidence for climatic changes was suggested by Gaetano Palloni in the Georgofili. Climate, he proposed, was a function of habitation and cultivation; thus settlement and agriculture had changed Germany from the frozen waste it was in Caesar's time to the comfortable, temperate country of today (speech of 5 August 1795 in *Atti Georgofili*, III, 282 f.). But none of the better naturalists ever suggested such a theory.

[101] Note review of *Il disinganno dei sistemi delle nuove filosofie* (« . . . the systems of the new philosophies badly deduced from the much-flaunted natural law, and here smashed

Meanwhile the academicians acquired a detailed knowledge of the physical character of their country, as the naturalists appended detailed charts to their publications and academic reports and as they prepared for the government greatly improved maps of Tuscany.[102] At the same time, they concluded from the mutations of the terrain in the past that they themselves might effect changes in the future and they turned again to problems of hydrostatics which had interested most of their predecessors, from Leonardo to Torricelli, and which now had become especially urgent as Pietro Leopoldo attempted to reduce the swampy plains to cultivation.[103] Some of the proposals, it is true, were a bit bizarre — like that of the Venetian engineer Antonio Belloni, who proposed to the Georgofili in 1777 that the beneficent "system of nature" be restored by tearing down the levies and letting the rivers find their "natural" course. But certainly Targioni Tozzetti clearly perceived that flood control depended ultimately upon the replanting of the forests so ruinously destroyed by centuries of misuse; while the researches of Perelli and Ximenes into the measurement of water velocity made possible the construction of the dykes and canals that have left a permanent mark on the Maremman and Pisan landscapes.[104] Such projects may have far

down by indisputable Catholic doctrine . . . Ironic arguments addressed to the scientific philosophers and free thinkers ») (Florence, 1778), in *Giornale fiorentino istorico politico letterario,* I (1778), 198.

[102] An excellent reproduction of one of the many maps (1773) preserved in ASF (e.g., Reggenza 985.4, and 780.53: Memoria indirizzata a . . . Botta Adorno [Governor of Tuscany for Francesco Stefano] intorno alla costruzione delle nuova carta geografica) is appended to Imberciadori, *La campagna toscana nel '700*; the progress in cartography can be seen by comparing it to the one of 1547 reproduced in the frontispiece. Cf. Attilio Mori, « Studi trattative e proposte per la costituzione di una carta geografica della Toscana . . . », *Archivio storico italiano,* XXXV (1905), 369-424. This work was carried much further in the following century: see Giuseppe Parenti in *Rassegna storica toscana,* IV (1958), 63-65.

[103] *Raccolta d'autori che trattano del moto dell'acque* (3 vols.; Florence, 1723; 2 vols. added: 1765-66). Note the *Avviso* of G. B. Clemente Nelli in *Novelle letterarie,* XVII (1756), 481-83, offering to « quegl'ingegneri, che vanno applicandosi all'idrostatica » the use of his collection of « una non piccola quantità di relazioni sopra simili materie . . . de' famosi mattematici [*sic*] Galileo Galilei, D. Benedetto Castelli, Vincenzo Viviani, D. Guido Grandi, ed altri geometri italiani . . . ».

[104] Georgofili problem for 1777 with the others listed in *Atti,* I (1791), 36 f. A. Belloni, *Memoria idrometrica sopra l'Arno* (which won the prize) (Florence: Stecchi, 1778), criticized by *Giornale fiorentino istorico politico letterario,* I (1778), 313-16, and especially by Francesco Puccinelli, *Analisi della memoria idrometrica sopra l'Arno pubblicata in Fi-*

exceeded the technical and financial resources of Settecento Tuscany; but at least the naturalists proved the "utility" of their discipline by holding forth the promise of restoring the terrain from the ravages of offended nature, just as medicine saved human lives from the menace of smallpox.[105]

On occasions, to be sure, the academicians forgot all about their pledges to public utility and practicality and succumbed to the popular passion for freaks and *scherzi della natura* which swept the country in the second half of the century:

> Un saltimbanco in piazza
> facea vedere al popolo
> un animale d'Affrica (*sic*)
> di sconosciuta razza...
>
> A bocca spalancata
> ed inarcando il ciglio
> la plebe ignorantissima
> ascolta, ammira, e guata....[106]

The "eruditi" might scoff at the "pardonable vanity of the public" for "columns of perpetual motion" and scorn the *ingegno perspicace,* "neither philosopher, nor physicist, nor man of letters," who turned his scientific jabber into handsome profits; but alas! they themselves

renze l'anno 1778 (Brescia: Masi, 1778).   Belloni is somewhat better known for his *Analisi del progetto del sig. colonnello Lorgna modificato dai signori matematici ab. Frisi, ab. Ximenes . . . sopra la regolazione del fiume Brenta* (1783).   L. Ximenes on hydrometry in *Atti Fisiocritici*, III, 17 f., and VII, 1-18, and *Della fisica riduzione della Maremma senese* (Florence: Moücke, 1769), esp. pp. 157 f.   His prize essay on river dykes of 1777 in published in *Atti Georgofili*, I (1791), 196 f.   Note *Giornale de' letterati* (Pisa), XXX (1778), 52-74, on the hydrostatics textbook of Ottaviano Cametti, *Mechanica fluidorum* (Florence, 1777).   On the work of Pompeo Neri and Tommaso Perelli on the control of the Arno: Antonio Zobi, *Storia civile della Toscana dal 1737 al 1838* (Florence: Molini, 1850-52), I, 115, and A. Fabroni, « Elogio di Tommaso Perelli », *Giornale de' letterati* (Pisa), LIII (1784), 1-65; on the hydrostatics of Giovanni Bottari: G. Gasparoni, *Di alcune fonti essenziali per la storia della cultura in Toscana* (Florence: Chiari, 1936), pp. 22-24.

[105] « Chi ama dunque la giustizia, la verità, la ragione, la salubrità dell'aria, la fertilità delle campagne, il bene, e l'utile privato, e pubblico, attenda a questa arte, e a questa scienza »: *Raccolta d'autori che trattano del moto dell'acque,* I, xxxvii.

[106] Giovanni de Coureil (of the Colonia Alfea), *Opere poetiche* (Florence: Grazioli, 1790), I, favola ii, no. iv: « I due ciarlatani »: « A mountbank in the public square showed the people an African animal of unknown race . . . With mouths hanging open and eyebrows arched, the ignorant rabble listens, admires, and gapes ».

were all too willing to watch with delight the butterfly invasion of 1741 and to gaze with fascination at the frightening pictures of a mammoth seal acquired by the Colombaria in 1778.[107]   Earthquakes and volcanic eruptions, for instance, provided a constant subject of discussion, which Nature herself encouraged by perpetrating considerable damage in Siena in 1693 and 1697 and in Livorno in 1742; but few of the many speculations on the "causes" of these tragedies advanced much beyond those of Anton Maria Salvini, since usually the lengthy descriptions, after a brief recording of the exact time and duration, dwelt largely upon the terror and panic of the populace.[108]

Equally incomprehensible, and therefore equally intriguing, were such atmospheric wonders as thunder, lightning, and the aurora borealis, which was observed in Florence on 16 December 1737. Some attributed them to the sun; others supposed them to be the remnants of an aboriginal fire still subsisting in sublunary bodies and made momentarily visible by climatic disturbance; and still others argued that lightning was simply an exhalation of mineral fumes (hence its frequency in mountain areas) and that it went from the earth up rather than from the heavens down.[109]   Then, when

[107] *Gazzetta toscana*, XII (1797), « Firenze », 9 June, and XIX (1784), 29 May. G. Targioni Tozzetti, *Lettera ... sopra una numerosissima specie di farfalle vedutasi in Firenze sulla metà di luglio 1741* (Florence: Buscagli, 1741); Colombaria: Annali 32, 7 September 1778. Note also the six huge volumes, beautifully illustrated by hand, of Saverio Manetti, Lorenzo Lorenzi, and Violante Vanni, *Storia naturale degli uccelli, trattata con metodo* (Florence: Moücke, 1767-76) (for which Pietro Leopoldo probably paid the bill).

[108] Fisiocritici: * Lezioni, 6 and 29 March 1698, 15 September 1699 (Salvini); * Deliberazioni, 27 February 1761, etc.; Giovanni Bottari in the Crusca: * Diario, 21 July 1729; *Lettera scritta ... in cui si dà ragguaglio dei terremoti seguiti in Livorno, dal 16 al 27 gennaio 1742 ... dal rev. sig. Pasqual Ranieri Pedini ...* (Livorno, [1742]), and Giovanni Gentili, *Osservazioni sopra i terremoti ultimamente accaduti a Livorno, descritte ... in una lettera al dott. Antonio Cocchi* (Florence: Bruscagli, 1742), and in *Atti Fisiocritici*, V, 301 f. (Bartaloni on Vesuvius), and VII, 200 f. (Ambrogio Soldani on the « terreno ardente » in Romagna — probably natural gas, for which the area has just recently become famous).

[109] Michel'Angelo Carmeli, minor osservante, « Ragionamento fatto ad un suo discepolo sopra il fenomeno apparso la notte del dì 16 dicembre 1737 », Calogerà, *Raccolta d'opuscoli*, XVIII, 465-81. Crusca: * Diario, 14 August 1763 and 30 August 1764; Fisiocritici: * Lezioni, 28 September 1692, 19 January 1702, *et al.* Much of the argument goes back to the preposterous nonsense in Benedetto Rozzinesi, *La filosofia a rovescio, ovvero dialogo intorno agli elementi per cagione del fulmini* (Pisa: Bindi, 1699), from which Gori accused

Giovan Battista Beccaria and Benjamin Franklin at last revealed the
"truth" about these spectacles and demonstrated their identity with
electricity, the academicians burst into grateful song:

> Franklin, o tu dell'Indico emisfero,
> Prometeo novel, che la fatale
> fiamma rapisti.[110]

But for Tuscans the voice of authority was not enough. On the
night of 18 April 1777 an excited crowd gathered beneath the Torre
del Mangia in Siena, which, to the delight of the Fisiocritici and the
scornful warnings of the marchese Alessandro Chigi, had just been
equipped with a lightning rod by command of Pietro Leopoldo.
Slowly the clouds gathered. Suddenly a bolt struck, lit up the Campo,
ran down the rod, and disappeared into the ground — all without
so much as scratching a brick of the famous tower. Experiment,
hazardous though it was, had proved Franklin right. Within a few
days the Fisiocritici had begun drawing up lengthy reports and
observations, some of which they published in the next volume of

Maffei (*Risposta . . . a Maffei* [Florence: Albizzini, 1739], p. 50) of having borrowed his
supposedly « new » theory (inverse lightning) in *Della formazione de' fulmini* (Verona: Tumermanni, 1747) (on which see Giuseppe Silvestri, *Un Europeo del Settecento: Scipione
Maffei* [Treviso: Canova, 1954], pp. 239-48). Hence the relevance, in Tuscany, of the
remark of Charles Burney: « Electricity is universally allowed to be a very entertaining and
surprising phenomenon, but it has frequently been lamented that it has never yet, with
much certainty, been applied to any very useful purpose »: *The present State of Music in
France and Italy* (London: T. Becket, 1771), p. 304. Another report on the aurora borealis
was written by Ximenes: « Osservazione dell'aurora boreale del dì III febbraio MDCCL . . . »,
in *Symbole litterariae opuscola varia,* ed. Anton Francesco Gori (10 vols.; Florence: Giovannelli, 1747-53), X, 73-92.

[110] Anon., *L'origine del fulmine, poemetto* (Pisa: Pizzorni, 1777): « Franklin, O thou
of the Indic hemisphere, new Proteus, who hast snatched the fatal flame »; now quoted
by Antonio Pace in his superb *Benjamin Franklin and Italy* (Philadelphia: The American
Philosophical Society, 1958), p. 211. This book is one of the best surveys of science and
scientific thought in Italy in this period. According to Pace (p. 41), who has examined
every scrap of material on the subject, Tuscans learned about Franklin only after the
publication of Beccaria's *Dell'elettricismo artificiale e naturale* (Torino: Campana, 1753).
His and other's work in electricity became a subject of academic discussion, however, only
in the 1770's: note the report of Luigi Eustachio Polidori on Beccaria in the Accademia Fiorentina (1783): * Registro, 31 January 1788, and also Infecondi: * Atti, 17 January 1777.
An Introduction to Electricity by James Ferguson (London: W. Strahan and T. Cadell, 1770;
2d ed., 1778) was translated as *Introduzione alla elettricità* and published by Cambiagi in
1787, of which the *Giornale fiorentino istorico politico letterario* wrote an enthusiastic
review (I [1778], 238-40), calling the author the « gloria inestinguibile del presente nostro
secolo ».

Atti and distributed all over Italy; and within two years the Georgofili were busy considering how to repeat, not now for the advance of
science, but for the edification and amusement of Florentines, the
experiments just previously performed in France by Jean-Paul
Marat.[111]

A still greater wave of excitement broke out some six years
later. In January of 1784 a certain Francesco Henrion of Pistoia
launched an "aerostatic globe" from the Ponte alla Carraia in Florence
by holding a skin-covered frame over iron filings in a solution of
sulphuric acid. Immediately the "youth and nobility" of every town
in Tuscany set to constructing "new balloons of various ingenious
shapes," which floated out across the Valdichiana and disappeared
into the Casentino accompanied by the wild applause of the assembled
citizenry and the extemporaneous sonnets of the Accademia Etrusca.
The fashion soon became a hazard, especially when one of the
balloons crashed into the Campanile of Giotto; and by April the
Grand Duke was obliged to prohibit further "experiments" without
special permission. The academic orators, of course, hailed the new
invention and its imminent improvement with steering devices as
proof of how the "sciences" in this "memorable epoch" were governed
by "la sola e vera utilità"; but in fact, as Pietro Leopoldo correctly
observed, they served far "more for entertainment than for study." [112]

Nevertheless, it was in terms of practical utility and of service to
"all the classes of inhabitants in Tuscany" [113] that science in the Set-

---

111 *Atti Fisiocritici*, VI (1781), 253-88 and *Giornale letterario di Siena*, III (1777), 257-
68. The incident is recounted by Pace, *op. cit.*, pp. 29 ff. A similar case is reported by Domenico Bartaloni in « relazione sopra un supposto fulmine caduto nella Cappella della
Piazza di Siena » (7 June 1784), *Atti Fisiocritici*, VII (1794), 61-68. The discussions of the
Georgofili are summarized in Marco Tabarrini, *Degli studi e delle vicende della R. Accademia dei Georgofili* (Florence: Cellini, 1856), p. 23 (7 July 1779).

112 *Gazzetta toscana*, XIX (1784), « Firenze » 21 January, *et seq.*, esp. « Cortona »,
8 May. The *Notificazione* of the auditore fiscale is given under "Florence", 17 April.
Another edict of 13 April is preserved in the collection of *Leggi Granducali* in the New
York Public Library (VI, No. 766). Gabbriello Grimaldi, *Memorie sopra la direzione, utilità ed invenzione dei globi aerostatici recitate nella R. A. Fiorentina* (29 May 1788) (Florence: Cambiagi, 1788) pp. 37-38. It is not surprising that the balloons were found to
be "inflammable," for from the description it is apparent that they were filled with
hydrogen.

113 Georgofili: * Petition of 4 October 1783.

tecento realized its most lasting accomplishments. Agriculture had long been the chief occupation of the Tuscan nobility. For over a century it had been almost the exclusive source of national income, from which not only the various branches of government, but the universities, churches, charities, and all other endowed institutions drew their sustenance.[114] Being one of the oldest urban peoples of Europe, moreover, Tuscans had been among the first to appreciate the amenities of the countryside, which Arcadia had now made even more attractive than ever; and the heirs of Boccaccio, Coluccio Salutati, and Leon Battista Alberti could still sympathize with shepherds fleeing from the "flattering mob" to the "blessed woods" and await themselves the call of "the freshness of the first rains" to "sweet repose" from "the troublesome mania for novelty that reigns in the city":[115]

> Dolce, caro alle Muse, almo Paese,
> padre di viver riposato....
>
> ...per te l'Alma mia, di spirti accensa,
> vaghi di pace, ha le cittadi a vile
> co i lor tumulti, e a se medesima pensa.[116]

[114] See Niccolò Rodolico, « Le condizioni materiali della Toscana prima delle riforme lorenesi », *Atti Georgofili*, Ser. V, Vol. V (1908), pp. 401-27; Antonio Anzilotti, « L'economia toscana e l'origine del movimento riformatore del secolo XVIII », *Archivio storico italiano*, LXXIII (1916), 82-119 and 308-53 (whose thesis can no longer be accepted without qualifications); Luigi Dal Pane, « Orientamenti e problemi della storia dell'agricoltura italiana del Seicento e del Settecento », *Rivista storica italiana*, LXVIII (1956), 165-85; and the great quantity of precise information scattered through Imberciadori, *Campagna toscana nell '700* (note 63) (on which note the unqualified eulogy of R. von Albertini in *Historische Zeitschrift*, CLXXXIV [1957] 645, and the more cautious observations of Marino Berengo in *Movimento operaio*, VII [1955], 328). In general: Jean Meuvret, *et al.*, « L'agriculture en Europe aux XVIIe et XVIIIe siècles », *Relazioni del X Congresso Internazionale di Scienze Storiche*, IV, 139-226, on agriculture in northern Europe. An indispensable guide to Tuscan literature is Marco Lastri's *Biblioteca georgica* (chap. ii, note 59).

[115] A. F. Adami, *Poesie*, p. iv: « I boschi »; G. Fabbroni, *Gli ozj della villeggiatura*, p. 3. Even the "scientific" agriculturalists and naturalists of later decades could still appreciate the amenities of the countryside. Can. Serafino Volta, for instance, in « Sull'origine, struttura, e rivoluzioni di Montebaldo di Verona, », *Atti Fisiocritici*, VII, 233 f., speaks of « le delizie del luogo » that provoke « l'ammirazione dei passeggieri »; but he quickly add: « ma questi non sono gli oggetti, che mi propongo a considerare » (p. 233).

[116] A. M. Salvini, *Sonetti* (1728), No. 371 (in honor of the villa of Gio. Lorenzo Pucci): « O sweet country that nourishes us, dear to the Muses, father of the life of ease.... For thee my soul, pressed on by spirits desirous of peace, looks with disdain upon the cities and their tumults ».

Occasionally, during the first half of the century, references to the fields and their products had slipped into the discourse of both the scientific and literary academies, whose members called attention to the agrarian origins of the Saturnalia among the Romans and the literary excellence of Cinquecento bucolic verse.[117] Still, for most Tuscans agriculture was a matter of pure business and the hills and valleys of pure pleasure, with no evident bearing upon "learning." Not until the botanists had demonstrated the adaptability of many new plants to Tuscan soil and not until the naturalists had exposed the "error" that Tuscan agriculture had reached its capacity did they realize that "he who studies nature in the part that most benefits us is really a practical philosopher." When Sallustio Bandini began to apply the experimental method of his teacher and predecessor Gabbrielli to the economic problems of the Maremma, agriculture had become a science, based firmly on "the most solid foundations of experiment" and guided by "chemical and physical discoveries."[118] In the sessions of the Georgofili, the Fisiocritici, the Accademia di Agricoltura of Pistoia, and even, at times, the Crusca, "gentle Flora" had "given way to Ceres."[119]

The foundation of the Georgofili occurred at a particularly critical moment in Tuscan history. For centuries the fields of Tuscany had produced just enough grain to feed its sizable urban population, with an occasional surplus which the few proprietors fortunate enough to secure an exemption from the prohibitions on exportation sold abroad for substantial profits. But periodically, every five or six years, either

---

[117] Fisiocritici: * Lezioni, 5 July 1691; Crusca: * Diario, 21 January 1712. Note also Sepolti: * Deliberazioni, 1764. Cf. Benedetto Croce, Storia dell'età barocca in Italia (2d ed.; Bari: Laterza, 1946), on agricultural "precepts" in the Seicento. Giovanni Salvini of Osimo in 1775 complimented the Etrusca for having considered « not only speculative matters, but also agrarian arts »: Istruzione al suo fattore di campagna (dedicated to the academy) (Osimo, 1775), p. iv.

[118] G. Targioni Tozzetti, Ragionamenti sull'agricoltura toscana (dedicated to the Georgofili), chap. i; Ottaviano Targioni Tozzetti, Lezioni di agricoltura, p. 13; Georgofili: * Ragguaglio del regolamento; Saverio Manetti, « Lezione accademica ... [in cui] si fa ... vedere come l'agricoltura possa fare dei progressi, e possano ai medesimi molto contribuire anche quelli che meno frequentano la campagna » (given in the Georgofili, 5 August 1767), Magazzino toscano, I (1770), 1-16.

[119] « L'amabile Flora avendo ceduto a Cerere »: O. Targioni Tozzetti, Lezioni di agricoltura, p. 2.

man or nature, through an invasion, a special levy, a frost, or a drought, interrupted the normal course of production. Prices soared well beyond the reach of most of the urban poor, and desperate peasants swarmed into the cities in the hope of obtaining from charity what their labor had failed to extract from the blighted land. Before the sixteenth century a timely exchange of abundant gold florins for Apulian, Sicilian, or Po Valley grain had usually averted a crisis; but now that agriculture itself, and not commerce and industry, furnished whatever liquid capital Tuscans might draw on and now that stringent regulations had cut off the supply from neighboring states, a marked decrease in one year's crop meant only one thing: famine, which all Tuscans, enlightened by the figures gathered each fall by the agents of the Abbondanza, could look forward to all winter with increasing anxiety. Moreover, during the eighteenth century the periodic famines had increased in frequency; and the three successive crop failures of 1764-66 resulted in a disaster of almost unprecedented proportions.[120]

Thus the academicians set out to accomplish with the help of science what a few individual proprietors and the city councils had failed to effect with isolated attempts at land improvement and centuries of legislation. They sought first of all to raise the productivity of the areas already under cultivation — by experimenting with various kinds of fertilizers, by adapting to Tuscan needs such new implements as the cylindrical plow of "the modern Columella," Duhamel, and the ventilator of Stephen Hales, and by proposing remedies for the weeds and for the plant diseases described by Targioni Tozzeti, which so long had impaired the quality and diminished the quantity of harvests. Most of the productive land in Tuscany was devoted to two crops: wheat and grapes. Accordingly, they showed how certain more resistant grains like *gran nero,* barley, and oats — some already "common in the bread of our poorer peasants"[121]

[120] Cf. Giuseppe Parenti, *Prezzi e mercato di grano a Siena, 1546-1765* (Florence: Cya, 1942).

[121] Saverio Manetti, *Delle specie diverse di frumento, e di pane, siccome di panizzazione* (Società Botanica) (Florence: Moücke, 1765), p. 93, *et passim.* Montelatici's « Ragguaglio dell'istituzione », in *Atti Georgofili,* Ser. V, Vol. III (1906), pp. 467-72, on Forzoni Accolti and Intieri; and consideration of Stephen Hales, *A Description of Ventilators* (2 vols.;

and others selected from Micheli and Linnaeus with proper Latin titles — might provide a good substitute in times of want; and they made lengthy investigations to find how best to prune and tie vines and to protect them from frost, as well as how to test wine during fermentation and to preserve it in bottles for exportation — investigations which in Pistoia occupied most of the sessions of the Accademia di Agricoltura in 1790 and incidentally led to the perfection of the exquisite *vin santo* still too little known outside Tuscany.[122]

But an intensified cultivation of the two traditional crops would still not adequately protect the economy of the country in case either of them should fail; and the academicians insisted even more strongly upon the urgency of diversification. The great variety in soil, terrain, and climate in Tuscany, after all, made the country admirably suited to a great variety of natural products — a "new species of bean," for instance, which Attilio Zuccagni had successfully grown in the Botanical Garden; bulb flowers, which one member of the Georgofili had learned about from a Dutch friend; and even two unidentified plants "in use among the Chinese." [123] Most fruits, it was discovered, could be raised on the mountain sides above Pistoia and Florence, provided they were correctly pruned and tilled; mulberry trees, for

London: W. Innys, 1743 and 1758; French translation, Paris: Poirion, 1744), by Bartolommeo Intieri, *Della perfetta conservazione del grano, discorso* (Naples: Giuseppe Raimondi, 1754). Gio. Domenico Olmi, « Se il loglio . . . sia prodotto . . . dalla semenza del grano », *Atti Fisiocritici*, IV, 297 f.; extracts from letter to F. Bartolozzi on *succiamele*: ASF Arch. Tolomei, 191 ins. VII, 637; Giovanni Lapi (« socio dell'Accademia Fisico Botanica Fiorentina e di quella di Cortona), *Metodo sicuro per distruggere i succiameli . . .* and *Discorso sull'esterminio del loglio* (both by Stecchi & Pagani: Florence, 1767). The first work on this subject was by none other than the botanist P. A. Micheli: *Relazione dell'erba detta da' botanici orobanche e volgarmente succiamele, fiamma e mal d'occhio . . . nella quale si dimostra . . . il modo di estirparla. Scritta a benefizio degli agricoltori toscani* (even Micheli's Latin catalogues, then, had a "practical" end), first published in 1723 and reprinted in Montelatici's *Ragionamento sopra i mezzi più necessari per far rifiorire l'agricoltura* (1752), pp. 65-127. See also D. M. Manni, *Nuova proposizione per trarre dall'agricoltura un maggior frutto* (in Georgofili, 6 September 1775).

122 Giovanni Fabbroni, *Metodo di conoscere alcune delle più dannose adulterazioni che si fanno ai vini . . .* (Florence: Pagani, 1785); ASF Arch. Tolomei, 191,no. 2; Agricoltura: * Atti, 21 December 1788, 23 September 1789, 13 May 1790, *et seq.*; *Gazzetta toscana*, XIX, (1784), "Pistoia," 29 May (*vin santo*); G. Targioni Tozzetti, in *Atti Georgofili*, I, 94 f., and 138 f.; and Fisiocritici: * Deliberazioni, 15 April 1760.

123 *Giornale fiorentino di agricoltura*, I (1786), 41; ASF Arch. Tolomei 191, ins. VII, 672 and 661; *Gazzetta toscana*, XIX, (1784), "Firenze," 15 May (Giovanni Fabbroni).

use not only as feed for silk worms but also as fertilizer, would grow abundantly along the banks of the Arno, with the added advantage of making the still important waterway to Pisa more attractive to the eye; and both *rubbia,* from which dye was extracted, and even cotton were found to be adaptable to certain parts of the Senese. One of the new plants, indeed, is honored even today in the wiry *toscani* cigar, still smoked by those of stronger digestions all over Italy: it was the Georgofili, with the encouragement of the government, who first successfully introduced tobacco in the hilly regions of the country.[124] The Academy gave particular importance, finally, to the encouragement of olive culture and to the raising of cattle; and they offered prizes, in 1788 and 1789, to whoever could plant the greatest number of trees and sow the greatest acreage of artificial meadows for grazing.[125]

Still, the academicians realized that intensification and diversification alone were not enough. The foreign travelers who returned with glowing reports, they noted, had not left the main thorough-fares: actually, much of Tuscany consisted of "vast stretches of country... completely uncultivated, without a tree, without a field, without a farm, without a habitation,... populated only by an occasional flock of sheep."[126] Much of this waste land simply lay

[124] Commission of the Georgofili on request of the Grand Duke to draw up « istru-zioni per la coltivazione del tabacco permessa con la legge » of 18 March 1789: Georgofili: Appunti, 6 May 1789; *Giornale fiorentino di agricoltura,* I, (1786), 73, and III (1788), 9; and Marco Lastri, *Della coltivazione e manifattura libera del tabacco in Toscana, discorso economico letto* . . . 6 July 1774 (Florence: Bonducci, 1789), which prepared for the legisla-tion of 1789. On fruit: Agricoltura: * Attti, 6 July and 18 August 1788; L. Tramontani, (3 June 1784), *Atti Georgofili,* II, 65 f. On mulberry tress: Agricoltura: * Atti, 22 April 1789 and 9 January 1790; D. M. Manni, *Della piantagione e coltivazione de' mori, o gelsi in Toscana, cagione di ricchezza* (Florence: Viviani, 1767); Anton Maria Fineschi, *Disserta-zione sopra la maniera di coltivare i mori* . . . (Siena: Mucci, 1783); the Georgofili prize for 1774 was awarded to Giuseppe Ricci of Fermo for his *Saggio sopra la replicata raccolta della foglia del gelso* (1775). Instructions for the planting of cotton were presented to the Academy by Eduardo Berlinghieri on 4 January 1790 and published in *Atti,* III, 1 f.

[125] Prize essay of Filippo Andreucci, *La moltiplicazione del bestiame toscano,* bound with runner-up by Luigi Tramontani with the same title (Florence: Stecchi, 1773); *Giornale fiorentino di agricoltura,* I (1786), 209 and 401 (Menabuoni), and G. Fabbroni (1784) in *Atti Georgofili,* II (1795), 49 f.

[126] Jacopo Ambrogio Tartini, "Memoria" (3 August 1785) from Geo Letture Acca-demiche II, in Imberciadori, *Campagna toscana nel '700,* p. 385. Note Agricoltura: * Atti, 25 January 1789.

fallow, due to an "intolerable error," which Paolo Franceschi, in response to the Georgofili contest of 1775, proposed to correct with proper fertilization, crop rotation, and more workers. Much of it was abandoned as sterile; but actually even the steep mountain sides, the swamps, and the alkaline clay of the Valdorcia could be made profitable, according to Targioni Tozzetti, Candido Pistoi, Domenico Niccoletti, and others, if subjected to special treatment.[127]   South of Siena, moreover, from Massa Marittima to Mt. Amiata and the Papal borders, extended the barren hills and plains of the Maremma. This area alone, the Georgofili supposed, could produce enough food for the entire country; but it still attracted only a few seasonal workers, who descended in the winter (often from as far as Parma) to graze sheep, reap an extra harvest of wheat, or gather *manna,* and then fled at the beginning of summer to avoid almost certain death from heat and malaria. The problem of how to bring the Maremma under cultivation had attracted the attention of many of the Medici princes; it provoked, in the eighteenth century, the first essays in political economy in Tuscany; it was to stimulate, under Pietro Leopoldo, some of the most courageous measures of political and economic reform; and it became, from the middle of the century on, one of the principal concerns of the Georgofili and the Fisiocritici.

Certainly this, and many other questions posed by the academies, far exceeded their competence. Only the chemical sprays of a later age would combat grain rust effectively; modern insecticides would more efficiently extract worms from fruit trees than a flexible wire inserted into the worm holes one by one; and simply plowing up the Maremma or even channelling the waters of the Ombrone, the Georgofili themselves admitted, would not alone achieve the repop-

---

127 [P. Franceschi], *Dissertazione coronata dalla R. A. dei G. di F. in soluzione del problema sui maggesi* (Florence, 1788). Gio. Francesco Pagnini, *Lettera d'un socio onorario dell'A. di Agricoltura di Firenze ... sopra il riposo dei terreni e i principj della vegetazione* (Florence: Pagani, 1785); *Atti Fisiocritici,* IV, 251 ff.; replies to Fisiocritici competition of 1770 on the problem of 1768: « in alcuni strati della campagna senese, come per esempio nei colli di Malamerenda, lungo la valle dell'Orcia, si ritrova una quantità di terra cretacea affatto sterile .... In qual maniera si possa rendere feconda? » — one answer: throw vinegar on the alkaline soil.

ulation of the deserted province.[428] Their success in raising the productivity of Tuscan agriculture cannot accurately be determined; for they must share the credit for whatever progress was actually realized with the government and with individual proprietors. Moreover, food shortages did not by any means disappear: a particularly serious one, in fact, occurred in the summer of 1790. But certainly, by applying scientific methods to agriculture, the academies laid the indispensable foundation for the expansion and diversification of Tuscan agriculture in the following century.

Thus scientific agriculture marks the culmination of a whole century of thought and research, in which the academies played a conspicuous, although not necessarily a dominant part. Science in the Settecento had begun with the general laws of nature revealed by the Seicento philosophers and with the method by which they had discovered them. First botany and anatomy had demonstrated that the same laws applied in all the various parts of the physical and organic world; then natural history and hydrostatics had shown that their operation produced continual mutations in the earth's surface; and finally agriculture had proved that man could manipulate these laws for his own material benefit. The opening of the Settecento found Tuscans gazing in wonder at the magnificence of the cosmos; the close of the Settecento found them tilling their own gardens in the firm conviction of having mastered it.

[128] Georgofili: * Ragguaglio (10) (*tarlo*).

Chapter V

ANTIQUITIES, ARCHEOLOGY, AND HISTORY

"I rather expect, virtuous academicians" — so begins the lecture on the antiquities of Siena by the later famous Sienese historian Uberto Benvoglienti before the Fisiocritici on 15 September 1699 — "I rather expect that you will greet the new subject I have chosen with little applause, since such matters are (I confess) not totally in harmony with our institution; ... I only hope that at the end you will not find it displeasing." Undoubtedly the assembly did applaud, at least out of politeness and respect for anything "learned"; they may even have admitted with Benvoglienti that "many excellent philosophers and physicans" had "combined very well the speculative sciences with the most flowering erudition." But evidently they agreed that history and science had very little in common, for no such titles appear in their records thereafter.[1] Only twice, indeed, during the three decades after 1690 did any of the other scientific or literary academies show the least interest in the events of the past; and during the 1720's the Crusca ignored even the immense editorial venture that was soon to make one of its most active lexicographers, senator Filippo Buonarroti, the founder of a major field of Sette-

---

[1] Fisiocritici: * Lezioni, 15 September 1699 (BCS L.III.2, p. 182); « Parmi d'antivedere, virtuosi Accademici, che alla novità del mio assunto poco siate per applaudire, non essendo (il confesso) materia totalmente adeguata al nostro istituto: nulladimeno avendo io osservato, che molti filosofi e medici eccellenti . . . anno congiunto così bene con le scienze speculative la più fiorita erudizione, non dispero . . . che alla fine non siate per non gradirlo . . . ». On Settecento historiography in general, see Virgilio Titone, *La storiografia dell'Illuminismo in Italia* (Palermo: Edizioni Del Prisma, 1952); Giulio Bertoni, « La storiografia del secolo XVIII », in *Miscellanea di studi muratoriani*, XI (1933), ix-xii; Benedetto Croce, « La storiografia dell'Illuminismo », in his *Teoria e storia della storiografia* (6th ed.; Bari: Laterza, 1948); and E. W. Cochrane, « The Settecento Medievalists », *Journal of the History of Ideas*, XIX (1958), 35-61. The best guide to historical literature in Tuscany is Domenico Moreni, *Bibliografia storico-ragionata della Toscana, o sia Catalogo degli scrittori che hanno illustrata la storia delle città, luoghi, e persone della medesima* (2 vols.; Florence: Ciardetti, 1805), in spite of its numerous lacunae and its inclusion of much frivolous matter.

cento historiography.[2] If, in the first part of the eighteenth century, the academicians were already consciously embarked on the conquest of space and on the establishment of a *perfetta poesia,* they still cared little, if anything, for time.

The curiosity of Tuscans about the origins and development of their cities, to be sure, was nothing new in the Settecento. Indeed, it had begun soon after the republican communes first asserted their authority over the surrounding countryside in the early thirteenth century.[3] In few countries of Europe, indeed, had historiography played so important a part in the political and social life of the community. Few peoples, moreover, could boast so illustrious a line of historians — from the great chroniclers like Malespini and the Villani of the Trecento to the humanists like Leonardo Bruni, Poggio Bracciolini, and Matteo Palmieri in the Quattrocento, to the political historians of the generation of Machiavelli and Guicciardini, to the scholars, Varchi, Segni, Borghini, and Ammirato, in the mid-Cinquecento. Then, almost abruptly, Tuscans had lost all interest in their past. Except for one or two compilations of the "diverse ancient facts," which already by 1700 had become rare, almost nothing was written about the growth and vicissitudes of the cities of Tuscany for the next 150 years.[4] When, in 1711 and 1714, Lodovico Antonio Muratori, then librarian to the Duke of Modena, traveled through Tuscany in search of documents for his history of the House of Este, he found many of the libraries and archives shut tight and most cities without "anyone who knows anything about old parchments."[5]

---

[2] Crusca: * Diario, 22 July 1706 and 28 January 1717.

[3] Cf. N. Rubinstein, « The Beginnings of Political Thought in Florence: A Study in Medieval Historiography », *Journal of the Warburg and Courtauld Institutes,* V (1942), 198-227.

[4] Orlando Malavolti, *Historia de' fatti e guerre de' Senesi* (Venice, 1599); Giugurta Tommasi, *Historia di Siena* (Venice, 1625). Muratori describes his vain effort to procure copies of these books in *Lettere a Toscani,* pp. 61, 257, 333. For Arezzo: Pietro Farulli, cittadino fiorentino, *Annali, ovvero Notizie istoriche dell'antica, nobile e valorosa città di Arezzo* . . . (Foligno, 1717); for Cortona: Domenico Tartaglini, cortonese, *Nuova descrizione dell'antichissima città di Cortona con l'aggiunta di diversi fatti antichi ed altri particolari della medesima* (Perugia: Costantini, 1700).

[5] Muratori to Leibniz, 8 April 1711 (« non v'ha chi s'intenda di pergamene antiche ») and 19 December 1714, in *Corrispondenza tra L. A. Muratori e G. G. Leibniz,* ed. Campori (Modena: Vincenzi, 1892), pp. 155 and 212-13.

What had happened to history in Tuscany? It is perhaps not yet possible to give a full explanation; but that proposed by the Settecento historians themselves is at least plausible. First of all, they suggested, the "mutation of states" — that is, the fall of the Florentine and Sienese Republics — had destroyed the illusion nurtured by most of the historians from Leonardo Bruni to Machiavelli, that what they learned about the past might assist them in effecting the improvement or modification of the institutions of their own times. The tragic events of 1530 and 1556 then left them to "bewail the tragedy of their country" and their helplessness before "the barbarism" which would soon "inundate our city and all the rest of Italy." At the same time, Cosimo I was fully convinced that even the most minute details of historical erudition had a direct bearing on the stability of his newly-founded regime. He did not forbid the study of history, to be sure. He simply transformed it into a servant of the crown by means of the same policy so effectively applied to the literary studies of the Accademia Fiorentina: subsidies and favors. Accordingly, even Scipione Ammirato, who "surpassed all others in critical ability," was forced to disfigure his text with false eulogies and unwarranted lacunae; the Grand Duke was paying him, after all, not to reconstruct the past, with its memories of liberty, republican government, and insurrections, but to replace it with a mythology. Thus, according to Adami, "the political jealousy of the Medici sovereigns was the cause of a great void in our historiography and of a great sterility among our historians." The Tuscan *letterati* evidently preferred to give up history altogether rather than expose themselves to the "persecution suffered by those writers not disposed to conform in everything" to the will of their rulers — for which Adami found ample evidence in the letters of Benedetto Varchi. History, in other words, had been suffocated by the Medici princes, who fully realized the dangers implicit in the concept that change had occurred in the past and might again occur in the future. By the end of the following century they had been completely successful. Their subjects had become so convinced of having escaped the historical process and so reconciled to living in an eternal present that they accepted without question the irrelevance of the past to the joys and sorrows of their own times and its relegation, therefore, to the realms of idle curiosity.[6]

Fortunately, the loss of interest in the past itself in no way affected the somewhat more recent fascination for the relics of the past. All during the Seicento the nobility and citizenry of the Tuscan cities had followed the example of their princes in amassing vast collections of "rare curiosities" — of gems, urns, vases, manuscripts, and incunabula, some of which can still be seen plastered into the courtyard walls of palaces and villas all over Tuscany. Such collections continued to flourish all through the eighteenth century: Manni, for instance, found ten devoted to ancient seals alone in 1739, and that of the enigmatic German exile Philipp von Stosch eventually won fame through the printed catalogue composed by none other than Winckelmann himself.[7] Some of this material, to be sure, had occasionally been the subject of learned inquiry even during the Seicento; indeed, the scholars of the following century were well enough aware of the merits of, say, the *Inscriptiones antiquae* of Giovan Battista Doni or, even better, the *Cenotaphia pisanae* of Enrico Noris (1631-1704) to have them published or reprinted. Still, little of this work rose above the level of annotation and description, and even less of it attained the quality of that of such contemporary

---

[6] Anton Maria Bandini, *Memorie per servire alla vita del senator Pier Vettori* (Livorno: Santini, 1756), pp. 33-34. Anton Filippo Adami, *Dissertazioni critiche ... in cui molti importantissimi argomenti si trattano sopra le antichità etrusche, romane, e de' mezzi tempi, appartenenti alla città di Firenze, e si esamina il genio, e lo spirito de suoi scrittori, e specialmente degli storici ... Si dà un metodo per compilare una diffusa, ed estesa Istoria Fiorentina* (Pisa: Pizzorno, 1766) (lectures delivered in the Apatisti), pp. 47 and 52.

[7] The private collections are described in *Novelle Letterarie*, I (1740), 36, and XI (1750), 197; by Gori in the Dedication to G. Averani, *Lezioni toscane*, II, vi-vii (Feroni); by D. M. Manni in Preface to *Osservazioni istoriche sopra i sigilli antichi de' secoli bassi* (22 vols.; Florence: Albizzini, 1739-86 [Accademia Fiorentina], I, ix f.; in Notizie del museo ... Niccolini: Mar A. 197, 15, and A. 284 (Guarnacci); by Pecci in a letter to Gori, 1 June 1733, 27 April and 20 May 1734: Mar B.7,66. A MS « Raccolta universale di tutte le iscrizioni, arme, e altri monumenti sì antichi come moderni », of Pecci himself, in 3 vols., is described by P. Guglielmo Della Valle in *Lettere senesi ... sopra le belle arti,* II (Rome: Salomoni, 1785), 31-32. On Stosch, see the very thorough study of Carl Justi, « Philipp von Stosch und seine Zeit », *Zeitschrift für bildende Kunst,* VII (1872), 293-308, 333-46, De Brosses, *Lettres familières,* I, 193; and *Description des pierres gravées du feu Baron de Stosch ... dédiée à son éminence mons. le cardinal Aléxandre Albani par M. l'abbé Winckelmann,* bibliothécaire de son éminence (Florence: Bonducci, 1760).

Transalpine scholars as Philipp Klüwer (*Sicilia antiqua* [1619], *Italia antiqua* [1624], etc.), Adam Rupertus, or Johann Andreas Bose.[8]

Not until the third decade of the eighteenth century did the Tuscan academies begin to consider the possibility of using the items in their members' private collections for academic exercises. Gradually it occurred to them that pious reflections on the Madonna of Impruneta or the Girdle of the Virgin at Prato might be improved somewhat by the inclusion of a documentary appendix. They found further that the examination of ancient gems and inscriptions would inevitably cause "delight" because of the "many new things" they contained, and that meditations upon former events could "move our hearts... to imitate that which must be done in civil life" much more effectively than mere "precepts."[9] Finally, they discovered that the consideration of such subjects offered a particularly promising way for Italians to recover their former prestige in the European Republic of Letters. "Because of our lack of adequate means," remarked Pietro Giulianelli (as well as Scipione Maffei and many others), "foreigners [*Oltramontani*] have gone well beyond us in the sciences. But in *antiquaria*, as even a learned Parisian had admitted, no one has yet arrived at the excellence of Italians."[10] Thus

---

[8] See Gervasoni, *Linee di storia della filosofia classica in Italia*, p. 57, and Sandys, *A History of Classical Scholarship*, II, 279-82 (from which it is clear that most of this work was devoted to collecting). Doni's (1594-1657) *Inscriptiones antiquae* was first published (*nunc primum editae notisque illustratae et indicibus auctae*) by A. F. Gori (Florence: Ex Regia Typographia, 1731); note also A. M. Bandini, *Commentariorum de vita ed scriptis I. B. Donii libri quinque ... Accedit ejusdem Donii literarium commercium nunc primum in lucem editum,* ed. Gori (2 vols.; Florence: Typis Caesareis, 1755). The *Cenotaphia pisana Caii et Lucii Caesarum dissertationibus illustrata* of Cardinal Noris of Verona, sometime professor at Pisa, first published in 1681, was republished in Vol. III of *Opera omnia nunc primum collecta atque ordinata* (Verona: Tumermanni, 1729), and later separately (Pisa, 1764).

[9] Note Giuseppe Bianchini, *Notizie istoriche intorno alla sacratissima cintola di Maria Vergine* (Florence: Manni. 1722), and G. B. Casotti, *Memorie istoriche della miracolosa immagine dell'Impruneta* (Florence: Manni, 1714). Giovanni Lami, *Lezioni di antichità toscane* (Florence: Bonducci, 1766), p. 303 (from lezione 9: Crusca: * Diario, 13 September 1749), and D. M. Manni, *Le veglie piacevoli,* I, x.

[10] Introduction to Giuseppe Averani, *Lezioni toscane,* III, xiv. Cf. Maffei, *Istoria diplomatica che serve d'introduzione all'arte critica in tal materia* (Mantova: Tumermanni, 1727), I. 113

the study of antiquities, although at first still disguised under the more customary literary and philosophical titles, soon assumed an important place in academic curricula.

As objects of learning, then, antiquities could no longer be arranged according to the whims of those who, like Goldoni's Don Anselmo, had valued their parchments and stones not as a way of acquiring an understanding of bygone times, but solely as a means of gratifying their taste for the curious and the unusual. No longer could a twelfth-century charter be placed between a Roman coin and a pressed flower; for, as the German-born painter Anton Raffaello Mengs pointed out, it was the "assembling of medals and engraved stones" that first had rescued Italy from "German barbarism."[11] As the botanists were arranging the vegetable world into *classes* and *genera,* therefore, so now also the collectors set out to separate "the important" from "the useless" and to put "everything in its proper place" — or else to hire a competent scholar, like Angelo Maria Bandini or Anton Maria Biscioni, to do it for them, and to compile the immense catalogues of which some are still in use today.[12] Many of them were sufficiently impressed by the importance of their collections to make the initial donations that since have become the Biblioteca Comunale of Siena (1759), the Museo Guarnacci of Volterra (1761), the Magliabechiana and the Marucelliana of Florence (1747 and 1752), and most of the other rich libraries and museums

---

[11] Mengs, *Opere* (Parma: Stamperia Reale, 1780), I, 99. Mengs's inverse patriotism aside, Germany can claim a certain priority over Tuscany — at least in such monumental works as the *Commentarii de Augustissima Bibliotheca Caesarea Vindobonensis* (Vol. I, 1679), undertaken by Peter Lambeck, historiographer to the Emperor Leopold I (see Bursian, *Geschichte der classischen Philologie in Deutschland,* pp. 311 f.).

[12] *Giornale de' letterati* (Pisa), XXXVIII (1780), 62. Among the principal catalogues: Anton Maria Biscioni, *Bibliothecae ebraicae graecae florentinae, sive Bibliothecae Mediceo-Laurentinae catalogus* (Florence: Typis Caesareis, 1767); A. M. Bandini, *Biblioteca Leopoldina Laurentiana, seu Catalogus MSSorum qui iussu Petri Leopoldi . . . in Laurentianam translati sunt . . .* (3 vols.; Florence: Typis Caesareis, 1791-93); Ferdinando Fossi, *Catalogus codicum saecolo XV impressorum qui in Publica Bibliotheca Magliabechiana Florentiae adservantur* (3 vols.; Florence: Cambiagi, 1783-95). Probably the first museum in Tuscany to be arranged "rationally" was that of the Grand Duke himself, which is described in Vol. I (« Graecae et romanae [inscriptions] quae visuntur Florentiae in vestibulo Regii Musei Magni Etruriae Ducis ») of *Inscriptiones antiquae in Etruriae urbibus exstantes,* ed. A. F. Gori and A. M. Salvini (Florence: G. Manni, 1727-43).

that now adorn the cities of Tuscany.[13]   At the same time, both local and central governments began to realize the value of their archives, not only for the purposes of "public and private law" but also for "scholarship" and "history."   As Iacopo Inghirami and the later historian Lorenzo Cecina reorganized those of the Palazzo dei Priori and the Cathedral at Volterra and as Giovan Antonio Pecci catalogued those of the Balìa in Siena, so, in 1778, Pietro Leopoldo ordered the deposition of all documents not pertaining to the current business of monasteries, hospitals, and municipal magistracies in a central *Archivio diplomatico,* now the *Archivio di Stato* of Florence.[14] Thus the generosity of a few private persons and the efforts of the public authorities transformed the once private collections of miscellaneous curiosities into museums, libraries, and archives, all arranged and catalogued in at least some sort of intelligible order, and readily available to all those persistent enough to secure official permission to consult them.

To be sure, the study of antiquities was not necessarily the study of history.   Indeed, the academies devoted much of their time exclusively to the assembly and description of single objects, without any attempt to see them as manifestations of times gone by.   For the chief interest of the antiquarians lay not in the past itself, but in the individual remnants of the past— in an ancient columbarium found in the Via Salaria, in a cut stone in the collection of Marcello

---

[13] Among many contemporary and modern titles, note: A. M. Bandini, *Lettera . . . sopra i principi e progressi della Biblioteca Laurenziana* (Florence: Allegrini, 1773); « Elogio dell'abate Francesco Marucelli », *Magazzino toscano* (Livorno), I (1754), 278 ff.; Francesco Fontani, *Elogio di Giovanni Lami* (Florence: Cambiagi, 1789) (Riccardiana); A. F. Gori, *Musei Guarnaceii antiqua monumenta . . .* (Florence: Albizzini, 1744), and Giuseppe Riccobaldi Del Bava in *Novelle letterarie,* XXIII (1762), 88 f.   The inscription on the Biblioteca Comunale of Siena reads « Sallustius. Archid. Bandini, Patritius. Senensis . . . huius Bibliotecae. fundamenta. jecit. An. MDCCLIX . . . » (cf. Glauco Tozzi, *Sallustio Bandini, economista senese* [Rome, 1933], p. 81).   In general: Carlo Angeleri, *La gloriosa tradizione delle biblioteche fiorentine* (Florence: Vallecchi, 1947), and the Introduction to Cesare Guasti, *Le carte strozziane nel R. Archivio di Stato di Firenze* (Florence: Cellini, 1884).

[14] Volterra: *Novelle letterarie,* I (1740). 705-9; Siena: [Antonio Pecci], *Elogio istorico del cav. Gio. Antonio Pecci* (Siena: Bindi, 1768), p. xi; quotation from Motuproprio of 24 December 1778, *Bandi e ordini,* LX, lxxvi (printed separately by Cambiagi in 1779).   In general: Giuliana Giannelli, « La legislazione archivista del Granducato di Toscana », in *Notizie degli archivi toscani (Archivio storico italiano,* CXIV [1956], 258-89, esp. 263-64).

Venuti, or in an "ancient grasshopper" belonging to the Baron von Stosch, of which Girolamo Boni had printed sketches distributed to the members of the Etrusca in 1750; and they frequently produced what Giulio Natali has justly termed "historical studies without history." [15] A few contemporary critics, it is true, later complained that cabinets of antiquities were really "not very useful," "pleasant" though they might be to the owners, and that "so far the rich mines of venerable antiquity have been penetrated only by the eye of grammar and sterile scholarship." [16]

But such accusations were not wholly justified; for it was only through the study of antiquities that the Tuscan academicians could learn about history. Unlike the botanists and physicians, the historians could not draw upon a continuing tradition, for the tradition had been interrupted in the Cinquecento. Nor, moreover, could they rely upon the encouragement of the universities, none of which included a chair of history. [17] The Jesuits, it is true, continued to teach at least the ancient historians. But after two centuries of classroom exercises, imitation had apparently lost its creative force even more in historiography than in literature; and the study of Thucydides,

[15] Etrusca: * Atti, 27 March and 3 November 1751, 8 November 1745, 7 October 1750, 11 November 1754 (cf. A. F. Gori, « Monumentum sive colombarium libertorum et servorum Liviae Augustae et Caesarum Romae detectum in Via Appia anno MDCCXXVI... adjectis notis... Antonii Mariae Salvinii », in Giovanni Poleni, Utriusque thesauri antiquitatum romanarum graecarumque nova supplementa... (3 vols.; Venice: Pasquali, 1737), III, 1-292, with exquisite illustrations mostly paid for by various Tuscan noblemen). Further: Crusca: * Diario, 7 September 1724. Giulio Natali in Il Settecento, p. 359. As late as 1801 the Colombaria gave over the entire third volume of its Memorie to the annotation of « monuments observed » in its sessions, with no other order than that of presentation. On the difference between « antiquities » and « history » note Etrusca: * Atti, 23 January 1776, and Lami in his Sanctae Ecclesiae Florentinae monumenta, I, 1; « Monumenta, seu Memorabilia, non Historiam vel Annales Ecclesiae Florentinae inscripsi »; and in general: Arnaldo Momigliano: « Ancient History and the Antiquarian », now in his Contributo alla storia degli studi classici (Rome: Edizioni di Storia e Letteratura, 1955), pp. 67-106.

[16] Giovanni Fabbroni, in « La derivazione e coltura degli antichi abitatori d'Italia », Memorie due lette nella Società degli Amatori della Storia Patria, pp. 3-96, esp. p. 3. Giulio Perini in inaugural address: ASF Reggenza 1052.58: « Credo che finora nelle ricche miniere della veneranda antichità sia penetrato soltanto l'occhio grammatico, e sterilmente erudito... ».

[17] Not until 1788 was a chair of « Istoria patria e geografia » even proposed at Pisa: Romolo Caggese. Firenze dalla decadenza di Roma al Risorgimento d'Italia (3 vols.; Florence: Seeber and Lumachi, 1912-31), III, 528.

Sallust, or even Aulus Gellius, which had been so fruitful in the days of Bruni and Biondo, could now inspire nothing more than the pale, and quickly forgotten, *Historiarum sui temporis* of the would-be Settecento Livy, Giovan Vincenzo Lucchesini (*S. J.*, to be sure), the Latin secretary to Clement XI.[18] It is not surprising, then, that the academicians saw little in common between their schoolbooks and their collections, except, perhaps, insofar as certain passages in a Roman author might help them to identify an Etruscan votive figure. At the same time history suffered from the glorification of the present in the eighteenth century almost as much as it had from the passive acceptance of the present in the seventeenth; for *illuminismo* "awakened in the hearts" even of the new historians themselves "a compassionate pity" for "the past ages," whose "scientific notions" were "enveloped in a darkness of confusion, credulity, and falsehood." [19] Thus an interest in the past could begin only when the academicians, tired of the more traditional arguments, stimulated by a desire for scholarly achievement, and encouraged by the still prevalent ideal of *enciclopedia,* found themselves surrounded by great quantities of previously untouched material, which the academies now admitted into the realm of *erudizione.*

Then, during the twenties, two important discoveries suddenly made the academicians aware of the still greater potentialities of their collections. In 1720 a visiting Englishman, Thomas Coke (later Earl of Leicester) acquired in Florence a long-forgotten MS treatise of the emigrant Scots scholar, Thomas Dempster (1570-1635), who, while teaching at Bologna and Pisa early in the seventeenth century, had gathered together a variety of strange artifacts and illegible inscriptions along with a number of passages from Roman authors and had deduced from them the existence of a highly developed civilization in Italy before the rise of Rome. Coke turned the manuscript over to his friend senator Filippo Buonarroti, who had already attained some competence in such matters through a study of ancient

---

[18] . . . . *ab Noviomagensi pace tomus primus* (—*tertius*) (Romae: Mainardi, 1725-38). The author is better known for his Latin translation of Demosthenes (1712).

[19] Lorenzo Guazzesi, « Lezione sopra il conclave di Papa Gregorio X », Calogerà, *Nuova raccolta d'opuscoli,* XIV, 409-440, p. 411.

vases. Buonarroti, following Coke's suggestion and assisted by his liberal purse, set out to supplement the text with many careful *explicationes* and corrections and, most important of all, with a great quantity of copper-plate illustrations of monuments like those mentioned by Dempster — something that "neither Dempster nor anyone else ever thought of doing."

After four years of hard work, the two-volume work was ready. Just then the Bishop of Gubbio ordered the printing of a set of ancient Umbrian tables known as the *Tavole Eugubine,* which had attracted some attention during the century after their discovery (1444), but which had lain neglected in the archives of the commune ever since. Buonarroti quickly added a lengthy appendix interpreting the tablets in the light of what he had learned from Dempster; and at last, in the summer of 1726, *De Etruria regali* was broadcast to the Republic of Letters, "plaudente universo litterario orbe." [20]

By November of the following year the nobility of Cortona, impressed by the importance given their city by Dempster, had transformed their recently founded Accademia degli Occulti into a new society with the name *Etrusca,* to which they elected none other than Buonarroti himself as *lucumone* (from the Etruscan *lauchime,* Latinized *lucumo,* "prince"); and Scipione Maffei rushed back to Verona to announce in his *Istoria diplomatica,* then in the process of publication, "a new source of marvelous and precious knowledge; ... the documents of another people until now unjustly omitted from the

---

[20] A. F. Gori, *Museum etruscum, exhibens insignia veterum Etruscorum monumenta* (3 vols.; Florence: *in aedibus auctoris,* 1737-43), I, xiii. *Thomae Dempsteri De Etruria regali libri VII nunc primum editi curante Thoma Coke Magnae Britanniae armigero Regiae celsitudine Cosmi III magni ducis Etruriae* (2 vols.; Florence: Tartini & Franchi, 1723). Vol. II is dedicated to Giangastone (Cosimo III having died in the meantime); the preparation of the plates prevented the issuing of the volumes until 1726. Note especially Preface to Vol. I by Coke (here quoted) and Dedication of Buonarroti to his « Ad monumenta etrusca ... explicationes et coniecturae » in appendix to Vol. II, pp. 3 f. See Pericle Ducati, « Tommaso Dempstero ed i primi studi etruschi », *Atti del Primo Congresso Internazionale Etrusco* (Florence: Rinascimento del Libro, 1929), pp. 313-29, and on the beginnings of Etruscology in Tuscany: A. F. Gori, *Storia antiquaria etrusca.* Buonarroti's, *Osservazioni sopra alcuni frammenti di vasi antichi ... ne' cimiteri di Roma* had been published anonymously by Guiducci in 1716; a report of it was made to the Crusca by A. M. Salvini: * *Diario,* 28 January 1717.

study of antiquities." [21] Modern Tuscans had discovered ancient Etruria.

At the same time, some of the members of the Crusca began to notice that the "language texts" they were preparing for citation in the fourth edition of the *Vocabolario* contained material of other than purely linguistic value — that the *novelle* of Sacchetti, for instance, might furnish not only new words for the enrichment of current Tuscan, but also "much information for the investigators of the ancient customs of our illustrious city." Thus, by 1731, Domenico Maria Manni dedicated almost the whole preface of the Chronicle of Donato Velluti to a demonstration of its importance for the history of the Trecento, with only a few marginal remarks on the language in which it was written.[22] Tuscans had discovered — or rather rediscovered — the Middle Ages. Consequently, what had formerly been admired as "antiquities" now became historical documents, to be valued not in themselves alone but as links between the past and the present.

As the academicians became interested in finding out exactly what had happened in the past, they discovered that, fortunately, their contemporaries outside Tuscany had already formulated a clear, precise method by which the documents in their possession could assist them in their quest. Actually, they observed, methodical, or "scientific" historiography had first been adumbrated as early as the Quattrocento by such scholars as Flavio Biondo and Lorenzo Valla; it had been further developed in the mid-Cinquecento by Carlo Sigonio, Scipione Ammirato, Vincenzo Borghini, and Pier Vettori; it had been kept alive beyond the Alps after the decease of Italian historiography by Casaubon and the Bollandists; and it had been brought back to Italy by the learned Benedictines Mabillon and Montfaucon just at the moment of its rediscovery by the Italian Benedetto

21 Maffei, *Istoria diplomatica* (above, note 10) . . . . *Appresso per motivi nati dall'istessa opera* (exactly what Gori denied in his *Risposta a Maffei* of 1739) *segue un Ragionamento sopra gl'itali primitivi,* I, 9. Gori's arguments are very convincing, especially considering the character of Maffei; but Silvestri, who does not cite Gori's tracts, attributes the whole quarrel to Gori's own jealousy (*Un Europeo del Settecento: S. M.,* p. 43).

22 Sacchetti, *Delle novelle,* Preface; *Cronaca di Firenze di Donato Velluti dall'anno MCCC in circa fino al MCCCLXX* (Florence: D. M. Manni, 1739); « Stampatore a chi legge ».

Bacchini. Then, finally, in the first decades of the Settecento, it had been perfected by Lodovico Antonio Muratori, whom Tuscans had already known as a moralist and a literary critic and whose merits as the author of "learned and scholarly productions" in historiography they now recognized by electing him to honorary membership in all the more important academies.[23] Thus, as Tuscans began once again to study history after an interval of almost two centuries, they turned for guidance and inspiration to the tradition of patient, scholarly archival research rather than to the reflective, interpretative historiography of Bruni, Palmieri, Machiavelli, and Guicciardini, which once had flourished in their cities.

The historical method, according to Adami, Manni, and others, who adapted it from Muratori (and to some extent from Scipione Maffei) to the particular requirements of Tuscan history, began with suspended judgment. The historian, they insisted, must be aware that most of what previously had passed for history was in fact little more than "an immense miscellany of stories woven from false tales, often copied haphazardly and uncritically, and not seldom adorned with strange and miraculous marvels." [24] He might avoid such errors himself by following one simple rule: "reject absolutely anything that appears to be opposed to the ordinary course of nature":[25] that is, attribute any supposed occurrence not explicable in terms of the orderly Galilean-Newtonian universe either to the

[23] Among the many titles on this subject, see Ezio Raimondi, « I Padri Maurini e l'opera del Muratori », Giornale storico della letteratura italiana, CXXVIII (1951), 429-71 and CXXIX 1952), 145-78. On Muratori, see now Sergio Bertelli, Erudizione e storia in Ludovico Antonio Muratori (Naples: Istituto Italiano per gli Studi Storici, 1960). Gori to Pecci (on Leon Battista Alberti), 16 July 1748: Mar B 77. Note letters of Mabillon and Montfaucon to Anton Maria Salvini published by Gori in Symbolae litterariae, II, 191-208. Muratori was elected to the Intronati in 1700, to the Colombaria in 1745, to the Etrusca before 1744, to the Crusca in 1746 (quotation from letter of 26 July 1746; Cr A.29, 155). His Antiquitates italicae was republished by Bellotti in Arezzo in 17 vols., 1773-80. Gori's tribute to his precedessors in Inscriptiones antiquae in Etruriae urbibus exstantes, I, xx ff.

[24] Giuseppe Pelli, in « Epoche di storia fiorentina », Memorie due lette nella Società degli Amatori di Storia Patria, p. 99.

[25] D. M. Manni, Metodo per istudiare con brevità e profittevolmente le storie di Firenze (2d ed., from 1st ed. of Livorno, 1755; Florence: Moücke, 1755), p. 19. The argument of this paragraph is taken from this book and from A. F. Adami's Dissertazioni critiche.

imagination of the ancient Roman or Trecento authors who reported it, or to the credulity of the Cinquecento compilers who blindly repeated it. He had then to examine the circumstances of composition to ascertain any possible bias and to distinguish carefully between those events witnessed by the author and those reported on the authority of others. Giovanni Villani, for example, might be very reliable when describing the *Bianchi* and *Neri* of the early Trecento; but his reminiscences of the Guelfs and Ghibellines were evidently one-sided and his account of the foundation of Florence was obviously fantastic. Once the definitely false had been cleared away from the probably true, "common sense" or "nature" might again be brought forth to deduce a number of propositions which, although not explicitly stated in the text, at least bore some degree of plausibility, if not probability. Lami, for example, supported his hypothesis of the Etruscan origin of Florence by pointing out: (1) that the absence of any word to the contrary in even the proudest Latin author sustains the easily observable fact that the Romans built no cities in Etruria; (2) that where modern Florence stands is an obvious place to build a city, and that "it would certainly be strange if in so commodious a site, in so fertile a plain, on so advantageous a river, in so temperate and beneficent a climate...," etc.; (3) that the Etruscans frequently built cities in plains, to wit, Populonia and Pisa; and, finally, (4) that Fiesole was an Etruscan city and the Fiesolani, being Etruscans and therefore a commercial people, must certainly from the very beginning have established an emporium at the point where the first rapids interrupt the navigability of the Arno. This hypothesis could then be further corroborated by analogy from similar circumstances: the still visible *campidogli* (capitols) in Verona, Toulouse, Narbonne, and even wholly non-Roman cities like Benevento and Babylon (!) show them to have been a common feature of all Mediterranean cities and not necessarily a Roman invention. Therefore one must have existed in Florence also, as Villani supposed, which must have been built by the Etruscans and obliterated in the Middle Ages by the artificial raising of the ground level around it. The academicians usually qualified such an argument as a "conjecture"; but at least, they affirmed, it was more "reasonable" than the mere "opinion" of Leonardo Bruni, for no classical text would, they declared, support the theory that Florence had been founded by Sulla.[26]

Still, the word of even the most highly esteemed author could guarantee no more than the probability of any statement. "Conjectures" would receive the "force and stability" of certainty only when confirmed, as Lami himself admitted, by "the various and diverse ancient monuments... that have been found in Florence";[27] and should any doubt arise concerning the validity of even the most tested hypothesis, there was but one solution: "imbattersi in più antiche cartapecore."[28]   The academic critics carefully distinguished between all written accounts on one hand — either of an interpreter of earlier events or a chronicler of those of his own times — and what they called "documents" or "monuments" on the other — either official papers and inscriptions, that is, or stones, ruins, statues, and artifacts.   The first would inevitably bear the imprint of the author's point of view; the second would have been made with no intent to influence the judgment of the observer.

It was, indeed, this rigorous distinction of historical records into wholly reliable sources and unreliable opinions that induced the academies to devote so much time and money to the preservation and classification of *vetera monumenta,* which Gori, Passeri, Venuti, and many others annotated and published with elaborate copper plates in various continuations of Muratori and in costly tomes like the *Museum etruscum* and the *Thesaurus gemmarum.*[29]   Several of the new societies, indeed, were organized specifically for the purpose of

[26] *Lezioni di antichità toscane,* p. 3 (on the site), and pp. 42 and 262 f. on Bruni.
[27] *Ibid.,* p. 35.
[28] G. Targioni Tozzetti in *Memorie Colombaria,* II, 154.
[29] Among the many works of this kind, *Museum cortonese, in quo vetera monumenta comprehenduntur anaglypha, thoreumata, gemmae inscalptae, insculptaeque quae in Academia Etrusca ceterisque nobilium virorum domibus adservantur in plurimis tabulis aereis distributum, atque a Francisco Valesio romano, Antonio Francisco Gori florentino et Rodulphino Venuti cortonese, notis illustratum* (with seal of the Etrusca) (Rome: Salomoni, 1750); Gori, Michele Moücke, Antonio Pazzi, *et al., Museum Florentinum exhibens insigniora vetustatis monumenta quae Florentiae sunt* (12 vols.; Florence: Nestenus, 1731-62); Gori, *Museum etruscum;* Gori and Passeri, *Thesaurus gemmarum antiquarum astriferarum, quae e compluribus dactyliothecis selectae,* and *Thesaurus veterum diptychorum consularium et ecclesiasticorum* (both published in 3 vols. by Albizzini in Florence, 1750 and 1759).   Others are mentioned in the notes following.

"putting into their Annals" — like those of the Colombaria in Florence and Livorno and of the Notti Coritane in Cortona — "as in a secure depository ... to be transmitted ... to posterity" the "noble, scholarly notices ... of bygone centuries," which their individual members had rescued "from voracious time."[30] It was the recognition, moreover, of the importance of all the authentic relics of the past that encouraged Filippo Venuti to search through archives and libraries all over France for manuscripts pertaining to Cortona. And it was the fear that the disappearance of documents would obliterate history that led the same academicians not only to deplore the recent destruction of ancient temples and arches, but even to publish miscellaneous dissertations in the arts and sciences of their own times for the benefit of future historians, to whom the eighteenth century would in turn have become "antiquity."[31] For they realized that only such records as these could provide the basis for "rigorous demonstrations," free from the prejudice and credulity that had marred the pages of most pre-Muratorian historiography.[32]

The identification and interpretation of a document, to be sure, often posed serious difficulties. A small statue found in a field near Cortona, after all, would remain a mere "antiquity" until a comparison with other figures of similar appearance and reflections upon the passages in Latin authors describing the Etruscan religion could show it to be an Etruscan votive offering to the goddess Juno.[33]

---

[30] Colombaria: Annali 28, 15 May 1760. Note Reginaldo Sellari's MS volumes of medieval seals presented to the Etrusca (* Atti, 6 October 1751).

[31] Etrusca: * Atti, 16 July 1745, 14 March 1744, 10 February 1745, and Saggi Etrusca, I (2d ed., 1742), No. 11, in the destruction of the Arco di Portogallo in Rome by Alexander VII for the widening of the Via Flaminia. The Academy's function as a clearing house for the interpretation of documents and inscriptions is illustrated by the following article (No. 12), in which Fontanini replies to the queries of a canon of Aquileia. Note introduction to Sernini's translation of Desaguliers (John Theophilus, 1683-1744), Dissertation sur l'électricité des corps (Bordeaux: P. Brun, 1742), « Dissertazione sopra l'elettricità dei corpi », in Dissertazioni e lettere scritte sopra varie materie, I, 13 (Etrusca: * Atti, 24 October 1749), and Francesco Antonio Zaccheria, « Sopra alcune antichità di Pisa », in Symbolae litterariae, IV, 177-207, which describes the delay caused in the preparation of this supplement to Muratori when Gori found he had to correct all the entries of the earlier compilation of Enrico Noris (note 8).

[32] Saggi Etrusca, IV (1743), ix, and IX (1791), viii-ix, and Pecci to Gori, 21 February 1752: Mar B.7, 25.

[33] Museum cortonense, No. 5.

Ancient inscriptions could be read only after each letter had been deciphered, and they could be understood only after a thorough study of all the customs and institutions to which they might refer.[34] Medieval manuscripts, similarly, could be properly interpreted only by carefully applying to each passage the criteria set down by Muratori and Maffei in their guides to the "science of diplomacy." Occasionally, it is true, the date and authority of a document could be established simply by examining the language in which it was written. Thus Venuti placed the inscription on the Cortonese Cross somewhere before the sixth century by comparing the words and phrases to those used in the time of Justinian, and Lami rejected the validity of the supposed Decree of Desiderius in Viterbo because its terminology differed from that in an authentic Lombard inscription in Monza.[35] At the same time the academicians discovered that the past had left its imprint upon many things not previously included within the limits of historical documentation: upon city walls, for instance, which in Cortona might reveal the successive ages of their construction; on place names, which in the Po Valley might still recall their Etruscan origin; on coins, through which the chronology of the Roman emperors could be established; on the names of persons, which might permit Cantini to date an inscription shortly after the Roman conquest of Florence by observing the absence of the non-Etruscan second *nomen*.[36] Thus the Tuscan scholars helped to redefine the very nature of historical sources by adapting archeology,

---

[34] Note L. Cantini, *Iscrizioni che si trovano negli Atti dell'Accademia Colombaria di Firenze*, I, 1 f.

[35] [F. Venuti], *De Cruce Cortonensi, dissertatio* (2d ed. from 1st of Livorno, 1751; Florence: Allegrini, 1781), p. 18 (cf. Etrusca: * Atti, 9 November 1752); and Lami, *Lezioni di antichità toscane*, p. 301.

[36] Cross section of the walls at Cortona in *Museum cortonense*, p. 1: « Cortonensis urbis moenia etrusca »; Passeri on Hebrew and Greek place names in *Symbolae litterariae*, IV, 10; on those of the Po: Alessio Stimmaco Mazzocchi of Naples in *Saggi Etrusca*, III, No. 1. On the coin collection of the Etrusca: * Atti, 10 February 1745 and 14 September 1752 (when it numbered 500 coins of the Roman Empire alone). Note comment of Ridolfino Venuti in *Osservazioni sopra il fiume Clitunno* (Rome: Bernabò & Lazzarini, 1753), pp. 1-2: « Altrettanta maggior lode . . . portar dee colui, che prima di discorrere delle cose a lui lontane, o non mai vedute, e soltanto lette negli antichi autori, va esaminando le origini, e le antichità del proprio Paese, la Religione, l'antica situazione dei luoghi, dei tempj, ed altri monumenti dell'antichità ».

toponymy, numismatics, and comparative linguistics to the needs of historiography.

The similarities between the method of the natural sciences and that of historiography did not escape the Settecento historians. The origins of the two methods, to be sure, were quite distinct, since one descended from Galileo and the Cimento and the other from Sigonio, the Benedictines, and Muratori. But even Anton Maria Salvini had recognized the necessity of "looking at the source and not relying on the citations of others," not only in Redi's experiments, but in all other disciplines including linguistics.[37] Many of the scientists, indeed, were themselves historians, and, like the botanist Micheli in the Società Colombaria, "often applied [their] diligent observations to historical or antiquarian researches." The historians in turn acquired dissertations in physics, medicine, and anatomy "for the assistance and illustration of antiquities" and abjured "systems" and "metaphysics" — along with which they apparently included such questions as "le principe actif de l'univers" admitted by the much-praised Académie des Inscriptions — with as much righteous disdain.[38] Like the anatomist and the physicist, the historian could propose generalizations only by induction from a great number of individual data; he could rely only on the single objects perceived by his senses; and he could «admit only that which according to the evidence is certain and secure.[39]

The historians were as convinced as the scientists, moreover, of the value of "truth" for its own sake, even when it regarded a relatively inconspicuous moment of the past; they were as scornful of all their predecessors who had not yet been enlightened by their own stand-

---

[37] A. M. Salvini, *Prose toscane*, II, 41: « Vedere in fonte, non istarsene alla fede di chi gli cita . . . ».

[38] « Godeva anco molto d'ascoltare eruditi ragionamenti, ai quali ei non mancava di contribuire, applicando bene spesso alle ricerche istoriche od antiquarie le sue diligenti osservazioni . . . »: Cocchi in *Discorsi e lettere*, I, 119. Letter of G. Targioni Tozzetti on Gori's library, 4 August 1757, in Colombaria: Annali 28, Appendix: « Questi sono stati principalmente raccolti dal Gori per aiuto ed illustrazione dell'antiquaria ». *Memorie Colombaria*, I (1747), 165 and 167. On the Académie des Inscriptions, note Badolle, *L'Abbé Jean-Jacques Barthélemy*, pp. 168-69.

[39] Girolamo de' Bardi, *Prospetto sugli avanzamenti delle scienze fisiche*, p. 5: « Poiché la verità della storia non ammette se non ciò che evidentemente è certo e sicuro ».

ards; they were as impatient with those "who speak and write what they wish, and not what in fact is"; and they were as relentless in their attacks on "received opinions," like the common attribution of certain Trecento paintings to St. Luke the Evangelist, which Lami and Manni showed to have no foundation either in common sense or in the documents.[40] The objects of investigation may have been tombs and manuscripts instead of petals and planets; the results of investigation may have been to establish the date of an event rather than the classification of a plant; but the method was the same.

By defining historiography as a science, the academicians accepted implicitly the resolution of the Maurists and Muratori to the doubts posed during the seventeenth century and even as early as Francesco Patrizi concerning the possibility of historical knowledge. As long as a historian sought only the establishment of the "facts," they supposed, and as long as he abstained from drawing hypotheses about their causal relationships, his conclusions would be free from all doubt. Hence they remained completely oblivious to the philosophical difficulties that increasingly bothered their contemporaries beyond the Alps and that would soon lead, in Italy, to the new Pyrrhonism of Melchiorre Delfico. Indeed, they avoided the question altogether — or else they assumed it to have been so definitely overcome that any further efforts to prove the scientific basis of Muratorian historiography, like that still pursued as late as the 1770's and 80's among the members of the Accademia Sampaolina of Torino, were unnecessary.[41] Voltaire, then, might go on warning

---

[40] Lucatelli in *Saggi Etrusca,* VII (1758), No. 8: « Talmente però è amabile la verità, che niente si deve trascurare per iscoprirla ». Giuseppe Fabiani, secretary of the Fisiocritici, letter of 24 August 1763, in Filippo Angellieri Alticozzi, *Risposta apologetica al libro dell'antico dominio del vescovo d'Arezzo sopra Cortona* (2 vols.; Livorno: Coltellini, 1763-65), II, 27: « coloro che . . . dicono, e scrivono quello che vogliono, e non quello che di fatti è ». D. M. Manni, *Del vero pittore Luca Santo* (written for the Accademia dei Sepolti) (Florence: Viviani, 1764). The legend was accepted by A. M. Salvini, who complained, in 1716, of the loss of the « azioni del Santo Pittore » (« Se fossero stati da altri colla stessa diligenza raccolti, con cui egli scrisse quei di San Paolo, del quale fu strettissimo amico »): « In lode di Santo Luca », *Prose sacre,* pp. 13-23, esp. p. 17.

[41] Note Sergio Bertelli, « La crisi dello scetticismo e il rapporto erudizione — scienze agli inizi del secolo XVIII », *Società,* XI (1955), 435-56; Massimo Petrocchi, *Razionalismo storiografico,* published with his *Razionalismo architettonico* (Rome: Edizioni di Storia e Letteratura, 1947), pp. 45 ff.; and especially on Delfico, whose *Pensieri sulla storia e su la*

that the word "certain" "ne doit guère être employé qu'en mathé-
matiques"; but to the academicians the age of "critical, sincere, and
impartial history" had now dawned. "An easy road is opening
before us," announced Adami to the Apatisti, "to learn the truth
by means of original monuments, and to abandon the sentiments
of the old authors . . . . It will be our duty, with secure proofs, to
make ourselves judges without passion." [42]

Unfortunately, passion did occasionally mar the judgment of
even the best historians, especially in matters that concerned the
honor of their country. When, for instance, in 1746, the academicians of Cortona came upon some passages in the works of the
English Hellenist Humphrey Hody that seemed somewhat slighting
to the "literary and civil history" of Tuscany, they rose in fury, and
commissioned Lorenzo Mehus "to make known," in a Latin rebuttal
addressed to the learned of all Europe, "the excellence [of Tuscans]
in every kind of literature." [43]   Similarly, in 1778, they found that
William Robertson, whose *History of America* had just become available in an Italian translation, had attributed the principal merit for
the discovery of the New World to the Genoese Christopher Columbus, whereas it rightly belonged, as Anton Maria Salvini had declared
in his memorial plaque of 1719, to the Florentine Amerigo Vespucci.
Even Columbus, whose priority in crossing the Atlantic Bandini
admitted as early as 1745, "had been moved," he insisted, "principally
by the arguments of a certain Paolo Fiorentino [i.e., Paolo Tosca-
nelli], an expert in the mathematical disciplines," and had discovered
the Caribbean Islands more by chance than by the "greater know-

incertezza ed inutilità della medesima (with a long discussion of Fontenelle and D'Alembert)
was first published in Forlì, 1806; Giovanni Gentile, *Storia della filosofia italiana dal Genovesi al Galluppi* (2d ed.; Milan: Treves, 1930), I, 65-89.   On the Sampaolina: C. Calcaterra, *Il nostro imminente Risorgimento* (Torino: Internazionale, 1935), pp. 121-80.

[42] Adami, *Dissertazioni critiche,* p. 73.   Voltaire quoted from *Nouvelles considérations
sur l'histoire* (1744) by J. H. Brumfitt, *Voltaire Historian* (New York: Oxford University
Press, 1958), p. 99.

[43] Comments in Etrusca: Atti, 8 May 1746.   The book mentioned, *De viris illustribus,*
may refer to his *De graecis illustribus,* published posthumously by Samuel Jobb, which is
in the Magliabechiana, and was therefore probably available there to Mehus, but which
is not in the present library of the Etrusca.   Humphrey Hody (1659-1707) was involved
mostly in English ecclesiastical controversies (*DNB*), and it is doubtful that he consciously
offended Tuscan scholars.

ledge of geography, navigation, and astronomy" that had led Vespucci to discover the continent. Then, in the late 1780's a generous
contribution from the French representative in Florence and honorary member, Louis Durfort, gave the Accademia Etrusca its long
awaited opportunity, and its offer of a prize for the best biography
brought forth eight essays, which fully vindicated its illustrious
compatriot once and for all. For it was their "duty," the academicians declared, "to look after everything that may increase the
prestige of our nation." [44]

Quite as often such disputes involved not Tuscany as a whole,
but its individual cities, where the memory of former independence
still lived on in the form of local patriotism, or *campanilismo*. In
1760 the Aretine Lorenzo Guazzesi, who, as former governor of
Cortona and *lucumone* of the Etrusca, should perhaps have been
more considerate of his former subjects and associates, published a
dissertation in which he claimed that in the thirteenth century the
bishop of Arezzo had held civil as well as ecclesiastical jurisdiction
over Cortona. Such ingratitude! retorted the offended Cortonesi,
as they called for a "defender" to "rise up" against so outrageous an
attack upon "the incomparable antiquity of Cortona, the glory of
the principal Etruscan cities." Cortona may well have had no bishop
of its own before 1325, they replied, but it had been as much a
"city" as Arezzo in the thirteenth century and was still quite as
"estimable" in the eighteenth, especially since both the reigning
grand duke and Tuscan civil law declared all Tuscan cities to be
absolutely equal. Then, in order to "annul" once and for all "the
pretentions of some modern writers" according to the severest prescriptions of the historical method, they produced an inscription of
1225, found in the Palazzo Comunale, which referred to Cortona

---

[44] Guglielmo Robertson, *Storia d'America*, tr. Antonio Pilloti (4 vols.; Florence: Cambiagi, 1777-78), with a life of Columbus in Vol. I. Angelo Maria Bandini, *Vita e lettere
di Amerigo Vespucci* (Florence: All'Insegna d'Apollo, 1745) and *Compendio della vita di
A. V., gentiluomo fiorentino, tratto in gran parte dalla vita e memorie di detto illustre
navigatore pubblicate dall'eruditissimo . . . Angelo Maria Bandini, e dato ora in luce da
F. B. A. A.* (Florence: Stecchi & Pagani, 1779), pp. 4 and 12. Salvini's plaque is printed
in the Preface. The eulogies of Vespucci are preserved in Etr 460, and the announcement
of the prize is published in the Preface (p. 3) of Marco Lastri, *Elogio di Amerigo Vespucci*
(Florence, 1787) (but Stanislao Canovai was the winner, not Lastri).

as an independent city. At least, added Filippo Alticozzi in his *Risposta Apologetica,* Guazzesi might have had the good taste to refrain from so offensive a word as *dominio,* "which might make an impression on the weak spirits of persons incapable of looking beneath the surface of things."[45] Meanwhile the controversy had spread to Siena, where Pecci promised to defend "each city in the State [of Siena]" with an eleven-volume history and called for the renewal of a league, like that proposed by Gigli some decades before, among the "Ghibelline" cities — Siena, Cortona, Pistoia, and even Perugia — against the "Guelfs" of Florence and Arezzo.[46]

At times these interurban wars ended in personal animosities — a frequent failing among the Settecento letterati, and one which the academies did their best to overcome. Guazzesi disdained even to reply to the "ridicolo libro cortonese," which "all those with any common sense" among his friends at Pisa brushed aside as "una solenne C—"; and the Vespucci contest soon turned out to be such an "apple of discord" — with the Accademia Etrusca playing the ungrateful role of Paris — that the public authorities had to intervene.[47] The "excessive partiality" of "diverse writers... for their own cities," deplored by a few more conscientious observers like Della Valle and even Pecci, may have been justified partially

---

[45] [Filippo Venuti], *Vita di Fra Elia da Cortona* (Livorno: Santini, 1755), p. 341. Lorenzo Guazzesi, *Dell'antico dominio del vescovo di Arezzo in Cortona* (Pisa: Giovannelli, 1760 [2d ed., 1761]). Alticozzi, *Risposta apologetica,* Preface. This dispute had nothing to do with jurisdiction or property rights, like that between Muratori and Fontanini over Comacchio earlier in the century. The difficulty lay perhaps in a certain pugnacious character that led Muratori to remark (*Scritti autobiografici,* p. 65) that « one Florentine is worth ten Venetians, but a hundred Florentines brought together, each with his own hot head and each in love with his own personal opinion, can do far less than the quiet prudence of a single Venetian ».

[46] Pecci's letter in Appendix to Alticozzi, *Risposta apologetica.* « Accademici Uniti » to Gigli, in 1717, and the Risvegliati to the same, 4 January 1717: BCS Y.I.19, fol. 10 f.

[47] Guazzesi to A. M. Bandini, 23 May and 3 June 1763: Mar B.2, 27, 17, 19. Remark of Moreni: « Il programma dell'elogio del Vespucci fù, come ognun sà, per le penne toscane il pomo della discordia », in *Bibliografia storica,* I, 94. Many of the papers and petitions, including the request of the secretary for government intervention, are in ASF Reggenza 1054.B.1. The Academy's position in the controversy is stated in *Monumenti relativi al giudizio pronunciato dall'A. E. di C. di un elogio d'Amerigo Vespucci* (Arezzo: Bellotti, 1787), including the original, uncorrected text submitted for the prize.

by the quantity of historical research it provoked.[48] But all too often
it encouraged the sacrifice of "truth" to purposes not entirely in
keeping with the ideals of scholarly impartiality demanded by
Manni and Adami.

Yet the scholarly quarrels of the Aretines and the Cortonese
would in themselves have been harmless, had they not at times
led the participants to betray in their texts the principles of
"scientific" historiography so eloquently professed in their prefaces.
The criticism of both medieval and ancient authors, first of all,
frequently depended more upon the support they apparently lent to
an attempt to magnify the antiquity and the glory of a Tuscan city
than upon the plausibility of what they said. Villani and Malespini,
for instance, could "shed great light on these things" by referring
to the antiquity of the Florentine towers, and Pliny could speak of
the tiny, seasonal Cecina River as navigable. Obviously such statements were true, for they proved that the towers were Etruscan and
that the site of Volterra had been chosen for its proximity to water
transportation. But should a chronicler erroneously locate the Roman
baths in the Via della Terma, the reader had to be warned that his
"authority can well be abandoned without scrupule." And should
the Roman historians suggest that Hannibal had been stopped by the
marshes of the Arno and Chiana valleys, their Settecento critics would
accuse them of "fables," since it was unthinkable that so industrious
a people as the Etruscans would have let the rivers overflow.[49]

At times, indeed, the academic historians disregarded the reservations even of their authorities. Giorgi, for instance, cites Thucydides
to prove that the Cyclops were the first inhabitants of Sicily; but he
overlooks completely the conclusion of the same sentence in the
Pelopennesian War (Bk. XVIII, chap. 2), which suggests that the
whole pre-Hellenic history of the island was a matter more for poets
than for historians. Most of them, moreover, all too easily burdened

[48] Della Valle's criticism of Gigli, in *Lettere senesi*, II, 30; Pecci to Gori, 9 December 1752: Mar B.7, 25.

[49] Lami, *Lezioni di antichità toscane*, pp. 147, 21, and 62; cf. [Bottari?], « In difesa
di Tito Livio, che narra varj prodigj nella sua storia », *Memorie Colombaria*, I, No. 5,
giving « scientific » explanations for the rain of stones on Monte Calvo. L. Guazzesi,
« Passaggio di Annibale per la Palude », *Saggi Etrusca*, VI, No. 2.

their works with documents that really had no relevance to their theses, or else they filled up embarassing lacunae with vague superlatives: Fra Elia of Cortona had had a "stupendous number of disciples," for example, and "there was perhaps no one in Italy who equalled him." [50] Indeed the multiplication of "must have been's" and "without doubt's" sometimes reached absurd proportions, especially in the works of the greatest offender of all, Lorenzo Guazzesi of Arezzo. The remains of Etruscan buildings were still visible in various other Tuscan cities, he mused. Therefore, "the Tuscans [i.e., Etruscans], among whom the Aretines without doubt were very prominent, must have built large and majestic edifices for their spectacles," supported by columns in the "Tuscan" ("or rather Herculean") order, the "most ancient, most robust," and most perfect in its "simplicity," which the Romans had simply copied in their own structures. A word in Vitruvius seems to indicate that they performed tragedies. Therefore, they must have celebrated games and they undoubtedly staged comedies, with dancers like those pictured on their urns... etc., etc. Then after a few pages of such imaginative conjectures, the conditional quietly gives way to the indicative, and what has been qualified as merely "probable" becomes "true" simply by default. [51]

Almost all the academicians, furthermore, were at times guilty of stretching their sources. It might be somewhat plausible, for example, that "an almost divine man could not be born except in a climate able to influence the formation of [his] inimitable genius." It might even be possible that no country was "more healthy, more fertile, more delicious" than the plains north of Lago Trasimeno. And it was almost certain that the Phoenician alphabet contained no vowels. But the temperate climate and good air of Tuscany could not, in all fairness, prove that Pythagoras in fact had been born in Cortona; nor, really, could the aspirated

[50] Antonio Giorgi, *Dissertazione accademica sopra un monumento etrusco* (Sepolti) (Florence: Bonducci, 1752), p. 12. [F. Venuti], *Vita di fra Elia di Cortona*, p. 4: « Ebbe stupendo numero di discepoli », « non vi era forse allora in Italia che l'uguagliasse ».

[51] L. Guazessi, « Dissertazioni intorno agli anfiteatri », in *Tutte le opere* (4 vols.; Pisa: Pizzorno, 1766), I, 1-2.

c of modern Florentine and the frequency of consonants in Etruscan prove that the Phoenicians had founded Florence.[52]

Finally, the inflexibility with which the Tuscan historians insisted upon separating "truth" from "falsehood" blinded them completely both to the meaning and to the historical significance of the myths and symbols which they collected with such assiduousness. Either they dismissed all the "fables of the ancients" as nothing but the work of superstition, or else they assumed them to be literally true accounts of real human beings, most of whom possessed all the virtues of the heroes of contemporary tragedies. Thus they worked out elaborate genealogical charts, beginning with Atlas (there were three of them, not one, as Hesoid erroneously supposed) going through his daughter, wife of Corito, king of Italy (whence *Cortona,* his capital), to his grandchildren — Fiesole, the nurse of Bacchus (who was portrayed on a vase found in Fiesole itself), and Dardanus, the founder of Troy — and usually ending with Aeneas.[53] *La boria de' dotti!* None of the academicians apparently ever read Vico; but a few of them eventually came to the conclusion that "the fantastic pleasure of deducing the origin of cities from the darkness of remote centuries" might more profitably be left "to the poets and the novelists." "It would indeed please me," confessed Luigi Lanzi in 1789, "to defend an opinion so advantageous to the Italic name"; unfortunately, "the arguments do not convince me."[54] For the documents themselves frequently led astray the very scholars who rightly would admit no other basis for their researches; and the new historical method, far from restraining their mental and sentimental flights of fancy, simply lent their patriotic speculations an aura of "scientific" accuracy.

[52] Filippo Laparelli, « Sopra la nazione, e la patria di Pitagora filosofo », *Saggi Etrusca,* VI, No. 4, pp. 92-93. Lorenzo Cantini, *Storia del commercio, e navigazione dei Pisani* (2 vols.; Florence: Albizzini, 1797-98). Lami, *Lezioni di antichità toscane,* 20 ff. The different dates of these publications show that such arguments continued from the 1740's to the end of the century.

[53] Lami, *Lezioni di antichità toscane,* p. 25. Etrusca: * Atti, 14 October 1776 and 31 January 1777 (where Sellari establishes the exact date of the foundation of Rimini (364 years before Rome) and gives the names of its kings — all from a monument found at Chiusi in 1773); *Museum cortonense,* p. vii.

[54] Della Valle, *Lettere senesi,* II, 11, and Luigi Lanzi, *Saggio di lingua etrusca e di altre antiche d'Italia per servire alla storia de' popoli, delle lingue e delle belle arti* (1st ed.; Rome: Pagliarini, 1789, here cited in 2d.; Florence: Tofani, 1824-25), I, 137.

Yet the very nature of the documents admitted by the new method led at the same time to a broadening of the scope of history itself well beyond its more traditional limitation to political events. The libraries and museums contained remnants of many phases of human life in the past; therefore, the historian had now to attend not only to the births and feats of princes, but also to "the clothing, banquets, funerals,... public festivities, spectacles, games,... and many, many other things of this nature,... following in the luminous footsteps of the immortal Lodovico Antonio Muratori."[55]   To be sure, the academicians overlooked a number of lateral fields that might easily have complemented their historical studies. They failed, first of all, to develop their interminable academic eulogies into anything approaching biography, that is, the recreation of a real person in a plausible historical setting. They gave no more than passing attention, secondly, to the history of language, since they were far more interested in freeing that of the Trecento from the corruption of time. They gave even less to the history of literature, which was just then being so ably written outside Tuscany. And, strangely enough for the descendants of Vasari and the associates of Della Valle, Bottari, and Lanzi, they ignored almost completely the history of art.[56]   Their occasional interest in the history of law, finally, was so limited by current concepts of natural law that, while they found little difficulty in understanding the statutes of the Florentine Republic, they could listen without murmur to Guarnacci's account of how a committee of Roman senators in the fifth century B. C. toured the civilized states of the Mediterranean in order to assemble the best laws of each into the first universal code — the Law of the Twelve Tables.[57]

[55] [A. F. Gori], *La Toscana illustrata nella sua storia con varj scelti monumenti e documenti per l'avanti o inediti o molto rari* (Livorno: Santini, 1755), pp. iv-v. Similarly: Giorgi, *Dissertazione accademica sopra un monumento etrusco*, pp. 1-2.

[56] Manni's *Addizioni necessarie alle vite de' due celebri statuarj....* (Michelangelo and Cellini) (Florence: Viviani, 1774), given in the Crusca, is one of the very few *lezioni* with any bearing on art history after those of Baldinucci (above. chap. i, note 19). A few were delivered at inaugural sessions of the Accademia delle Belle Arti, which was not an "academy" in the sense used here; and others were presented to the Accademia Pistoiese at the beginning of the next century.

[57] *Memorie Colombaria*, I, No. 4. The story, of course, is Livy's; note St. Augustine, *De Civitate Dei*, II, xvi. Gregorio Fierli, « Sul governo dei Romani relativamente

Nevertheless, the Tuscan academicians were among the first to consider the "rites and customs" of the past in an historical context — the clothing of the Etruscans, for instance, the celebrations of medieval Florentines, the origins of schools and churches, and the sea and land routes used by the Romans.[58] Some of them, indeed, specialized specifically in economic history, writing of the viticulture and the weights and measurements of the ancients and illustrating the failure of Quattrocento Tuscans to solve the question of food supply and their success in preventing the deflation of the currency.[59] And others dedicated themselves to the history of the sciences, recounting the progress of geography and astronomy in the fifteenth century and of physics in the sixteenth and seventeenth.[60] Thus during the course of the Settecento historians came to include institutions, systems of transportation and communication, family life, agriculture, legislation, and even the carts used in the annual feast of San Giovanni as subjects of historical investigation.[61]

alle arti e al commercio », and Bernardo Lessi, « Le leggi etrusche e l'adozione che ne fecero i Romani », in Saggi Etrusca, IX, Nos. 2 and 8.

[58] Saggi Etrusca, III (1741), x: « i riti e i costumi di que' secoli de' quali vi è memoria di uomini ». L. Guazzesi, « De vesta etruscorum dissertatio », Calogerà, Raccolta d'opuscoli, XVIII, 249-73. Giuseppe Averani, « Del principio, e progresso della navigazione e della grandezza dell'antiche navi » and « Dell'armate navili, e prestezza di fabbricarle, e della navigazione degli antichi », in his Lezioni toscane, Nos. 6 and 7, and Crusca: * Diario 17 July 1727; and Guazzesi's dissertation « sulla Via Cassia » published with Dissertazioni sugli anfiteatri di Toscana, etc. (Pisa: Giovannelli, 1761).

[59] F. Venuti and L. Lorenzi in Saggi Etrusca, I, Nos. 7 and 9; Vincenzo Fineschi, Istoria compendiata di alcune antiche carestie, e dovizie di grano occorse in Firenze, cavata da un diario MS in cartapecora del secolo XIV (Florence: Viviani, 1767), with historical preface; G. Targioni Tozzetti, « Del Fiorino di sigillo, e delle riflessioni sulle cause dell'accrescimento di valuta del fiorino d'oro della Repubblica Fiorentina » (Crusca: * Diario, 20 April 1747), in Memorie Colombaria, II, 127-204, reprinted in Guid'Antonio Zanetti, Nuova raccolta delle monete e zecche d'Italia (8 vols.; Bologna: Volpe, 1775), I, 247-354.

[60] Ottaviano Guasco and Stanislao Canovai in Saggi Etrusca, VIII, No. 4, and IX, No. 13, and G. Targioni Tozzetti, « Brevi notizie intorno alle infreddature epidemiche », in Prima raccolta, p. 174-76, with reference to a catalogue he was preparing on epidemics similar to that of 1752 which had occurred after 1323.

[61] Note D. M. Manni, Ragionamento istorico sopra i carri, che si conducono al Tempio di San Giovanni Battista di Firenze la mattina del Santo (Florence: Stecchi, 1766, and in Osservazioni istoriche, Vol. XXI). A number of studies, both in and out of the academies, were devoted to the origins of printing, e.g., Manni, Della prima promulgazione de' libri in Firenze (in the Apatisti, 5 February 1761). (Florence: Viviani, 1761).

Nothing, it is true, would necessarily have prevented the academicians from applying their new methods to the history of the entire world. They might well have followed their contemporaries, both foreign and Italian, into the study of ancient Greece, Egypt, and Mesopotamia or of contemporary China and America; the works of the Jesuit missionaries, after all, of the Spanish historians of the New World, and of the scientific explorers, as well as the publications of the principal learned societies across the Alps were all available in their libraries. Yet neither Magalotti's popular account of "that wise Empire of China," nor the translations of De Solis' *History of Mexico,* of the *American Gazetteer,* or of Robertson's *History of America,* which all attracted considerable attention during the century, had any apparent influence on the historical research of the academies.[62] History in Tuscany began with artifacts and documents; and since the academicians had found no visible remnants of the Egyptians, the Chinese, or the Aztecs among the antiquities found on Tuscan soil, they simply relegated all the literature pertaining to such distant peoples to the realms of aesthetics, linguistics, or pure curiosity.

Rome, on the other hand, was much closer to Tuscany. All through the Seicento and well into the Settecento the discourses by Carlo Dati and Filippo Baldinucci on the painting of the ancients and by Giuseppe Averani on their religion, food, and drink had kept alive among the academicians at least some of the enthusiasm for Roman art and literature that had so animated their ancestors of the Quattrocento.[63] The publication of *De Etruria regali* in 1726

---

[12] On De Solis, above, chap. i, note 37. [Lorenzo Magalotti], *Notizie varie dell'Impero della China* (Florence: Manni, 1697). One of the few exceptions in the academic diaries is the discourse of Luigi Lorenzi, French chargé d'affaires, to the Crusca: *Diario, 20 September 1764. In general, see E. W. Cochrane, « Il 'Gazzettiero americano' di Livorno e l'America nella letteratura del Settecento », *Quaderni di cultura e storia sociale,* III (1954), No. 1; Guglielmo Procacci, « Rivoluzione americana e storiografia italiana », *Rassegna storica del Risorgimento,* XLI (1954), 565-71; as well as chap. vi of Pace, *Benjamin Franklin and Italy.*

[63] Note comment of Baldinucci in *Raccolta di alcuni opuscoli* (Florence: Bonducci, 1755), p. 96 (lecture to Crusca of 29 December 1691); Carlo Dati, *Vite de' pittori antichi* (1st ed.; Florence: Della Stella, 1667; 2d ed. with notes of the author and the seal of Crusca; Naples: Ricciardo, 1730). In general: Antonio Minto, *Le vite dei pittori antichi di Carlo Roberto Dati e gli studi erudito-antiquari nel Seicento* (Florence: Olschki, 1953).

gave a new impulse and a completely new direction to these traditional studies by changing their bases from literary to archeological sources. Inspired by the example of Buonarroti, Gori and Salvini set to work almost immediately assembling and annotating the inscriptions and art works of the Roman period then scattered in various private collections all over the country. The interest aroused by their project was further enchanced by the discovery of two marble tablets near Volterra in 1732, by the detailed description of Roman remains in Capua brought back by Gregorio Redi in 1737, and by the many reports sent in by correspondents of the academies of the current excavations in Rome, which soon produced, among other treasures, an entire burial chamber filled with funeral urns and the theater of Hadrian's Villa.[64]

Then, in 1748, the most spectacular discovery of all sent a wave of excitement throughout Italy. As early as 1711 the Prince d'Elbeuf had uncovered several marble pieces, including a statue of Hercules, while searching for construction material for his villa outside Naples. Lack of funds and the indifference of the viceroys prevented any further digging until 1738, when Carlo III ordered systematic excavations of the site. When the Royal Librarian, Marcello Venuti of Cortona, had himself lowered by rope into a long shaft to compare the inscriptions that had been found with appropriate passages in Pliny, the conclusion was unavoidable: this was the buried city of Herculaneum. For some time the discovery remained a secret, carefully guarded by the express prohibition to remove or even to sketch any of the objects then being transferred to the Royal Museum. But enough information evidently leaked out to permit the Accademia Etrusca to decorate its *Saggi* in 1742 with culs-de-lampe of fairly accurate Pompeian motifs; and when Venuti returned to Cortona on family business in 1748, he presented to the Academy a full description of the successive excavations, which he published the following

---

[64] See *Giornale de' letterati d'Italia*, XXXVIII (1726-27), 315-30, on the *Inscriptiones antiquae in Etruriae urbibus extantes* (above, note 12). Lami in *Saggi Etrusca*, I (2d ed.), No. 6; Gregorio Redi in *ibid.*, II. No. 6, and the MS in Mar Redi 51 (date given in the catalogue); *Saggi Etrusca*, II, No. 8, and the discussions in the Notti Coritane on the Villa Adriana in *Symbolae litterariae*, VIII, chap. ix.

year with the texts of hundreds of inscriptions and with many drawings.[65]   In September 1758, Gori delivered an equally glowing résumé
to the Crusca of the reports he had received from several correspondents; and thereafter academic sessions were dedicated ever more frequently to the analysis of frescoes, statues, and stones, which by 1755
had already attracted enough attention to provoke several rather
violent literary controversies.[66]   A new "Antiquity" had suddenly
emerged — not merely "small remnants and fragments, but... an
entire city, complete with magnificent and precious decorations, with
theaters, temples, pictures, houses," [67] which could tell the academic
historians far more about the life and customs of the *antichi* than
could the classical texts upon which their previous discourses had of
necessity been based.

Unfortunately, the enthusiasm aroused by "these remarkable discoveries," of which the members of the Etrusca, the Crusca, and the
Colombaria justly complimented themselves for having been "the first
to give notice," soon died out, and by the 1760's the academicians seem
to have forgotten all about them.[68]   Few Tuscans, first of all, could
fully appreciate the romantic charm of the "imposing ruins" of the
Eternal City, which Giambattista Piranesi, the friend and collaborator
of the Cortonese antiquarian Ridolfino Venuti, was just then rescuing

[65] Marcello Venuti, *Descrizione delle prime scoperte dell'antica città d'Ercolano* (Venice: Baseggio, 1749) (translated as *A Description of the First Discoveries of the Ancient City
of Heraclea* [*London*, 1750]), and Etrusca: * Atti, 22 May and 18 November 1748.

[66] [A. F. Gori], *Notizie del memorabile scoprimento dell'antica città di Ercolano vicina
a Napoli . . . avuto per lettera da vari celebri letterati* (Florence: Stamperia Imperiale, 1748),
and Crusca: * Diario, 16 Semptember 1748, and his « Admiranda antiquitatum Herculanensium
descripta et illustrata » in *Symbolae litterariae*, I, 1-192 which, together with Venuti's *Descrizione*, gives a much more thorough history of the discoveries than any more recent account.
Novelle letterarie, XVII (1756), 144; *Saggi Etrusca*, VII, No. 10; Etrusca: *Atti, 18 April and
29 June 1754, etc.   Among the controversies: see Lami's account (*Novelle letterarie*, I [1740],
663-67), of the attack « senza carità cristiana, e civiltà ancora » of P. D. Giovan Grisostomo
Scarfò (1685-1740?) of Mammola in Calabria on Ridolfino Venuti's *Collectanes antiquitatum
romanarum* (Rome, 1736), to which Filippo Venuti addressed an anonymous *Risposta* « alla
nobile Accademia di Cortona » in 1740.

[67] « Una intera città, corredata di magnifici, e preziosi abbellimenti. con teatri, templi,
pitture, case . . . »: M. Venuti, *Descrizione delle prime scoperte*, p. ix.

[68] « Si mostra . . . essere stati i fiorentini i primi a dare avviso . . . di queste insigni
scoperte »: Gori in *Symbolae litterariae*, I, 52. In general: Arnaldo Momigliano, « La formazione della moderna storiografia sull'Impero Romano », *Rivista storica italiana*, XIV[1]
(1936), 35-60, and xix, 19-48.

from "the barbarism in which they had been hidden" and learning
to "regard with the eye of an artist."[69] Almost no Roman ruins, after
all, survived on Tuscan soil; and the standards of "scientific" historiography would permit neither the use of mere reports in place of
direct observation nor the intrusion of aesthetic or sentimental considerations into matters of scholarship. Rome, moreover, could add
very little to the pride of local patriots, whom Dempster had now
inspired to look for the foundation of their cities far earlier than
the Catilinian conspiracy or the flight of Remus to Siena. Even the
much-applauded paintings at Herculaneum, it was found, disobeyed
the strict rules of "design based upon reason," which Winckelmann
and Mengs were just then imposing upon Italian art; while neo-
classicism soon condemned the elaborate composite style of Roman
architecture, which the infallible Vitruvius had so berated, in favor of
the simplicity and solidity of "Etruscan" columns.[70]

Yed the academicians accused the Romans of far more than bad
taste. Rome, they insisted, had grown through plunder and blood-
shed alone. The Republic may have produced a few virtuous citizens,
true; but it also had ruined and depopulated Italy. The Empire may
have facilitated the growth of Christianity; but it had systematically
despoiled the entire Mediterranean solely to satisfy the lusts of irre-
sponsible aristocrats and idle plebeians. Among the subjects of an
enlightened monarch, who had long since lost any nostalgia for their
own republican liberties, both regimes were equally despicable. The
moralists condemned the Romans as avaricious, intemperate, cruel,
and incapable of governing themselves. The economists blamed them
for neglecting agriculture, disdaining commerce, and failing to invent
even so fundamental an instrument of economic activity as the bill of
exchange. And to these charges the historians added the most un-
forgivable crime of all: the conquest of Etruria, the destruction of

---

[69] « Scotendo la barbarie, nella quale si occultavano, incominciò a guardare con occhio
d'artista queste imponenti rovine . . . »: Preface to 2d ed. of Ridolfino Venuti, *Accurata e suc-
cinta descrizione topografica delle antichità di Roma* (from 1st ed. of 1763 [Bernabò e Laz-
zarini]; Rome, 1803), I, ix (most of the illustrations are by Piranesi). Even Venuti admits,
however, that « il fervido genio di questo valente artista, lo fece alle volte cadere in qualche
svista ».

[70] Della Valle, *Lettere senesi*, I, 45.

its cities and monuments, and the obliteration of its language, which not even such esteemed "antiquarians" as Cicero and Varro had bothered to transmit to posterity.[71]

It is not surprising, then, that the still more fruitful discoveries at Pompei some years later passed unnoticed in the records of the academies; for their members were now far too busy avenging the defeat of their own ancestors to contemplate any further the monuments of a "foreign" conqueror. During the two previous centuries the curiosity of a few isolated scholars — Giovanni Annio da Viterbo, for instance, Teseo Ambrosio, Pier Francesco Giambullari, Curzio Inghirami, and even Dempster himself — concerning certain passages in the Latin authors and certain monuments that occasionally turned up in the fields of Tuscany had encountered little more than scorn or ridicule; for their contemporaries had been far too preoccupied with the Romans themselves to bother with speculations about the peoples that preceded them.[72] Then, in the Settecento, the resurgence of literary *campanilismo,* the emphasis of the new historical method upon primary sources, and the demand of the academies for scholarly

[71] Etrusca: * Atti, 30 December 1746; Fierli on Roman commerce: note 57; Filippo Venuti in *Memorie Colombaria,* II, 18-19; and Bindo S. Peruzzi, « Se più convenga lo studio dell'antica o della moderna storia », donated to the Colombaria in 1763 (Tarpato I, p. 88). Cf. Giovanni Fabbroni, *Dei provvedimenti annonarj* (Florence, 1804), pp. 228-29, and Pompeo Neri, « Roma, che non conobbe altri mezzi di farsi grande che quello della conquista . . . »: *Discorso sopra la materia frumentaria* (written in 1776, here referred to in S.C.I.E.P. edition), pp. 17-18. There were, of course, a number of exceptions to the more general condemnation of Rome, although mostly outside the academies: note, for instance, many of the passages of Stefano Bertolini quoted by Giorgio Giorgetti in « S. B.: L'attività e la cultura di un funzionario toscano del sec. XVIII », *Archivio storico italiano,* CIX (1952), 84-120. Note Frederic Mascioli, « Anti-Roman and Pro-Italic Feeling in Italian Historiography », *Romanic Review,* XXXIII (1942), 366-84, which observes similar tendencies in Denina, Giuseppe Micali, and Vincenzo Cuoco and emphasizes the importance of Etruscology in this connection.

[72] On the early history of Etruscology: Pericle Ducati, *Le problème étrusque* (Paris: Leroux, 1938), pp. 26 f. (a very sympathetic review); Part I of Raymond Bloch, *The Etruscans* (English translation; New York: Praeger, 1958); Preface of Lorenzo Cantini to *Memorie Colombaria,* III; and other works cited in note 20 above. On the popularity of Etruscology, note Maffei's plea that Dempster be translated into Italian: *Osservazioni letterarie,* III (1738), 242. Gori found that some of the charges against Inghirami were valid, but that the real objection to his book, published in 1636, was the quality of his Latin prose: *Documenti raccolti dal can. Niccolò Maria Lisci . . . intorno all'antichità toscane di Curzio Inghirami* (Florence: Viviani, 1739), pp. 1-23. Note further Gaetano Gasperoni, « Primato, onore e amore d'Italia negli storici ed eruditi del Settecento », *Convivium,* XI (1939), 264-73.

production quickly dissipated the former indifference of Tuscan audiences. Nothing flattered the citizens of Cortona so much as the thought that their city had been the capital of a great Italic kingdom long before Romulus had settled on the banks of the Tiber;[73] and few fields of study could offer a comparable opportunity for originality or so attractive a possibility of reconstructing an entire civilization without the aid of written accounts.

The initial enthusiasm aroused by the publication of *De Etruria regali,* therefore, spread rapidly. Within a few years extensive excavations were begun in the countryside around Volterra, Siena, Cortona, and Arezzo; and Anton Francesco Gori toured all the cities of Tuscany, tramping through the fields on foot and leaving behind local artists charged with sending him drawings of all that had been or might be found.[74] The excavators overlooked, it is true, the rich treasures which the Maremma yielded to the archeologists of the following century, partially because of their assumption that the cities of ancient Etruria had been in the same location as those of modern Tuscany. But they succeeded within a few years in uncovering a number of important tombs, complete with the original furnishings and decorations; and by the middle of the century they had filled the museums of Tuscany with paintings, vases, statues, and utensils of a people which thirty years before had been almost completely unknown.

Yet what really fascinated the academicians was not so much the monuments themselves as the characters that the Etruscan artisans had rather sparingly inscribed upon them. The letters posed the first problem, for they differed considerably from those of the known ancient languages. Although some had already been identified by the scholars of the Cinquecento (and some others simply invented

---

[73] Alticozzi in Etrusca: * Atti, 3 January 1744. On the origins of Volterra: Giuseppe Riccobaldi Del Bava, *Dissertazioni istorico-etrusche sull'origine, antico stato, lingua, e caratteri dell'etrusca nazione, e sopra l'origine, e primo, e posteriore stato della città di Volterra* (Sepolti: hereafter cited as *Dissertazioni istorico-etrusche*) (Florence: Viviani, 1758), Nos. I, VI, and Appendix.

[74] All thoroughly described in the long "Ad lectorem" of Gori's *Museum etruscum,* and documented by his correspondence with Pecci from 1733 to 1749 in Mar B.7.66. Gori frankly acknowledged his debt to Buonarroti in a letter to Pecci of 1 June 1733. On the excavations at Volterra: Sepolti: * Deliberazioni, 16 February 1756.

to fill out the remaining letters of the Greek and Roman alphabets), not until the 1730's had enough inscriptions been copied and compared to permit a reliable compilation. First Buonarroti and then the Swiss antiquarian Louis Bourguet drew up alphabets based on the material in Dempster and on the Tavole Eugubine; and finally, by 1737, Gori had sufficiently improved on the work of his predecessors to publish one in the *Museum Etruscum* which is remarkably close to that accepted by scholars today. In spite of the violent (and largely unjustified) attacks of Scipione Maffei, Gori's alphabet soon won the approval of the Accademia Etrusca, of the *Acta Eruditorum,* and of Giovanni Cristoforo Amaduzzi, one of the most accomplished contemporary authorities on ancient writing. Indeed, except for one or two archaic letters, which are omitted, and except for the inverse E, which is confused with the Roman E, it differs from that recently published by Professor Pallottino only in confusing such close sounds as F and PH and in giving as contemporary variants what actually are successive modifications.[75]

Understanding the words into which the letters were arranged posed much more serious difficulties, although their success with the alphabet made the Etruscologists confident of eventually being able to read them. A few were almost self-evident — like place names, which had remained substantially the same, and the names of deities, which the Romans themselves had confessed to have taken from the Etruscans. Sometimes even grammatical inflections and

[75] Gori's alphabet of 1737 is printed in his *Museum etruscum*, I, xlviiii; it is reprinted in simplified form, together with all the other earlier alphabets, including Maffei's, in his anonymous *Difesa dell'alfabeto degli antichi toscani* (Florence: Albizzini, 1742; first published in 1739 according to his *Storia antiquaria etrusca*, p. v), opposite p. cxxxviii; in the Appendix is printed the judgment of the *Acta eruditorum*. Cf. M. Pallottino in *The Etruscans*, English translation by J. Cremona in the Pelican edition (1955), p. 259. Note Lodovico [Louis] Bourget, *Saggi Etrusca,* I (2d ed.), No. 1. He cannot really be credited with having "discovered" the alphabet, as claimed in Michaud. Amaduzzi's approval in letter to Bianchi in Gaetano Gasperoni, *Settecento italiano* (Padova: Cedam, 1941), p. 42. Cf. Preface to his *Alphabetum veterum etruscorum et nonnulla eorundem monumenta* (Rome: Propaganda Fidei, 1771). Gori here cited on his controversy with Maffei in *Storia antiquaria etrusca*, pp. x-xi; note his *Osservazioni critiche sopra alcuni paragrafi del Ragionamento degli itali in cui dal marchese S. M. si procura d'investigare . . .* (Florence: Albizzini, 1740). Maffei's « Della nazione etrusca e degl'itali primitivi » is published in his *Osservazioni letterarie*, Vols. IV-VI, with another article in *Saggi Etrusca*, III, No. 5.

peculiarities of orthography could be identified by careful observation:
Gio. Battista Passeri, for example, succeeded in recognizing the final
particle AL as a sign of the genitive; and he correctly concluded that
some words were syncopated, although for the somewhat dubious
reasons that clusters of consonants would have offended the ears of
ancient as much as modern "Etruscans." [76] But the language as a
whole threatened to remain incomprehensible unless it could be
related to some known tongue. A few scholars, like Bourguet, suggested that it was a form of archaic Greek. Others, like Lami and
eventually even Passeri, supposed it to be connected with Latin. And
a few thought it to be a combination of both and freely translated
the words Frater and Erak in the same inscription respectively as
"brother," through the Latin homonym, and "desolation," through
the Greek   ἐρημόω.   This assumption, indeed, appeared for a
time to be correct; for when Gori applied it to what he thought to be
the Etruscan portion of the Tavole Eugubine (which is really Umbrian, as Buonarroti had suspected, written in modified Etruscan
characters) he managed to turn out a fairly elegant word-by-word
translation very similar to the religious hymn that Bourguet, supposing the Latin tablets to be a translation of the others, had read
into the texts some years earlier.[77] Still others, on the other hand,
proposed an even more lofty origin: Etruscan was perhaps the first
"gentile" dialect to emerge from Hebrew, the language of Noah,
which certain Egyptian words and certain place names in Asia Minor
suggested was once spoken all over the eastern Mediterranean. Etruscan, then, would have been the "Language of the gods" mentioned

---

[76] Passeri in *Memorie Colombaria,* I, No. 1, esp. pp. 37-38, on the word Thvphlthm,
« voce, che tanto aborre dal dolcissimo suono della nostra etrusca favella » (he is probably
mistaking the sound of the H). It might well have been the absurdity of an inscription
"talking" (« I commemorate so-and-so ») that prevented his guessing the meaning of MI
(e.g., p. 40), which Pallottino has identified as the first person singular pronoun.

[77] *Museum etruscum,* I, xlvii ff.: « Prolegomena ad interpretationem etruscae Tabulae
Eugubinae »; the translation follows a reproduction of the original on p. lv, with a note
to support the rendering of each word. Passeri's final views (next note) are given in his
In Thomae Dempsteri libros de Etruria regali Paralipomena (Lucca: Venturini, 1767). A
possible similarity to Phoenician, already noted by Lami in *Lezioni di antichità toscane,*
p. 20, is suggested by G. Guyot de Marne, « Sopra un'inscrizione [*sic*] punica e greca » and
by Michèle Fourmont (1690-1746), professor of Syriac at Paris), « Sopra una iscrizione fenicia

by Homer, who, according to Gori, had "traveled all over Etruria and had learned much of what he wrote in the Iliad and the Odyssey from the Etruscans." It therefore would have engendered Greek about the time of the Trojan War and have subsequently produced the dialects of the various Italic peoples, including Latin, all of which Guarnacci insisted had once been merely local variants.[78] Hence, it could easily be understood simply by choosing apparent homonyms from any of the other ancient languages.

In practice, unfortunately, these hypotheses proved to be of little use. Most of the "texts" consisted of no more than short funeral or votive inscriptions full of proper names. No two scholars, moreover, even if they held the same theory of the origin of the language, could agree on the interpretation of any one of them: when Passeri, for instance, dismissed the first two letters of the name TLENAIEIM as a conventional formula in order to define the rest of it as "born of Enalia," Lami scrawled in the margin: "what a miserable explanation! who told you such nonsense!"[79] Some of then eventually recognized the hopelessness of the task, lamenting the "deep night" that obscured "the occult language of the Etruscans" as thoroughly as it shrouded "the Egyptian hieroglyphics";[80] and not until Luigi Lanzi at the

---

trovata a Malta », *Saggi Etrusca*, I, No. 2, and III, No. 3; or to the language of Palmyra by Barthélemy, *Ibid.*, VII, No. 1.

[78] Mario Guarnacci, *Origini italiche, ossiano Memorie istorico-etrusche sopra l'antichissimo Regno d'Italia e sopra i di lei primi abitatori nei secoli più remoti* (3 vols.; Lucca: I & II: Venturini, 1767; III: Giusti, 1772), esp. Part II, p. v (on whom note the meeting of the Sepolti in * Deliberazioni, 21 August 1785). Passeri, « De hebraismo aegyptiorum dissertatio », (p. 3: « Ad linguam etruscam explicandam maxime confert non modo lingua greca, sed etiam hebraica »), and « De hellenismo etruscorum », both in *Symbolae litterariae*, IV, 1-104, and II, 35-76; the position is fully explained in his « Lettere roncagliesi », Calogerà, *Raccolta d'opuscoli*, Vols. XXII, XXIII, XXVI and XXVII. Gori in *Museum etruscum*, I, xxvii: « . . . satis constare arbitror, Tuscos perspectam habuisse Troiani Belli Historiam: & facile crediderim, Homerum, qui teste Strabone, ut mox suo loco ostendam, Etruriam peragravit perlustravitque, multa quae narrat in Iliade & in Odissea, ab Etruscis didicisse ». Luigi Lanzi finally demonstrated the dissimilarity between Etruscan and the other Italic laguages in his *Saggio di lingua etrusca*. The attempt to trace all languages back to Noah, of course, was already centuries old: see Don Cameron Allen, *The Legend of Noah* (Urbana: University of Illinois Press, 1949).

[79] In the copy of *Memorie Colombaria*, I, in the BNF, 3-41: « Che meschina spiegazione . . . Chi ve l'ha detto? che semplicità! ».

[80] Anton Maria Vannucchi, *Dissertazione del metodo d'acquistare la giurisprudenza critica* (Florence: Bonducci, 1750), p. 41.

end of the century did the work of translation begin to make any appreciable progress. For instead of considering the possibility that Etruscan might have been a completely independent language, the academicians wasted their energies in the vain search for an *Ursprache;* and instead of continuing to examine patiently each word in all available contexts — the method by which most of the words understood today have at last been defined — they looked hopefully for a single key, which would suddenly remove the veil of mystery and enable them to understand all the words at once.

Thus the interpretation of the language inevitably involved the question of the origin of the people who spoke it. If Etruscan was a form of Hebrew, then Dempster's hypothesis that the Etruscans were completely indigenous could not be accepted. On the other hand, no patriotic Tuscan could admit the proposal of Nicholas Fréret, secretary of the Académie des Inscriptions and honorary member of the Etrusca, that the similarity of the name *Rasena* mentioned by Dionysius of Halicarnassus and that of the Roman province *Rhaetia* proved that the Etruscans had descended from Gaul.[81] Perhaps they they were really Egyptians, who brought across the sea the philosophy they later taught to Pythagoras; or perhaps they were Canaanites, who had acquired the wisdom of Moses from the invaders of their homeland. More probably, thought Gori — and this was the explanation most pleasing to the academicians of Cortona, Florence, and Volterra — they were the same as the Tyrrhenians and Pelasgi (hence: *Peloponnesus*) who had once occupied all Greece and Asia Minor and who then passed into Syria and Egypt, whence they were chased by the Phoenicians to Crete and finally to Italy. It might still be possible, to be sure, that they descended from a certain Giano, who had come to Italy soon after the Flood (or at least [Gen. 10: 1-5] from Kittim son of Japheth and brother of Javan, founder of Athens, since Bochart found Hebrew texts mentioning, apparently, Pisa and

---

[81] Reginaldo Sellari, for instance, showed that modern Rhaetian or Tyrolian dialects bore no resemblance to Etruscan: Etrusca: * Atti, 4 February 1754. See Fréret, « Recherches sur l'origine et l'histoire des différents peuples de l'Italie », in *Histoire de l'Académie des Inscriptions,* XVIII (1753), 72-114.

Siena); that a unified Etruscan kingdom had been firmly established by the time of the Confusion of Tongues and had spread all over Italy and the Mediterranean Islands (Lami found signs of a colony even in Spain); and that Etruscan colonists had been the first inhabitants of the Greek mainland — so, at least, maintained Mario Guarnacci of Volterra, honorary president of the Sepolti, although most of his compatriots hesitated to accept all his conclusions unconditionally.[82]

Actually, any of these theories might be correct, for they all apparently confirmed the suspicion of the academicians that the Etruscans had built the temples of Magna Graecia and made the so-called Attic vases found in their tombs, and that, therefore, the similar temples and vases found throughout the Mediterranean proved the Etruscan origin of all Greek civilization.[83] It was the Etruscans, the academicians claimed, who discovered philosophy, which they passed on to Plato through the "Etruscan" Pythagoras; it was they who founded jurisprudence and architecture, which they taught to the Romans; it was they who invented navigation, which Cadmus took back to Phoenicia with his Etruscan wife Ermonia, sister of Dardanus of Troy; and it was they who laid the basis of natural science, which the modern Etruscan, Galileo, had recently rediscovered. They were probably also the first to create a written literature, which the "jealous" Latin authors consciously obliterated, and to raise sculpture to an art, in which "who knows that [they] did not surpass the Greeks." Indeed, the word "Etruscan" often gave way to "ancient Tuscans"

[82] Note the reserve of Angelo Fabroni reviewing Guarnacci's *Origini italiche* in *Giornale de' letterati* (Pisa), I (1771), 54-77; cf. Luigi Gasperetti, *Le "Origini italiche" di M. G. e l'utopia della "sapientia antichissima"* (Genova, 1926: reprinted from *La rassegna*), with interesting observations on other contemporary theories. The Chaldean origin was suggested by Alessio Mazzocchi of Naples in an article « Sopra l'origine de' tirreni » in *Saggi Etrusca*, III, No. 1, while Gianantonio Ciantar contended that certain Maltese antiquities proved that the Etruscans once occupied the island: Etrusca: * Atti, 29 December 1745, and *Saggi*, VIII, No. 2. Lami in Crusca: * Diario, 10 September 1757, and Ridolfino Venuti, « Sopra l'antica città di Cortona e suoi abitatori », *Saggi Etrusca*, IV, No. 1. Note further the theory of Paolo Fenci that the Etruscans were pre-Trojan War emigrants from Greece (16 May 1805) in *Atti dell'Accademia Pistojese*, I (1808), 27-28.

[83] Such hypotheses are demolished by Lanzi in *De' vasi antichi dipinti volgarmente chiamati etruschi* (Florence: Fantosini, 1806).

13

as the Settecento scholars attributed to their little-known ancestors
the virtues and wisdom they hoped to attain in their own times.[84]

These fantastic speculations about questions that were mistaken
in their very formulation and therefore impossible to solve eventually
brought discredit upon Etruscology as a whole. As early as 1738,
Maffei had ridiculed the attempts to credit the Etruscans with having
invented everything short of breathing; and in 1766, Adami claimed
to have found enough "enormous errors and contradictions" in
Dempster and his followers to fill "an entire volume of fallacious
puerilities." Such arguments, concluded Angelo Fabroni and Giuseppe Pelli soon afterwards, were "obscure, uncertain, and useless,"
unworthy of "studious men ... devoted to things of greater advantage," and destined to "remain hidden in the darkness of eternal
night"; and the academicians gradually gave them up.[85]

Still, the aberrations of *etruscheria* cannot be blamed so much on
the Etruscologists themselves as upon a number of misconceptions

[84] Note Gio. Maria Lampredi in Etrusca: * Atti, 27 April 1756, *Dissertazione istorico-
critica sopra la filosofia degli antichi etruschi* (Florence: Bonducci, 1756), and *Del governo
civile degli antichi toscani e delle cause della lor decadenza: Discorso* (Lucca: Giusti, 1760),
as well as his « Sopra il genio di Socrate », in *Saggi Etrusca*, VIII, No. 10; and Bernardo
Lessi, « Sopra le leggi etrusche e l'adozione che ne fecero i romani », *ibid.*, IX, No. 2.
Many of these opinions come right out of Dempster, e.g., chap. ix: « Etruscorum fama,
opulentia, ac potentia: Italiam totam domuerunt: Romae tributum imposuerunt, trecentas (!)
umbrorum urbes subegerunt: cum Jasone et Argonautis pugnaverunt ... ». Note further
A. M. Ricci in Crusca: « Diario, 2 August 1749, ascribing the invention of a double twenty-
four-hour day to them, and L. Fabbri, * Diario, 19 August 1752; Gregorio Fierli, « Sopra
il merito degli scultori etruschi paragonato con quello dei greci », *Saggi Etrusca*, VIII, No. 14:
p. 281 (cf. Passeri, « Della pittura degli etruschi », Calogerà, *Nuova raccolta d'opuscoli*,
XVI, 113-44). Before Lanzi (on whose arrangement of periods in Etruscan art see Onofrio
Boni in the biographical Preface to his *Opere postume* [Florence, 1817], I, 26 ff.) the academicians generally failed to distinguish between different periods, ascribing archaic pieces
either to poor workmanship or to a decay during the years of Roman expansion. This
fundamental difference between the Etruscologists and Winckelmann is noted by Lessing
(*Briefe antiquarischen Inhalts*, 131-32 [No. 18]).

[85] Maffei in *Osservazioni letterarie*, III (1738), 235: « per poco non si attribuisce a gli
etruschi d'aver'inventato anche il respirare ». Adami in *Dissertazioni critiche*, pp. 90-91:
« un intiero volume di puerilità, e di fallacie ». A. Fabroni in *Giornale de' letterati* (Pisa),
III (1771), 58, and G. Pelli, *Saggio istorico della Real Galleria di Firenze* (Florence: Cambiagi, 1779-80), I, 335. The speculation did not stop entirely, to be sure: Gianrinaldo
Carli's *Delle antichità italiche*, for instance, appeared in Milan in 1788 and 1793; and even
in Tuscany, in 1803, the editor of the *Memorie due* of the Società degli Amatori di Storia
Patria commended Giovanni Fabbroni for the « nuove facelle per accrescere gloria all'Etruria, Maestra dei greci medesimi » (p. v).

about the nature of historical development almost universally accepted at the time. All the authors cited in their footnotes, after all, from Gerardus Joannes Vossius (1577-1649) to Dionysius Petau and Peter Huet, supposed as much as they that a fully civilized nation could suddenly be born at the beginning of time, that it could continue for several centuries without any substantial modification, that languages could be imported, exported, and preserved in as great a purity as Trecento Tuscan, and that a people could wander over thousands of miles without changing its character. Their contemporaries in other parts of Europe — Rapin de Thoyras, for instance, in his *Histoire d'Angleterre* of 1724-27 — were as convinced as they that an analysis of language could furnish conclusive, historical proof for the direct descent of their respective nations from Noah. The search for an *Ursprache* and an *Urvolk,* indeed, has continued to enjoy scientific respectability right up to the present, even though one may be called Indo-European instead of the Tongue of Noah and the other the Illyrians instead of the Pelasgi. Some scholars, finally, still hesitate to accept Pallottino's argument that the whole question of origins has simply obstructed the understanding of what the Etruscans really were; and some are as unwilling as the Settecento academicians themselves to admit that wherever the various settlers of Etruria may have come from, the culture by which they became identified as a single people could have arisen only after their settlement on the soil of Etruria.[86] It is easy to laugh at the academic Etruscologists; but the laughter has all too often obscured their real accomplishments. Even Luigi Lanzi, who far surpassed his predecessors as a philologist and a historian, admitted that "to the members of this illustrious academy [the Etrusca] we owe what we know of Etruscan."[87] For it was they who drew up the first workable alphabet, who initiated the first systematic excavations, who founded the first museums, and who first described with accuracy many aspects of the religion, the customs, and the character of the ancient inhabitants of

[86] Compare M. Pallottino, *L'origine degli etruschi* (Rome: Tumminelli, 1947), with Ernst Pulgram, *The Tongues of Italy: Prehistory and History* (Cambridge, Mass.: Harvard University Press, 1958), Part IV, chap. xv, esp. p. 191.

[87] *Saggio di lingua etrusca,* I, 809.

Italy.   And it was they who first aroused the enthusiasm for the Etruscans that would animate the labors of scholars for many generations thereafter.

The very remoteness of Etruria had inspired much of this enthusiasm; for, after some 150 years during which Tuscans had almost completely forgotten the past, Etruscology had suddenly presented them with the possibility of spanning not just a few years, but more than two millenia.   Then, as the time-span narrowed, the enthusiasm waned.   While some of their studies, like Lami's investigations of medieval religious practices and of painting before Giotto, were undoubtedly motivated by problems current in the Settecento, most of the academic historians approached the ages nearest their own with sober caution.[88]   They used the term *mezzi tempi* or *secoli di mezzo* — meaning the centuries between the first appearance of the Tuscan communes and the fall of the Florentine and Sienese Republics — without any connotation of sympathy or antipathy; and they studied this period principally because the necessary documents were wanting for everything earlier, and because many of those regarding the political history of the Principato were still locked up in the *Archivio Segreto*.[89]   The paucity of written material about the Etruscans had stirred the imagination of the academicians; but the quantity of charters, contracts, private papers, and chronicles left by their ancestors of the eleventh to the sixteenth centuries forced them to spend much of their time simply exploring the archives and annotating the contents.   The novelty of Etruscology, similarly, had tempted them with the prospect of originality; but they found it difficult to make any real contribution of their own to the history of Florence until they had pondered and evaluated the record and interpretation of the principal events already compiled by their predecessors of the Quattrocento and Cinquecento.   Etruria, moreover, had long since disappeared, but the *mezzi tempi* still lived on into the Settecento — in

---

[88] On the Middle Ages in Settecento historiography, see Giorgio Falco, *La polemica sul Medio Evo* (Torino: Fedetto, 1933); Luigi Sorrento, « Medio Evo: Il termine e il concetto », in *Medievalia: Problemi e studi* (Brescia: Morcelliana, 1943); and E. W. Cochrane in the *Journal of the History of Ideas*, XIX (1958), 35 ff.

[89] Note Adami on the *Archivio segreto* in *Dissertazioni critiche*, p. 169.   For similar motivations in historiography, note Muratori in *Scritti autobiografici*, p. 55.

art, in buildings, in laws, in institutions, in customs and prejudices. Finally, an occasional transgression of Muratorian principles might perhaps be tolerated in the contemplation of the distant past; but study in the field in which Muratori himself had led the way demanded a strict adherence to his standards of scholarly objectivity.

Unable, therefore, to project an idealized eighteenth century back into the thirteenth, the Settecento medievalists limited themselves to the consideration of specific problems and events. Instead of attempting a general summary of medieval economy, for instance, they traced the penetration of Pisan merchants into Corsica and reviewed the monetary and fisical legislation of the Florentine Republic. Instead of considering the political development of Tuscany as a whole, they examined the tyrannies of the Casali in Cortona and of Pandolfo Petrucci in Siena and compiled chronological lists of the captains of Volterra. Instead of writing about religion and art, they studied the furnishings of the churches in Florence and the frescoes of Santa Margherita in Cortona. Instead of expounding on the achievements of their ancestors in architecture and engineering, they investigated the construction of the Ponte Vecchio and of the bridge built across the Po during the wars against the Visconti. Only in Volterra and in Pisa, indeed — cities, that is, whose histories had not previously been written — was an attempt ever made to transcend the limits of a monographic study; and even then the volumes of Riccobaldi Del Bava, of Lorenzo Cecina, of the Dal Borgo, and of Lorenzo Cantini are essentially series of specific monographs.[90] For the medievalists

[90] Besides those titles already mentioned, see « Del dominio antico pisano sulla Corsica », *Saggi Etrusca,* VII, No. 11 (by an anonymous professor at Pisa); and [Gian Francesco Pagnini], *Della decima e di varie altre gravezze imposte dal Comune di Firenze* (4 vols.; Lisbon & Lucca [but problably Florence], 1765-66), on which: Luigi Dal Pane, « Uno storico dell'economia nella Toscana del Settecento: G. F. P. », *Studi in memoria di Gino Borgatta* (Bologna, 1953), I, 143-69. Etrusca: *Atti, 14 December 1750, and G. A. Pecci, *Memorie storico-critiche della città di Siena che servono alla vita di Pandolfo Petrucci* (4 vols.; Siena: Pazzini, 1755-60); Lorenzo Cecina, *Notizie istoriche della città di Volterra, alle quali si aggiunge la serie de' potestà, e capitani del popolo di essa* (Pisa: Giovannelli, 1758), on which: Luigi Pescetti, « Volterra nell'opera di due eruditi settecenteschi », *Rassegna volterrana,* XVII (1946), 3-24; Anton Filippo Giachi, *Saggio di ricerche sopra lo stato antico e moderno di Volterra* (Florence: Allegrini, 1786). The earliest of these chronologies was the much-praised *Della serie cronologica degli antichi duchi e marchesi di Toscana . . . raccolta da Cosimo Della Rena, accademico fiorentino e della Crusca* (Florence: Cocchini,

were too busy compiling sources and correcting errors to respond to the pleas of Adami for a new history to replace those of Varchi and Ammirato; and not until 1793, when Lorenzo Pignotti began writing his *History of Tuscany before the Principato*,[91] did anyone propose a reconstruction or an interpretation of the period as a whole in the manner of, say, Tiraboschi or Bettinelli.

Some general conclusions, nevertheless, were unavoidable. The academicians could not but notice, for instance, a regular progression from episcopal, to aristocratic, to popular, to tyrannical, and finally to monarchical government in most of the Tuscan cities; for such patterns of political change had already been elaborated in the works both of the ancient authors, which they read in school, and of those of the Cinquecento, which they read as historians. Nor could they fail to observe that Florence, Siena, and Pisa had been both more wealthy and more populous in 1300 than they were in 1750 and that the Florentines had been one of "the first [nations] to apply themselves to trade"; for the problems of population and prosperity were among the most urgent of their own times.[92] Indeed, their very definition of the *mezzi tempi* reflects their preoccupation in other fields of study with such questions as literary creativity, political vitality, and economic prosperity. The age opened, according to most of the academicians, "about the beginning of the eleventh century," when "the Florentines happily threw off the hard yoke of servitude," that is, freed themselves from imperial authority. It culminated in the thirteenth and fourteenth centuries, when the gold florin assured the commercial expansion of Florence, when all classes of Sienese, as Della Valle noted with pride, formed "a sole body and society, intent upon enriching the city with agriculture and commerce and upon embellishing it with buildings, pictures, and sculpture," and when Boccaccio and Petrarch gave the Tuscan

---

1690, republished in 1764 and 1780). D. M. Manni, « Intorno alle pile dell'acqua santa di Firenze de' secoli bassi », *Memorie Colombaria*, II, 227 ff.; *Della vecchiezza sovragrande del Ponte Vecchio di Firenze* (in the Etrusca, 9 September 1763) (Florence: Viviani, 1763), and Lezione . . . detta nell'Accademia degli Apatisti . . . 1738 », in Calogerà, *Raccolta d'opuscoli*, XVIII, 209 ff.; Gori, *Symbolae letterariae*, VIII, chaps. v, ix, and x.

[91] *Storia della Toscana sino al Principato* (2d ed.; Florence: Marchini, 1821), I, iv.
[92] G. Targioni Tozzetti in *Memorie Colombaria*, II, 151.

language its literary masterpieces.[93] It declined during the Quattrocento, when Latin replaced Tuscan as the principal literary language, when civil strife endangered the unity of the commonwealth, and when foreign competition forced the magistrates to alter the value of the currency. And it ended, finally, in the early Cinquecento, with the collapse of trade and manufacturing, which the academicians attributed wholly to the opening of sea routes to India and America, and with the invasions of the French and the Spanish.

This definition, to be sure, had obvious shortcomings, even in Settecento terms, for it overlooked completely the "Risorgimento delle belle arti" described by the art historians in the years between Brunelleschi and Michelangelo, and it ignored the achievements of the Quattrocento humanists, whose scholarship, although still unadorned with documentary footnotes, had impressed such editors as Mehus, Bandini, and Fossi.[94] But at the same time the emphasis in this concept upon politics and economics made the academicians fully aware that even the greatest moments of the Middle Ages had not been free of grave evils; and their hope for the imminent realization of domestic harmony and international peace made them shrink from the "abominable sects" that had "kept the city miserably divided" even at the height of its power and prosperity. "When I turn my thoughts... to the fifteenth century," confessed Lastri, "I am confronted with the vision of Italy, enviable for its advantageous position and success in commerce, [but at the same time] torn by bloody factions, internal and foreign war, atrocious schisms, and vicious massacres and death...."[95] The academicians had learned too much about their medieval ancestors either to exalt them, as they did the Etruscans, or to condemn them, as they did the Romans.

---

[93] *Ibid.*, p. 127, and Della Valle, *Lettere senesi*, II, 12.

[94] Note, for example, the reference of the author of « In difesa di Tito Livio » (above note 49) to Giovanni Domenici not in the original but through a quotation of St. Antonino. Cf. A. M. Bandini, *Memoria per servire alla vita del senator Pier Vettori*, and in general, above p. 85.

[95] Adami, *Dissertazioni critiche*, p. 28, and Lastri in *Monumenti ... Accademia Etrusca*, p. 12.

In many ways this view of the Middle Ages reflects the general limitations of all the historical work of the Settecento academicians. They had first become interested in history not because of any dissatisfaction with the present or any nostalgia for the past, but simply because the publications of Buonarroti and the Crusca had suggested the possibility of using the contents of their collections as a means of fulfilling the demands of the academies for scholarly contributions. Throughout the eighteenth century academic historiography retained the marks of its origin. It remained monographic, first of all, preoccupied with the particular rather than the general, with analysis rather than synthesis, capable of mixing fantasy with logic in deducing the names of Riminesi kings from a single vase, but incapable of combining many single observations into a comprehensive view of any one people or age. It remained scholarly, secondly, burdened with interminable footnotes and innumerable digressions on points of minor importance, concerned more with the description of single documents than with reflection upon their significance, and insouciant of the appearance or the style of the narrative. It remained national, or regional, finally, confined in scope exclusively to the history of Tuscany and of its individual cities and unconcerned with the relation of such subjects to the history of other nations or of the world as a whole — except, of course, for the admission that all nations proceeded from a common ancestor.

The same limitations in turn explain the indifference of the academicians to many of their predecessors and foreign contemporaries whose works would long outlive their own. Historiography, they insisted, was not a form of literature, since any intrusion of aesthetic or oratorical considerations into a narrative would inevitably compromise the fidelity with which the "facts" were recorded. They read the chronicles and Ammirato, therefore, but they considered Bruni and Guicciardini above all as masters of prose writing and as historians only in those few passages describing events of which the authors themselves were witnesses.[96] Historiography, moreover,

---

[96] Their coolness to Guicciardini may in part be explained by the omission even in the contemporary Venetian edition of the passages condemned by the Inquisition: see C. Pellegrini in *Giornale storico della letteratura italiana*, CXVI (1940), 8, describing Lami's cor-

was not an *instrumentum* either for the furtherance of dynastic ambitions, as it had been as late as 1711 during the Comacchio controversy, or for the promotion of political and economical reforms, as it became elsewhere in Italy and Europe during the eighteenth century.[97] While they applauded many of the dissertations of the Académie des Inscriptions (of which some of them were members), therefore, they paid no attention whatever to the polemical treatises written in the 1720's at the behest of the Grand Duke himself for the protection of Tuscan independence against Imperial claims, and they noted the publication of Giannone's *Istoria civile,* many years after its appearance, with detached coolness. Historiography was not a means of destroying the past by revealing its errors and ignorance; and while they applauded *Zaïre* and *Oreste,* none of them ever commented on the *Essai sur les moeurs.* Historiography was not a means of understanding the general course of nations or the origins and development of civilization; consequently, they ignored not only Vico, whose citations are often the same as theirs, but also Montesquieu, whom some of them knew personally, and Gibbon and Robertson, whose works were published in translation by Tuscan printers in the last decades of the century.[98] The academicians were interested not in the meaning of the events but in the events themselves, not in history in general, but in the history of ancient Cortona and medieval Volterra. Hence, they showed little interest in the work even of scholars elsewhere in Italy — in the Sampaolisti of

respondance on the subject in 1742. The only Settecento edition of Donato Giannotti's *Della Repubblica Fiorentina* was published in Venice (Herz, 1731), not in Florence, where perhaps the editor's admiration of Giannotti's reluctance « nella patria ritornare per viver in ischiavitù in compagnia degli stolti » (Preface) may have still been dangerous. By the time of Pietro Leopoldo, however, the danger must have vanished, for the *Discorso sopra i modi di riordinare la Repubblica Fiorentina* was published in Vol. XXIII of *Le delizie degli eruditi toscani.*

97 Cf. Massimo Petrocchi, *Razionalismo architettonico e razionalismo storiografico,* pp. 47 ff.

98 See *Novelle letterarie,* XXV (1763), 157-58, and N .S., XVIII (1786), 316-17, and *Giornale de' letterati* (Pisa), IV (1773), 225-27. The academic records make no mention whatever of the translation of the *Decline and Fall* published in Pisa in 1779-86. The interest in Robertson, except for a few oratorical flourishes of Giulio Perini in the Fiorentina, was confined solely to the Vespucci controversy. Giuseppe Averani, *De libertate civitatis Florentiae ejusque dominii* (Pisa, 1721).

Torino, for instance — whose principles and objectives were very similar to their own.[99] They studied history for one reason only: to find out exactly what had happened in their own country during the past centuries; and they simply passed over everything else in silence.

Yet within these limitations the academic historians succeeded in making an important contribution to the culture of their age. They may have been preoccupied with particulars; but they made available during the course of the century great quantities of previously neglected or unknown information about the past which, as Momigliano has shown, could be used by writers like Gibbon to rescue history from the philosopher's impatience with detail.[100] They may themselves have written no general histories; but they provided manuals with which those that already had been written might profitably be read, and they published the chronicles upon which many of them had been based. They may have sacrificed the readability of their dissertations to the apparent interests of *erudizione,* and they may never have sought, like the Georgofili, to communicate their learning to peasants;[101] but they were to some extent justified in supposing that ordinary educated citizens would find the "truth" alone sufficiently attractive to require no further ornament.[102] They may have failed to attribute any but a purely informative value to history and have ignored the inquiries of many of their contemporaries, both Italian and foreign, into its nature and purpose; but, in spite of an occasional remark on the importance of "a prudent, regular conduct of life," [103] they freed history from the role given it by Vossius, by Mascardi and the Jesuit *trattatisti* of the Seicento, and even by such Settecento writers as Galeani Napione — the role,

---

[99] Carlo Calcaterra, *Il nostro imminente Rinascimento,* chap. ii, pp. 121-80 — to which most of this chapter can profitably be compared.

[100] Arnaldo Momigliano, « Gibbon's contribution to historical method », *Contributo alla storia degli studi classici,* pp. 195-211.

[101] Above, chap. ii, note 56.

[102] Gori to Pecci, May 1746, Mar B.3, 66.

[103] L. Cantini, *Iscrizioni che si trovano negli Atti dell'Accademia Colombaria* (1801), pp. iii-iv. Note in the *Atti dell'Accademia Pistojese,* I (1808), 6: « Servirà forse questo nobile ufficio [history] d'incitamento nel tempo stesso . . . alla gioventù che sorge alle migliori speranze della patria, quando a lei si presentino il genio e la virtù trionfante ».

that is, of providing moral examples for the promotion of virtue and the perfection of the soul.[104]

Still more important, the academic historians gradually abandoned the traditional systems, based on mathematics or theology, of dividing the past into series of ten or hundred-year periods from the Creation or the Incarnation,[105] and replaced them with a new scheme of periodization based on the events themselves — or at least upon those events that interested them. A few, to be sure, still sought to interpret history in the light of particular disciplines and to see "an almost absolute void" between the School of Alexandria and Copernicus, for instance, if they were scientists, between Columella and Luigi Alamanni if they were agriculturalists, or between Sacchetti and Bembo if they were linguists.[106] All history before the foundation of Etruria, moreover, remained strictly within the limits of Mosaic chronology, for no one ever suspected that the suggestions of the naturalists concerning the antiquity of the physical world had any relevance for the history of man.[107] But most agreed in discerning three successive periods of growth, organization, and prosperity, separated by two of disintegration and poverty: first, the age of the Etruscans, which was destroyed largely by the "divisions, perverse customs, and effeminacy" brought in from Greece and by the ruinous agrarian laws of the Romans;[108] then, the age of the free communes, which began with the introduction of Christianity and which rose from the depths of Lombard domination to the cultural and economic brilliance of the thirteenth and fourteenth centuries; and, finally, the age inaugurated by Galileo, which during the eighteenth century had already shaken off the lethargy

[104] On Vossius, note Gentile in *Studi sul Rinascimento,* pp. 275 ff., and in general the excellent study of Giorgio Spini, « I trattatisti dell'arte storica nella Controriforma italiana », in *Contributi alla storia del Concilio di Trento e della Controriforma* (Florence: Vallecchi, 1948), pp. 109-36.

[105] Repeated even as late as 1745 by Maffei in Calogerà, *Raccolta d'opuscoli,* XXXII, xxxi-xlvii.

[106] Frisi, *Elogio di Galilei,* p. 7, and Lastri, *Biblioteca georgica,* pp. vii ff. Note G. Calcaterra, *Il Parnasso in rivolta* (Milano: Mondadori, 1940), pp. 261-62.

[107] Note Ridolfino Venuti in *Museum cortonese,* p. 30.

[108] Riccobaldi Del Bava, *Dissertazione istorico-etrusca,* pp. 34-35. This book is a good example of the chronological scheme here described.

of the Seicento and which, with the help of a scientific method unknown to the ancients and of an economy based securely upon agriculture, would without doubt go on indefinitely to ever greater achievements in the future. Thus in spite of their reluctance to generalize, the academicians, simply by their selection of certain periods for special study, arrived at a general interpretation of history which, although applicable only to Tuscany and devoid of any concept of continuity among the several ages, at least presented the past in terms easily comprehensible to their contemporaries.

At the beginning of the eighteenth century Tuscans had known little and cared less about the history of their country; by the end of the century, even though the record of former ages was still far from complete, they had learned much and were anxious to learn even more. Moreover, they were gradually becoming aware that the past was not simply a matter for the "delight of the scholars." Historiography had disappeared in the late Cinquecento because the Medici princes feared what the historians themselves no longer believed possible, that is, that historiography might contribute to the solution of the concrete problems of the time. It had reappeared in the 1720's as a purely scholarly activity completely free of any political implications and disassociated from any consideration of the present. Could what happened in the past again have any bearing on what happened in the present? The historians themselves gave no explicit answer. Not only did they never seriously consider the philosophic question of the nature of history and time, but few of them, before Riguccio Galluzzi's *Istoria del Granducato* (1781), ever extend their studies beyond the mid-Cinquecento — the moment, according to Riccobaldi Del Bava, when the establishment of the Principato on the ruins of the republics had given "to all Tuscany the peace so long hoped for and . . . a respite from so many ills." [109] The present had not yet been incorporated into the past. Nevertheless, by emphasizing the achievements of the two former "great

---

[109] *Ibid.*, p. 144. Note G. Tiraboschi, *Memorie storiche modenesi* (Modena: Società Tipografica, 1793), I, xi: « . . . fino a' primi anni del secolo XV, ne' quali vide pacifico possessore di ambedue queste principali città . . . D'allora in poi queste provincie non ci offrono cosa degna di storia ».

ages," the historians suggested to their contemporaries that, in spite of its advances in science and philosophy, the eighteenth century in Tuscany did not compare favorably in many ways with the sixth century B.C. or the thirteenth century A.D. By drawing attention to the changes that had occurred in the past, they suggested that the eighteenth century was as subject to change, and therefore as much a part of history, as the thirteenth. By attributing the fall of Etruria and the medieval republics to human rather than natural causes, they suggested that although change was inevitable, it might not necessarily be independent of human control. The historians set up the premises. They left to the political economists and the legislators of the Leopoldine era the task of drawing the conclusions.

CHAPTER VI

ECONOMICS AND POLITICS

Giuseppe Maria Buondelmonti, professor of civil law at Pisa, did not surprise his fellow-Cruscans with a wholly new subject when, on 30 August 1755, he proposed for their consideration certain differences between Hobbes and Grotius on points of international law.[1] As early as 1728 the young lawyer Corso de' Ricci had spoken at length about ancient agrarian legislation, and ever since then the usual exegeses of Dante, Homer, and the Scriptures had occasionally digressed into question of the law in ancient Greece or medieval Italy. Such matters, indeed, had long found favor among the antiquarians, who remembered Gori's admonition that the reconstruction of the past required a study of all phases of human life; and dissertations on subjects like the "spirit of autonomy" in the Greek cities and the magistracies of the Roman Republic always formed an important part of the programs of the Etrusca and the Colombaria.[2]

But until the middle of the century the interest in such questions remained exclusively literary or historical. The long fight waged in the 1720's and 30's by all the prominent law professors from Giuseppe Averani to Borgo Dal Borgo, for instance, over the famous Florentine MS of the Pandects of Justinian — a fight that erupted unexpectedly into at least one academy with Bernardo Tanucci's diatribe against Guido Grandi — sought neither to further an under-

[1] Crusca: * Diario, 30 August 1755, published as *Ragionamento sul diritto della guerra giusta* (Florence: Bonducci, 1764), republished in 1767 along with his *Lettera sulla misura dei dolori e dei piaceri*. On Buondelmonti, see below, note 15.

[2] Crusca: * Diario, 4 and 15 January 1728, 11 July 1744, 11 September 1745, 2 and 9 September 1747. Ottaviano Guasco, « Sopra l'autonomia de' popoli e delle città greche e latine », and Bernardo Lessi, « Sopra le leggi etrusche e l'adozione che ne fecero i Romani », in *Saggi Etrusca,* V, No. 4, and IX, No. 2; Colombaria: Annali 22, 7 July 1756, and 23, 22 June and 3 July 1757; Bindo Simone Peruzzi, De' magistrati romani: Etr 455, 8.

standing of the texts nor to suggest principles for the guidance of modern legislators. The various authors were intent chiefly upon rescuing the glories of Pisa from the implied insults of the Dutch jurist Hendrik Brenkman, upon proving or disproving the story of the capture of the documents from Amalfi, and upon convincing the *Repubblica Letteraria* that the Pandects should be called *Pisan* rather than *Florentine,* or vice versa.[3] Hence, the academicians never entertained the possibility that what they learned of the civic spirit of the Athenians or the *annona* regulations of the Romans might have some relevance to Tuscany in the Settecento.

Questions of the content and the nature of the law and of its application to contemporary situations had, it is true, once attracted the best minds of Tuscany. It was in Florence, after all, that Colluccio Salutati, three centuries earlier, had begun the attack upon those jurists of his time, particularly the Bartolists, who ignored both the methods of Accursius and the texts of Justinian and who referred every question uncritically to the authority of the glossators. It had been Angelo Poliziano who first applied the techniques of philology to the long-treasured Pandects and who, by insisting upon an historical interpretation of Roman law, laid the foundations upon which Budé, Alciatus, Bodin, and Zasius established the juridical framework of the modern state in the following century. But by the mid-Cinquecento this vigorous intellectual effort had died out — partially, as Domenico Maffei has suggested, because of a divorce

---

[3] The quarrel is recounted by Enrica Viviani Della Robbia in *Bernardo Tanucci ed il suo più importante carteggio,* I (Florence: Sansoni, 1942), 28-37 (of which chap. i contains a good review of the Florentine and Pisan juridical world at the time). All the relevant literature is reviewed by Borgo Dal Borgo, in *Dissertazione sopra l'istoria de' codici pisani delle Pandette di Giustiniano* (Lucca: Giusti, 1764), pp. 1 ff. Only Dal Borgo's ruffled *campanilismo* could have led him to infer from a very few passages in *Henrici Brencmanni, jc. et academici fiorentini, Historia Pandectarum* (Ultrech: Van de Water, 1722), p. 55, that the author wished to « far comparire la Repubblica Pisana un aggregato di gente rozza e negligente (p. 24). The *Ad nobiles socios cortonenses qui Academici Etrusci dicuntur Epistola . . . de Pandectis* (Lucca, 1728) of Bernardo Tanucci, then professor at Pisa and later first minister to the King of Naples, was so vituperous (but that of his opponent Guido Grandi was even more so) that the government soon suppressed it. This was the first work dedicated to the new academy; but so little did it fit in with the other interests of the members that they simply registered its reception and payed no further attention to the argument.

of practical from theoretical law, and partially, according to Luigi Firpo, because the peculiar conditions of Italy discouraged the learned from taking any further interest in social or political improvement.[4] In Tuscany, the Medici felt little need to justify by rational argument the position they had acquired through force and diplomacy, and the jurists, resigning themselves to an identification of law with the will of the prince, gave up any attempt to explain his separate edicts as part of a logical system. Hence, the bold speculations of Machiavelli and Donato Giannotti concerning the purpose and structure of political society soon dwindled into *ragion di stato*.

To be sure, the practice and teaching of law, both Roman and statutory, still went on, and lawyers continued to participate in the academies. But so thoroughly had law become a matter of purely professional interest that even so prominent a professor and so active an academician as Giuseppe Averani never once saw fit, in the early Settecento, to include reflections on his work in the University among his numerous discourses before the Crusca on literary, religious, and scientific subjects. Neither he nor his contemporaries, indeed, seem even to have noticed the eulogy of Poliziano included in Brenkman's *Historia Pandectarum,* the work that touched off their lengthy polemics on the origins of the Pandects.[5] For the

---

[4] See Domenico Maffei, *Gli inizi dell'umanesimo giuridico* (Milan: Giuffrè, 1956), esp. chap. ii, secs. 4 and 5, and Luigi Firpo, « Il pensiero politico del Rinascimento e della Controriforma » in *Questioni di storia moderna,* ed. Rota (Milan: Marzorati, 1948), pp. 345-408. On the debt of Guillaume Budé to Poliziano, as well as to Valla, see Louis Delaruelle, *Guillaume Budé, les origines, les débuts, les idées maîtresses* (Paris: Champion, 1907), pp. 104-5. On the jurists of the sixteenth century, see Myron Gilmore, *Argument from Roman Law in Political Thought, 1200-1600* (Cambridge, Mass.: Harvard University Press, 1951).

[5] On Averani, see Angelo Fabroni, *Vitae Italorum,* II (1769), 4-44, and Averani's own « Oratio de jurisprudentia, medicina, theologia », in his *Monumenta latina postuma* (Florence: Albizzini, 1769) (and above, p. 32 f.). The existence of several forensic "academies" at Pisa at the turn of the 1700's further illustrates the continuing separation of law and letters; though organized as academies, their membership consisted wholly of students, and their activities were intended to perform much the same function as mock trials in modern law schools. See Giuseppe Niccolai, « Antiche accademie universitarie pisane », *Bollettino storico pisano,* I (1932), 64-74. Poliziano mentioned in Brenkman, *Historia Pandectarum,* p. 306. The first Settecento Tuscan to recognize Poliziano's contribution to jurisprudence was apparently Angelo Maria Bandini in *Ragionamento istorico sopra le collezioni delle fiorentine Pandette fatte da Angelo Poliziano* (Livorno: Fantechi, 1762).

Tuscan jurists wrote either textbooks for students of Roman and canon law or detailed opinions of specific cases, and they carefully avoided any speculation of the difference between what the law was and what it ought to have been.

Then, during the first half of the Settecento, at least one of the impediments to the application of intellect to politics gradually disappeared. The Medici family, which for two centuries had identified itself with the political entity it had created, died out. But it was not so much the jurists or the academicians who first realized the consequences of the change in dynasty. It was rather the government itself: first that of Giangastone, which abandoned the painful attempt of Cosimo III to turn the country into a monastery, and then that of the Regency, which increasingly found itself obliged to act in practice as if the state were something more than the personal property of the ruler. To be sure, politics remained the exclusive concern of those designated by the prince; and none of the royal ministers ever referred to their official activities when participating in the academies. But such problems as the disposition of the Medici inheritance and the jurisdictional conflicts with Rome at least suggested to all Tuscans the necessity of distinguishing between the Crown and the person of the prince and of asserting, if not yet defining theoretically, the absolute sovereignty of the state in internal affairs; while the change in dynasties itself invited their criticism of everything associated with the political and economic order of the past two centuries. Not in committing themselves to statements of principle, then, but rather in limiting the creation of inalienable landholdings, in codifying the press and heraldic laws, and in punishing dishonest officials, the ministers of Francesco Stefano came to assume that whatever was, was *not* necessarily right and that their political authority might be employed for some higher purpose than merely preserving the status quo.[6]

---

[6] See Ernesto Sestan, « Il riformismo settecentesco in Italia », *Rassegna storica toscana*, II (1955), 19-46, and Niccola Carranza, « Polemica antimedicea dopo l'istaurazione lorenese », *Bollettino storico pisano*, XXII-XXIII (1953-54), 122-62, which shows further the importance of the change in dynasty in reviving interest in matters of law and the state.

Meanwhile, the new fields of study introduced into the academies during the first half of the century were gradually leading at least some of the *letterati* to conclusions capable eventually of furnishing these practical measures with a theoretical justification. The study of history, first of all, had taught them that Tuscany once had supported a much greater population in much better conditions and that this former prosperity had resulted not from fate or chance but from the "good maxims drawn up by our ancestors" and properly applied "to the circumstances in which they found themselves." Reflecting, then, that "the country is the same and the men born in it are the same," they concluded, like Pagnini, that "it should not be wholly impossible to achieve the same ends" by "adapting the same general rules to the different circumstances of our own times."[7] History could also provide some indication of just what these general rules had been. It could show, for instance, that the value of the gold florin had depended more upon public confidence in the seal it bore than upon the quality of its component metals; and it could suggest that therefore any attempt to fix the price of money artificially would succeed no better in Settecento Tuscany than it had in Quattrocento Lombardy.[8] History could prove further that ideas, institutions, and even religious practices of the present had in fact arisen at particular moments of the past in response to particular needs and that, even though still "religiously adhered to," they could safely be discontinued if these needs had

---

[7] G. F. Pagnini, *Della decima,* Part III, chap. i (Vol. II, p. 2), and Editor's Preface to Vol. I of *Memorie istoriche per servire alla vita di più uomini illustri della Toscana* (Livorno: Santini, 1757): « Poichè essendo essi riusciti sotto il medesimo clima . . . ». On Tuscany past and present, note impressions of P. Bernardino Vestrini, S.P., on the Valdichiana in 1444 as described in documents in the Cancelleria of Asinalunga: *Etr Notti Coritane,* X, 65-66 (6 August 1753).

[8] G. Targioni Tozzetti, in « Del fiorino di sigillo », *Memorie Colombaria,* II, 137 ff., and Pompeo Neri, *Osservazioni sopra il prezzo legale delle monete, e le difficoltà di perfinirlo, e di sostenerlo* (n. d. [but Florence, 1751], chap. vi, Art. IV (« . . . delle monete istesse e della sua forza superiore alle leggi »); the reference on p. 70 is probably to the tables printed in Filippo Argelati, *De monetis Italiae variorum illustriorum virorum dissertationes* (6 vols.; Milan: Palatina, 1750), III, 134-35. Note similar studies by Ignazio Orsini, accademico fiorentino, apatista, e socio colombario, *Storia delle monete della Repubblica Fiorentina* (Florence: Viviani, 1760).

been satisfied or rendered obsolete.[9] Finally, it could suggest that since "ignorance" alone had brought the last two great ages to an end, so "wisdom" might both create and perpetuate another great age in the near future.[10] Ancient Vetualia, then, might "under a benign star rise again, a new city," and the Maremma might soon regain "its ancient flourishing condition, of which we are assured by many authentic documents."[11] For the present, Tuscans began to realize, was as much a part of history as the past, and neither the feudal domains nor the guilds were any less immune to alteration in the Settecento than they had been at the moment of their creation several centuries earlier. Constructive change, abolished by the Principato, once again became possible.

By 1753, secondly, the natural sciences had taught Tuscans the necessity of drawing hypotheses only from observable phenomena and of considering them valuable only in relation to their practical utility for the whole of society. Increasingly they had become interested in agriculture, which seemed to them the most empirical and the most useful of all the sciences; and agriculture in turn had drawn their attention to the most serious problem faced by all Tuscan governments over the preceding three centuries: famine.[12] The Georgofili remembered what the Sienese scientist and economist Sallustio Bandini had preached to deaf ears in 1737: that, as long as the existing tax and administrative structure remained in force, all attempts to restore the prosperity of the Maremma by dikes, canals, and even large-scale colonization would succeed no better than the

[9] Manni in *Memorie Colombaria*, II, 240, and Neri in *Relazione* of 1763: ASF Gabinetto 122, fol. 8-9 and 17: « Ma in oggi per verità non ha verun'altro uso pratico . . . » as well in Neri Badia, *Decisiones et responsa juris*, II, 604, on feudal domains.

[10] F. Paoletti, *I veri mezzi per render felici le società* (S. C. I. E. P.), p. 332 (below, p. 236 ff.: hereafter cited as « *I veri mezzi* »).

[11] « Sotto benigna Stella [Pietro Leopoldo] / sorgerai città novella, / così vaga, e così bella / che ciascun t'ammirerà »: Pasquale Parrini, *Veturia fra le umbre* (Siena: Bindi, 1779), p. 23; progetto of 1762: ASF Reggenza 780.21, fol. 654: « al suo antico florido stato, di cui ci attestano più documenti autentici », and Ximenes, *Della fisica riduzione della Maremma senese*, Preface: « come sarà rilevato dall'antica storia della Maremma ».

[12] Montelatici's *Regolamento* of 1753, in *Atti Georgofili*, Series III, Vol. V (1906), p. 462.

order of Julian the Apostate to rebuild the Temple of Jerusalem.[13]
Technology alone was not enough. If "formerly heavily populated
and happy areas of Tuscany" have "long since become deserted,"
noted Targioni Tozzetti in 1768, the causes were human rather than
natural. "The poverty of the land," insisted Roberto Pucci, "resides
not in the perversity of nature nor in the malignity of certain
classes of men," but in "the latent poison of old systems." "Unless
assisted by philosophy and the laws," concluded the Georgofili, even
the most vigorous efforts to extend cultivation were doomed to
failure.[14] It was these very "old systems" and "laws," to be sure,
that the Principato had, two centuries earlier, pretended to remove
from the vicissitudes of time and the control of men. But if they
were not modified or abolished, the academicians now pointed out,
the increasingly grave crises they produced would soon complete the
ruin of the country. Thus the scientists began calling for legislative
solutions to questions originally posed in purely scientific terms,
and they proclaimed that constructive change, which the historians
had shown to be possible, was in fact an urgent necessity.

Increasingly, therefore, the academicians turned to the study of
those disciplines upon which the salvation of Tuscany now seemed
to depend. They urged linguists and philologists to stop "writing
boring treatises about an inflection or a diphthong" and to bring
their knowledge to bear upon "the greater arguments" which "concern directly the common happiness and good of mankind." They

---

[13] *Discorso economico* (S. C. I. E. P.), p. 200. This work was finally published
in 1775.

[14] G. Targioni Tozzetti, *Relazioni d'alcuni viaggi* (2d ed. of 1768: the date is significant), Preface to Vol. I, p. xi; Pucci quoted by Tabarrini, *Degli studi e delle vicende della
R. A. dei G.*, p. 25; and *Atti Georgofili*, I, 5: « Se la Filosofia e le leggi non si uniscono
a favorire il genio per la cultura de' terreni, egli non può mai divenir costante, nè generale ». There was always, to be sure, some dissent. Ximenes, for instance, in his *Della
fisica riduzione della Maremma senese*, held that unless the swamps were drained even the
best laws would be ineffective (*e.g.*, p. 31), and Gregorio Fierli pointed out, in 1797, that
the good intentions of the government would never bring prosperity to agriculture and
manufacturing as long as they « were thwarted by the prejudices and the particular interests
of the people » and as long as « the public good is lost sight of and the love of country
does not unite all hearts » (*Atti Georgofili*, IV, 257). Law, in other words, depended upon
morality and civic spirit, rather than morality upon law. It must be noted, moreover, that
all discussions of political subjects ceased in the Georgofili during the Napoleonic period.

pressed historians to consider "the legislation and the public economy of various nations" in relation not to the peculiarities of time and place, but to "the true principles of science." Their pleas were soon heard. By 1760, Giovanni Maria Lampredi had shown that the materials previously used only by the Etruscologists to reconstruct the manners and customs of an ancient people could also serve to illustrate the universal principles of civil government.[15] Jurisprudence thus emerged, in academic sessions, as a field of investigation independent of the literary and historical questions in which it formerly had been presented.

The academicians then discovered that the law had nothing to do with the volumes of "decisions" decorated with "many bits of wonderful erudition drawn from Greek as well as Latin authors." It had less to do with the painful tomes of "those miserable glossators who, trying to explain the laws with useless distinctions and ridiculous commentaries, have done little but alter and corrupt them."[16] The law, they realized, was rather "the discipline that teaches the manner in which men may live peacefully in society." It had been completely transformed by such "celebrated thinkers" beyond the Alps as Grotius, Pufendorf, and Wolff, who, like Galileo in science and Muratori in historiography, had applied "rational philosophy" in jurisprudence to sweep away "the chimerical systems of the ancients."[17] It rested no longer upon "useless and vain contro-

---

[15] [A. M. Vannucchi], in *Accademia funebre di arcadici componimenti per la morte del cav. frà G. M. Buondelmonti . . . fatta dagli Arcadi della medesima colonia* [Alfea] *nella loro adunanza tenuta il dì 17 maggio 1757* (Pisa: Giovannelli, 1757), p. xv: « non già per scrivere noiosi trattati sopra una inflessione, o un diftongo . . . ma per penetrare . . . i più grandi argomenti, che direttamente riguardano la comune felicità, ed il bene del genere umano ». Perini in ASF Reggenza, 1052.58. Lampredi, *Del governo civile degli antichi toscani* (1760). On Lampredi (1732-93), see Piero Ranucci, *Elogio di G. M. L.* (Florence: Cambiagi, 1793), the Introduction of Defendente Sacchi to the 1818 translation of his *Diritto pubblico universale,* and Francesco Foggio, « Saggio sugli scritti di G. M. L. », *Atti della Accademia Italiana,* I (1808), 205 ff.

[16] « Piena ancora di molte belle erudizioni tirate da autori sì greci che latini »: *Novelle letterarie,* XXVI, (1765), 162-63 (reviewing with approval Leopoldo Guadagni, *Institutiones juris civilis* (Pisa: Giovannelli, 1758-62): « Quei miseri glossatori », etc.: Vannucchi in *Accademia funebre,* p. xiv.

[17] Vannucchi, *Dissertazione del metodo d'acquistare la giurisprudenza critica* (above, chap. v, note 80), pp. 27 and 12.

versies," "distinctions," and "subtleties," but upon a rigorous method similar to "the admirable manner of reasoning of our immortal Galileo."[18] It was no longer the exclusive domain of a closed profession specially trained to memorize authoritative texts and to cite forgotten edicts in support of a client. It had now become the proper concern of "all the citizens"; and it was therefore, the academians concluded, a subject well suited for consideration in those institutions in which the most distinguished citizens were assembled.[19]

No sooner, then, did the academicians turn their attention to law than they found that what the historians had shown to be possible and the scientists to be necessary, the jurists now showed how to accomplish. The law, they discovered, consisted of "a few, simple, true, and unalterable principles," founded not upon the "authority of Greek and Roman authors" nor upon "the [specific] customs of nations," but upon "reason alone." [20] These principles, "from which are derived all the rules and the laws of natural jurisprudence," possessed the same certainty as those governing the physical universe. First of all, they depended upon the self-evident axiom that all human actions spring from "self-love guided by right reason" and, consequently, that all civil societies have originated solely in response to the necessity of providing for the "common defense" and of protecting "the particular interests of each individual." [21] "The laws of nature are engraved on the heart of man," said Paoletti, and can be perceived by "the sole light of reason, that light which lighteth

[18] Lampredi, *Juris publici universalis, sive Juris naturae et gentium theoremata* (Livorno, 1776-78, 2d ed.; Pisa, 1782; Italian translation in note 15 above), chap. viii, 1; chap. xi, 5; chap. xvii, 25. Antonio Niccolini, « Delle lodi di Giuseppe Averani » (first published separately in Rome, 1745: Crusca: * Diario, 28 April 1745), in G. Averani, *Lezioni toscane* (2d ed), II, xi: « L'ammirabil maniera di filosofare del nostro immortale accademico il gran Galileo ». The similarities of these statements seems to indicate a close connection between the jurisprudence of the first and of the second half of the century, although considerable differences in emphasis have been noted by Piano Mortari (below, note 99).

[19] Vannucchi, *Dissertazione,* p. 80.

[20] Ferdinando Paoletti, quoted by Abele Morena in *Rassegna nazionale,* XXIX (1886), 328.

[21] Braccio da Filicaja in the Crusca: * Diario, 2 September 1747.

every man that cometh into the world." (!) [22] Secondly, they rested upon the same "spirit of analysis" and the same "geometric method" that had already proved so profitable in the natural sciences.[23] Finally, they could be confirmed by experience. "No one can fully master jurisprudence," insisted Targioni Tozzetti, "unless he knows the history of the governments and of the actions of various peoples." [24]

The law, to be sure, was not historical: it was not equivalent to the sum of the statutes and court decisions of any one state, and it did not develop through time with the increasing complexity of political organizations. Even Roman law, which had so long been venerated for its "true, undeniable principles of equity," was actually but a series of generalizations drawn from the positive laws of a particular people, whose warlike character had little in common with the peaceful sentiments of modern Tuscans. According to the *Giornale letterario* of Siena, in fact, Justinian had simply assembled all the edicts of all the emperors, whether still in force or not, into one large volume that might, with some justice, be dismissed as a "mass of absurd frivolities." [25]

In pointing out the discrepancies between Roman and natural law, the jurists seem often to adopt much of the anti-Roman sentiment

---

[22] Paoletti, *I veri mezzi*, p. 301: «... quella luce, che illumina ogni uomo, che nasce al mondo...». Similarly Ranucci in *Elogio di G. M. Lambredi*, p. 22. «that science of which the seeds and principles we carry in our hearts». Lampredi «found moral philosophy... reduced to a rigorous system of universal justice through the immutable principles of natural law, whence derive the rights and duties of men in their various states and in all the circumstances of human life».

[23] Vannucchi, *Dissertazione*, p. 12.

[24] Targioni Tozzetti to Giuseppe Gori, 4 August 1757, in Colombaria: Annali, 28. Appendix.

[25] *Giornale letterario di Siena*, III (1777), v-viii, reviewing Neri Badia's *Decisiones et responsa juris*. Similarly, Pompeo Neri in Memoria of May 1749: ASF Reggenza 29 bis, fol. 40, and Uccelli, speaking of Leopoldo Guadagni in *Elogio di Alessandro Bicchierai*, p. 18: «Ma per quanto il Codice, i Digesti di Giustiniano inspirino rispetto, e venerazione poichè in sostanza non sono che il resultato della ragione umana applicata ai diversi casi particolari...». Guadagni (on whom note A. Fabroni, *Historia Academiae Pisanae*, I, 12) carried out an historical interpretation of Roman law in his *Institutiones juris civilis*, which proceeds chronologically from the Tarquins to Justinian. On similar views in Muratori, Vasco, Beccaria, *et al.*, note Luigi Salvatorelli, *Il pensiero politico italiano dal 1700 al 1780* (3rd ed.; Torino: Einaudi, 1935), pp. 38 ff.

of contemporary Etruscologists, especially when, like Lampredi, they were themselves Etruscologists as well.[26] But the jurist had nevertheless to be "a good historian," because only history could provide him with the means of "consulting nature in the facts," of observing the consequences of the greatest possible number of specific laws and of inducing them from the constant relationships of cause and effect that govern them. Deduction and induction thus coincided; and the principles he might observe in even so small an area as the Maremma might, as Bandini and Montelatici had supposed, "with discretion be applied generally to every art, to every profession, to all conditions of men in all times and in all provinces." [27] It was the jurist's obligation then to follow the example of Machiavelli — whom Baldelli could now rescue from two centuries of opprobrium — to do in politics, that is, "what the philosophers of our times do in the physical and natural sciences" [28] and to free what had existed unaltered since the Creation from the blind clouds in which it had so long been enveloped.[29] As Tuscan botanists had applied the system of Tournefort to the flora of Tuscany, so now Tuscan jurists began to compare the laws of Tuscany "to the natural rules of right reason." What they found was not a well-ordered code deduced from "just, eternal, stable, and universal" principles, to which "the positive laws of each society," Tuscany included, were bound to conform.[30] They found instead a "labyrinth" [31] — a hopeless jumble of contradictory statutes and customs administered through many overlapping jurisdictions, which neither the scientific standards of simplicity nor the mere burden of work in the law courts could long endure. The acade-

[26] Ranucci, *Elogio di Gio. Maria Lampredi,* p. 25.

[27] B. S. Peruzzi, Sul problema se per essere buon legale si debba essere buon istorico, in Colombaria: Tarpato, I, 88. Bandini, *Discorso economico,* pp. 130-31, and Montelatici, *Ragionamento,* p. 1.

[28] Baldelli, *Elogio di Machiavelli,* p. 18.

[29] The unfortunate metaphor is the author's: « quod . . . caeca adhuc erat caligine circumfusum »: L. Guadagni quoted by A. Fabroni in *Vitae Italorum,* II (1769), 15.

[30] *Giornale de' letterati* (Pisa), XXXVII (1779), 79, commenting on the *De jure criminali* of the Sienese Luigi Cremani, and Vannucchi, *Dissertazione,* pp. 9-10 (« . . . a cui devono tendere ed avere sempre rapporto le leggi positive »).

[31] The word is Lampredi's in *Del commercio dei popoli neutrali in tempo di guerra* (Florence, 1788), here cited in second French translation, *Du commerce des neutres* (Paris: H. Agasse, an X [1802]), Preface, p. 9.

micians concluded, then, that all previous efforts to increase agricultural productivity had failed simply because a "misunderstood concept of legislation" had led their fathers to attack the effects rather than the causes.[32] The new jurisprudence thus offered an easy and efficacious remedy for the ills that so long had afflicted their country: let the positive laws of Tuscany, they proclaimed, be brought into harmony with the universal laws of beneficent nature, and poverty, famine, injustice, and confusion would disappear automatically.

The academicians were, therefore, quick to respond when a change of government in the midst of the economic crisis of 1765-66 provided the long-awaited opportunity to put Bandini's principles into practice. For two years the government of Botta Adorno had simply repeated the age-old prohibitions against the exportation of grain, increased the vigilant controls over harvesting and marketing, and doubled the savage penalties for even minor infractions — all with no other effect, apparently, than of discouraging further planting and of aggravating the already perilous food shortages. At last the academicians were forced to face the bankruptcy of the traditional formulas — just what the Balìa of Siena had often pointed out, what Neri, Gianni, and a few other royal officials had already proposed, and what the inquiry ordered by the Grand Duke in November 1766 would soon make perfectly clear.[33] Almost immediately Tuscan proprietors received the right, unconditionally in the Maremma and subject to a liberal maximum price in the other provinces, to sell their produce where they pleased, even beyond the borders of the Grand Duchy; and by September of the following year royal decrees

[32] Giuseppe Sarchiani in *Ragionamento sul commercio* (1781), quoted by Hermann Büchi, *Finanzen und Finanzpolitik Toskanas im Zeitalter der Aufkärung, 1737-1790* (Berlin: Ebering, 1915), p. 203 (one of the best works on the economic history of the period) and Bandini, *Discorso economico*, p. 39. Cf. Paoletti, *I veri mezzi*, p. 128: « Divine Providence, in establishing the admirable order of nature, has ordered and directed everything to the needs of man ».

[33] See L. Dal Pane, « I lavori preparativi per la grande inchiesta del 1766 sull'economia toscana », *Studi storici in onore di Gioacchino Volpe* (Florence: Sansoni, 1958), pp. 261-313, especially the recommendation of Ugoccioni and Federighi quoted on p. 274 that « since there is in Tuscany an Academy of Agriculture, it would seem appropriate . . . to ask its opinion on how to make the agriculture of Tuscany more flourishing », and the conclusion of Dal Pane (p. 313) on the general sentiment among Tuscans favorable to the abolition of existing economic regulations.

had abolished many of the measures by which the medieval city states had once sought to assure themselves, albeit in vain, a steady supply of cheap food.[34]   At last, it seemed, the government itself would lead the way in rewriting the laws of Tuscany in accordance with the laws of nature.

When, then, the royal ministers began seeking the advice of those who supposedly knew the most about natural law, or at least about the many unfortunate effects of *un*natural law on agriculture, the academicians hastened to modify their programs and statutes to provide for their assumption of new responsibilities.   By 1767 the Fisiocritici had supplemented their scientific dissertations with "similar researches" "profitable to ... the improvement of industry, the increase of commerce, the comforts of life, and, consequently, the opulence and population" of the realm;[35] the Colombaria had begun expanding its collection of historical documents to include the texts of the more important Tuscan statutes;[36] while the Georgofili, electing the first minister Orsini Rosemberg to the presidency, inserted a special clause in their new constitution on "the political and economic subjects accessory to agriculture."   "It would be most opportune," they proposed, that the members study such questions as "the physical and moral impediments to prosperity," "ways to facilitate, politically and economically, the marketing of produce at home and abroad," "the relation of population to land under cultivation," and "the increase of natural products [proportionate to] the progress of industry and manufacturing."[37]   Just the next year, in fact, they were contem-

[34] Principal legislation, especially the law of 18 September 1767, is reviewed in detail by Morena in *Rassegna nazionale*, XXVIII (1886), 638-39.   Typical of the traditional *annona* regulations is that of 6 July 1719 in Siena, found, significantly enough among the papers of Bandini and reproduced in part by Tozzi, *Sallustio Bandini*, p. 9.   On the purpose of the *annona* in the Middle Ages, see Gino Luzzatto, *Storia economica d'Italia*, I: *L'antichità e il medio evo* (Rome: Leonardo, 1949), pp. 259-60, and *Storia economico dell'età moderna e contemporanea* (3d ed.; Padova: Milan, 1955), Part II, pp. 151-52.

[35] *Atti Fisiocritici*, III, v-vi (dedication by Carlo Tonini to Pietro Leopoldo).

[36] Col. IV.II.III.I and 6, and Col. IV.II.56, described by U. Dorini, *Inventario dell'archivio e degli altri manoscritti della S. C.* (1915: those that survived the destruction of the former seat of the society during World War II are listed in his typed "Elenco degli mss. ricuperati").

[37] Georgofili: Constitution of 1767, chap. iii, Art. 2.   On requests for assistance from the government, see above. p. 52 ff.

plating the possibility of undertaking themselves the compilation of "the agrarian laws of Tuscany." [38] For "taken in its greatest extension," the solution of problems in agriculture of necessity comprehended the full consideration of "public" as well as "private economy." [39]

Nevertheless, while claiming the whole of "political economy" as their domain, the academies at first limited their inquiries to a relatively small number of specific problems. It had been the specter of famine, after all, rather than a fascination with the law itself, that had led them to consider using legislation as a way to increase the wealth and happiness of their fellow citizens. They began, therefore, by asking not how to remodel society as a whole or even how to raise agricultural productivity in general, but rather how to encourage the breeding of cattle, how to make the forests economically profitable without destroying them, and how to lower the costs of transportation through the construction of public highways. [40] The answers, moreover, were often as specific as the questions themselves. The candidates for the prize of 1767, for instance, agreed that a growth in cattle-raising required nothing more than the removal of the existing procedures for buying and selling. No amount of scientific information or official encouragement, they thought, would induce proprietors to augment their flocks unless they could fairly and easily dispose of them. But even when this proposal proved inadequate, when it was found, that is, that simply leaving the parties free to draw up any terms they wished resulted in even greater litigation, Gregorio Fierli, speaking for the Academy, would go no further than to put forth "a new, very simple law," designed to do no more than reduce the number of legally recognized defects in cattle. [41]

[38] Lecture of 22 June quoted in ASF Reggenza 170: Ragguaglio di documenti

[39] Georgofili: Constitution of 1783, chap. i (Geo I.I.I.6): « L'agricoltura presa nella sua massima estensione in rapporto al territorio toscano, congiunta coll'economia tanto pubblica, che privata . . . ». On the Tuscan economists, see the excellent preface and introductions to selections from the writings of Bandini, Neri, Gianni, and Giovanni Fabbroni in *Illuministi italiani*, III: *Riformatori lombardi piemontesi e toscani*, ed. Franco Venturi (Milan: Ricciardi, 1958), pp. 883-1134.

[40] See list of prizes offered in competition in *Atti Georgofili*, I, 16 ff.

[41] *Ibid.*, III, 125-37: Address of 10 April 1793 by Gregorio Fierli. See above, chap. iv, note 125. on cattle-raising.

Yet in spite of the reluctance to generalize that they shared with all other "scientists" of their age, the academic economists soon realized that some of these specific problems would require solutions considerably more extensive than merely adjustments in those statutes immediately involved. The persistence of the fallow field system, for instance, which the new experiments in crop rotation now showed to be wasteful, derived less from the anachronistic regulations concerning the season and methods of planting than from "political and human causes"; for, as Paolo Franceschi pointed out in 1775, the system did not exist in the neighborhood of the cities, where agriculture benefited from a nearby market and an abundant labor force. He proposed, therefore, not only the instruction of proprietors in the advantages of planted meadows and the removal of vexatious subaltern officials, but above all the promotion of urban industries, the improvement of roads, the opening of foreign markets, and the protection of the cultivators — all measures designed, that is, to raise the demand for agricultural products, to make the demand effective even at distances, to insure a readily available supply of liquid capital for land improvements, and to provide an adequate rural labor force.[42] Overcoming but one of the many defects of the Tuscan economy, in other words, apparently depended upon overcoming them all.

Thus the academicians were led to entertain propositions involving a thorough reform of the entire economic, and to some extent even the political, structure of the country. They all agreed, first of all, that the population of Tuscany was too small. "The land," declared the judges of the competition of 1775, "lacks men, not men land." One contestant, indeed, managed to place at exactly 122,578 the number needed solely for the conversion of the fallow fields.[43] Some question arose, to be sure, as to whether an increase in population were the cause or the effect of prosperity. A few, citing certain passages in Quesnay and in the first chapter of the *Ami des hommes* of the Marquis de Mirabeau, arrived at positions similar to those of the

---

[42] Franceschi, *Memoria sui maggesi*, published first in the *Magazzino toscano* and then separately in 1778, is reviewed in Imberciadori, *Campagna toscana nel '700*, pp. 184 f.

[43] « In Toscana mancano gli uomini alla terra e non la terra agli uomini », quoted in Imberciadori, *op. cit.*, p. 183. The population estimate is in Appendix iv.

English and French "populationists" of the earlier decades of the
century: they supposed, like Mengotti, that the national wealth
could be calculated simply by multiplying the cost of subsistence by
the number of inhabitants, and that the first would automatically rise
in proportion to the second. Others, following Lastri in attributing
the low birth rate in the 1730's to Giangastone's dissipation of tax
revenues, maintained that proper fiscal policies could bring about a
growth in population.[44] Still others accepted the position of Manetti
— and in part, therefore, of the Neapolitan economist Antonio Genovesi to whom he frequently refers — that the activity of the population
was as important as its numbers, and that poverty resulted largely
from the presence of men, "either noble or plebeian," who, like
Pignotti's housefly, defended

> con un nobile orgoglio
> il privilegio illustre
> di vivere ozioso

and boasted

> Non fo, non feci e non farò mai nulla.[45]

This last hypothesis, indeed, had one further advantage. The
presence of swarms of beggers — 781 in Florence alone according
to a survey of 1766 — and of many more "underprivileged," whom
contemporary artists invariably paint pestering fashionable tourists
before Florentine palaces, seemed to indicate that the real trouble lay
in the distribution rather than in the size of the population. A solu-

---

[44] Francesco Mengotti, feltriense, *Il colbertismo, ossia della libertà di commercio de'
prodotti della terra* (winner of Georgofili competition of 1791, here cited in S.C.I.E.P. edition
of 1804), pp. 325-26. On "populationism" in Quesnay and Mirabeau, see Adolphe Landry,
« Les idées de Quesnay sur la population », in *François Quesnay et la physiocratie* (Paris:
Institut national d'études démographiques, 1958), I, 11-49, esp. 12-18. Marco Lastri, *Ri-
cherche sull'antica e moderna popolazione di Firenze*, pp. 89 and 91.

[45] Saverio Manetti, « Lezione accademica » (1767), *Magazzino toscano*, I¹ (1770), 1-16,
p. 12. Note articles by Mario De Vergottini, Paolo Fortunati, Giovanni Lasorsa, and Guido
Sensini on Genovesi's theories of population growth in *Studi in onore di Antonio Genovesi*,
ed. Domenico Demarco (Naples: L'Arte Tipografica, 1956), Lorenzo Pignotti, « L'uomo,
il gatto, il cane e la mosca » in *Raccolta di favole* (London, 1850), p. 189: « with noble
pride / the illustrious privilege / of living in idleness »; « I do nothing, I have done nothing
and I will never do anything ».

tion to the rural labor shortage, therefore, might simultaneously do away with what had long been deplored as an incurable evil in the cities.[46]

Whatever theory of population growth they might accept, the academicians recognized that no one would stay on the land unless encouraged to do so by the prospect of receiving some reward for his labor. They recognized further that the creation of such prospects would require a considerable investment in buildings and equipment and a large expenditure to implement the Academy's projects for the scientific improvement of agriculture. But no proprietor, obviously, could be induced to make such efforts unless he were free to plant what he pleased in the manner he pleased and to buy and sell property according to his means. Thus from 1770 on the Georgofili pressed continually for the abolition of the privilege of creating inalienable landholdings (*fidecommissi*), which the Regency had already compromised by limiting to the nobility; they demanded the withdrawal of all transfer taxes on the grounds that they discouraged the acquisition of property by those most willing and able to exploit it; and they called for the repeal of the various laws requiring the planting of so many mulberry trees per square mile, the maintenance of pastures for public use, the harvesting of grapes within certain dates, and the issuance of special licences for water and forest rights on privately owned land.[47] The academicians agreed further that the rights of

---

[46] Among previous proposals: Lorenzo Magalotti, *Il mendicare abolito nella città di Montalbano* [Montaubon] *da un uffizio di carità* (Florence: Cecchi, 1693). The words *meno facoltosi* are those of the semi-official *Governo della Toscana sotto il regno di S. M. il re Leopoldo II* (Florence. 1790, here cited in 2nd ed. of 1791 by Bonducci), p. 68 (translated as *Die Staatsverwaltung von Toskana* [Gotha, 1795]). Figure for 1766 given in « Prospetto delle occupazioni nella città di Firenze » published by Zobi, *Storia civile,* II, doc. v. For beggars in art, note Giuseppe Richa, *Notizie istoriche delle chiese fiorentine* (10 vols. in 5; Florence, 1754-62), V, frontispiece, and Vol. III of John Richardson, *Traité de la peinture,* entitled *Description de divers fameux tableaux qui se trouvent en Italie* (Amsterdam: Uytwerf, 1728), p. 148. The first prize for the Georgofili competition of 1770 was awarded to L. Andreucci, *De' mezzi per impiegare i mendichi in vantaggio dell'agricoltura e delle arti* (n.d.). On the concept of a proper "balance" in population: Gianni, *Cagione e progresso dello sbilancio degli interessi tra la capitale e le provincie di Toscana:* ASF Carte Gianni XIII, ins. 278. On the problem of mendicancy in general, see the introduction and notes to Neri's *Memoria* in *Illuministi italiani,* III, 967 ff.

[47] On landholding: Memorial of Paoletti in *Giornale fiorentino di agricoltura,* I (1786), 353-54. Giuseppe degli Albizi on *fidecommissi* (7 October 1772) and on the freedom of cul-

proprietorship necessitated a clarification of the relationship between landlord and tenant, a question of particular importance in a country where the very nature of the terrain favored the traditional system of sharecropping, or *mezzadria.*[48]

It was certainly to the interests of the landlord, and to the whole of society, that the *mezzadro* produce as much as possible. But whether his willingness to work depended upon his security and personal prosperity, as Paoletti maintained, or upon his fear of expulsion and his "freedom" from the perils of luxury, sloth, and immorality, as Luigi Tramontani held, remained a matter of debate.[49] The first thesis lent support to the proposals of Gianni, Francesco Paolini, and Francesco Mormorai to stimulate the growth of peasant proprietorship, which Pietro Leopoldo tried to put into practice, for social and humanitarian as well as for economic reasons, by alienating or converting into perpetual leases (*allivellazione*) much of the public domain. The second would support the plea of Giuseppe Pelli, Tramontani, and other members of the Georgofili commission of January 1788 for the preservation of large landed estates; it would support also the successful attempt of the Academy to shorten the time permitted a peasant to evacuate a farm after the cancellation of his *mezzadria* contract.[50] But in any case, all special impositions on the peasantry

tivation (3 August 1774) in *Atti Georgofili,* I, Nos. 5 and 6. Note Giuseppe Sarchiani, in *Elogi di accademici defunti* (from *Atti,* V), p. 23 f. These suggestions were incorporated into the laws of 14 March 1782 and 3 February 1789 (*Leggi e bandi,* XI, No. 17, and XIV, No. 5). In generale: Imberciadori, *Campagna toscana nel '700,* pp. 148 ff., reviewing the principal literature on these arguments and on the consequent legislation.

[48] Cf. W. K. Hancock, *Politics in Pitcairn* (London: Macmillan, 1947), chap. ii: « Italian metayage ». Present changes in Tuscan agriculture suggest that this judgment of *mezzadria* is somewhat too favorable. Note also the inconclusive and somewhat opinionated article of Luigi Bologna, « Origine e sviluppo della mezzadria toscana sino all'editto leopoldino » (of 2 August 1785), *Rivista di diritto agrario,* III (1924), 73-84, 224-40.

[49] Paoletti from *Pensieri sopra l'agricoltura,* pp. 18 f.; Tramontani speech of 7 August 1794 in Imberciadori, *Campagna toscana nel '700,* Appendix xviii.

[50] Gianni's opinions (e.g., « che le vaste possessioni di terreni . . . sono opposte al progresso della ricchezza nazionale », fol. 27) in Memoria of 17 October 1782: ASF Carte Gianni XXVII, 518. The opposite opinion of Tramontani in Imberciadori, *Campagna toscana nel '700,* Appendix xviii, pp. 395 f. In general: Antonio Anzilotti, « Piccola o grande proprietà nelle riforme di Pietro Leopoldo e negli economisti del secolo XVIII », *Bullettino senese di storia patria,* XXII (1915), 339-69, and the recent criticism of Anzilotti's thesis by Mario Mirri, « Proprietari e contadini nelle riforme leopoldine », *Movimento operaio,* VII (1955), 173-299, who shows that in a few areas around Pisa almost all the alienated land

— from tithes, communal taxes, and the offerings demanded by mendicant friars to the *corvée,* which the Georgofili specifically ruled out as a possible means of maintaining the roadways — were recognized as "prejudical to agriculture" and detrimental to an increase in the number of agricultural laborers.[51] Hence the Academy insisted upon their abolition — with the condition, of course, that such impositions not simply be transferred to the landowners in the form of higher taxes.

Yet no one supposed that any of these measures would succeed in the long run unless the misguided policy of forcing agriculture to produce independently of demand gave way to one which permitted it to produce in response to the stimulus of a free market. They therefore called first of all for the withdrawal of all restrictions on the movement and sale of crops within the borders of Tuscany: "deve lasciarvi oprar la natura," as Bandini had taught, "let nature work," for she "knows well how to revenge offenses against her providence."[52] They called secondly for the replacement of indirect with direct taxes, for the abolition of the innumerable duties and tolls levied on commerce in favor of impositions upon productive wealth — a change that would have the added advantage of reducing the great number

ended up in the hands of large proprietors, thus thwarting the intention of the legislation. Mirri's identification of the position of the Georgofili with the class interests of landed proprietors, however, must be accepted with some reservation. As late as 1808, Vincenzo Agostino in the Academia Pistoiese attributed the growth in prosperity and population to « the *allivellazione* of land undertaken by order of the immortal Pietro Leopoldo . . . This most enlightened prince fully recognized the truth that the multiplication of the means of subsistence resulted necessarily in an increase in population, and that the happiness of the state lay not in big estates [*latifondi*], but in limited and restricted landholdings, which in proportion give a greater product »: *Atti dell'A. P.,* I (1808), 191. Note further Targioni Tozzetti's concern for the proper housing of peasants in his *Ragionamento sull'agricoltura toscana* (1759), p. 7. On agrarian contracts: Agricoltura: * Atti, 11 January and 22 April 1789, and Gregorio Fierli, « Sopra le licenze, e disdette dei coloni » (8 February 1792), *Atti Georgofili,* III, 100-114.

[51] Prize of 1778-79 (above, note 40): « senza servirsi delle comandate, state riconosciute pregiudiciali all'agricoltura, e perciò proibite dalle veglianti leggi ». Crusca: * Diario, 5 August 1762: Buondelmonti on the *decime ecclesiastiche* (tithes); G. Sarchiani, « Intorno al sistema delle pubbliche imposizioni » (13 July 1791). *Atti Georgofili,* III, 46-84. Note Georgofili: Appunti, 13 November 1771, and letters of Angelo Tavanti to the Academy of 8 October 1771: ASF Archivio Tolomei 191, ins. VII, No. 711, on taxes which « posandosi sopra i contadini pregiudicano all'agricoltura ».

[52] Bandini, *Discorso economico,* pp. 12, 167.

15

of tax collectors, condemned by Giuseppe Sarchiani as "a double burden on the state." [53] They called thirdly for the unconditional and permanent guarantee of freedom to import and export, for, they pointed out, any interference in international trade simply encouraged contraband and gluts, and would therefore be wholly inefficacious.[54]

Let no one complain, the academicians warned, should freedom provoke an initial rise in the price of food, for freedom would also assure an eventual fall in prices by attracting products to the most favorable market. Supply and demand, after all, and not the decrees of a prince or an artificial estimate of intrinsic value, determined the natural, and therefore the just price of any commodity. Let no one complain, moreover, should the eventual level of prices turn out to be somewhat higher than that established by the former *annona* officials in years of relative plenty: a steady price, after all, was most certainly preferable to the disasterous fluctuations that once discouraged producers and starved consumers. The prosperity of agriculture, upon which the entire Tuscan economy rested, would result almost immediately in a corresponding prosperity of industry and commerce — providing, of course, that they also were freed from the restrictions that had long kept alive a number of unprofitable and parasitical enterprises at the expense of those capable of expansion.[55] The Georgofili therefore supported enthusiastically all those measures by which the government of Pietro Leopoldo, well before that of even such a progressive state as Austrian Lombardy, put these

[53] Sarchiani in *Atti Georgofili*, III, 51.

[54] Giovanni Lessi, « Della inefficacia e dei dannosi effetti delle leggi, che escludono dagli stati le manifatture esteri » (7 September 1791), *Atti Georgofili*, II, 85 ff. In general: R. Mori, *Le riforme leopoldine nel pensiero degli economisti toscani del '700* (Florence: Sansoni, 1951), pp. 80-88. Opinion on such a drastic measure, which went against a century old tradition, was by no means unanimous. Note the arguments, for instance, of Adami in his *Della necessità di accrescere e migliorare l'agricoltura* of 1767.

[55] Note Gio. Francesco Pagnini, *Saggio sopra il giusto pregio delle cose, la giusta valuta della moneta, e sopra il commercio dei romani* (Florence, 1751), and Gianni, * Ricordi per l'Accademia (ASF Carte Gianni XIII, 302). On freedom of manufacturing and commerce: Luigi Dal Pane, *Il tramonto delle corporazioni in Italia. Secoli XVIII-XIX* (Milan: Istituto per gli Studi di Politica Internazionale, 1940), and Attilio Oblath, *La camera di commercio, arti e manufatture di Firenze, 1770-82* (Bologna: Cappelli, 1932). The *arti* (corporations) were dissolved gradually by the edicts of 1 February 1770 and 29 May 1781 (*Leggi e bandi*, V, No. 180, and X, No. 117).

principles into practice; they rushed to the defense of the Leopoldine legislation as soon as, in 1790, a series of riots forced to frightened Regency to re-establish the long-abrogated controls; and they continued, well into the following century, to look back with admiration on this "celebrated epoch in the history of modern monarchies."[56] "Long live the freedom of commerce," exclaimed Giovanni Fabbroni in 1799, "the only true remedy to the scourge of famine, the sure source of public quiet, the lifeblood of the countryside, the nourisher of workers, and the cause of general prosperity."[57]

Obviously all these proposals rest ultimately upon certain philosophic assumptions concerning nature, man, and society. They presuppose first of all that "reason" and utility are in perfect harmony, and that any specific measures deduced from the "few, perfectly evident principles" from which all public economy derives automatically further the well-being of the nation.[58] These proposals assume secondly that the interests of society coincide perfectly with those of its individual members, that they are best served by leaving each citizen in perfect freedom to determine what is most advantageous to him and by guaranteeing him complete control over the means necessary to achieve it. The principal of these means is private property. Any attempt to abridge the rights of property, therefore, even for such well-intentioned purposes as the preservation of for-

[56] The principles of free trade in Lombardy, outlined in Art. III of the edict on the Supremo Consiglio di Economia of 20 November 1765, were not even partially applied until 1771; and not until the edict of 4 April 1786 was the free circulation of grain fully permitted. See C. A. Vianello in introduction to *Considerazioni sull'annona dello stato di Milano nel XVIII secolo* (Milan: Giuffrè, 1940), pp. xi-xii. Pietro Verri's recognition of the leadership of Tuscany in free trade in his « Nuova proposizione sul piano d'annona », of 1768, *ibid.*, p. 132. Note the Georgofili program of 1791 (won by Mengotti, above, note 42): « If . . . it is more advantageous . . . to favor manufacturing by the regulation of commerce in foodstuffs, or to leave such products in the complete and perfect freedom of natural commerce ». On the other competitors, see Morena in *Rassegna nazionale*, XXXI (1886), 487-88.

[57] Fabbroni, *Gli ozi della villeggiatura*, p. 109.

[58] Pietro Ferroni, speech to the Georgofili of 2 March 1796, *Atti Georgofili*, IV, 316: « Pochi ed evidenti principj ». 'Discorso' of Vittorio Fossombroni, 12 May 1792: « No maxim, no law can have any effect if private interest is not in accord with public interest », in his *Scritti di pubblica economia*, ed. Morena (2 vols.; Arezzo, 1896), I, 12.

ests,[59] will simply diminish the potential contribution of the citizens to the society. Property, moreover, and above all landed property, is the chief stimulus to activity. Hence proprietors are by definition the most active citizens, and they should be both permitted and encouraged to contribute on their own initiative to the formulation of public policy and to take complete responsibility for those affairs that properly fall within the domain of local government.[60]   Thirdly, the proposals of the academicians assume that agriculture is the « basis of the prosperity and the power of the state," [61] and that any attempt to control it for the benefit of industry or commerce, which are essentially derivative or secondary occupations, will simply diminish the productivity of the economy as a whole.   They assume further that the state is basically a voluntary association for the pursuit of the individual and collective advantage of its members.   Since this advantage is largely material, politics and political economy are the same thing, and all laws must be judged according to their effect on the national wealth.   Princes, in fact, as Pietro Leopoldo himself declared (without obliging himself always to observe the declaration in practice), are "simples particuliers et serviteurs de l'Etat." [62]

The actual form of the state (which the academicians indeed almost never discussed) is a matter of minor importance, since it can vary according to the peculiar circumstances of time and place.   "The

[59] Dissertation of Onofrio Goretti: Infecondi: * Atti, 25 June 1776; Georgofili prize for 1793: « salvo il diritto di proprietà ».

[60] Note Paoletti, *Pensieri sopra l'agricoltura*, p. 30.

[61] Saverio Manetti (above, note 45) in *Magazzino toscano*, I^1 (1770), 15.

[62] Letter to Joseph II, 7 June 1787, in *Joseph II und Leopold von Toskana: Ihr Briefwechsel von 1781 bis 1790*, ed. Alfred von Arneth (2 vols.; Vienna: Braumüller, 1872), II, 69-62.   Denunciations of "tyranny," usually in fairly vague terms, increase rapidly in the secondo half of the century, from the discourse of Feroni to the Crusca (* Diario, 22 August 1750) to Gianni's Meditazione sul despotismo: ASF Carte Gianni XX, 441 (now partially published in *Illuministi italiani*, III, 1065-75), and the tragedy *Agide* (Florence: Cambiagi, 1787) of Cosimo Giotti, where death is prescribed as the just reward for oppressors.   Contrast the opinion of the Jansenist Bishop of Pistoia and Prato, Scipione de' Ricci, for whom all political authority descended directly from God to the prince alone (« a Dio solo della esecuzione del medesimo [his office] ha da render conto, non ai privati cittadini »): Arturo Jemolo, *Stato e chiesa negli scrittori italiani del Seicento e del Settecento* (Torino: Bocce, 1914), p. 47.   Similar opinions among the Tuscan Jansenists are described in Part III of Ettore Passerin d'Entrèves, « La politica dei giansenisti in Italia nell'ultimo Settecento », *Quaderni di cultura e storia sociale*, II (1953), 359-65.

system of government," after all, as the Accademia Etrusca admitted in 1787, "which those Republicans [in the United States] are about to adopt may well resemble closely those laws of interior economic administration now in force under the philosophic reign of Pietro Leopoldo." [63]   Still, the best constitution is probably monarchical. Monarchies, as the historical speculations of Lampredi and Orazio Maccari suggested, were the first governments ever to be established, and the authority of the immediate descendants of Noah is not to be disregarded.   Monarchy, moreover, offers the best guarantee against the division or alienation of sovereignty that so often has oppressed the citizens and blocked the exercise of political authority.[64] The function of government consists solely in making possible the free operation of the physical and moral laws of nature.   Any transgression of these limits, in the regulation of commerce, for instance, or in "commanding that 100 lire of depreciated money" equal "100 lire of good money," has the same effect, as Neri pointed out, as "commanding that 10 be a number equal to 12."[65]   All government, finally, derives its authority solely from the will of the governed, who as men "are naturally born free."   No man, therefore, can be induced to give up "his natural liberty" except "by his own consent, either expressed or tacit" and by the offer of a "greater security under the legislative power of civil society." [66]

[63] Program of 1796, printed in Preface to Lastri, *Elogio di Amerigo Vespucci*, in *Gazetta toscana*, 15 April 1778, No. 15, p. 59, and elsewhere.

[64] Maccari in Etrusca: * Atti, 26 February 1776.   Bandini: « l'essere molti a commandare non giova niente al miglior servizio del sovrano . . . », in *Discorso economico*, p. 112.

[65] Neri, *Osservazioni sopra il prezzo legale delle monete* (S.C.I.E.P.), p. 163.

[66] Filippo Alticozzi, *Risposta apologetica* (1763), Preface, p. vii: « . . . gli uomini nascono liberi naturalmente: non vi è cosa, che possa metterli sotto il dominio di un altro, se non il proprio consenso ».   A man « rinunzia alla libertà naturale per sua maggior sicurezza, sotto la potenza legislativa della società civile ».   Alticozzi, of course, intended these rather bold assertions to do no more than deflate the claims of Arezzo to be more "ancient" than Cortona.   The transition from enlightened despotism to constitutionalism has been noticed above all in Lampredi (note E. Passerin d'Entrèves, « L'ambiente culturale pisano nell'ultimo '700 », *Bollettino storico pisano*, XXII-XXIII [1953-54], 54-121, citing Lampredi's letters of 1789-90 in the Bibliothèque Royale at Brussels), but the question needs much more study.   Many of the statements in Lampredi's publications are already a bit hold; but, as Cantimori has observed (*Utopisti e riformatori italiani*, chap. x, esp. pp. 130 ff.), those in his classroom may have gone much further.   One of his pupils, after all, was none other than Filippo Buonarroti, the associate of Balbeuf in the Conspiracy of Equals of 1797.

None of these theoretical propositions, to be sure, is particularly remarkable for its originality. The distinction of Roman from natural law had already been accomplished by the humanists of the Quattrocento, the derivation of individual rights from human nature rather than from God by Grotius and Pufendorf, and the interpretation of the state as a contract between subjects and sovereign, at least as echoed in Paoletti and Alticozzi, by Locke.[67] The concept of public happiness as the aggregate of that of all the citizens, the definition of the monarch as merely the chief representative of society, the supposition of a causal relationship between wealth and population, the limitation of legislation to the discovery rather than the creation of law, free trade, nature, *lasciare andare,* peasant prosperity, the primacy of agriculture — all such theses can be found much more fully developed in the works of the more famous contemporaries of the Tuscan academicians, from Filangieri and Genovesi in Naples to Mirabeau and Le Mercier de la Rivière in France.[68] From the Physiocrats, indeed, the Tuscan economists seem to have borrowed not only such theories as the single land tax, but even some of the mythology. They never tire, for instance, of repeating Sully's *mot* about a chicken in every pot every Sunday, of denouncing "Colbertism," or of marveling at the happy domains of "that wise Emperor of China." [69]

[67] Above, note 4, and Paoletti, *I veri mezzi,* p. 138.

[68] Note Dino Fiorot, *La filosofia politica dei Fisiocratici* (Padova: Cedam, 1954), especially I, v (p. 97 ff.), the similar titles in Gaetano Filangeri, *Scienza della legislazione* (here cited in the edition of Milan: Classici Italiani, 1822), I, chaps. iii, iv, xxxiv — on whose concept of monarchy: Enrico Malato, « L'anti-assolutismo di G. F. », *Nuova antologia,* CDLXXI (1957), 81-90. The closeness of Genovesi to the Tuscan economists is suggested by his having reprinted Montelatici's *Ragionamento* in Naples, 1753; it is probably through him, indeed, that they learned much of what they knew of the political philosophy of Locke.

[69] E.g., Mengotti in *Il colbertismo*; Paoletti, *Pensieri sopra l'agricoltura,* p. 59 (« quando ciaschedun contadino si fosse trovato in grado di far bollire una gallina nella sua pentola ogni domenica » as « diceva Sully »); and Montelatici, *Ragionamento,* p. 23, note 2. Tuscan authors would have found similar statements about China in Wolff, whom they frequently cite: cf. Donald F. Lach, « The sinophilism of Christian Wolff (1697-1754), *Journal of the History of Ideas,* XIV (1953), 561-74. See Mario Mirri, « Per una ricerca sui rapporti fra 'economisti' e riformatori toscani: L'abate Niccolini a Parigi », *Annali dell'Istituto Giangiacomo Feltrinelli,* II (1959), 55-120, especially pp. 107-8 on the exchange of literature between the government of Turgot and the Georgofili and Fisiocritici.

This apparent similarity is by no means a coincidence. Tuscan writers, after all, freely admitted their debts by filling their discourses with citations to French, German, Neapolitan, and even to some extent English jurists and political economists, whose works circulated rapidly in Tuscany throughout the second half of the century. Continuing the practice of the historians and scientists of popularizing the contributions of foreigners to their own field of study, the Georgofili printed résumés in their journals of all current publications received from beyond the Alps and sponsored translations of the more important of them: the *Avviso al popolo* of Baudeau, for instance, the *Lettere ad un amico* of Le Trosne, and the many others that appeared, usually within a few months of the publication of the original, in the series entitled "Short treatises of interest to mankind and the public and private well-being." [70] They also adopted the practice of the Etrusca and the Crusca of bestowing honorary membership upon foreign philologists and antiquarians; thus as Brenckman had been elected to the Accademia Fiorentina in recognition of his "History of the Pandects," so the name "il marchese di Mirapoux" or "Mirabeaux" appeared on the Georgofili rolls as early as 1762. [71] Meanwhile Tuscan printers were themselves busy satisfying the demands of the domestic market — with Mirabeau's *Amico degli uomini* (1783), with Filangieri's *Scienza della legislazione,* with a collection (*Raccolta*) of the decrees of several French parlements "regarding the perfect and complete liberty of commerce." [72]

[70] See above, pp. 48-50. The anonymous *Avviso al popolo sul bisogno suo primario* (Florence: Stecchi & Pagani, 1768), translated from Nicholas Baudeau, *Avis au peuple sur son premier besoin, ou petits traités economiques* (Amsterdam and Paris: Hochereau jeune, 1768); *Lettere,* etc., (Florence: Pisoni, 1770), from Guillaume François Le Trosne, *Lettres à un ami sur les avantages de la liberté du commerce des grains* (Amsterdam [but Paris]: Dessaint, 1770); on the *Opuscoli interessanti l'umanità e il pubblico e privato bene delle popolazioni e provincie agrarie* (n.d., [but Florence from 1773 on]), see L. Dal Pane, *La questione del commercio dei grani nel Settecento in Italia.* I, *Parte Generale: Toscana* (Cotignola: Tampieri, 1932), pp. 256-63.

[71] B. Dal Borgo, *Dissertazione . . . delle Pandette,* p. 55; Georgofili roll in Tabarrini, *Degli studi e delle vicende della R. A. dei G.,* pp. 63 f.

[72] *Amico degli uomini, ovvero Trattato della popolazione* (Siena, 1783), from *L'ami des hommes* (Avignon, 1756-58; Paris: Hérisant, 1759-60); Filangieri, *La scienza della legislazione* (Florence: Pagani, 1786, from Neapolitan edition of 1785); *Raccolta di decreti, partiti, e lettere di alcuni parlamentari della Francia spettanti alla perfetta e intera libertà nel commercio de' grani* (Florence: Allegrini, 1769). Pufendorf, it should be noted, was

It is not surprising therefore, that by 1765 a canon of the Florentine Cathedral should think it fitting to honor the memory of the
late Emperor-Grand Duke with lengthy references to Locke, Grotius,
Cumberland, Vattel, Hobbes, and Pufendorf and to hail the "holy
law of nature, daughter of the Eternal Mind, soul of the world";
nor is it extraordinary that Giovanni Neri should have begun his
brilliant career as an economist when, as a young man absorbed in
the management of his estates, he stumbled upon the works of Mirabeau and Quesnay and found, "to his amazement," so many "vaunted
prodigies" swept away "in a few lines." [73] For the academies of
the first half of the century had already broken down the barriers
that once had isolated Tuscany from its neighbors; and the Tuscan
political economists after 1750 could accept with little difficulty the
meditations of their foreign colleagues as valid contributions to the
same European cultural community of which their own country was
an integral part.

Yet the frequency of such citations is not necessarily a sign that
Tuscans were wholly passive in their reception of external influences.
First of all, the very multiplicity of citations in their writings, both
in and out of the academies, has so far thwarted all attempts to identify all or even some of them with any of the Transalpine schools or
doctrines. With surprising lack of discrimination they heaped praise
not upon a few, but upon *all* their contemporaries, apparently un-
aware of the contradictions among the various theses they cited. Their
admiration for the Physiocrats, for instance, did not prevent their
applauding the *Ami des hommes,* which appeared before the conversion of Mirabeau to the *Ecole,* or even the *Homme aux quarante
écus,* which Gianni admitted to be a "most violent attack upon the

---

available in Italian, translated, but alas! also *rettificato* by the Brescian G. B. Almici (Venice: Valvasense, 1757-59). though Tuscans usually read the original.

[73] Giovanni Giorgio degli Alberti, in *Raccolta di tutto ciò che si è fin qui pubblicato
in Livorno e altrove in morte ... Francesco I ...* (Livorno: Strambi, 1765). Part. II,
pp. 178-211, quoted from p. 181. Sarchiani on Neri in an « Elogio », *Atti Georgofili,* IV,
52. Cf. A. Anzilotti, *Matteo Biffi Tolomei* (Bologna: Emiliano, 1915), p. 13: Biffi Tolomei
« conosceva perfettamente gli scritti di Quesnay, de la Rivière, Turgot, Le Trosne, Mirabeau ... ».

financiers";[74] their references to Turgot did not discourage their making others to the reforms of Joseph II, which, while possibly exerting some influence on the policies of his brother Pietro Leopoldo, had in fact quite different historical and philosophical origins.[75] At times they seem to accept the thesis of the sterility of manufacturing and commerce; at others, usually with reference to the past centuries when Florentine merchants were "the fifth element," they insist that both contribute to the national wealth and ascribe the preponderance of agriculture in their own times to the peculiar development of Tuscan history. Even the most doctrinaire "Physiocrats" among them recoiled at the proposal for a single tax, and even the most convinced proponents of the free exportation of grain at times questioned the advisability of the free importation of manufactured goods.[76] If viewed through definitions borrowed from Transalpine schools of economics or political theory, then, the Tuscans were mercantilists, liberalists, free-traders, and protectionists all rolled into one — to which perhaps the term "eclectics" can be applied, but to whom no coherent "system" can be attributed.[77]

[74] Gianni, *Pensieri sulla ricchezza nazionale* (1787), ed. Morena (Arezzo, 1894), pp. 7-8.

[75] Note Hans von Voltelini, « Die naturrechtlichen Lehren und die Reformen des 18. Jahrhunderts », *Historische Zeitschrift*, CV (1910), 65-104, and Fritz Valjavec's explanation of the reforms in Lombardy and Tuscany as parallel to but independent of those in Austria in *Der Josephinismus* (Munich: Oldenbourg, 1945), p. 13. The influence of Joseph II on his brother, between whom relations were generally cool at best, cannot fully be estimated until their voluminous correspondence, of which Arneth published only a part, has been studied: see François Fejtö, *Un Habsbourg révolutionnaire, Joseph II* (Paris: Plon, 1953), p. 101, where Pietro Leopoldo is described, though without any evidence being given, as « un homme d'état florentin ». For the origins of the religious aspects of Josephinism, see Eduard Winter, *Der Josefinismus und seine Geschichte* (Brünn: Rohrer, 1943).

[76] G. Fabbroni, *Gli ozi della villeggiatura*, 112-13, *et seq.;* Georgofili prize of 1798 for the improvement of dyeing, in *Atti Georgofili*, IV, 116-17; and Paoletti, *I veri mezzi*, p. 231: « Il coltivatore, il mercante, il manifattore, l'artista formano tutti una sola famiglia . . . ». Cf. Gianni, « Meditazione sulle teorie e sulla pratica delle imposizioni e tasse pubbliche » (1786), first published anonymously in 1793 and reprinted in his *Scritti di pubblica economia* (Florence: Niccolai, 1848), I, 10-45, and the summary of the various positions of Gianni, Paolini, and Biffi Tolomei on Physiocratic theory in Mori, *Le riforme leopoldine*, pp. 104-8. The paucity of references to Smith may be explained by the absence of any editions of the *Wealth of Nations* in Florentine libraries before that of London, 1788. The first (according to the editor) Italian translation is that of Naples, 1790-91.

[77] Characteristics similar to those described in the following paragraphs have been observed in contemporary Venetian and Neapolitan economists by Massimo Petrocchi, *Il*

Secondly, the Tuscan economists ignored many of the more important passages even in those works they most admired. While adopting almost all of Quesnay's proposals for the restoration of the French economy, for instance, they made no mention whatever of those pertaining to military service or religious toleration. While accepting in principle the distinction between crime and sin and while agreeing with Grotius that natural law would be valid even if God did not exist, they hesitated to accept the full consequences of concepts that had originally been elaborated in response to circumstances wholly foreign to their own experience. Tuscans, for instance, had never been obliged to search for rules of conduct acceptable to the adherents of different religious creeds.[78] They repeatedly proclaimed, therefore, that luxury (*il lusso*) was a social ill to be corrected by law, that a state was a moral entity charged with making men "good" as well as "happy" and with "maintaining the tranquil distinction of the different orders of citizens, the good conduct of private families, [and] the just recompense of merit and virtue." They thus applauded the "requests" of Pietro Leopoldo that only plain black clothing be worn at court, and they wept over the mounting evidence that the *popolo* lived no longer according to the traditional "national frugality" but "as Sybarites and Tarantines enervated by pleasure and softness."[79]

tramonto della Repubblica di Venezia e l'assolutismo illuminato (Venice: La Deputazione Editrice, 1950), chap. v, and by Guido de Ruggiero, *Il pensiero politico meridionale nei secoli XVIII e XIX* (2d ed.; Bari: Laterza, 1946), chap. ii.

[78] *Giornale de' letterati* (Pisa), X (1773), 220-21 and 227. On the distinction between law and religion in Grotius and Pufendorf, a question upon which modern scholars have disagreed, see Antonio Corsano, *U. Grozio* (Bari: Laterza, 1948), pp. 273-88, and Mariano Campo, *Cristiano Wolff e il razionalismo prescritto* (Milan: Vita e Penisero, 1939), pp. 417 ff. (and 415-16 on the origins of this distinction in the religious divisions of Northern Europe and in the contacts of Christian with non-Christian peoples overseas). On Pufendorf's thesis that natural law and revelation, if distinct, are still united in God and therefore perfectly reconcilable, a thesis heartily endorsed by Tuscans, see the introduction of Walter Simons to his *De jure naturae et gentium* (Oxford: The Clarendon Press, 1934), II, 19a.

[79] Bindo Peruzzi, *Dissertazione letta nell'A. de' G. sopra l'uso giusto del lusso relativamente all'agricoltura, arti, e commercio* (2 September 1767) (Florence: Cambiagi, 1768), distinguishing between « useful » and « harmful » luxuries: and Infecondi. * *Atti,* 19 September 1774: « far gli uomini felici e buoni ». Ildefonso di S. Luigi in *Delizie degli eruditi toscani,* VII, xxii-xxiii: « la tranquilla distinzione degli ordini diversi de' cittadini, il buon conducimento delle private famiglie... ». Decrees of Pietro Leopoldo on dress in court printed in the *Gazzetta toscana* for 27 January 1787 (Vol. XX) and another of 10 August 1781

While speculating, moreover, on the futility of political action in those areas governed by the law of nature alone, they dismissed a somewhat more thorough attack on the "abuses of government" in defiance of "the rights of man," submitted by a French correspondent in 1796, with the smug admonition that the author "does not appear to have a sufficiently clear grasp" of the "particular circumstances of our state." [80] Indeed, they regarded many propositions with considerable suspicion, especially those which, "even though sustained by the most able writers," were based upon the calculation of "men as they ought to be and not as they are." All others, as Adami pointed out in 1768, "even though in appearance well thought out, must be thoroughly discussed by all sides before being approved and copied in our own country." [81] Tuscany soon dissolved what little armed force it ever had supported; it had never had any Huguenots to expel; and the academicians had no quarrel either with a social order in which they lived so comfortably or with a monarchical regime that so well responded to their petitions. They saw little reason, therefore, to concern themselves with these matters. In political economy, as in all the other sciences, Tuscan writers adopted from the writings of their foreign colleagues only what corresponded to questions they themselves were asking.

Their citations, finally, are by no means limited to foreigners. Bandini, for instance, whose *Discorso* was written some nineteen years before the publication of Quesnay's articles in the *Encyclopédie,* supported his theses almost exclusively with references to the conditions of the Sienese Maremma, both past and present. In spite of some generalizations reminiscent of Boisguilbert and Vauban, he proposed as a solution no more than the permanent and unconditional enactment of a measure already conceded temporarily and condition-

appended to Colombaria: Annali 33, Appendix 8. Vittorio Fossombroni in the « Discorso » of 12 May 1792, *Scritti di pubblica economia,* I, 11, and Luigi Fiorilli's memorandum read on 8 April 1795 in Imberciadori, *La campagna toscana nel '700.* Doc. XX, p. 408: « al sibarita e al tarantino snervato dalla voluttà e dalla mollezza ».

[80] ASF Archivio Tolomei, 191, VII, 690.

[81] Paoletti in the Georgofili, quoted by *Giornale fiorentino di agricoltura,* I (1786), 354 (11 November): « calcolati quali esser dovrebbero, non quali sono ». A. F. Adami, *Della necessità di accrescere e migliorare l'agricoltura,* p. 44.

ally by the Medici since as early as 1574. The methods of "la moderna filosofia," indeed, which permitted him to establish the relationship between public happiness and agriculture by "a bit of reflection" upon "the evidence" rather than upon "abstract metaphysical verities," may well have come from those methods already applied so fruitfully by his teacher Gabbrielli and his colleagues in the Fisiocritici to physics and medicine.[82] Paoletti, similarly, cites only two minor foreign economists, Bertrand and Thomas, in his first essay of 1767; almost all the argument, which his subsequent contact with the Physiocrats led him to modify only superficially, is based on his own observations of the agricultural conditions in the rural parish of Villa Magna, where he lived from 1746 until his death.

Yet Tuscans were not obliged to rely wholly on personal experience: they could find abundant support for their thesis in the authors with which they were already familiar as students of literature and history. Thus even in 1772, after he had extended his reading to the works of Montesquieu, Le Mercier, and John Cary, Paoletti still preferred to quote St. Antonino on the problem of mendicancy, Pliny and Columella on the importance of agriculture, and Cicero on the necessity of following "nature"; and he found the purely Christian arguments of the pious Bishop Ippoliti of Cortona on behalf of the peasants far more convincing than any scientific demonstration of the rights of the proprietors.[83] Tuscan authors may similarly have dis-

---

[82] On the comparison of passages in Bandini and Boisguilbert by Ulisse Gobbi, *La concorrenza estera e gli antichi economisti italiani* (Milan, 1884), note L. Dal Pane, *La questione del commercio dei grani*, I, 168. Glauco Tozzi points out that the works of Boisguilbert and Vauban were almost unknown in Tuscany at the time: *Sallustio Bandini*, pp. 112 f. The law of 31 July 1574 permitting limited exportation of grain from the Maremma is described by Büchi, *Finanzen und Finanzpolitik Toskanas*, pp. 35-36; the very similar edict of 4 October 1738 is outlined by Morena in *Rassegna nazionale*, XXVIII (1886), 231-40, where he emphasized the role of the Balìa of Siena in carrying on Bandini's teachings. Bandini is here quoted in *Discorso economico*, pp. 131, 141. Another experiment in free trade that might have inspired some of the subsequent proposals was that of the free port of Livorno: see Elio Fazzi, « L'economia livornese alla fine del '700 e durante il Regno d'Etruria », *Rassegna storica toscana*, I⁴ (1955), 1-25. Even Pietro Leopoldo admitted that the freedom accorded to manufacturing in 1775 (*Motuproprio* of 18 December: *Leggi e bandi*, VII, No. 98) was based on a similar edict issued as early as 1738.

[83] Paoletti's references in his *Pensieri sopra l'agricoltura* (first published in 1767) are probably to Jean Bertrand, *De l'esprit de la législation pour encourager l'agriculture* (Bern: Société Typographique, and Paris: Dessaint, 1766), and to Antonie Lionard Thomas, whose

covered the splendors of China not so much in the works of Wolff and Quesnay as in the accounts of missionaries mentioned in their own footnotes — in the same accounts, that is, that all Europe read in their day and that Lorenzo Magalotti had popularized in Florence several generations earlier. They may have found in Muratori, or even in the *precettisti* of the Seicento, the paternalistic concept of political authority to which they clung in spite of the much more "rationalist" views of their favorite Transalpine authors; it was Muratori, after all, who furnished them with much of the specific information included as examples in their treatises. Thus Tuscans did not reject or condemn their own cultural heritage when they took up political economy. They thought of their new discipline rather as an extension to somewhat different material of the methods and occupations of the antiquarians, botanists, and poets; and they looked forward to the perfection of government not in some happy time when the previous intellectual occupations of their compatriots would be swept into outer darkness, but in the near future, if not in the present, when the *eruditi* would be kings or the kings *eruditi*.[84]

culogy of Sully won the prize announced by the Académie Française in 1762 and was published in 1763 (on which: G. Weulersse, *Le mouvement physiocratique en France*, p. 11). *I veri mezzi* (first published in 1772) begins with a long response to an anonymous critic of his first book in which the author explains that what he *really* meant by just price in the first volume was that price established by « the free and general competition between buyers and sellers » unimpeded by tariff barriers (S. C. I. E. P., pp. 115 and 113). The introduction begins with a quotation from Cicero: « In hoc naturam debemus ducem sequi ». His praise of the « illustre parroco della Val di Chiana » (*Pensieri*, p. 14) refers to Giuseppe Ippoliti, bishop of Cortona, who published his reflections in a *Lettera parenetica, morale, economica di un paroco* [*sic*] *della Val di Chiana a tutti i possidenti o comodi, o ricchi* . . . *concernente i doveri loro rispetto ai contadini* (« nuovamente impressa »; Florence: Stecchi & Pagani, 1774).

[84] Montelatici, for instance (above, note 67), refers to Thomas Salmon (1679-1767), *Lo stato presente dello Imperio della China*, which forms Vol. I of his immense *Modern History, or the Present State of All Nations*, (London: For the Author, 1735), first published in Italian translation in 1737 (the edition to which he refers) and, since the first eight volumes were already exhausted, in a 2d ed. as *Lo stato presente di tutti i paesi e popoli del mondo* in some twenty-three volumes (Venice: Albrizzi, 1740-61). He refers also to « Padre Duval », probably Jean-Baptiste Du Halde, whose *Description géographique historique* . . . *de l'Empire de la Chine* appeared in the Hague in 1736. On Muratori, note Salvatorelli, *Il pensiero politico italiano dal 1700 al 1870*, pp. 6 ff., with comments on passages from the *Annali d'Italia*. On the political *precettisti* of the Seicento: B. Croce, *Storia dell'età barocca in Italia*, pp. 149-51; on the connection between *erudizione* and politics, of which an excellent example in Tuscan literature is Lampredi's dedication to Gaetano An-

The similarity of their own doctrines, then, with those of their foreign contemporaries does not indicate mere imitation on the part of Tuscan authors, nor does the freedom with which they borrowed from often contradictory sources necessarily condemn them as indiscriminate eclectics. Most of their writings and scribblings, to be sure, are painfully dull. Their magniloquent naïveté, their loquacious over-simplification, and the self-righteousness with which they knock down their straw men are often tedious, if not actually annoying. But Tuscans became political economists not because at a given moment they happened upon certain books and pamphlets brought from across the Alps. They had read Grotius for decades, after all, without ever worrying about the discrepancies between Tuscan and natural law, and they had long been familiar with the economic policies of Louis XIV without ever proposing a mercantilist system for Tuscany. Rather, they became political economists for much the same reasons that, according to Adolphe Landry, first led Quesnay himself to search for the laws of prices and production — that is, by observing the actual economic conditions of their own country.[85]

It was their previous interest in history and natural sciences, moreover, rather than a desire to imitate foreign societies, that induced them to make such observations; and it was these same interests that persuaded them both of the possibility and of the necessity of altering what they observed. Only then did they turn, like the historians and the scientists before them, to the works of those foreign authors who had dealt with problems similar to their own. What they found was a number of specific criticisms which, though directed at unfamiliar institutions and practices, could be applied as well to those of Tuscany because of a fortuitous similarity between "Colbertism" and the economic regulations of the medieval Tuscan communes. They found also a full theoretical elaboration, stated in terms of the standards they had long accepted in the other "sciences," of the hypotheses they themselves had arrived at only empirically. They

tinori of his *Del governo civile degli antichi toscani*, note remarks of Mario Fubini in « Dall'Arcadia all'Illuminismo: Francesco Algarotti », in *La cultura illuministica in Italia*, pp. 73 ff.

[85] In *François Quesnay et la physiocratie*, I, 39.

found further a wealth of detailed information about political and economic conditions in other countries which, added to what they had already learned about those in Tuscany, could endow their propositions with somewhat more universal validity. Above all, they found a confirmation of the basic assumption that made possible all their endeavors — the assumption, that is, that the ills of society were caused not by the stars but by institutions, and that it was in their power to alter the institutions and thus cure the ills. The realization that their work bore the sanction of the most celebrated writers of the century then inspired them with the firmness and the enthusiasm to continue their investigations and to press for the adoption of their programs. The logical connection among their various citations is to be found, therefore, not in some argument or point of view common to William Petty, Adam Smith, St. Jerome, and Cicero, but in the search for a solution to the economic problems of Tuscany that induced them to make the citations.

Yet Tuscans claimed to be original not so much in formulating theories as in putting them into practice — in adapting, that is, to the special circumstances of Tuscany "a method everywhere advocated in so many books [but] never before executed," and in carrying it out cautiously and slowly in order to test its consequences and assure its acceptance.[86] In France, they maintained, the *philosophes* talked, or, like Turgot, tried to impose vast schemes overnight on an unprepared country. In Tuscany "one of the most active and enterprising governments of the world" had, over a period of some thirty years, gradually but effectively wiped out one order and created another in its place.[87] Tuscans found, therefore, that they had little to learn from the French about the practice of political economy. They had

---

[86] « L'esempio di un metodo da per tutto studiato con tanti libri e mai eseguito »: Gianni quoted by Morena in *Rassegna nazionale*, XXIX (1886), 608. On the policy of gradual application: Paoletti, *I veri mezzi*, p. 114.

[87] Anon., Parere sopra l'operazione dell'abolizione della Tassa di Redenzione in Toscana: Archives des Affaires Etrangères, Paris, Toscane, 144A, 20 February 1789 (I have quoted this passage in the original in *Rassegna storica del Risorgimento*, XLV [1958], 203). Heinz Holldack ascribes the "practicality" of Tuscan and other Italian economists to the fact that most of them, unlike their Transalpine contemporaries, were constantly employed in affairs of state and administration: « Probleme des Risorgimento », *Historische Zeitschrift*, CLXXIII (1952), 505-28, pp. 511 f.

established free trade years before Vergennes finally discovered it in
1786; and almost all the provisions of the supposedly revolutionary
Code Rurale, as the Georgofili dryly reminded Napoleon in 1808,
already appeared in "the existing Tuscan economic laws," promulgated
three decades earlier "under the government of the Grand Duke
Leopoldo" with the encouragement and support of "our economists
and agronomes" in "the Florentine Academy of the Georgofili."[88]

Thus the academicians themselves recognized that only success in
application could ultimately confirm the soundness of their principles;
and, remembering that the empirical method was binding in their
own as well as in all other sciences, they sought carefully to evaluate
the actual effects of at least those laws which they had advocated.
A few measures, it is true, like those pertaining to agrarian contracts,
did not seem at first to produce the expected results; and the Academy
quickly initiated further investigations in order to determine what
amendments were necessary to the original text. But in most cases
it seemed to the academic observers that their program had succeded
beyond their fondest hopes. Already by 1774, less than ten years
after the first and still one year before the final decrees on free trade,
the Georgofili were somewhat shocked to learn that the new regime
had enriched the once-starving peasantry to the point even of endan-
gering their morals: simple farm girls could now afford the jewels
and silk garments once within the means only of ladies of quality.
While raising the income of the rural population, moreover, the new
price levels permitted by open grain markets had apparently benefited
the cities as well. Bricklayers who had formerly earned but three
paoli now earned five, as Fierli reported in 1797; the abolition of the
guilds had stimulated an unprecedented expansion of the silk industry; and unemployment had all but vanished, even though the
number of artisans had almost doubled.[89] Should any doubt remain
about the validity of their observations, the academicians brought forth

[88] Archives des Affaires Etrangères, Toscane, 142B, 10 November 1786: Memoria of
Seratti of 4 November. Georgofili comments on the *Code* in Imberciadori, *La campagna
toscana nel '700.* p. 393.

[89] *Ibid.,* Appendix iv, p. 333; V. Fossombroni, « Rappresentanza sull'arte della seta »
(1793-94), *Scritti di pubblica economia,* I, 114-15; Fierli's discourses of 1 March 1797 in *Atti
Georgofili,* IV, 261-62.

statistics. Between 1766 and 1791, they noted with pride, the population had risen from 945,063 to 1,058,931 (9 per cent), the annual grain harvest had grown from 6,098,868 to 8,032,534 *staja,* and the exportation of oil and other consumption goods was bringing in some 3,500,000 lire per annum.[90]

Thus not only the words of famous foreign economists, but above all the test of experience now assured them that the hypotheses they had induced from the particular conditions of their own country did indeed approximate the laws of nature. "The increased prosperity of Tuscany" had been reduced to "figures," and the academicians could therefore dismiss the all too audible voices of protest as merely the selfish cavillings of dispossessed bureaucrats or the expression of "those errors which long currency had given "a kind of apotheosis" and rendered impervious to the arguments of reason.[91] Let their enemies look about them: "everything is coming to life, everything is becoming beautiful. New roads, new bridges, new canals, new buildings, new lands open to cultivation..."; in a society once incapable of motion "there are now everywhere unmistakable signs of movement and energy."[92]

Subsequent students of the period have not, it is true, always shared the unqualified sanguinity of the Settecento political economists. Some have, indeed, found evidence of a considerable increase in grain production and as much as a threefold rise in the exportation of manufactured goods.[93] But at least one recent historian has pointed

---

[90] Statistics in ASF Archivio Tolomei 191, Inserto I, No. 1: Pubblica economia, 1761-1798 — with population figures furnished by the royal *auditore*; others in Tabarrini, *Degli studi e delle vicende della R. A. dei G.,* p. 30, and *Rassegna nazionale* (by Morena), XXXI (1886), 148.

[91] Gianni, *Ricordi per l'accademia (ASF Carte Gianni XIII, 302); Giovanni Lessi in Discourse of 7 September 1791, *Atti Georgofili,* III, 85.

[92] Fierli, *loc. cit.,* note 89 above: « ora tutto si rinnova, tutto si abbellisce. Nuove strade, nuovi ponti, nuovi canali, nuove fabbriche, nuove coltivazioni; e da per tutto si scorge un certo movimento, ed energia, che prima non vi era ».

[93] E. g., Antonio Fossati, *Lavoro e produzione in Italia dalla metà del secolo XVIII alla seconda guerra mondiale* (Torino: Giappichelli, 1951) pp. 18 ff. (without sources cited), and the figures of Morena quoted by Imberciadori in *Campagna toscana nel '700,* p. 152. Figures on the increase in the population of the Maremma after 1786 are given by Imberciadori, « Introduzione della mezzadria in Maremma », in *Rassegna storica toscana,* IV (1958), 7.

to the riots of 1790 as proof that free trade failed to overcome the peril of famine, while another has shown that production figures reflect more an extension than an intensification of agriculture and do not, therefore, indicate any substantial improvement in the lot of the peasantry.[94] Even the reports of the early nineteenth century often disagree: Sismondi's idyllic picture of the Tuscan countryside, for instance, conflicts in many ways with the admission by one of the Georgofili in 1824 that grain still had to be imported in lean years and that the conditions of the Maremma were still "deplorable" in spite of so much expense and experiment.[95].

Many of the reforms certainly did fail to fulfil the hopes of their authors — those pertaining to the alienation of state property, for instance, which still left Tuscany a land almost wholly of great land-owners, and those pertaining to liturgical practices and ecclesiastical polity, which the opposition of the principal ministers, the hostility of the majority of bishops in the National Synod of 1787, and the violence of the Pratesi forced Pietro Leopoldo eventually to abandon.[96] Some, on the other hand, undoubtedly succeeded; for by the end of the century what had been an agglomeration of petrified medieval communes, in which all action required the special intervention of the prince, had become a single centralized, bureaucratic state, relatively

[94] R. Mori, « Il movimento reazionario in Toscana alle riforme economiche leopoldine nel 1790 », *Archivio storico italiano,* C[2] (1942), 53-94, esp. p. 59, whose thesis is apparently based on Gianni's interpretation (« Memoria sul tumulto del 1790 », *Scritti di pubblica economia,* I. No. 11) of the riots as a protest against the economic and political, rather than the religious aspects of the reforms — an interpretation shared neither by the French envoy Durfort nor by the Papal legate Luigi Ruffo-Scilla (Vatican Archives: Nunziatura Firenze, No. 175, fol. 103 ff.

[95] Sismondi sent a copy of his *Tableau de l'agriculture toscane* to the Georgofili: the cover letter of 14 April 1801 is printed in *Atti Georgofili,* IV, 21-23. In another, unpublished report of 1799 he is much less optimistic: see E. Passerin d'Entrèves, « Un inedito saggio del Sismondi sui problemi dell'economia toscana all'inizio dell'occupazione francese del 1799 », *Rassegna storica del Risorgimento,* XXXVIII (1951), 546-62. Later reports: G. B. Thaon, « Dell'attuale stato economico della Maremma toscana » (1824), in *Scritti di pubblica economia degli accademici georgofili,* ed. Morena (Arezzo, 1899), I, 57-61, and Felice Francolini, « Dell'aumento generale di rendita e di prezzo dei terreni di Maremma dopo la metà del secolo XVIII », *Atti Georgofili,* Ser. II, Vol. XXII (1844), pp. 162-75 (attempting to prove thereby the benefits of free trade).

[96] Among the many studies of this question, see E. Passerin d'Entrèves, « Il fallimento dell'offensiva riformista di Scipione de' Ricci », *Rivista di storia della Chiesa in Italia,* IX (1955), 99-131.

free of debt and supported by an energetic minority of its subjects. Many of the economic doctrines current at the time may now, it is true, seem somewhat naïve. But they had the merit of provoking and justifying the abolition of a completely anachronistic system of regulations that previously had done little but accelerate the impoverishment of the country. In so far as they resemble the teachings of the Physiocrats, moreover, they contained certain basic principles still acceptable to some economists today;[97] and they rested upon the assumption, finally, that economic activities, once the object merely of ad hoc emergency remedies, could be calculated and controlled — an assumption indispensible to any lasting material progress. While a valid assessment of the reforms must, then, await the results of historical research into the still little-known social and economic conditions of the Settecento, [98] it is at least clear that many of the legislative changes adopted in Tuscany escaped the fate of those introduced in Spain, in Baden, and in other parts of Europe where native cultures proved too hostile to permit any but a superficial modification of traditional ideas and institutions.

Still, the work of the academies cannot be judged simply in terms of the relative success of the Leopoldine legislation, much of which went unnoticed in their sessions. Royal ministers like Gianni and Tavanti, for instance, seem to have said nothing in their communications to the academies about many of the bolder economic theories and many of the more vigorous proposals for reform elaborated in their memoranda to the Grand Duke. Similarly, academic records make no mention of the various projects, initiated by the Regency and carried on throughout the reign of Pietro Leopoldo, for the codification of municipal laws and for the restriction of the civil jurisdiction of ecclesiastical courts. Except for one or two outbursts of verse, they are silent concerning even such important measures as the reorganization of local government, which Cosimo I himself had not dared to touch, or the Criminal Code of 1786, which evoked the

---

[97] Note Luigi Einaudi in Preface to *François Quesnay et la physiocratie*, I, viii.

[98] Like that proposed, for example, by Renato Zangheri, « Per lo studio dell'agricoltura bolognese nel '700 », *Studi in onore di Armando Sapori* (Milan: Istituto Editoriale Cisalpino, 1957), pp. 124 ff., and in part carried out by Mario Mirri (above, note 50).

applause of all Europe.[99]　And they never refer, as has been noted, to the religious conflicts of the 1780's or to the preceding theological controversies among Jesuits, Jansenists, Molinists, Jurisdictionalists, Anti-Curialists, *et al.,* in which many of the academicians themselves were individually involved.[100]　The academicians did not, in other words, necessarily identify themselves with the whole of the government's program, and they cannot be held responsible therefore for the failure of the measures they did not initiate or support.

Nevertheless, Richard Cobden's tribute to the Georgofili in 1847 was not completely unjustified.[101]　Their achievement, indeed, lies not only in having urged the adoption of policies similar to those advocated half a century later by the Anti-Corn Law League in England or in having furnished much of the specific information upon which subsequent legislation was based.　It lies above all in having instilled in their contemporaries a mentality favorable to reform.　It was they who, to a large extent, made possible the peaceful transition from an old to a new political order.　It was they who encouraged the study of history and the natural sciences from which political economy in Tuscany first arose.　It was they who gradually drew the attention of the educated classes from balls, banquets, and "literary exercises" to problems of agricultural productivity, price fluctuations, and com-

---

[99] The first proposals for the codification of law are those of Pompeo Neri (« Discorso tenuto nell'adunanza dei Deputati alla Compilazione di un nuovo Codice delle leggi municipali della Toscana » of 6 July 1747, published in Neri Badia, *Decisiones et responsa juris,* II, 527-37) and of Canini in co-operation with Richecourt of 1753 and 1758: ASF Reggenza 29 bis and 196.2, all on commission from the Regency.　Pietro Leopoldo turned the work over to Lampredi, but it was never completed.　In general, see Vincenzo Piano Mortari, « Tentativi di codificazione nel Granducato di Toscana nel secolo XVIII », *Rivista italiana per le scienze giuridiche,* LXXXIX (1952-53), 285-387.　The criminal code of 30 November 1786 (on which: Carlo Calisse, *A History of Italian Law,* English translation [Boston: Little, Brown, 1938], pp. 471-72) appeared in London in 1789 (*Edict of the Grand Duke of Tuscany*); note the enthusiastic review in the *Mercure de France* quoted by Nicola Matteucci, *Jacques Mallet-Du Pan* (Naples: Istituto Italiano per gli Studi Storici, 1957), p. 143.

[100] See E. Passerin d'Entrèves, « La riforma 'giansenista' della Chiesa e la lotta anticuriale in Italia nella seconda metà del Settecento », *Rivista storica italiana,* LXXI (1959), 209-34 (to continue).

[101] *Adunanza ordinaria dell'Accademia dei Georgofili del dì 2 maggio 1847 alla presenza di R. Cobden* (Florence: Galileiana, 1847).　The speech of Raffaello Lambruschini on the occasion is published by Morena in *Scritti di pubblica economia degli accademici georgofili,* II, 225-36.

mercial restrictions. It was they who, by publicizing the most advanced economic doctrines among all literate Tuscans, undermined the resistance of proprietors, cultivators, and royal officials which might have, and still did on occasions, impede the execution of the new laws. It was they, finally, who created a governing class, who taught the noblemen, the professors, the lawyers, and the *abati* of Tuscany to abandon the indifference to public affairs they had learned during a century and a half of despotism and to dedicate themselves to furthering the happiness and well-being of all their fellow citizens.

Now that the tramway has been removed, the Piazza de' Giudici, of which one side opens onto the Arno just up river from the Ponte Vecchio, is one of the quieter corners of Florence — at least in comparison to the unbroken din that reigns in the Piazza della Signoria just two steps away. On the west side of the piazza, with its back touching the Palazzo degli Uffizi, stands a solemn medieval building, upon which is displayed, just to the right of the *portone,* a small white plaque bearing the names of the present occupants of the halls once used by the supreme tribunal of the Grand Duchy. A steep stone staircase (or a cage elevator if someone happens by with the key) leads past the entrance of the Museum of the History of Science, the sole objective of the few tourists who ever come into the palace, up several long flights to a barely lit doorway on the third floor, where another sign requests that the bell be rung for admission. Just inside, a short corridor opens on the right to the director's office, while on the left a door gives access to some nine or ten large rooms, following in series around the whole building, most of them lined with bookcases that reach up some twelve feet into the darkness of the high ceilings.

This is the Accademia della Crusca today. On the walls may still be seen the portraits of the Salviati and the Salvini, together with the emblems and *imprese* they once adopted amid declamations and song. But there is little else reminiscent of the boisterous weekly meetings, the orations from the *bugnola,* the recitations of sonnets. Gone are the crowds that once filled the courtyard of Palazzo Strozzi for the annual *stravizzo* and the special sessions in honor of distinguished foreign visitors. Gone also are the discussions of archeology, medicine, the law, the *Decamerone,* and all the other subjects once considered fitting for academic consideration; the Crusca now limits its activities to the occasional publication of philological monographs. Even the *Vocabolario* seems to have been forgotten; and indeed there may be some question of the possible utility of the fifth edition, begun in 1860 and still incomplete, in a day when Italian authors borrow words and expressions from wherever they please and when the *questione della lingua* has been buried once and for all. Except for the charming and learned director, Dr. Pagliai, for the kind and helpful custodian, and, from time to time, for Professor Castellani, Professor Volpi, and one or two other scholars, almost no one ever breaks the dusty silence that makes the halls of the Crusca the most pleasant place in all Florence for quiet reading. The membership is composed no longer of the whole aristocracy of birth and talent of the city, but of a small number of professors of linguistics. And the visitors from beyond the Alps or Ocean who now walk from the Uffizi to Santa Croce (or from the State Archives to the National Library) seldom even notice the modern seat of the once famous institution.

Unlike the sixteenth and the eighteenth, apparently, the twentieth century is not an academic age. Neither the Crusca nor the other academies that still survive today — the Colombaria, the Georgofili, the Etrusca, the Intronati, the Fisiocritici — makes any pretension of representing the cultural aspirations of an entire community or of furthering the advancement and the diffusion of learning. Each is dedicated to a carefully defined discipline — to philology, to archeology, to agriculture, to local history; and membership is usually limited to specialists in the field, who, unlike their forerunners in the Settecento, are seldom called upon to supplement from their own pockets the meager budget allotted by the state. Usually, indeed, they are far too busy with other occupations to devote much time to institutions that must occasionally seem anachronistic in the busy, prosaic postwar world. Yet their very adherence is a worthy tribute to the conspicuous role played by these same societies two centuries ago, when almost no other means were available through which educated Tuscans could join together of their own accord for the pursuit of common objectives.

This examination of the organization and activities of the Tuscan academies cannot by any means solve the many problems raised by recent students of pre-Revolutionary Italy; but it can at least offer a number of clarifications. It has suggested first of all that the Leopoldine reforms were in part the result of a gradual change in the attitudes of Tuscans over half a century — a change for which the academies deserve considerable credit. For although much of the legislation may have been inspired by foreign models, its success in application depended solely upon Tuscans — upon the landowners, jurists, and government officials who had already become convinced of its utility through their studies of history, of the sciences, and of the physical conditions of the country. It has suggested secondly that the "reawakening" of the Settecento was a social as well as an intellectual phenomenon, of which the academies themselves, the first institutions in over a hundred years to be erected independently of royal authority, were one of the principal manifestations. It has suggested thirdly that the word "Enlightenment" when applied to Tuscany must be defined in accordance with the connotation of the contemporary term *Illuminismo;* it must comprehend, in other words, not only those elements of a common European culture that Tuscans borrowed from beyond the Alps, but also the literary and linguistic heritage of the Trecento and the philosophic heritage of the age of Galileo, onto which they grafted whatever they borrowed. It is the loyalty of Tuscans to their heritage, in fact, and their conviction of its compatibility with the new ideas of their own times that account for many of the differences between the Enlightenment in Tuscany and that in France, Prussia, or Sachsen-Weimar-Eisenach.

This study has suggested further that Tuscan culture in the Settecento is somewhat more indebted to the achievements of the Renaissance than even its representatives would have admitted; for at least in such fields as historiography, jurisprudence, and political thought, the academicians often began by returning, at times unwittingly, to positions that had already been established by their ancestors of the Quattro- and Cinquecento. It has suggested also at least some of the reasons for the unenthusiastic, although not necessarily hostile reception of the changes imposed during the period of French domination; for most educated Tuscans seem to have regarded them merely as slight modifications of what had already been accomplished or what would soon have been accomplished more effectively under the government of the grand dukes. At the same time, the preoccupation with the concrete and the suspicion of the general that had been characteristic of all their thought for over a century made Tuscans insensitive to the slogans of Revolutionary propaganda.

This study will suggest finally that Tuscans of the eighteenth century prepared for the Risorgimento of the nineteenth not so much by proposing the unification of Italy (an idea completely foreign to even the most progressive of the academicians) but rather by realizing that of Tuscany — by creating, that is, on the ruins of the medieval city-states, a single political structure in harmony with the various social institutions (like the academies themselves) within it; and to this achievement the academies contributed by persuading the principal citizens of the possibility and the desirability of change and by calling upon them to assume the responsibility for its direction.

BIBLIOGRAPHICAL NOTE

The standard histories of the Risorgimento all contain introductory chapters on the Settecento, although the most recent, Giorgio Candeloro, *Storia dell'Italia moderna,* I: *Le origini del Risorgimento* (Milan: Feltrinelli, 1956) deals only very briefly with the years before the Napoleonic period. Most of them (e.g., Antonio Monti, *Il Risorgimento* [2 vols.; Milan: Vallardi, 1948]) consider the period almost exclusively in terms of preparation for the events of the nineteenth century, as do the somewhat older works of Ettore Rota, *Il problema italiano dal 1700 al 1815 (L'idea unitaria)* (2d ed.; Milan: Istituto per gli Studi di Politica Internazionale, 1941), and *Le origini del Risorgimento* (Milan: Vallari, 1938, and 1948), and of A. M. Ghisalberti, *Gli albori del Risorgimento italiano* (Rome: Cremonese, 1931), following the definition of the problem by Rota in *L'enigma del Settecento e il problema delle origini del nostro Risorgimento* (Milan: Dante Alighieri, 1918). The thesis that nationalism arose in the eighteenth century (and not, therefore, at the time of Napoleon) is turned upside down by Emiliana Pasca Noether in *Seeds of Italian Nationalism* (New York: Columbia University Press, 1951), who finds just as much of it, but calls it bad instead of good. The weakness of this approach is suggested by Gioacchino Volpe in « Principi di Risorgimento del '700 italiano », *Rivista storica italiana,* I (1936), 1-34. A more recent consideration of the problem of the debt of the Risorgimento to the eighteenth century is that of Heinz Holldack, « Probleme des Risorgimento », *Historische Zeitschrift,* CLXXIII (1952), 505-28, which takes into account, as the others did or could not, the vast amount of study that has been devoted to the period since the Second World War. General surveys of the Italian Settecento are few (indeed, it may be still too early for any new ones). Franco Valsecchi, *Gli stati dell'Italia centrale e meridionale nel periodo anteriore alle riforme* (Milan: La Gogliardica, 1953), an outline for a course in the university, gives a brief review of the political and economic situation in several of the states, as do, more thoroughly, the articles of Guido Quazza and Ettore Passerin d'Entrèves in Vols. II and III of *Storia d'Italia,* ed. Nino Valeri (Torino: Unione Tipografico-Editrice, 1959). The most comprehensive, although very brief, survey is Alfred Noyer-Weidner, *Die Aufklärung in Oberitalien* (Munich: Hueber, 1957). Basic for all investigations of the period is the huge bibliographical work of Giulio Natali, *Il Settecento* (2d ed.; Milan: Vallardi, 1944); and still of considerable interest are the various essays in his

Idee costumi uomini del Settecento (Torino: Sten, 1916 and 1926). The questions raised by Benedetto Croce in « La crisi italiana del Cinquecento e il legame del Rinascimento col Risorgimento», *La critica,* XXXVII (1939), 401-11, have yet to be explored thoroughly. Much more attention has been devoted recently to various phases of Settecento culture. Still of great value and unique in the subject is Gabriel Maugain, *Étude sur l'évolution intellectuelle de l'Italie de 1656 à 1750 environ* (Paris: Hachette, 1909). Of particular importance is the series of brief studies edited by Mario Fubini, *La cultura illuministica in Italia* (Torino: Radio Italiana, 1957) (on which see Enrico Malato, « L'illuminismo e la cultura italiana del Settecento », *Nuova antologia,* CXIII [1958], 342-66). Among the many excellent studies devoted to literature and criticism (which reflect much of the culture of the age) may be mentioned: Walter Binni, *Preromanticismo italiano* (Naples: Edizioni Scientifiche Italiane, 1947), Carlo Calcaterra, *Il Parnasso in rivolta* (Milan: Mondadori, 1904), and Mario Fubini, *Dal Muratori al Baretti: Studi sulla critica e sulla cultura del Settecento* (Bari: Laterza, 1954), and Bruno Migliorini, « Panorama dell'Italia settecentesca», *Rassegna della letteratura italiana,* LXI (1957), 373-437, and many other works by the same authors. An excellent consideration of *illuminismo* and a select bibliography on political and economic thought is to be found in the short introduction of Franco Venturi to *Illuministi italiani,* III: *Riformatori lombardi piemontesi e toscani* (Milan: Ricciardi, 1958).

Of the few histories of Florence that come down as far as the Settecento, the best is probably still Romolo Caggese, *Firenze dalla decadenza di Roma al Risorgimento d'Italia* (Florence: Seeber e Lumachi, 1912-31), Vol. III, although Alfred von Reumont, *Geschichte Toskanas* (Gotha, 1876) is still useful and the more recent *Storia di Firenze* (Florence: Sansoni, 1949) of Antonio Panella is helpful in spite of its brevity. Still the most thorough record of political events is to be found in Riguccio Galluzzi, *Istoria del Granducato di Toscana sotto il governo della Casa Medici* (Florence: Cambiagi, 1781, and Livorno: Vignozzi, 1820-21), and, from where it leaves off, Antonio Zobi, *Storia civile della Toscana dal 1737 al 1838* (Florence: Molini, 1850-52), which may be supplemented for the earlier years of the century by Niccolò Rodolico, *Stato e chiesa in Toscana durante la Reggenza lorenese* (Florence: Le Monnier, 1910), and *La Reggenza lorenese in Toscana, 1737-65* (Prato: Vestri e Spighi, 1908), and for the later by Abele Morena, « Le riforme e le dottrine economiche in Toscana », *Rassegna nazionale,* XXVII (1886), 265-98, *et seq.* through many following numbers. Still of great importance for the specific subjects they deal with are the two works of Hermann Büchi, *Ein Menschenalter Reformen der Toten Hand in Toskana (1751-1790)* (Berlin: Ebering, 1912), and *Finanzen und Finanzpolitik Toskanas im Zeitalter der Aufklärung, 1737-1790* (Berlin: Ebering, 1915) and the several of Antonio Anzilotti, particularly « Le riforme in Toscana nella seconda metà del secolo XVIII », in *Movimento e contrasti per l'unità italiana,* ed. L. Russo (Bari: Laterza, 1930). Among more recent contributions to the history of the reforms is the much-debated *Le riforme leopoldine nel pensiero degli economisti toscani del '700* by Renato Mori (Florence: Sansoni, 1951). Heinz Holldack, « Die Reformpolitik Leopolds von Toskana », *Historische Zeitschrift,* CLXV (1942), 23-46, may still be consulted.

The number of recent titles on the ecclesiastic and religious history of the time is too numerous to permit mention here of each of them; it is to be hoped that Ettore Passerin d'Entrèves, the most assiduous student of the question, will soon consolidate his many monographic articles into a general survey. For the time being, Arturo Jemolo, *Stato e Chiesa negli scrittori italiani del Seicento e del Settecento* (Torino: Bocce, 1914), is still probably the most comprehensive. A number of recent essays on the period as a whole, although of uneven quality, are included in the volume *Il Sei-Settecento* (Florence: Libera Cattedra di Storia della Civiltà Fiorentina, 1956). Great quantities of valuable, if incomplete and somewhat disorganized information on contemporary economic conditions may be found in Ildebrando Imberciadori, *Campagna toscana nel '700* (Florence: Accademia dei Georgofili, 1953). For glimpses into the social life of the time there are several miscellanies of anecdotes, of which Alessandro Ademollo, *Corilla Olimpica* (Florence: C. Ademolo, 1887), is superior to the occasionally amusing but often inaccurate accounts of the *va et vien* of princes by Giuseppe Conti (e.g., *Firenze dai Medici ai Lorena* [Florence: Bemporad, 1909]), and more valuable than the witty letters of Horace Mann, the English minister, recently published as *Horace Walpole's Correspondence with Sir Horace Mann,* edited by W. S. Lewis, W. H. Smith, and G. Lam (New Haven: Yale University Press, 1954) (Vols. XVII-XIX of *Horace Walpole's Correspondence*), with thorough notes but no index.

Works dealing with the specific subjects treated in this book are given at the appropriate places in the footnotes and need not be mentioned again here. There is no general literature on the Tuscan academies. The few published academic histories and all the other material both in MS and in print will be considered in the following volume.

INDEX

Agosto 1961

A. B E. T. E.

Azienda Beneventana Tipografica Editoriale

Roma - Via Prenestina, 683